ADOBE® PREMIERE® PRO 2.0 REVEALED

Chris Botello
Contributing Editor, Ann Fisher

THOMSON
COURSE TECHNOLOGY™
Professional ■ Technical ■ Reference

Publisher and General Manager of PTR:
Stacy L. Hiquet

Director of Marketing:
Sarah O'Donnell

Marketing Manager:
Heather Hurley

Manager of Editorial Services:
Heather Talbot

Contributing Editor:
Ann Fisher

Acquisitions Editor:
Megan Belanger

QA Manuscript Reviewers:
John Freitas, Serge Palladino

Project Editor:
Cathleen Snyder

Interior Layout Tech:
William Hartman

Cover Design:
Steve Deschene

Printed in the United States of America.

1 2 3 4 5 6 7 8 9 PH 09 08 07 06

For more information, contact Thomson Course Technology, 25 Thomson Place, Boston, Massachusetts, 02210. Or find us on the World Wide Web at: www.courseptr.com

ISBN 1-59863-028-8

Library of Congress Catalog Card Number: 2005929810

THOMSON
COURSE TECHNOLOGY™
Professional ■ Technical ■ Reference

Thomson Course Technology PTR, a division of Thomson Course Technology
25 Thomson Place ■ Boston, MA 02210 ■ http://www.courseptr.com

Revealed Series Vision

The *Revealed* series is your guide to today's hottest multimedia applications. These comprehensive books teach the skills behind the application, showing you how to apply smart design principles to multimedia products, such as dynamic graphics, animation, Web sites, software authoring tools, and digital video.

A team of design professionals, including multimedia instructors, students, authors, and editors, worked together to create this series. We recognized the unique needs of the multimedia market and created a series that gives you comprehensive step-by-step instructions and offers an in-depth explanation of the "why" behind a skill, all in a clear, visually-based layout.

It was our goal to create a book that speaks directly to the multimedia and design community—one of the most rapidly growing computer fields today. We feel that *Adobe Premiere Pro 2.0 Revealed* does just that—with sophisticated content and an instructive book design.

—The Revealed Series

Author's Vision

Pause for just a moment and consider how cool it is that you can edit your own video footage and create movies on your own computer. In the ten years since I first began playing with Adobe Premiere, computers have become faster, hard drive storage has become larger, and the ability to connect your video camera to your computer has become as easy as plug-and-play. And so, with Adobe Premiere Pro, the fantasy has become a reality: You can edit your own movies—real movies—with transitions, titles, and effects.

This book is a series of exercises that will take you on a fully guided tour of Premiere Pro 2.0—from basic concepts to complex techniques—all with a hands-on approach.

I had fun writing this. I had fun shooting the video footage that you'll be working with, and I had fun putting together the exercises that you will follow. You'll create a colorful countdown video, edit breathtaking footage of hang gliders flying over the beach in San Diego, and watch kids having fun at an amusement park.

And those are just the highlights! I think you'll have a blast.

I want to thank Megan Belanger, who shepherded the book through its many stages, and Thomson Course Technology PTR, for their vision and for their enthusiastic and dedicated staff who faced the many quality control challenges of producing this book.

I also want to acknowledge the QA manuscript reviewers for their input: John Freitas and Serge Palladino. Special thanks to David Rajter of Groovepod Experience for his great music and the song "Touch Another," which was used for the audio component of many exercises. Last but not least, this book is dedicated to my friend, location manager, camera operator, dog wrangler, and lead actor, Bill Miltenberger.

Step-by-Step Instructions

This book combines in-depth conceptual information with concise steps to help you learn Premiere Pro 2.0. Each set of steps guides you through a lesson where you will create, modify, or enhance a Premiere Pro 2.0 file. Step references to large images and quick step summaries round out the lessons.

CONTENTS

CONTENTS

CONTENTS

CONTENTS

READ THIS BEFORE YOU BEGIN

Opening Data Files

Premiere Pro project files have been supplied for working with the exercises in this book. Premiere Pro files work with source clips. Source files are video files, audio clips, still images, or titles that are housed in the Project panel and can be moved to the Timeline to be part of a video program. These clips are not themselves the Premiere Pro file; they are imported into the Premiere Pro file.

Every source clip for the exercises in this book is located in a single folder—named Source Clips—on the CD that comes with this book. Having every source clip in this single location should make it very easy to locate source clips.

When you open a Premiere Pro Data File, it needs to load all of the source clips used in the exercise. Most Data Files already contain imported clips. To locate all of the clips used in a Data File, you should navigate to the Source Clips folder and select the first item being asked for. Premiere Pro will then find all of the additional source clips in the same location, if necessary. Click OK and the Data File will finish opening.

Working with a Complex Timeline

The bulk of the work done in Premiere Pro occurs in the Timeline. You will find that Premiere Pro's Timeline is well-designed, straightforward, and intuitive. However, as you create increasingly complex programs, you may find it challenging to manage the contents of the Timeline. For example, as you add clips, you will find that you need to scroll left and right to view all the clips in the program. As you add tracks, you will need to scroll up and down to see the multiple tracks. There will be many times in this book when you'll be encouraged to zoom in on the Timeline for a better view of its contents. To do so, drag the Zoom Slider in the left corner of the Timeline panel. Scroll bars are available to scroll vertically through the Timeline when multiple tracks are being used.

Restoring Preferences

Preferences settings offer you options for customizing your workspace and choosing defaults (such as default fonts or default functions within a panel), among many other options. As you choose preferences in Premiere Pro, those settings are recorded and saved in a preferences file. Each time you start Premiere Pro, the preferences file is referred to in order to maintain your last settings.

The easiest way to revert to default preferences is to press and hold [Shift] [Ctrl] throughout the startup of the Premiere Pro application.

Working with Preferences for Still Images

When a still image is imported into the Project panel, it is imported at a duration that is specified by a preference setting. This setting is found by clicking Edit on the menu bar, pointing to Preferences, then clicking General. The default duration of a still image is 30 frames. To change the duration, enter a new number of frames in the Still Image Default Duration text box. This preference setting is important when working with titles. Titles are, by definition, still images. Thus, when they are created, their duration is that which has been set in the General preferences window.

Generating a Preview and Render-Scrubbing

When you generate a preview, Premiere Pro plays the contents of the Timeline—at the intended frame rate—in the Program Monitor. Depending on the complexity of the program and the speed of your computer, generating a preview can be time consuming.

Often, an exercise will call for the user to generate a preview along the way—before the exercise itself is completed—to preview an effect or an edit. If doing so requires 30 seconds to a minute, you should go ahead and generate the preview. However, if generating the preview becomes overly time consuming, you can simply render-scrub to preview the effect. Render-scrubbing is done by dragging the Current time indicator over the frames in the Timeline.

Previewing is a memory-intensive function. For that reason, the source clips supplied for the exercises have been saved at minimal file sizes. Nevertheless, previewing video requires substantial memory; if your computer is having trouble when previewing, or if the preview itself is choppy, the problem is most likely insufficient computer memory.

Choosing the Workspace

The workspace is the arrangement of panels on your computer screen. There are four types of editing workspaces: Editing, Effects, Audio, and Color Correction. The Editing workspace is efficient when you are doing just that—editing. However, if you are working with audio, you'll want to switch to the Audio workspace. This workspace features the Audio Mixer front and center above the Timeline. The Effects workspace is great for adding and modifying video or audio effects to clips in the Timeline. You can drag effects from the Effects panel on the left directly to the Timeline on the right. The Effect Controls panel sits directly above the Timeline so that you can easily make modifications to an effect over and over. Throughout this book, you are asked to choose various workspaces; however, it's best for you to work in the one most comfortable for you.

Working with Fonts

In Chapter 7, you will work with titles and be asked to choose fonts. If you do not have the font or fonts available on your computer, feel free to substitute one of your fonts that would also work.

NR 328

chapter 1

GETTING STARTED WITH ADOBE PREMIERE PRO 2.0

1. Explore the Premiere Pro workspace.
2. Work in the Project panel.
3. Explore the Source and Program Monitors.
4. Examine the Timeline elements.

chapter 1 GETTING STARTED WITH ADOBE PREMIERE PRO 2.0

Welcome to Premiere Pro 2.0!
You couldn't have picked a better time or place to develop your skills with digital video editing. Premiere Pro is a professional digital video editing application created by Adobe Systems Incorporated. If this name is familiar to you, that's because Adobe is an award-winning producer of graphics software for the personal computer. There's a pretty good chance that you have already been introduced to other Adobe software products, such as Photoshop or Illustrator. Like those two products, Premiere Pro is smart, fun, and boasts an intuitive workspace design. For anybody who is into movies or video, it's pretty much a dream application. Premiere Pro's role—its function—is very focused. Premiere Pro makes movies. As you learn its functions and abilities, you will come to appreciate that it is dynamic in both its role and its scope and can be a conduit for stunning visual artistry. Premiere Pro is a place where you gather loose artwork—video clips, bitmap images, and vector graphics—and bring them together to create a whole new video product.

Premiere Pro brings your artwork to life.

Tools You'll Use

Project panel

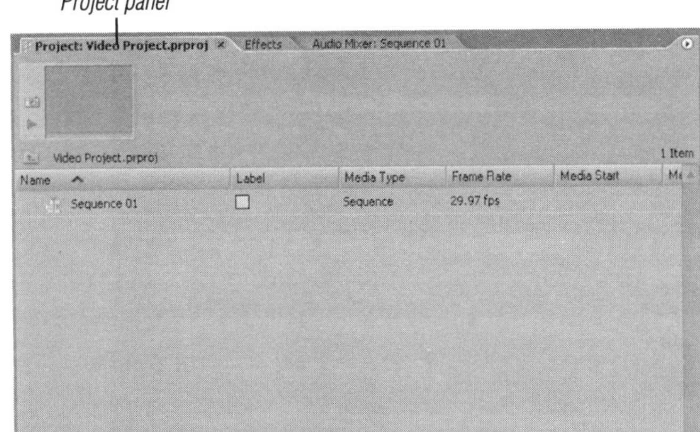

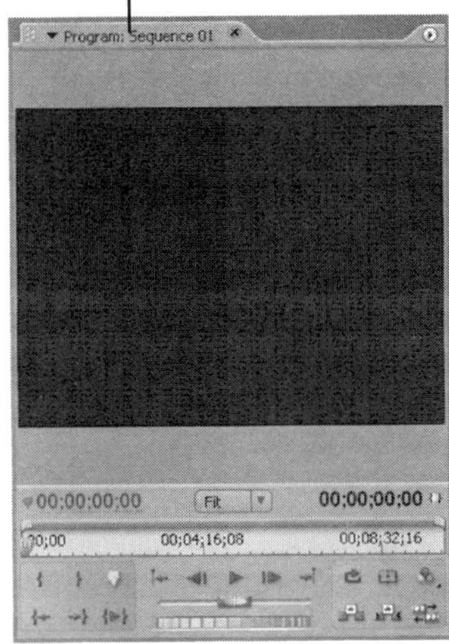

Source Monitor panel

Timeline panel

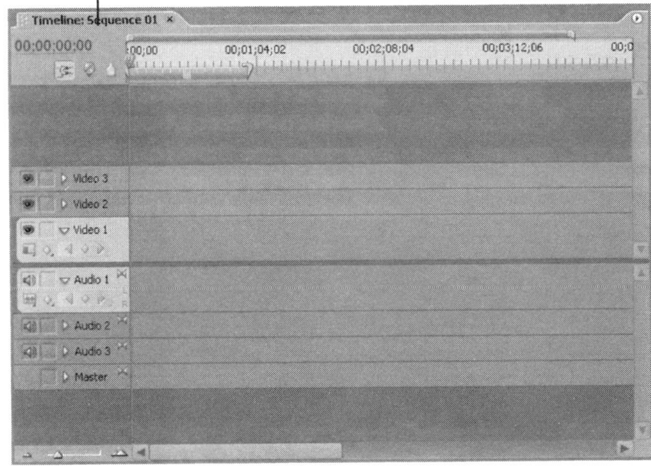

LESSON 1

EXPLORE THE PREMIERE PRO WORKSPACE

What You'll Do

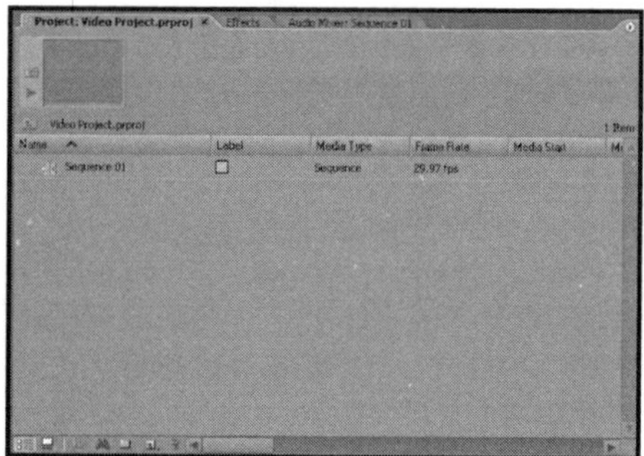

In this lesson, you will start Premiere Pro and explore the workspace.

Exploring the Workspace

The arrangement of panels on your computer screen is called the workspace. The workspace includes necessary panels and tools to create your project. Figure 1 shows the Editing workspace. It features the Project, Program Monitor, Source Monitor, and Timeline panels, as well as a number of other panels, such as the Info, History, and Effects panels. All panels are available on the Window menu.

Most of the panels have their own menus that are accessed by clicking the panel list arrow. Figure 2 shows the Project panel and its menu.

The most commonly used panels in Premiere Pro are as follows:

Project panel: The Project panel is where you import, organize, and store references to video clips, audio clips, and still imagery. It lists all of the source files that you import; however, you do not need to use all of them in your final video program.

Timeline panel: The Timeline panel is where you assemble and edit your video. It contains all of the source clips that are used in the project, including video and audio, as well as title cards, transitions, and special effects. When you start a new project, the Timeline is empty. Once clips have been added, the Timeline displays its contents sequentially from left to right, with clips to the left occurring earlier in the video program than clips to the right.

Source and Program Monitor panels: The Source and Program Monitor panels are where you preview both individual clips and the entire project. Use the Source Monitor panel to preview a source clip, and the Program Monitor panel to display the contents of the Timeline.

FIGURE 1
Editing workspace

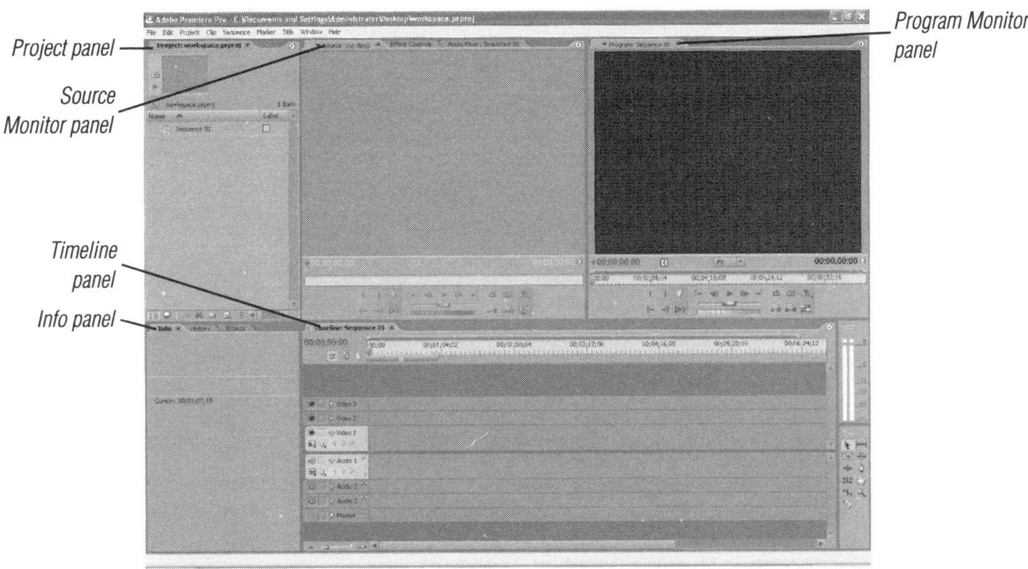

FIGURE 2
Project panel menu

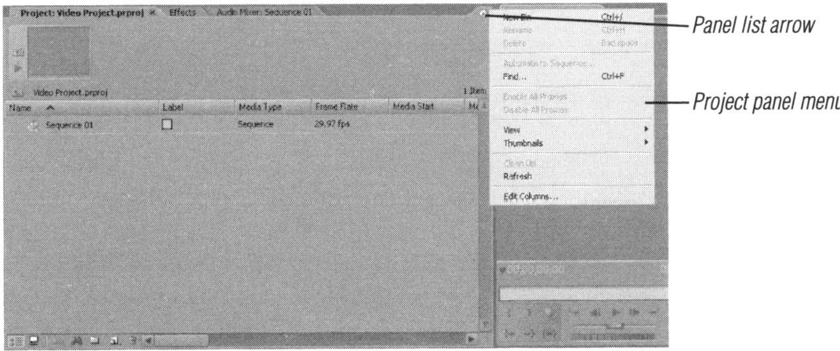

Effects panel: The Effects panel includes special effects that you can apply to your video. These special effects are categorized into folders: Presets, Audio Effects, Audio Transitions, Video Effects, and Video Transitions.

Audio Mixer panel: The Audio Mixer panel allows you to make adjustments to audio tracks while listening to them and viewing video at the same time.

QUICKTIP

A panel that is selected is highlighted in orange.

History panel: This panel allows you to go back to any previous state of the project since it (the project) was opened.

Info panel: As its name suggests, the Info panel provides information about a selected clip or source file, a location in the Timeline, or other notations.

Tools panel: The Tools panel offers tools for working in the Timeline, such as the Hand Tool, Zoom Tool, Selection Tool, and the Track Select Tool.

Effect Controls panel: The Effect Controls panel offers you options for changing an effect's settings.

QUICKTIP

All panels can be resized by placing the mouse pointer over a panel border, then dragging the border when you see a double arrow pointer.

Using Default Preferences

Preferences are common to most applications. Preference settings offer you options for customizing your workspace and choosing defaults (such as default fonts or default functions within a panel), among many other options. Activating and deactivating specific preferences can have a substantial impact on how you work, especially when you are working with more complex software, like Premiere Pro.

As you set preferences in Premiere Pro, those settings are recorded and saved in a preferences file. Each time you start Premiere Pro, the preferences file is referenced in order to maintain your last settings. You can revert your preference settings to their default settings by deleting the preferences file. You should use Premiere Pro's default preferences as you follow the exercises in this book, in order to maintain consistency.

QUICKTIP

The easiest way to revert to default preferences is to press and hold down [Shift] [Ctrl] throughout the startup of the Premiere Pro application.

Premiere Pro also allows you to save different preferences configurations. This is a handy feature that allows you to save different techniques—your preferences—for different types of projects. For example, let's say you are working on two projects simultaneously—a psychedelic music video for your sister's pop-rock garage band and a straightforward wedding video. You may want to revert to default preferences to work on the wedding video, then use a saved set of preferences for the rock video.

Working in Premiere Pro

The work that you do in Premiere Pro is called editing. You assemble individual source files or **clips**—video, audio, still pictures, and graphics—into a video project. The final product can be output as many things: film or digital video, for example. It can be an on-screen presentation that you play on your computer monitor or a downloadable video that you store on your Web site. You can present the project on a CD or a DVD to hand out to friends, or you can import it as a feature within a larger CD-ROM presentation.

QUICKTIP

You can only have one project open at a time.

There are four types of workspaces: Editing, Effects, Audio, and Color Correction. The appearance of the workspace changes based on the type of editing workspace you choose. Figure 3 shows the

FIGURE 3
Audio workspace

Audio workspace with the Audio Mixer being the focus of this workspace. Figure 4 shows the Color Correction workspace. The focus in this workspace is not the same as the Audio workspace. Using the Color Correction workspace you can compare frames using the Program and Reference Monitors. Notice in each figure, the Tools panel is made available.

Using the Adobe Premiere Pro Help System

Adobe Premiere Pro comes packaged with lots of helpful information. Clicking Adobe Premiere Pro Help on the Help menu will lead you to the Adobe Help Center. Here you will find the Contents, Index, Search, and Bookmarks tabs on the left side of the window. The Contents tab provides you with topics organized by category, such as Transitions. If you expand the Transitions category, you'll see a list of related topics. Choosing a topic will display that topic in detail on the right side of the Help Center window.

If you are looking for a specific item, type the keyword(s) you are looking for in the Search For text box, then click Search. You can also get help for other Adobe products in the Adobe Help Center by clicking the View Help Info for This Product List arrow, then clicking the appropriate program name.

FIGURE 4
Color Correction workspace

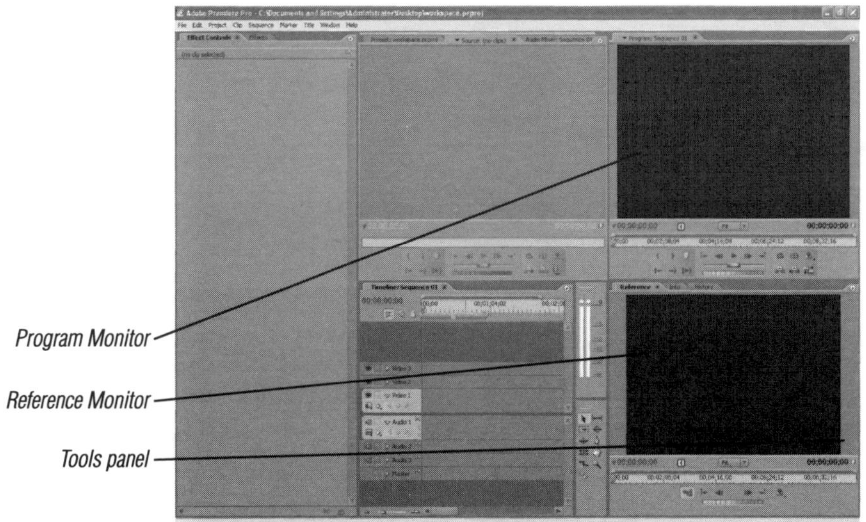

FIGURE 5
Starting Premiere Pro

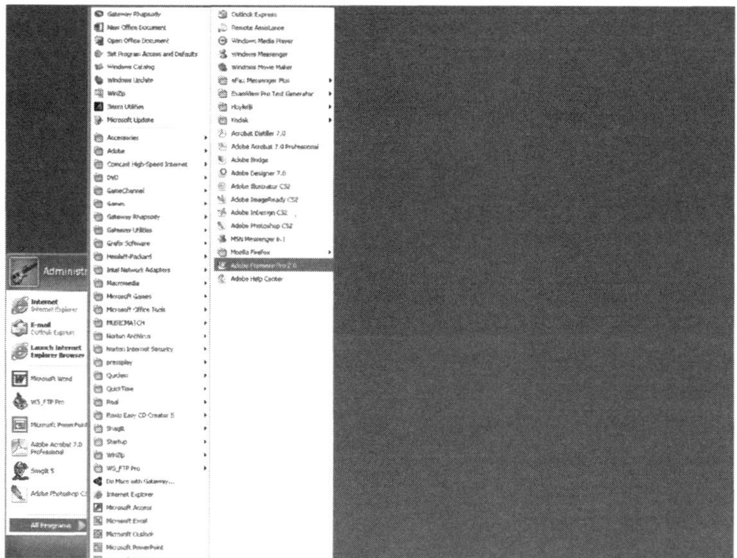

FIGURE 6
New Project dialog box

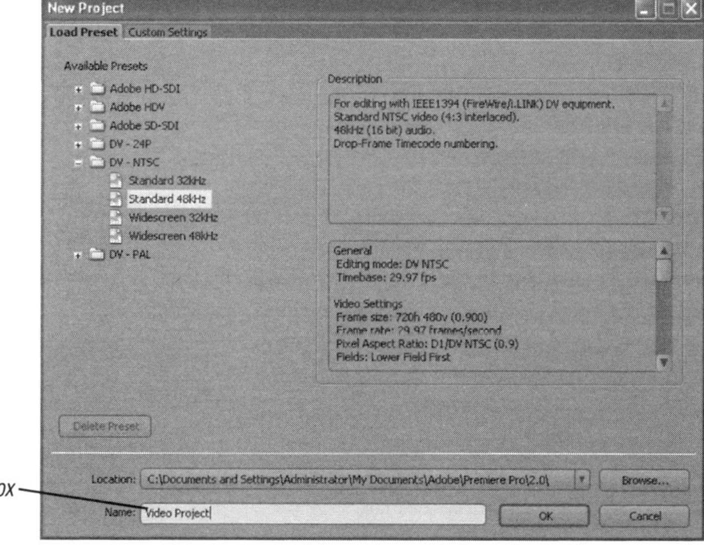

Start Adobe Premiere Pro

1. Click **Start** on the menu bar, point to **All Programs**, then click **Adobe Premiere Pro 2.0**, as shown in Figure 5.

   TIP Pressing and holding [Shift] [Ctrl] while starting Premiere Pro restores default preference settings.

2. Click **New Project** in the Adobe Premiere Pro 2.0 window, type **Video Project** in the Name text box of the New Project dialog box, as shown in Figure 6, then click **OK**.

   The Premiere Pro workspace appears.

3. Locate the Project, Source Monitor, Program Monitor, and Timeline panels.
4. Click **Window** on the menu bar, point to **Workspace**, then click **Color Correction**.

   Note the change in the workspace appearance.

5. Click **Window** on the menu bar, point to **Workspace**, then click **Editing**.
6. Click **File** on the menu bar, then click **Close**.

You started Adobe Premiere Pro, located the Project, Source Monitor, Program Monitor, and Timeline panels, changed the type of workspace, then closed the Video Project file.

LESSON 2

WORK IN THE PROJECT PANEL

What You'll Do

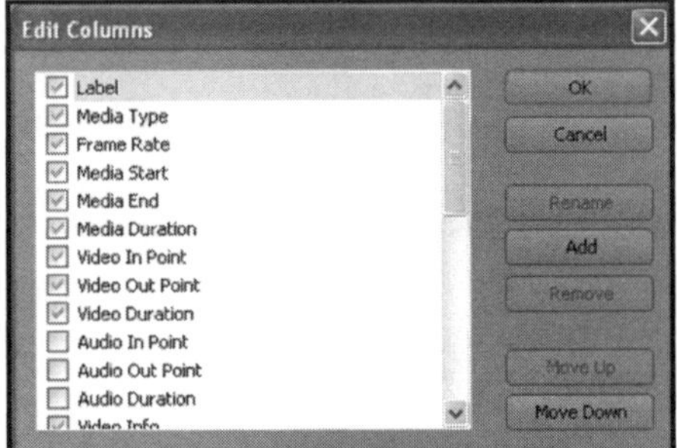

In this lesson, you will explore the Project panel and its options for storing and organizing clips.

Defining the Role of the Project Panel

In Premiere Pro, the project is the entirety of what you are working on. You will almost certainly refer to your project as a "movie" or a "video." Premiere Pro uses the more generic terms "project" and "video program."

The Project panel is your project, and you cannot have two projects open at one time. When you save your project, the name you give it appears in the title bar of the Project panel.

The Project panel contains all of the elements of your project. It is the storage site for source files or clips that you import into Premiere Pro—clips which you may or may not use in the movie you are creating. Source clips are usually thought of as video and audio clips; it's important to note that source clips can also include still images and graphics. Does that last sentence make your eyes widen with excitement? It should, because Premiere Pro is not only for video; it's a place where you can animate your work from graphics programs such as Photoshop and Illustrator. Think of the possibilities!

When you import source clips into Premiere Pro, you have the option of importing single or multiple clips, folders that contain multiple clips, or all the clips from another Premiere Pro project. Video files that are used in Premiere Pro projects are typically large in size and take up a substantial amount of memory. In order to keep your project's file size manageable, actual video clips or art files are not imported into Premiere Pro. Instead, the Project panel imports **reference files** that point to the original files on your computer. Otherwise, a typical project's file size might become so enormous that it would crash your computer!

Working in the Project Panel

Not much happens in the Project panel other than storage. However, it is important that you master the options available in the Project panel. These options are, essentially, all about organization. It's one thing to work with three or four clips that make up a 90-second movie. It's another thing altogether to work with hundreds of clips that make up a 30-minute movie.

The Project panel is divided into two sections. The top section includes the Preview Area, which allows you to preview a selected clip. The bottom section displays a list of individual clips and bins. **Bins** are folders that you can create using the Bin button, to store loose clips. You can assign descriptive names to bins to help you identify their contents. This option is helpful when you are working with dozens of bins. To view the contents of a bin, click the triangle to the left of it to expand it; click it again to collapse the bin.

The Project panel can be viewed two ways: List View or Icon View. Figure 7 shows the Project panel in List View. Figure 8 shows the Project panel in Icon View. In Icon View, you can choose a size for the thumbnails shown in the Project panel by clicking the Project panel list arrow, pointing to Thumbnails, then clicking Small, Medium or Large.

List View is the simplest—and the least memory-intensive—view. It lists the loose clips by name. List View offers 24 columns of information about the clips in the Project panel. The Name and Label columns should be visible if your Project panel is at its default size; however, if you resize it or scroll, you 'll see the Media Type, Frame Rate, and Media Start columns. Keep scrolling to the right to view all information pertaining to your clips. You can choose which columns you want to show in the Project panel by clicking the Project panel list arrow, clicking Edit Columns, then adding or removing check marks from the column names in the Edit Columns dialog box. You can even rename columns and change the order of the columns using the Rename, Move Up, and Move Down buttons, respectively.

QUICKTIP

You can easily locate a clip in the Project panel by clicking the Find button. The found item will be highlighted in the Project panel.

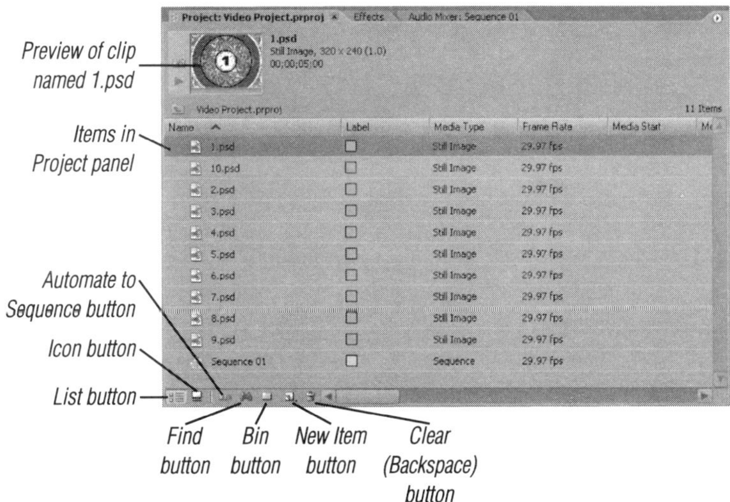

FIGURE 7
Project panel in List View

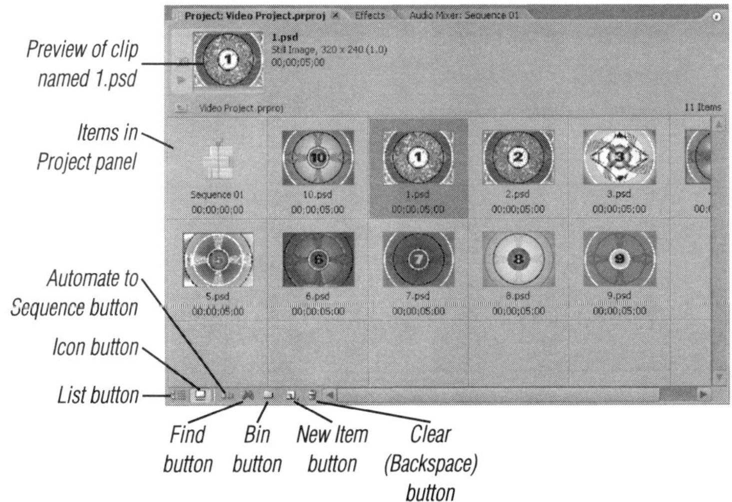

FIGURE 8
Project panel in Icon View

Explore List View options

1. Click **Open Project** in the Adobe Premiere Pro 2.0 window, open APP 1-1.prproj from your Chapter 1 Data Files folder, click **File** on the menu bar, click **Save As**, type **Rex vs. Blake** in the File Name text box, navigate to the drive where your Data Files are stored, then click **Save**.

   Premiere Pro files are saved with the Adobe Premiere Pro Project file type extension .prproj.

   > TIP Do not save your work to the Source Clips folder. Use the Source Clips folder only to locate source clips needed with your Data Files.

2. Click the **List View button** in the Project panel, if necessary.
3. Click the **triangle** to the left of the Loose Clips bin to view its contents.

   Your Project panel should resemble Figure 9.
4. Click the **Project panel list arrow**, then click **Edit Columns**.
5. Remove all of the check marks in the Edit Columns dialog box, except for the first six items, so that your Edit Columns dialog box matches Figure 10.

(continued)

FIGURE 9
Expanding the Loose Clips bin

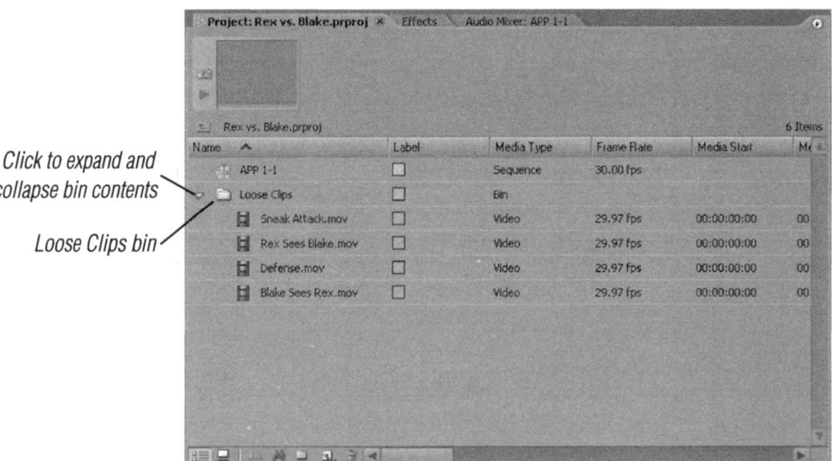

FIGURE 10
Edit Columns dialog box

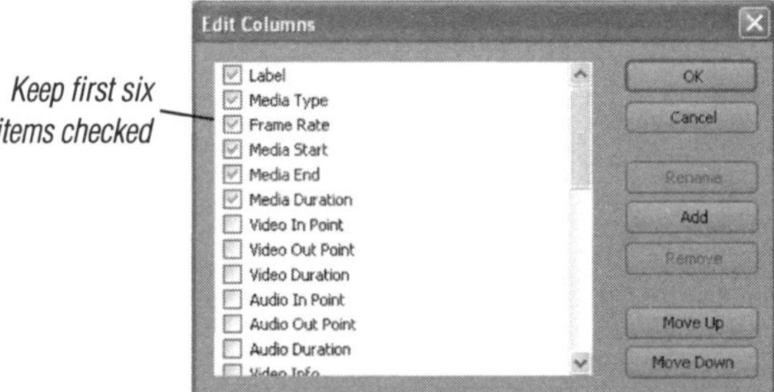

FIGURE 11

Moving Media Duration below Label

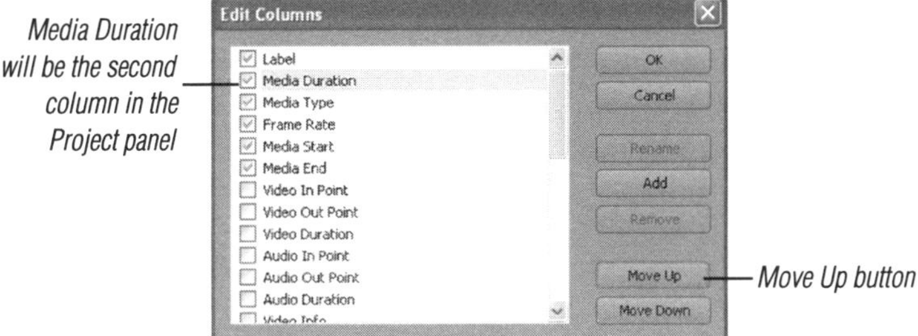

FIGURE 12

Viewing the length of Sneak Attack.mov

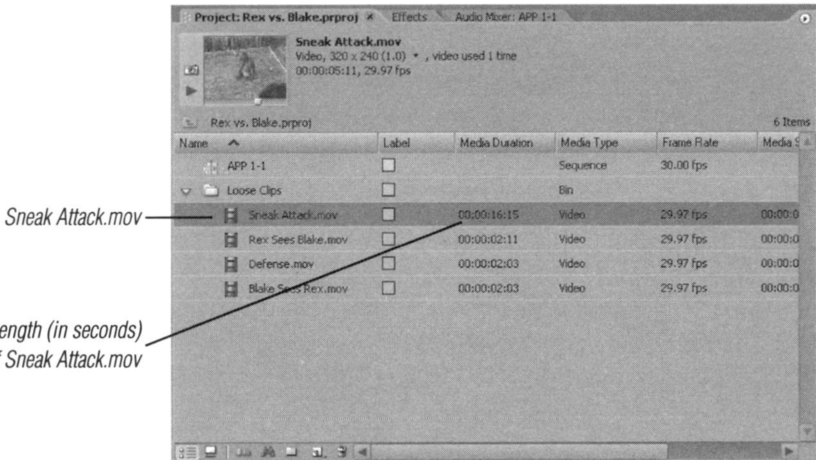

6. Click **Media Duration** in the Edit Columns dialog box.
7. Click **Move Up** four times so that Media Duration is below Label, as shown in Figure 11.

   Media Duration will be the second column in the Project panel when the Project panel is in List View.
8. Click **OK** to close the Edit Columns dialog box.
9. Click **Sneak Attack.mov** in the Project panel, then notice its duration under the Media Duration column.

   The length of the Sneak Attack movie clip is approximately 16 seconds, as shown in Figure 12.
10. Save your work.

You viewed the Project panel in List View, then changed the number and order of the information columns using the Edit Columns dialog box.

Explore Icon View options

1. Click the **Icon View button** [icon] in the Project panel.
2. Double-click the **Loose Clips bin**.

   Your screen should resemble Figure 13.
3. Click **Sneak Attack.mov**, then view the Preview Area in the Project panel.

   The Preview Area lets you preview a clip, whether it is a still image or a video clip.
4. Drag the **small slider** beneath the preview of Sneak Attack.mov all the way to the left, then click the **Play button** [icon] to view the video clip in the Project panel, as shown in Figure 14.

   TIP Previewing clips in the Project panel allows you to watch them before adding them to your project.

5. Click the **Folder icon** [icon] below the Play button in the Preview Area to view the Loose Clips bin.
6. Click the **List button** [icon] to return to List View.

You viewed the Project panel in Icon View, then previewed a movie clip in the Preview Area.

FIGURE 13

Viewing the Project panel in Icon View

FIGURE 14

Previewing Sneak Attack.mov in the Preview Area

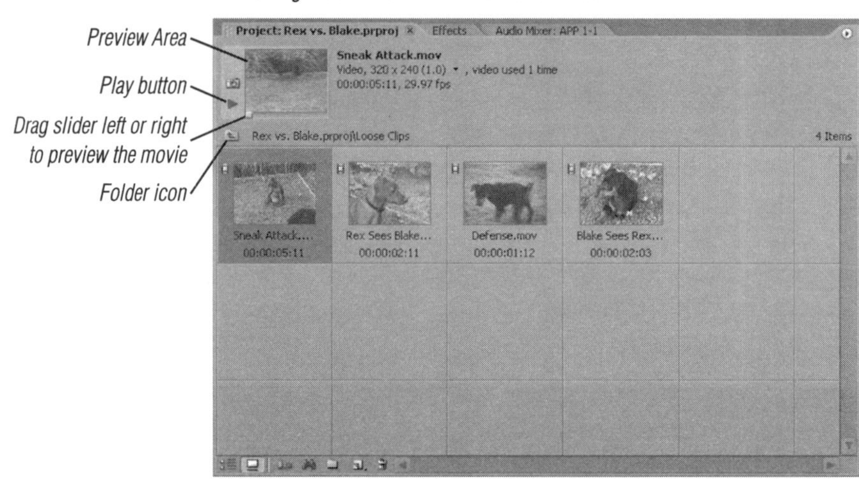

FIGURE 15

Mendelssohn.mov added to the Project panel

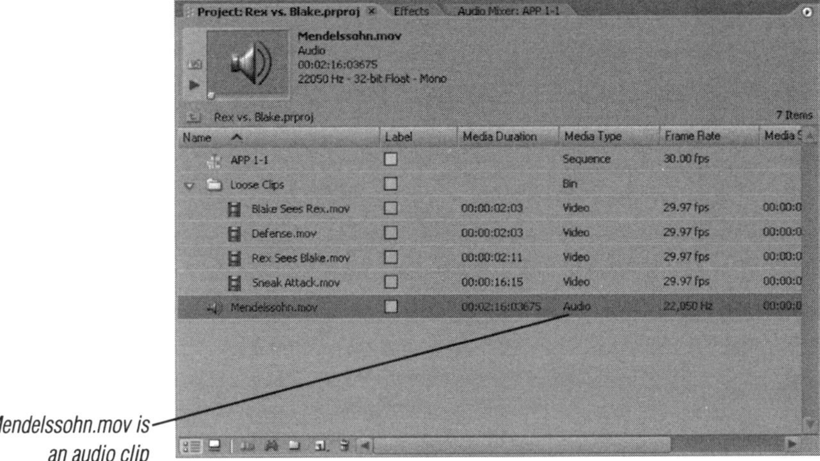

Mendelssohn.mov is an audio clip

Import clips into the Project panel

1. Click **File** on the menu bar, then click **Import**.
2. Navigate to the Source Clips folder, then click **Open**.
3. Click **Mendelssohn.mov**, then click **Open**.

   As shown in Figure 15, Mendelssohn.mov appears in the Project panel and it is listed as an Audio file in the Media Type column.

   TIP Items in the Project panel are labeled with different colors. Notice on your monitor that audio files are labeled green and video files are labeled blue.

4. Save your work.

You imported an audio file to the Project panel and noted its media type and label color.

Identifying How Premiere Pro Fits into Video Production

Video production generally breaks down into three recognizable phases. The first—pre-production—involves coming up with a concept, writing a script for dialogue and action, and possibly sketching a storyboard to help visualize some shooting goals. The second phase—production—involves the actual shooting of the scenes. The third phase—post-production—involves choosing the best scenes, or the best versions of scenes, and editing them into a rough cut. Post-production also includes enhancing the video or audio quality, fine-tuning the editing to improve the narrative and the flow of the program, adding music and sound effects, and adding titles. Once you decide that you have finished, you have produced the final cut. Premiere Pro is positioned in this third phase—post-production. If you are making a movie that you intend to run on your computer, or maybe upload to the Internet or distribute to your friends and family on a CD or DVD, Premiere Pro may be the only tool you will need in post-production. However, if your ambitions are to produce a final cut for broadcast or for film, you will require the consultation of professionals. Keep in mind that whenever your project involves outside vendors, such as a video production or post-production house, consult them first before starting any phase of production. In fact, that consultation should be your first step in pre-production!

LESSON 3

EXPLORE THE SOURCE AND PROGRAM MONITORS

What You'll Do

In this lesson, you will explore the Source and Program Monitor panels and their role in previewing clips.

Working in the Source Monitor

The Source Monitor is where you preview individual source files—clips that you may or may not use as part of your final movie. These can include video segments, still pictures, graphics files, and title cards.

To view a clip in the Source Monitor, you must first add it to the Source Monitor. To

Getting Paid to Play

Can anything this fun really be called work? The answer is a very big yes! If you relish the idea of working with video—of making movies for a living—you couldn't have picked a better time to get started. Just 20 years ago, if your ambition was to be an editor, you would have had to hustle for a job in a much smaller movie or television industry or try to find work in the newly developing world of video and video production. Now, we have entered a multi-channel, multimedia age, with so many venues that are all in need of the type of skills that you will hone with Premiere Pro. On the Internet alone, it is only a matter of time—and not much time—before online video is commonplace and people are trading video the way they now trade e-mail. The rapidly expanding world of animation, video games, and CD-ROM publishing offers a wealth of fascinating jobs and skill sets. So here you are, learning about video and editing, honing your skills, and sharpening your visual senses. You're in the right place at the right time. There's a whole multimedia world out there that will be more than happy to meet you. And you will find few things in the working world as sweet as getting paid to play.

do so, you can double-click the clip in the Project panel or simply drag a clip from the Project panel into the Source Monitor as shown in Figure 16. You can add multiple clips to the Source Monitor, then view the clip you want using the Source menu at the top of the Source Monitor.

Working in the Program Monitor

As you'll see by looking at Figure 17, the Program Monitor looks very much like the Source Monitor. The difference between the two is that, while the Source Monitor is used for viewing clips that are not already part of the sequence, the Program Monitor is used for previewing the actual movie being made. You'll preview your movie in the Program Monitor over and over, especially when you've added audio and special effects, to make sure that everything is in sync.

> **QUICKTIP**
>
> Premiere Pro uses the term "sequence" to refer to the contents in the Timeline. Some people use the term "movie" or "program" when referring to the contents in the Timeline. All mean the same thing; it's just a matter of preference.

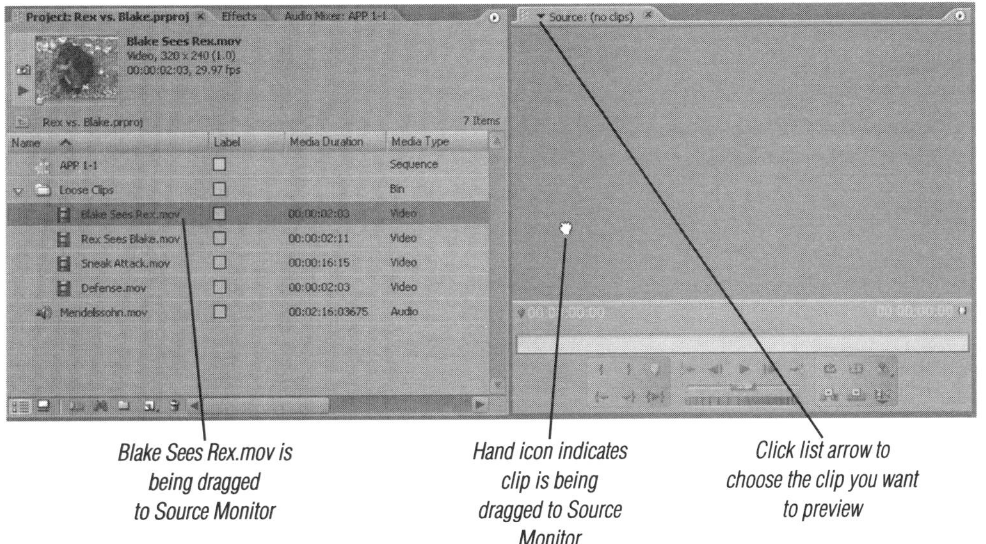

FIGURE 16
Dragging a clip into the Source Monitor for viewing

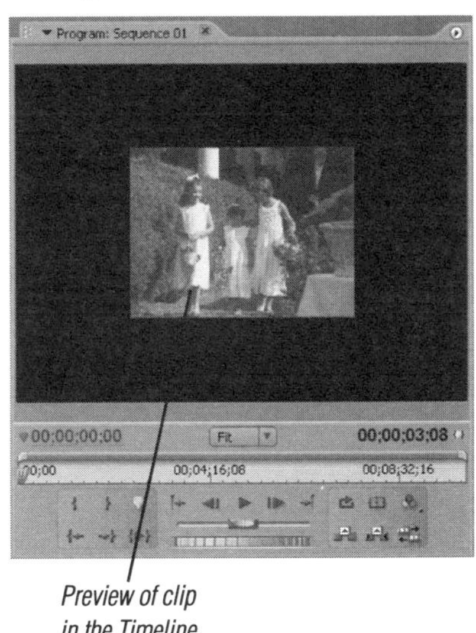

FIGURE 17
The Program Monitor

Understanding Preview Controls on the Source and Program Monitors

The Source and Program Monitors each have a set of buttons and controls for previewing clips. Figure 18 displays some of the basic controls for viewing your sequence.

The first set of buttons inside the red box in the figure are used for setting and navigating to **In points**, **Out points**, and **Markers**. In and Out points are places that you can set in the Timeline to crop part of a sequence. Markers are reference points that you create in order to isolate an important part of your sequence. For example, you may want to set a marker when the action changes in your sequence.

The **Play/Stop Toggle button** is used for playing and stopping the sequence. Once clicked, the Play button becomes the Stop button and vice versa. You can also click the **Step Back button** or the **Step Forward button** to move through your sequence one frame at a time. These buttons are useful if you are trying to find a specific frame. The **Loop button**, when clicked, plays a sequence repeatedly, until you click the Loop button again to turn off looping.

The **Shuttle slider** and the **Jog disk** are both used for manually previewing a sequence. You can drag the Shuttle slider or the Jog disk left or right to view your movie. If you use the Shuttle slider, the playback of the sequence becomes faster the farther you drag it from its original centered position.

FIGURE 18

Controls in the Program Monitor

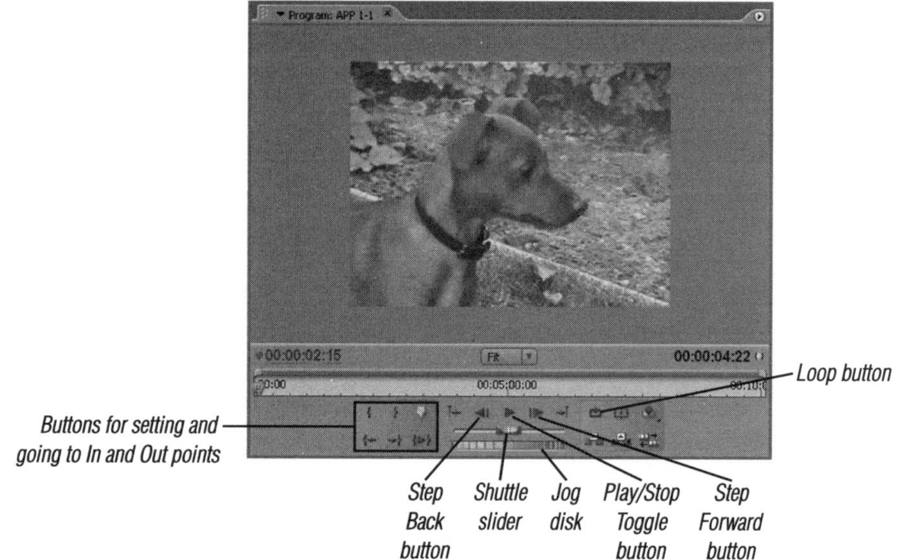

Understanding Time Controls on the Source and Program Monitors

The time controls in the Source and Program Monitors provide you with specific time information about your sequence or individual clip. Figure 19 shows these important controls in the Source Monitor. The **time ruler** displays the duration of a clip in the Source Monitor and the duration of a sequence in the Program Monitor. The time ruler is highlighted in blue for whichever monitor is selected. In this case, the time ruler is highlighted in blue because the Source Monitor is selected. The **Current time indicator** (light blue triangle) shows exactly which frame is being displayed. You can drag the Current time indicator to step through a clip or a sequence frame by frame, or watch it move automatically when you press the Play button. The **Current time display** identifies how far along you are into the clip during playback and the **Time duration display** indicates the total duration of the contents in the Timeline.

FIGURE 19
Time Controls in the Source Monitor

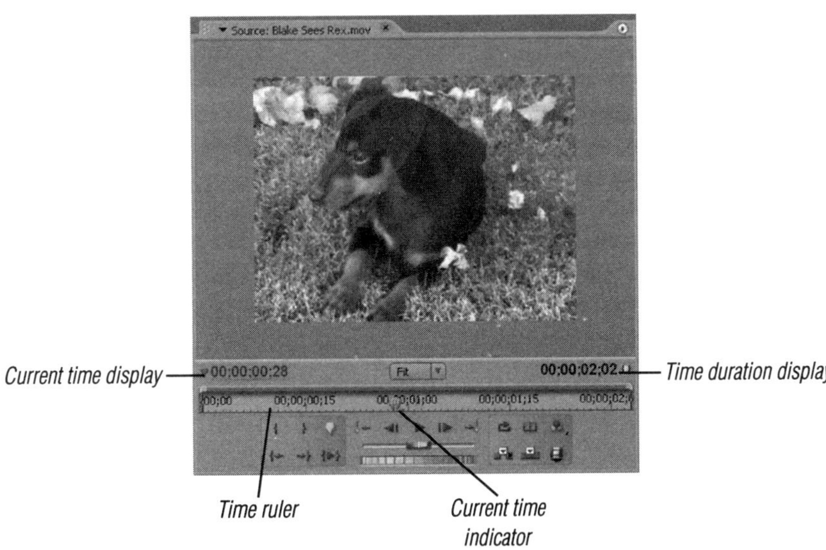

Preview clips in the Source Monitor

1. Verify that your Source Monitor is displayed.

   TIP If you do not see the Source Monitor, click Window on the menu bar, then click Source Monitor.

2. Double-click **Blake Sees Rex.mov** in the Project panel.

   The clip appears in the Source Monitor, as shown in Figure 20.

3. Press the **Play button** in the Source Monitor to view the clip once.

   TIP You can also press [Spacebar] to play and stop a clip.

4. Press the **Loop button** to play the clip continuously, then press the **Stop button** at any time.

5. Click the **Step Back** and **Step Forward buttons** in the Source Monitor to move backward and forward in the clip, one frame at a time.

   TIP You can use the right and left arrow keys on your keyboard to advance frames forward or backward.

6. Drag the **Shuttle slider** left and right, then all the way to the left.

You used the preview controls in the Source Monitor to view the clip.

FIGURE 20

Blake Sees Rex.mov in the Source Monitor

FIGURE 21

Sneak Attack.mov in the Video 1 track of the Timeline

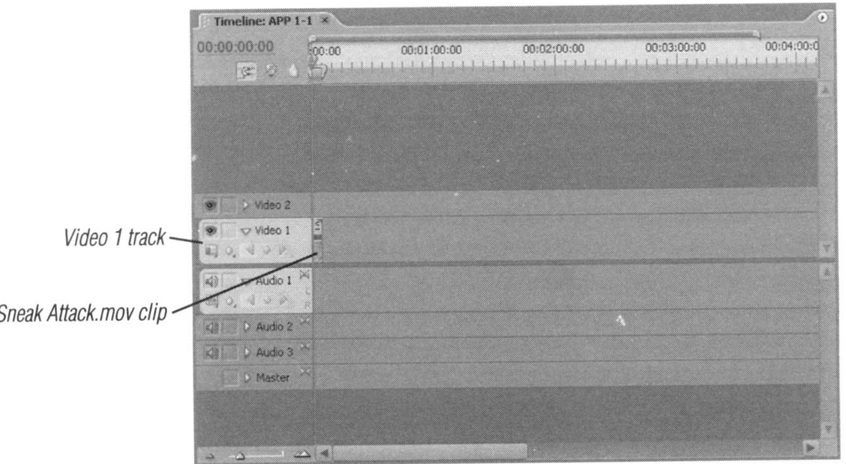

FIGURE 22

Stepping through a sequence using the Step Forward button

Preview contents of the Timeline in the Program Monitor

1. Verify that the Timeline is displayed.
2. Drag **Sneak Attack.mov** to the Video 1 track of the Timeline.

   Your screen should resemble Figure 21.
3. Press the **Play button** in the Program Monitor to view the contents of the Timeline.
4. Drag the **Current time indicator** in the Program Monitor left and right to view the sequence.

   > TIP Viewing the clip in this manner is referred to as **scrubbing** (so named because of the back-and-forth motion).
5. Drag the **Current time indicator** all the way to the left so that the timecode reads 00:00:00:00, then click the **Step Forward button** in the Program Monitor five times so that your Current time display matches that shown in Figure 22.

You dragged Sneak Attack.mov into the Video 1 track, then previewed it using the controls in the Program Monitor.

EXAMINE THE TIMELINE ELEMENTS

What You'll Do

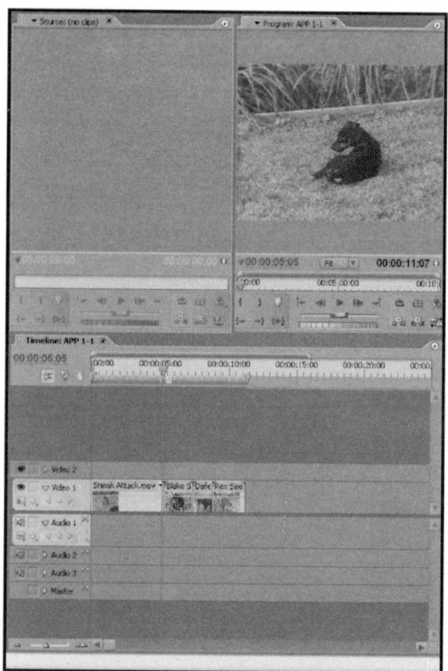

In this lesson, you will explore the Timeline, learn how to measure video time using timecode, and navigate to a specific frame.

Defining the Role of the Timeline

Much of the work you do in Premiere Pro will take place in the Timeline. The Timeline is where you assemble video clips, still art, audio clips, transitions, and video effects to produce a complete, edited sequence. In the Timeline, you move clips, duplicate them, adjust their lengths, and rearrange them, among other functions. Video clips and artwork that you import into Premiere Pro do not become part of your movie until you bring them into the Timeline.

The Timeline, as shown in Figure 23, offers you a visual representation of your movie.

FIGURE 23
The Timeline

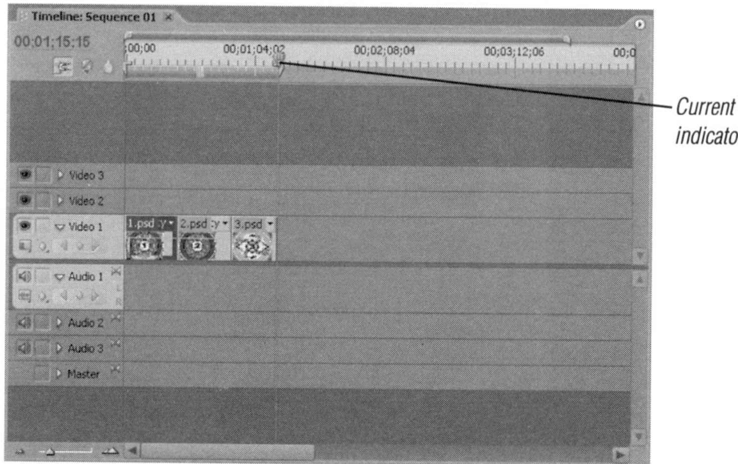

It uses icons to show the sequence of clips and the interaction of the clips with transitions, audio clips, and video and audio effects.

Working with the Timeline

When you look at the Timeline, you will note a vertical line that extends across all tracks. This is Current time indicator. At the top of the Current time indicator is a blue triangular handle, which you can drag left or right to scrub the movie.

The Timeline contains clips, and clips are made up of frames. The Current time indicator moves over clips in the Timeline, and that progress is shown in the Program Monitor. When the Current time indicator is still, it is stopped at a single frame, which is shown in the Program Monitor.

Working with Frame Rates

Frames are still images that, when viewed in sequence, create the appearance of motion. **Frame rate** is a measurement of the number of still images that make up one second of motion. Frame rate is specified as fps or frames per second.

When editing video, it is a good idea for you to remind yourself that movies are a series of still images, captured by a camera at a specific rate. The number of still images that a camera captures per second is called the source frame rate. For example, if your source frame rate is set to 30 fps on your video camera, the camera records one frame every 1/30th of a second. See Figure 24.

In a video project, a sufficient number of frames must be present to create the illusion of motion. For example, if the video camera were capturing visual data only once every second (1 fps), everything that happened between each second wouldn't be recorded. A lot can happen in one second. The action in the resulting video would be jumpy and would not create the illusion of continuous motion.

FIGURE 24
Video captured at 30 fps

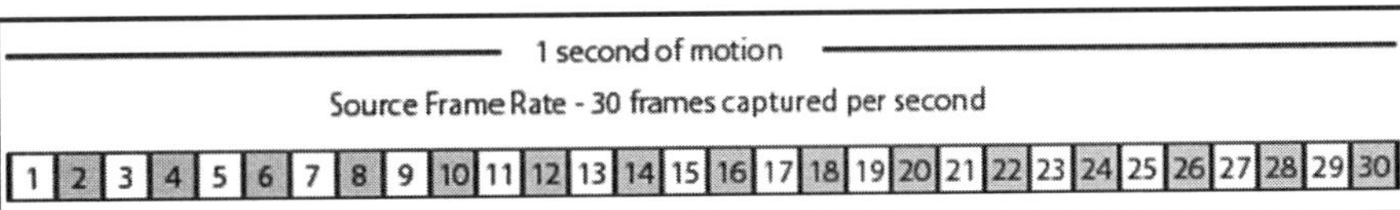

The timebase determines the increment at which time is measured in your current Premiere Pro project—you could say it is the project's frame rate. This is a very important determination, because edits can occur only at a time division. For example, if your timebase is set to 15, this means that the Timeline divides each second into 15 units, or frames. Thus, when a clip is brought into this Premiere Pro project, it can be edited only at 1/15th of a second intervals—regardless of the clip's source frame rate. For example, as shown in Figure 25, when a 30 fps source clip is brought into a Premiere Pro project whose timebase is set to 15 fps, every other frame of the source clip is discarded.

Finally, Premiere Pro uses the generic term frame rate to specify the rate at which it will generate frames from your project when it is output. For example, a project frame rate of 30 means that Premiere Pro will generate 30 frames from each second of your project to the output medium.

QUICKTIP

You may want to refer to the frame rate as the output frame rate to distinguish it in your mind from the timebase and the source frame rate.

Generally, you will determine the timebase and the frame rate when you begin a new project. The timebase is set in the Project Settings dialog box, as shown in Figure 26.

FIGURE 25
Every other frame is discarded

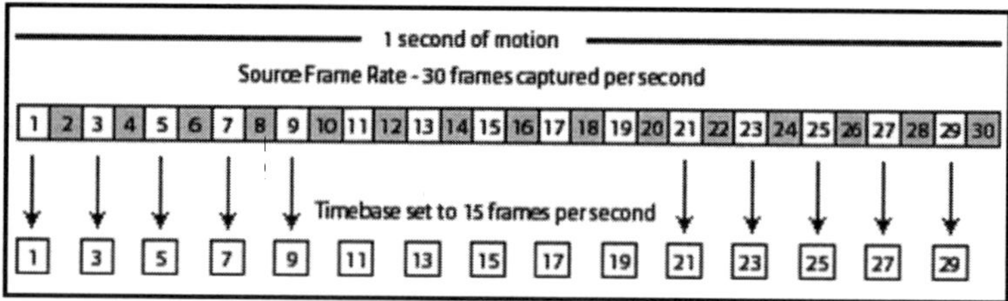

FIGURE 26
Project Settings dialog box

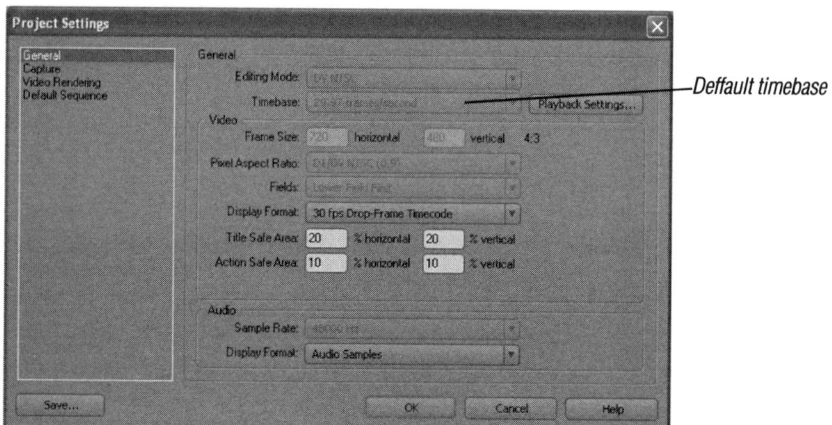

In the best-case scenario, the source frame rate, the timebase, and the (output) frame rate will all be consistent.

QUICKTIP

Premiere Pro uses the same timebase as NTSC: 29.97 frames per second.

Working with Timecode

Timecode is the method for counting frames and for measuring time in a video project. By default, Premiere Pro displays time using the SMPTE (*Society of Motion Picture and Television Engineers*) video timecode. Using this system, time is broken down into four increments: hours, minutes, seconds, and frames, separated by colons. Therefore, a movie whose duration is coded as 01:17:37:29 will play for 1 hour, 17 minutes, 37 seconds, and 29 frames.

The time ruler in the Timeline measures time in terms of timecode.

Timecode is also displayed in the Source Monitor and the Program Monitor. In the Source Monitor, the Time duration display on the left specifies the duration—in timecode—of the clip being viewed. The Current time display identifies the location of the current frame being viewed. In Figure 27, for example, the clip in the Source Monitor is 10 seconds in duration, and the image in the Source Monitor is located five seconds and 19 frames into the clip.

In the Program Monitor, the Time duration display specifies the duration of the sequence in the Timeline. The Current time display specifies how many hours, minutes, seconds, and frames the current frame is located into the movie.

Therefore, in Figure 28, the frame displayed in the Program Monitor is 20 seconds and 29 frames into a movie whose duration is one minute and four seconds.

FIGURE 27
Using timecode in the Source Monitor

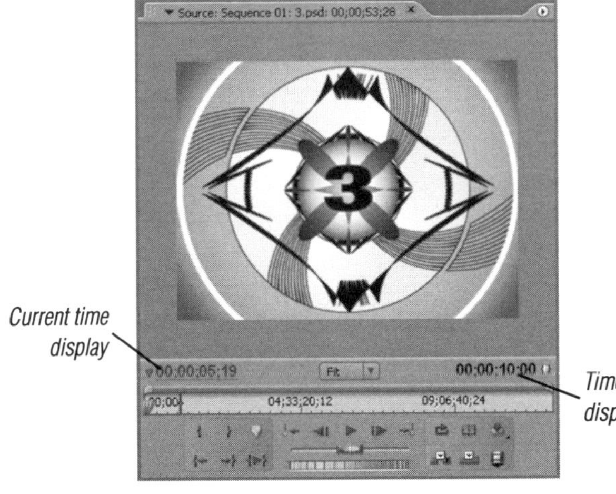

FIGURE 28
Using timecode in the Program Monitor

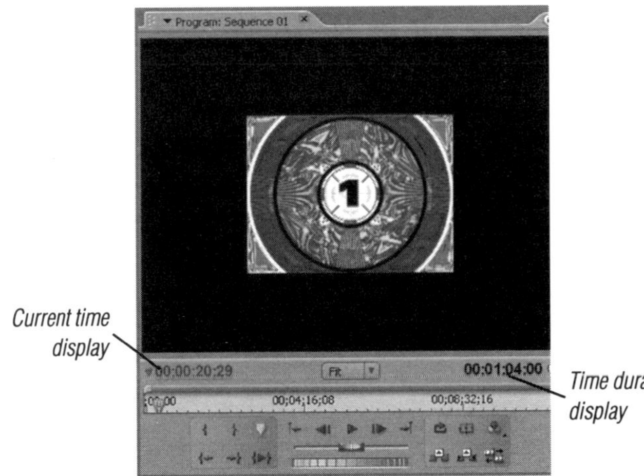

Entering Timecode

The Current time display in both monitors is interactive. You can enter the hour, minute, second, and frame that you want to go to. You do this by first selecting the numbers in the field. Then, type over the numbers, entering the timecode of the frame you want to preview.

For example, entering 1.3 in the Current time display will take you to a frame that is 1 second and 3 frames into the clip or the sequence. Entering 1.37.13 in the Current time display of the Program Monitor will take you to a frame that is 1 minute, 37 seconds, and 13 frames into the sequence. Note that when you enter this number, the Current time indicator in the Timeline window is positioned at the same frame. Understanding how to enter timecode will be crucial to making precise edits at specific frames.

Zooming In

The Zoom slider and Zoom In and Zoom Out buttons in the lower-left corner of the Timeline allow you to change your view of clips in the Timeline. Use the Zoom In button or drag the Zoom slider to zoom in on clips in the Timeline to see them with more detail, as shown in Figure 29. Use the Zoom Out button or drag the Zoom slider to the left to see all the clips in the Timeline at once. Working with a 20-minute movie, for example, you can specify the Timeline to show the movie's entire set of clips without your having to scroll. At the other extreme, you can specify that the Timeline shows you each frame of every clip!

Remember, the zoom level affects only the visual representation of the clip icons in the Timeline. Changing the zoom level does not affect the duration of the clips or the movie in any way.

Generally, you won't rely on the Timeline visuals alone to edit your movie. Instead, you will work in combination with the Source and Program Monitors and with the Info panel. In this manner, you can make your edits with necessary precision without having to enlarge the view in the Timeline.

FIGURE 29
Zoom controls in the Timeline

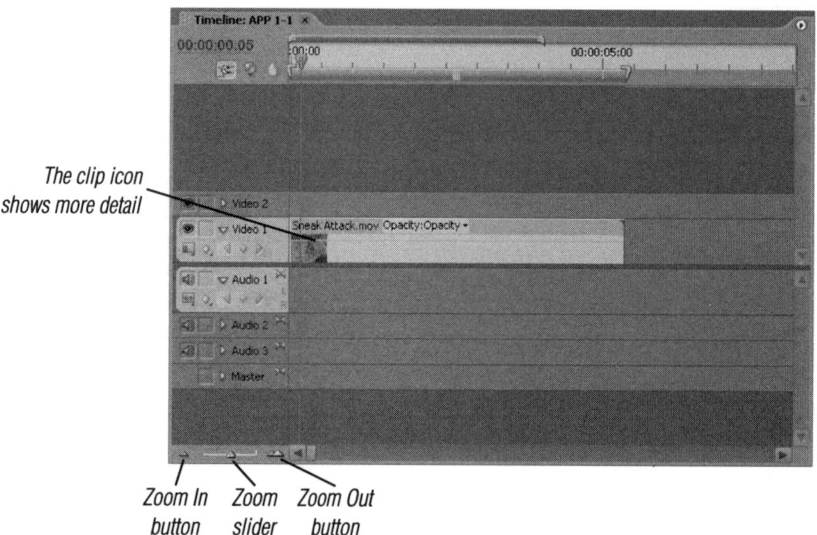

FIGURE 30
Zooming in on the Timeline

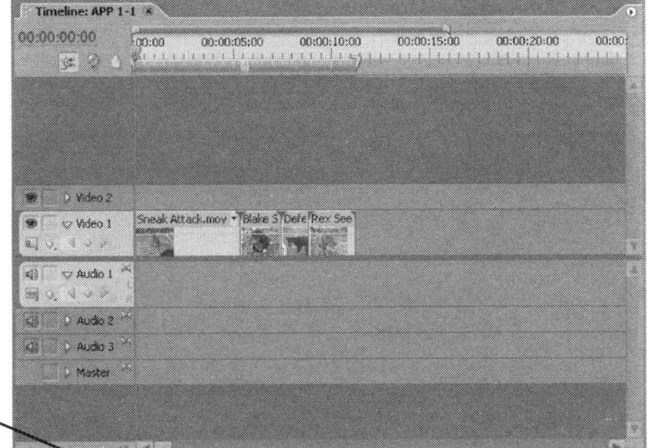

FIGURE 31
Using timecode to jump to a specific frame

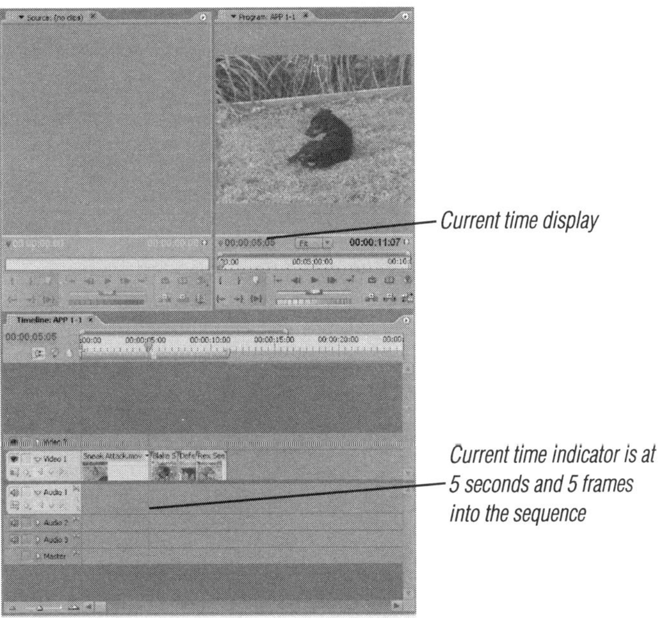

Work in the Timeline

1. Press and hold **[Ctrl]**, click **Blake Sees Rex.mov**, **Defense.mov**, and **Rex Sees Blake.mov** in the Project panel, then drag them next to Sneak Attack.mov in the Video 1 track of the Timeline.
2. Drag the **Zoom slider** slowly to the right until your screen resembles Figure 30.

   The clips are much easier to see. You can read the clip names in the Timeline, making it easier to recognize them.
3. Drag the **Zoom slider** left and right to see the impact of your moves in the Timeline.
4. Return to the approximate zoom level shown in Figure 30, then save your work.
5. Click the **Current time display** in the Program Monitor, type **5.5**, then press **[Enter]**.

   The Current time indicator jumps five seconds and five frames into the sequence, as shown in Figure 31.
6. Save your work, then close Rex vs. Blake.

You added more clips to the Timeline, then zoomed in and out to view them at different sizes. You then jumped to a specific frame by entering 5.5 in the Current time display.

CHAPTER SUMMARY

Adobe Premiere Pro is a video-editing software tool that allows you to create your own movies using still images, sounds, video and audio clips, and special effects, such as transitions. The Premiere Pro workspace includes the Project panel, which houses the elements you may use in your final project. It also includes the Source Monitor, Program Monitor, and the Timeline. You'll work mostly in the Timeline when putting your movie together. You can preview your work at any time during the process, using the controls in the Program Monitor. You can also preview clips that are not yet part of your sequence in the Source Monitor. The time controls in both monitors make it simple for you to see a specific frame of a clip or of an entire sequence at any time. There are other workspaces to choose from, and you can even save your own workspace that you've become comfortable with.

What You Have Learned

- How to start Adobe Premiere Pro 2.0
- How to identify the Project panel, Source Monitor, Program Monitor, and Timeline
- How to choose a workspace
- How to switch to List View
- How to switch to Icon View
- How to customize the Project panel using the Edit Columns dialog box
- How to preview a clip in the Preview Area of the Project panel
- How to import clips into the Project panel
- How to preview clips in the Source Monitor
- How to preview the contents of the Timeline in the Program Monitor
- How to add clips to the Timeline
- How to zoom in and out in the Timeline
- How to enter timecode in the Program Monitor

Key Terms

Project panel The Project panel is where you import, organize, and store references to video clips and still imagery. It lists all of the source files that you import; however, you do not need to use all of them in your final video program.

Timeline The Timeline is where you assemble and edit your video. It contains all of the source clips that are used in the project, including video and audio, as well as title cards, transitions, and special effects.

Source Monitor The Source Monitor is used for previewing still and video clips that are not necessarily part of the movie.

Program Monitor The Program Monitor is used for previewing the contents of the Timeline.

NR·328

PEPPER
SALT

chapter 2 WORKING WITH CLIPS

1. Import source files.
2. Work with still clips.
3. Bring clips into the Timeline.
4. Manipulate clips in the Timeline.

chapter 2 WORKING WITH CLIPS

In Premiere Pro, the Timeline is where you make it all happen. Like a canvas for a painter, or a sketchpad for a designer, the Timeline is where you do all your editing work, where you assemble your movie—and reassemble your movie. It's where you try out different clips—and different sequences of clips. From all the experimentation that you do in the Timeline, your final cut emerges.

The Timeline is nicely designed, intuitive, and easy to use. You can drag and drop clips quickly into the Timeline one at a time. But sometimes one at a time is just too slow. The Automate to Sequence command offers you the option to add multiple clips to the Timeline—in a specific sequence—with just one click! Once the clips are in the Timeline, you are free to rearrange and reassemble at will—select multiple clips, insert clips between other clips, add duplicate clips, and remove clips. You can have more than one Timeline panel open. Each Timeline panel is named "Sequence" followed by the next consecutive number available, such as Sequence 01, Sequence 02, and so on. To create a new Timeline panel, click File on the menu bar, point to New, then click Sequence. In the New Sequence dialog box, you can assign a new name to the sequence and choose the number of video tracks, as well as the number and type of audio tracks.

The Timeline is cool. It's smart. It's fun. It has to be—it's where you make your movie!

Tools You'll Use

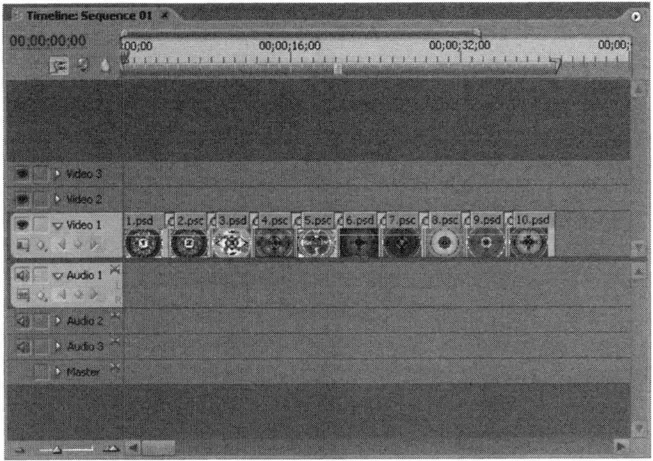

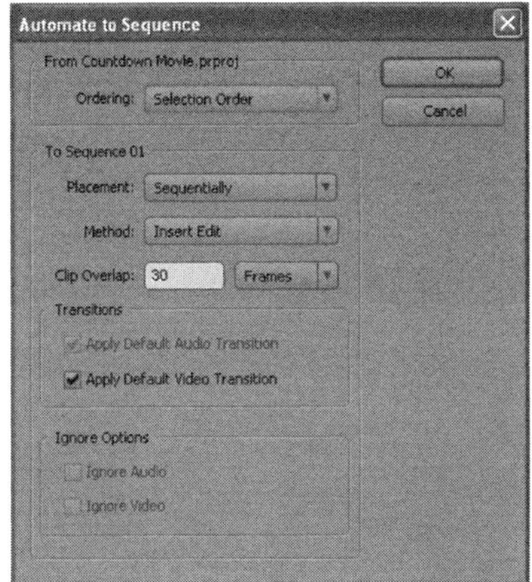

LESSON 1

IMPORT SOURCE CLIPS

What You'll Do

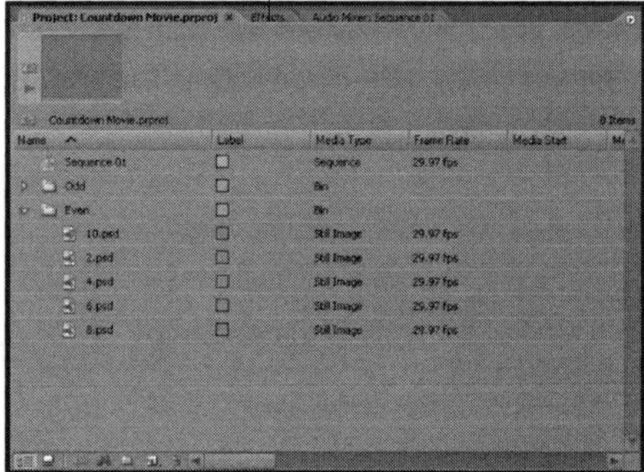

In this lesson, you will explore various methods for importing source files and organizing them in bins in the Project panel.

Using the Import Command

You import video and graphic files into Premiere Pro using the Import command. The Import command offers you the option to import a file, multiple files, a folder and its contents, or another Premiere Pro project.

QUICKTIP

You import multiple files by clicking File on the menu bar, pointing to Import, pressing [Ctrl], then selecting the files in the Import dialog box.

Working with RGB

Try this experiment: Dip your index finger in a glass of water, then flick a drop of water at your TV screen. The water will magnify the pixels that make up your TV image, and you will see that the image is composed *only* of red, green, and blue (RGB) pixels. That's right—all the color images you see on your TV are produced with red, green, and blue light. Red, green, and blue light (RGB) are the additive primary colors of light. The term **primary** refers to the fact that red, green, and blue lights cannot themselves be broken down or reduced. The term **additive** refers to the fact that they combine to produce other colors. For example, red and blue light, when combined, produce violet hues. As primary colors, red, green, and blue light are the irreducible component colors of light. All light sources, like your TV or your computer's monitor, use the RGB color model to produce color. Color video display is based on the RGB color model. Color film images have been created from colored light. Thus, when you are preparing still images for use in Premiere Pro, save them in Photoshop or Illustrator's RGB mode.

Most often, you will want to import multiple video clips and still images to use in a project. Having the option to import an entire folder and its contents is a very useful alternative to importing one file at a time. Before importing clips into Premiere Pro, you may want to organize them in folders by category. For example, you could place all still images that you plan on importing into a folder named Stills and all video clips into a folder named Video. Then, instead of importing the individual stills and video clips one at a time, you could import the two folders. This will not only save time but will ensure that you didn't leave an important clip behind.

QUICKTIP

You can import recently used clips by clicking the Import Recent File command on the File menu, then choosing a file from the list.

Organizing the Project Panel with Bins

Remember, the more source files you import for your movie, the more important it will be for you to keep them organized. Organizing source files in named bins makes them easy to find in the Project panel and easy to distinguish from other clips. To create a new bin, simply click the Bin button in the Project panel, then type a new name for it in the provided space. Bins can be expanded in order to view their contents and then collapsed to hide their contents. The ability to expand and collapse bins is another way to help keep the Project panel organized. Figure 1 shows the Project panel with two named bins: **Even Numbered Clips** and **Odd Numbered Clips**.

FIGURE 1
Using bins to organize clips

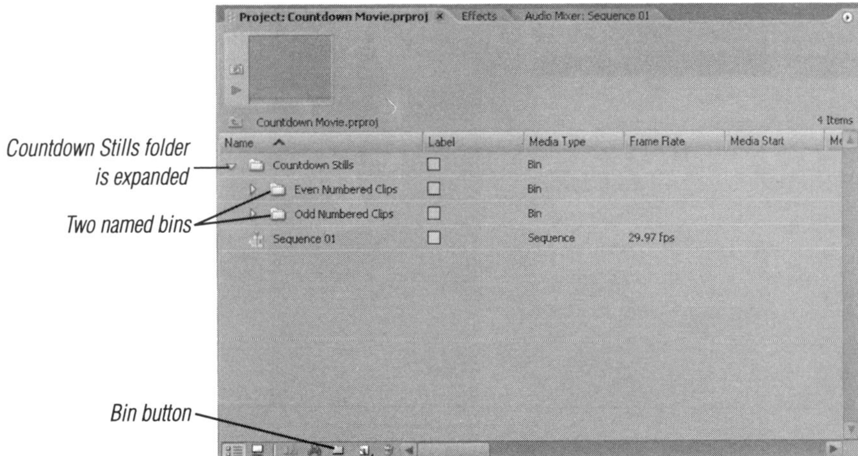

Notice that the Countdown Stills folder is expanded to show its contents: the two named bins. Clicking the triangle next to Countdown Stills would collapse the folder and hide the two named bins.

> TIP The Preview Area of the Project panel displays the name, media type, width, height, and duration of the selected clip. The Preview Area also identifies the name of the project and the bin that the selected clip is stored in, next to the folder icon.

Assigning Label Colors to Items in the Project Panel

Premiere Pro uses a labeling system to help identify program elements. For example, audio clips are assigned a label color of Green while still images are assigned a label color of Violet. Label colors appear as small squares in the Label column of the Project panel. If you prefer to rely on color to organize your Project panel, rather than storing like-items in named bins, you can feel free to change the default labeling system by changing the Label Defaults preference settings. Click Edit on the menu bar, point to Preferences, then click Label Defaults. Each category has a list arrow that you can click to select a new color. If you're really into color, you can click the Label Colors category on the left side of the Preferences dialog box, then create new label colors. For example, you can click the blue colored rectangle next to "Blue." Doing so opens the Color Picker, in which you can then create a shade of blue that you like using the options available. When finished, click OK and your new color will replace the old one. You can also rename the default colors by typing new names in the provided text boxes.

FIGURE 2

Project panel menu

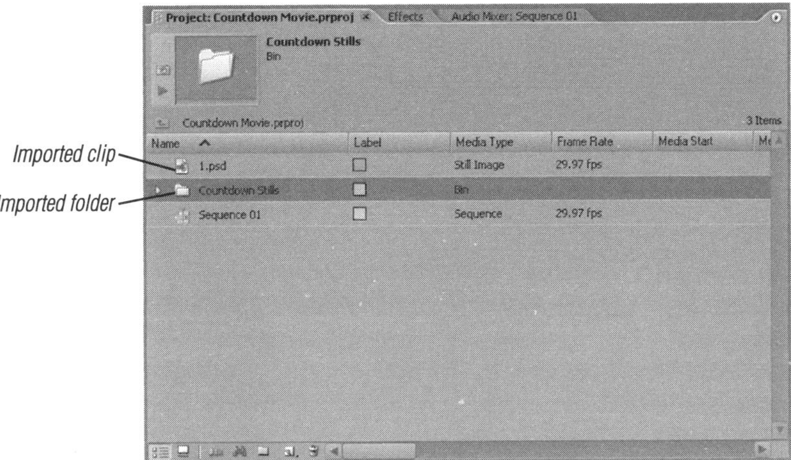

FIGURE 3

Expanding the Countdown Stills folder

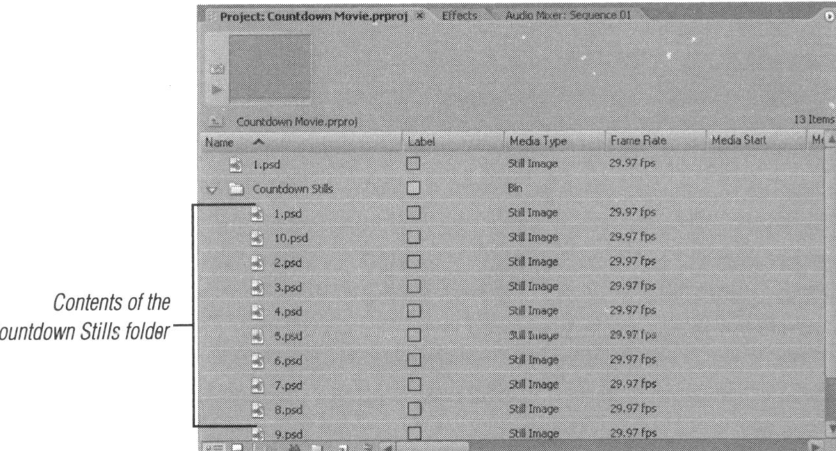

Import files and folders

1. Open APP 2-1.prproj, then save it as **Countdown Movie**.
2. Click **File** on the menu bar, then click **Import**.
3. Click the **Look In list arrow**, navigate to and open the Source Clips folder, click **Countdown Stills**, click **Open**, click **1.psd**, then click **Open**.

   1.psd is imported into the Project panel.
4. Click **File** on the menu bar, then click **Import**.
5. Navigate to and open the Source Clips folder, click the **Countdown Stills folder**, then click **Import Folder**.

   As shown in Figure 2, the folder is imported into the Project panel below 1.psd.
6. Click the triangle to the left of Countdown Stills in the Project panel.

   The contents of the Countdown Stills folder are displayed, as shown in Figure 3.

   TIP Bins are assigned a label color of Orange. To change the label color of bins, click Edit on the menu bar, point to Preferences, click Label Defaults, click the Bin list arrow, choose another color, then click OK.
7. Click **1.psd**, then click the **Clear button** in the Project panel.
8. Save your work.

You imported a single file and a folder into the Project panel. You viewed the contents of the folder, then deleted the single clip.

Create new bins and store clips

1. Click the **Bin button** ![bin] in the Project panel, type **Odd** in the space provided, then press **[Enter]**.
2. Drag **1.psd** from the Countdown Stills folder into the Odd bin by dragging it on top of the bin until the bin is highlighted, as shown in Figure 4, then release the mouse pointer.
3. Click **3.psd**, press and hold **[Ctrl]**, then click **5.psd**, **7.psd**, and **9.psd**., as shown in Figure 5.

(continued)

FIGURE 4

Dragging 1.psd into the Odd bin

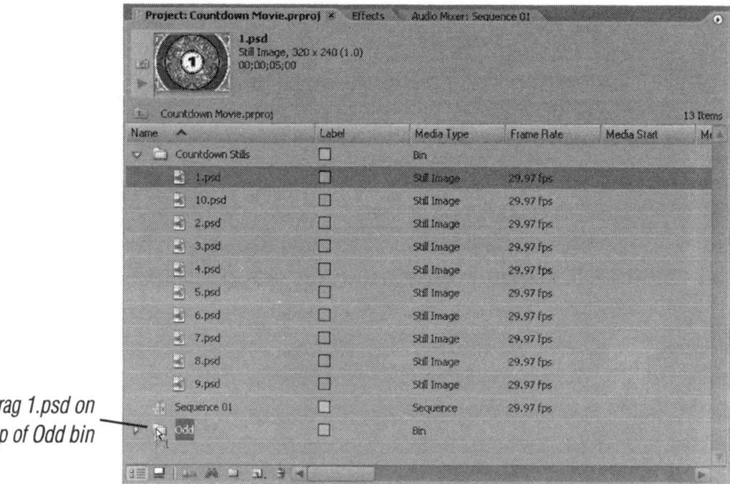

FIGURE 5

Selecting multiple clips

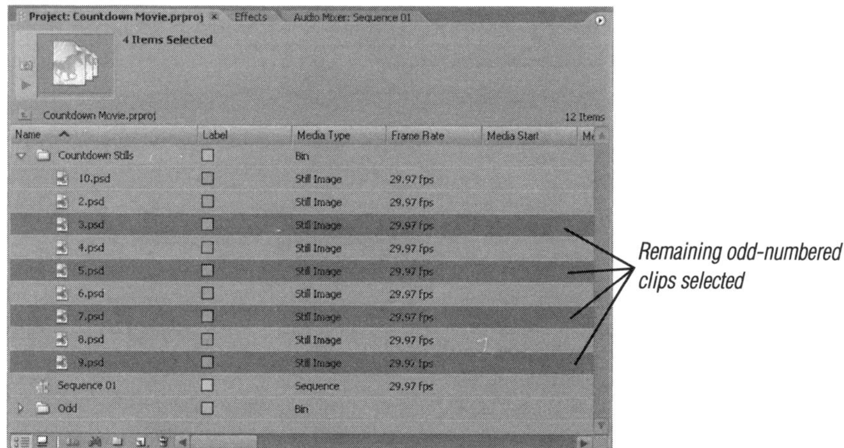

FIGURE 6
Expanding the Even bin

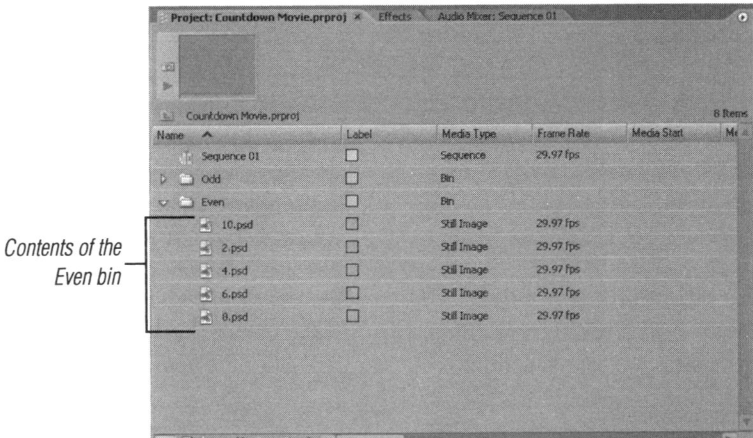

4. Release [Ctrl], then drag the four selected clips into the Odd bin.

   TIP Before you drag the clips, position the mouse in one of the four highlighted areas, then drag all of the clips; otherwise you may lose your selection.

5. Click the **Bin button**, name the new bin **Even**, then press **[Enter]**.
6. Select 2.psd, 4.psd. 6.psd. 8.psd, and 10.psd, then drag them into the Even bin.
7. Delete the Countdown Stills folder.
8. Expand the Even bin, then compare your Project panel to Figure 6.
9. Save your work.

You created two new bins, then dragged clips into them.

WORK WITH STILL IMAGES

What You'll Do

In this lesson, you will modify the duration of clips.

Changing the Duration of Still Images

Still images will often include key components of your project, such as logos, animations, title cards, or rolling credits. Think about it: When you import a one-minute video clip, its duration is ... one minute.

So what is the duration of a still image? In Premiere Pro, the duration of a still image is whatever you set it to be. When you import a still image, Premiere Pro applies the default duration that is specified in the General section of the Preferences dialog box. As shown in Figure 7, the still

FIGURE 7
Preferences dialog box

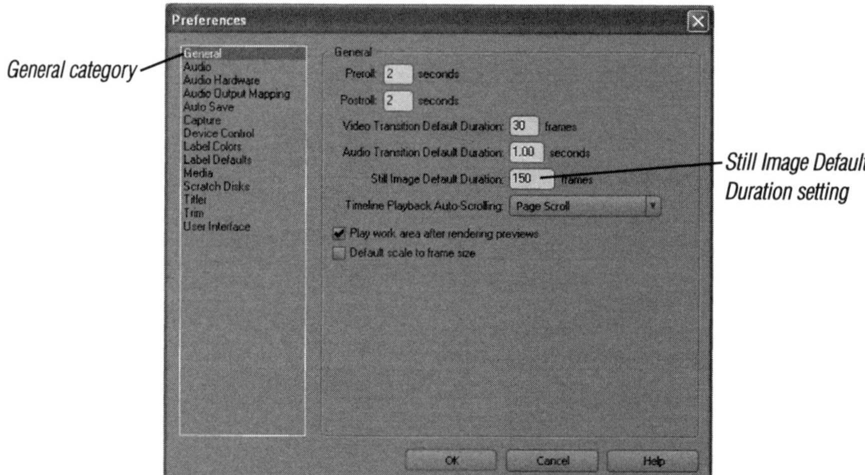

image default duration is 150 frames. At this setting, still images would appear for five seconds in a project that has a frame rate of 30 frames per second. You can change the duration of a still image after you import it; however, if you are importing many still images, it makes sense to change the preference setting before importing the stills.

Working with Parameters for Frames

All movies are series of still images or **frames**. Every frame is composed of pixels. **Pixels**—short for *picture element*—are the smallest components of a digital image. Pixels can be square or rectangular. The **pixel aspect ratio** is a measurement that specifies the ratio of width to height of one pixel in a frame. Square pixels are an NTSC (*National Television Standards Committee*) standard; the pixel aspect ratio of a square pixel is 1:1. Figure 8 shows two different pixel aspect ratios. Frames, too, can be different shapes. You are probably familiar with this if you've ever compared a "wide screen" version of a movie on DVD with what you see when it is broadcast on your relatively square television set. The **frame aspect ratio** specifies the ratio of width to height of the frames in a project. The NTSC standard frame aspect ratio is 4:3. Figure 9 shows two different frame aspect ratios.

FIGURE 8
Different pixel aspect ratios

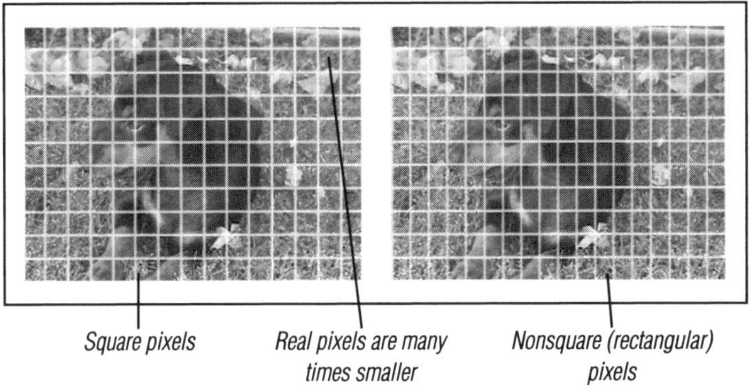

FIGURE 9
Different frame aspect ratios

Using NTSC Standards

The National Television Standards Committee (NTSC) is responsible for setting television and video standards in the United States. In Europe and most of the rest of the world, the dominant television standards are PAL (*Phase Alternation Line*) and SECAM (*Sequential Couleur avec Memoire*). The NTSC standards are just that—standards. There are many different pixel and frame aspect ratios for different formats. For example, some motion picture frame sizes use a more elongated aspect ratio of 16:9. Some formats also use rectangular rather than square pixels.

The pixel aspect ratio is decided upon when you create a new project. When you create a new project, the Load Preset tab is activated and the default pixel aspect ratio, D1/DV NTSC (0.9), is displayed on the right. To change this setting, you must first click the Custom Settings tab in the New Project dialog box, then click the Pixel Aspect Ratio list arrow to choose a new setting. To view the pixel aspect ratio for a project that is already created, click Project Settings on the Project menu, then click General. You can also view the frame size (or frame aspect ratio) in the Project Settings dialog box, as shown in Figure 10. The **frame size** is the number of pixels that make up the image. When working in video, you express the frame size in terms of total pixels. For example, a standard frame size of 640 × 480 means that each frame is 640 pixels wide and 480 pixels in height. Finally, should you need to adjust the pixel aspect ratio of a still image, you can do so by first selecting it in the Project panel, clicking File on the menu bar, clicking Interpret Footage, then making necessary adjustments in the Interpret Footage dialog box.

FIGURE 10

Project Settings dialog box

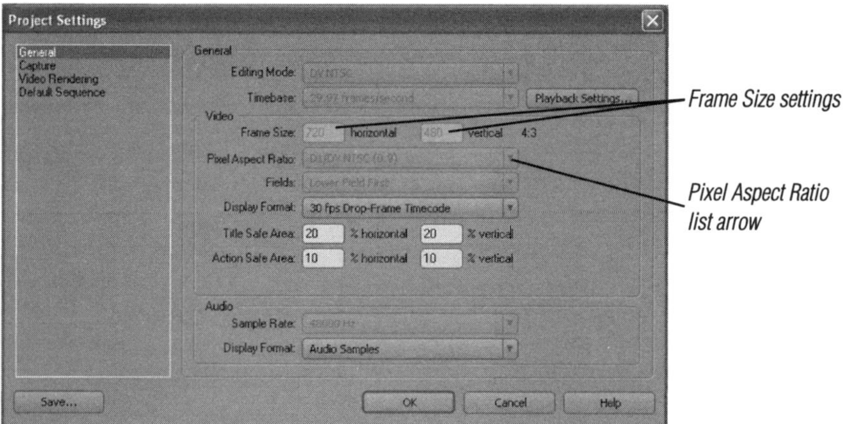

Creating Photoshop Documents for Premiere Pro

Creating Photoshop documents at a 4:3 ratio means that your Photoshop document and your Premiere Pro project's frames are the same shape—their widths and heights are proportional. It doesn't necessarily mean they are the same size. For example, if you create a Photoshop document at 640 × 480 pixels, it will not be distorted when imported into a Premiere Pro project whose frame size is 320 × 240; both sets of measurements have a 4:3 ratio. But the Photoshop image is twice the size of the Premiere Pro frame, so Premiere Pro will need to reduce the Photoshop image for use in the project. A good rule of thumb is that Photoshop is always the best choice for scaling an image. In the above example, you'd be better off reducing the image in Photoshop to 320 × 240 rather than leaving it for Premiere Pro to do the job.

Setting the Aspect Ratio in Other Applications

By default, when you import a still image, Premiere Pro will alter the width and height of the image to match that of the frame aspect ratio specified for the project. This means you'll want to create images with the same pixel aspect ratio as the frame aspect ratio chosen for your movie.

Director's Cut: *Goodfellas*

Director Martin Scorsese used still images to great effect in his magnificent 1990 Mafia epic, *Goodfellas*. One of the marks of Scorsese's brilliance is his understanding that what you see—and the way he makes you see it—elicits very specific feelings. Throughout the film, Scorsese stops the action of the film, and he uses those sudden stops to manipulate your emotions and your experience as a viewer.

(photo courtesy of Photofest)

Robert De Niro and Ray Liotta in a scene from Martin Scorsese's Goodfellas

Watch the scene toward the end of the movie, when our narrator, Henry Hill (Ray Liotta), meets Jimmy Burke (Robert De Niro) in a diner. Henry knows that Jimmy has been killing off their partners in crime to keep them from talking, and Henry knows that Jimmy wants to keep him quiet too. These are two old friends on the surface who both know they have become deadly enemies. The conversation is fairly casual, until Jimmy talks about sending Henry to Miami to "do a job." We see Jimmy as he slides a note with a name written on it across the table—and the action stops. In a voice-over narrative, Henry tells us that he knew at that very instant that he would never come back from Miami alive.

This scene could have been done without the still frame, but it would have been far less effective. Because, like Henry, we are suddenly paralyzed. We are forced to stay in this moment and bear the full implications of Jimmy's request. By freezing this moment—the passing of the note—Scorsese drives home the full thrust of the narrative, isolating a single action that signifies an old friend's kiss of death.

Modify the default duration of still clips

1. Click **10.psd** in the Project panel.
2. Click **Clip** on the menu bar, then click **Speed/Duration**.

   The duration of 10.psd is five seconds.
3. Click the existing duration in the Clip Speed / Duration dialog box to highlight it as shown in Figure 11, type **2.15**, then click **OK**.
4. Drag the **scroll bar** in the Project panel to the right until you see the Video Duration column, then stop scrolling.

   The duration of clip 10.psd is 2 seconds and 15 frames, as shown in Figure 12.
5. Expand the Odd bin, click **1.psd**, click **Clip** on the menu bar, then click **Speed/Duration**.
6. Click the existing duration to highlight it, if necessary, type **2.15**, then click **OK**.
7. Change the duration of the remaining eight clips in the Odd and Even bins to 2.15, then drag the scroll bar all the way to the left in the Project panel.

   TIP You cannot change the duration of multiple clips simultaneously.

You changed the duration of 10 still clips using the Clip Speed / Duration dialog box. You viewed the duration of clip 10.psd in the Video Duration column of the Project panel.

FIGURE 11
Clip Speed / Duration dialog box

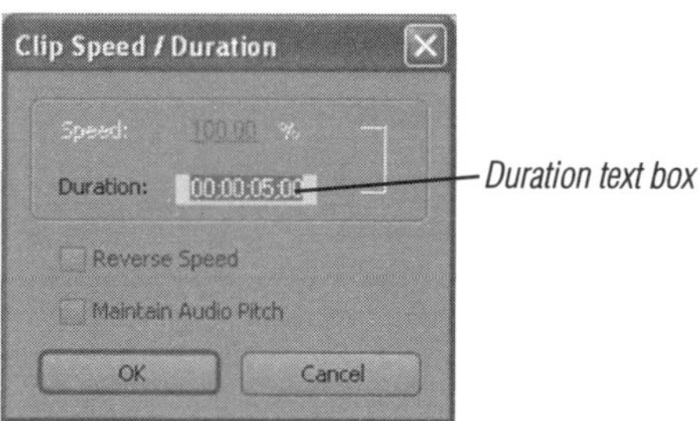

FIGURE 12
Viewing the duration of clip 10.psd in the Project panel

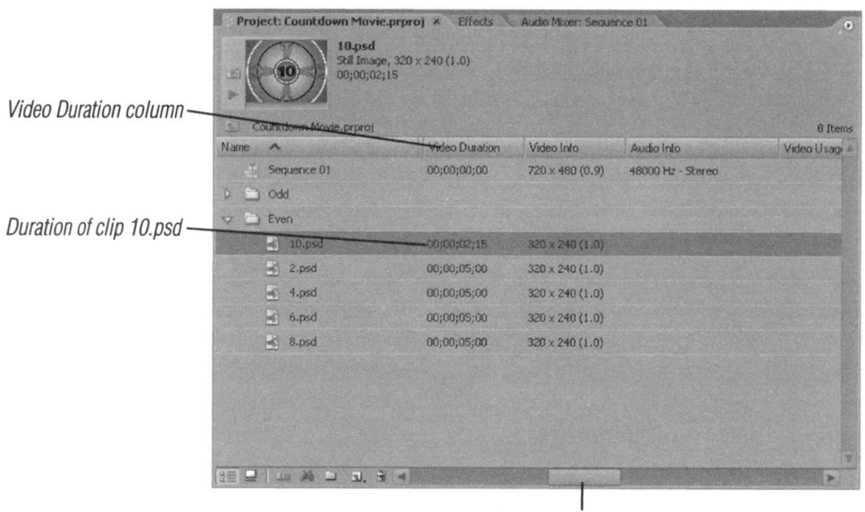

FIGURE 13

Locating the frame parameters of 1.psd in the Preview Area

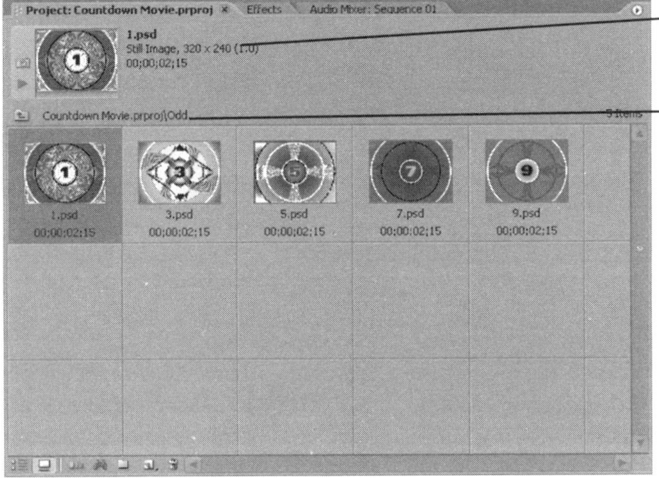

FIGURE 14

Interpret Footage dialog box

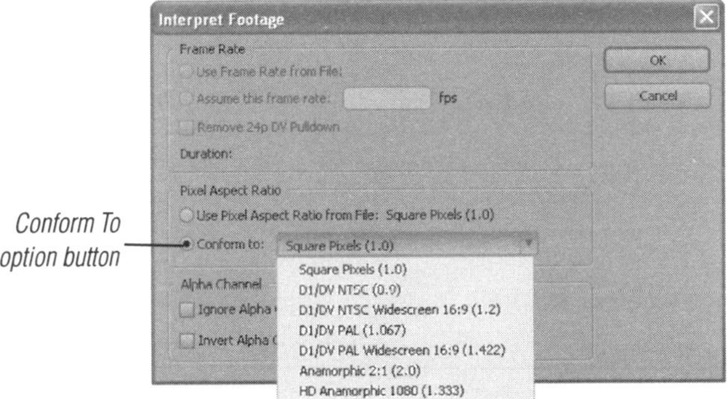

Explore frame parameters of a clip and view pixel aspect ratio of a still image

1. Click the **Icon button** , then double-click the **Odd bin**.

   The contents of the Odd bin are displayed as thumbnails.

   TIP When you switch to Icon View, bins are automatically collapsed. Double-click a bin to view its contents.

2. Click **1.psd** in the Project panel, then note the numbers 320 x 240 located in the Preview Area of the Project panel, as shown in Figure 13.

   1.psd is 320 pixels wide and 240 pixels tall.

3. Click **File** on the menu bar, then click **Interpret Footage**.
4. Notice in the Pixel Aspect Ratio section, that the Use Pixel Aspect Ratio from File: Square Pixels (1.0) option button is selected (the NTSC standard).
5. Click the **Conform To option button**, click the **list arrow** to view the other pixel aspect ratios, as shown in Figure 14, then click **Cancel**.
6. Click the **Folder icon** in the Project panel, then click the **List button** to return to List View.

   The Odd and Even bins should still be expanded.

7. Save your work.

You explored frame parameters of 1.psd, then viewed the pixel aspect ratio settings in the Interpret Footage dialog box.

BRING CLIPS INTO THE TIMELINE

What You'll Do

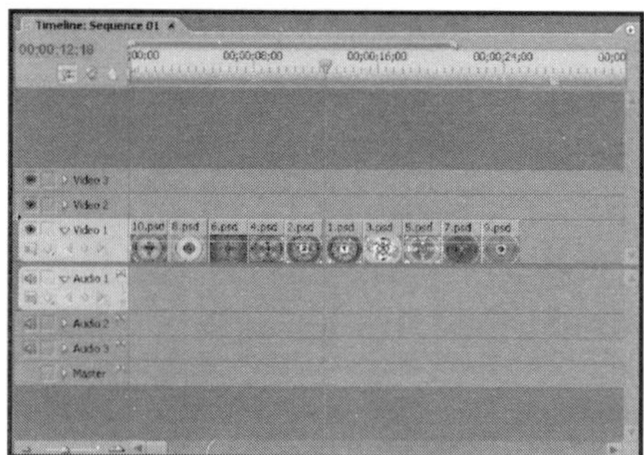

In this lesson, you will explore various options for moving source clips from the Project panel into the Timeline.

Adding Clips to the Timeline

You have many options for adding source clips to the Timeline. The most straightforward method is to simply drag a clip from the Project panel into the Timeline. If it is a video clip, you drag it to a video track. If it is an audio clip, you drag it to an audio track. It is important to note that the clips in the Timeline and Monitor panels are copies, or **instances**, of the imported clips in the Project panel. Whatever is done to a clip in the Timeline or a Monitor does not affect the clip in the Project panel. Many times, you will want to view a video source clip before adding it to the Timeline. You can preview the clip in the Source Monitor. Once you've done so, you can simply drag it into the Timeline. The mouse pointer becomes a fist pointer as you drag from the Source Monitor and then becomes a white arrow pointer it is placed in the Timeline. In Figure 15, the clip shown in the Source Monitor is being dragged into the Timeline.

The Clip menu offers alternatives to dragging clips to the Timeline. For example, the Insert command allows you to insert a clip at the location of the Current time indicator. The clip can be in the Project panel or in the Source Monitor before you execute the command. Just make sure you have the appropriate clip selected. This method can be very useful in that—once you have positioned the Current time indicator precisely—you know you are positioning the start of that clip in that specific location.

Inserting Clips between Clips in the Timeline

Inserting a clip between two clips is easy. You simply press and hold [Ctrl] while you drag the clip from the Project panel over the clips in the Timeline and "drop" the clip between two existing clips. The new clip will be inserted. Of the first two clips, the one on the left remains where it is in the Timeline, and the one on the right is "pushed" to the right the exact distance necessary to accommodate the inserted clip. If you do not press and hold [Ctrl] while inserting a clip between two others, the clip to the right of the insertion point will be replaced by the newly inserted clip.

Adding Clips Using the Automate to Sequence Command

Imagine that you had 15 clips to add to the Timeline—dragging and dropping each one would become, well, a drag. You can simply select all 15 clips in the Project panel, then drag them into the Timeline. But what if you want to add them to the Timeline in a specific order? A fast way to add lots of clips to the Timeline in one step is to select them in the Project panel in a specific sequence, then use the Automate to Sequence command. Using this command, you can add them to the Timeline— *in that sequence*—with one mouse click! Another option in the Automate to Sequence dialog box is how to deal with the other clips already in the Timeline. Choose Insert Edit from the Method list arrow to insert the selected clips at the location of the Current time indicator and push all existing clips to the right. Choose Insert Overlay to replace the existing clips in the Timeline at the location of the Current time indicator by the same amount of frames being overlayed.

FIGURE 15
Dragging a clip into the Timeline

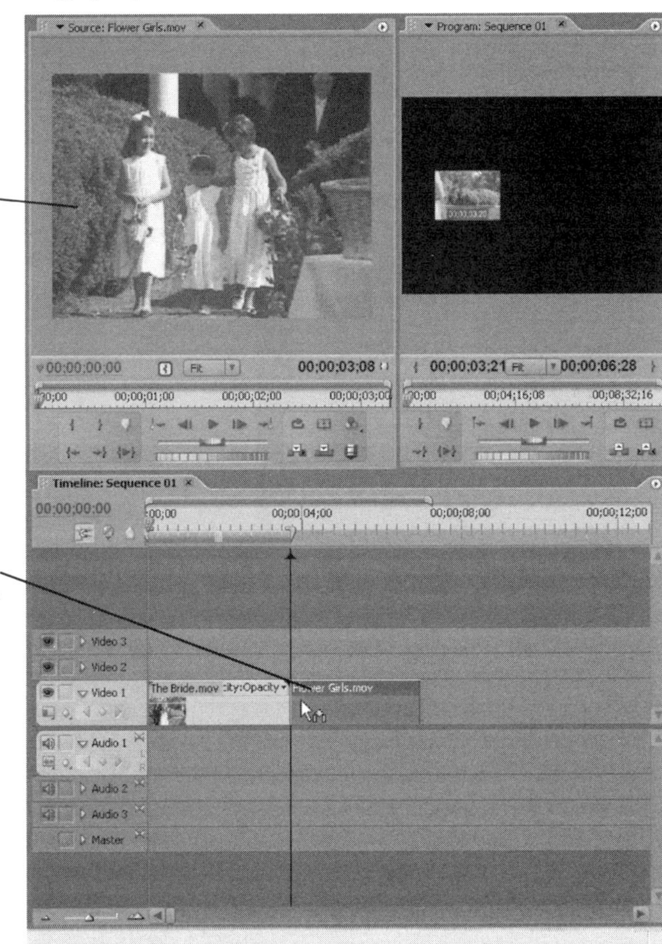

Add clips to the Timeline

1. Verify that the Even bin is expanded, drag and drop **10.psd** to the beginning of the Video 1 track in the Timeline, then drag the **Zoom slider** in the lower-left corner of the Timeline to enlarge the view of 10.psd, as shown in Figure 16.
2. Drag the **scroll bar** in the Project panel to the right until you see the Video Usage column, then locate the number 1 in the Video Usage column next to 10.psd.

   10.psd is being used once in the Timeline. This column may prove helpful to you while editing a long sequence. For example, if you are unsure if you have used a clip more than once in the sequence, this column will verify the number of times a clip has been used.
3. Drag the **scroll bar** in the Project panel all the way to the left.
4. In the Timeline, drag the **Current time indicator** over 10.psd to the right while watching the timecode change in the Current time display in the Program Monitor, then position the Current time indicator at frame 2:15.

   > TIP If you cannot drag the Current time indicator exactly to frame 2:15, you can type 2.15 in the Current Time Display text box in the Timeline or in the Program Monitor.

(continued)

FIGURE 16
10.psd in the Video 1 track of the Timeline

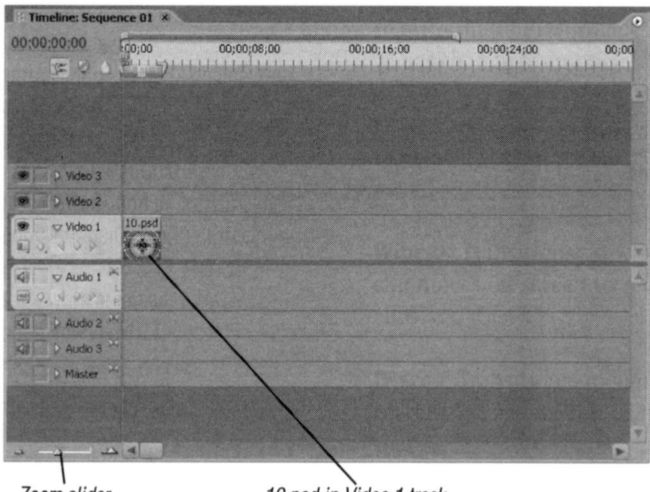

FIGURE 17
The Timeline with two clips inserted

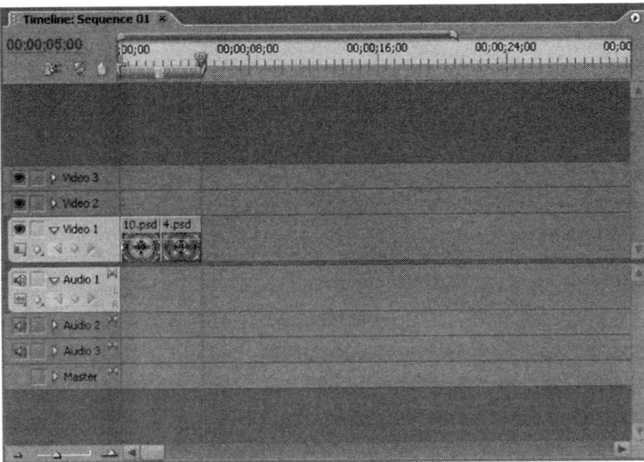

FIGURE 18
6.psd is inserted between 8.psd and 4.psd

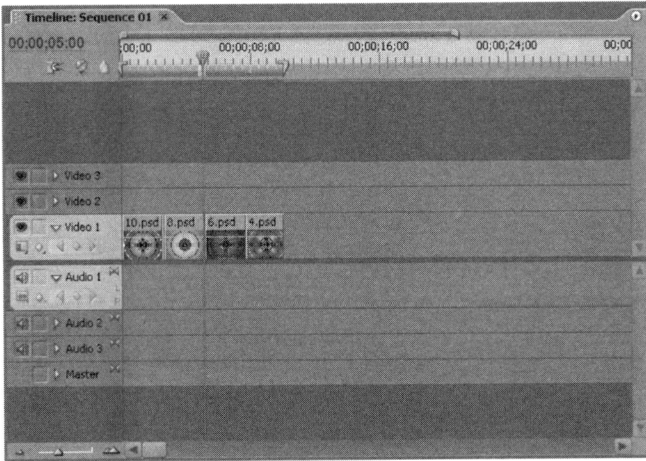

5. Click **4.psd** in the Project panel, click **Clip** on the menu bar, then click **Insert**.

   Your Timeline window should resemble Figure 17. Notice the violet label color above the two still-image clips.

6. Click **8.psd**, press **[Ctrl]**, drag **8.psd** and drop it between 10.psd and 4.psd in the Timeline, then release the mouse button.

7. Click **6.psd**, press **[Ctrl]**, drag **6.psd** and drop it between 8.psd and 4.psd in the Timeline, then release the mouse button.

   TIP If you press [Ctrl] before you click 8.psd, you'll select both clips. Make sure 4.psd is not selected.

   Your Timeline should resemble Figure 18.

8. Drag and drop **2.psd** immediately after 4.psd.

   TIP The Snap icon, directly below the Current time display in the Timeline, "snaps" clips to each other like magnets when they are placed next to each other. This icon is a toggle on/off. Clicking it once will turn it on or off, depending on its current status.

You added five clips to the Video 1 track in the Timeline.

Use the Automate to Sequence command

1. Drag the **Current time indicator** to 12:15 in the Timeline.

   Clips that are inserted using the Insert Edit method will be inserted at the Current time indicator location.

2. Verify that the Odd bin is still expanded so that you see its contents.

3. Click **1.psd**, press and hold **[Ctrl]**, then click **3.psd**, **5.psd**, **7.psd**, and **9.psd**.

   TIP Press and hold [Ctrl] to select clips that will be used in the Automate to Sequence dialog box, regardless of whether the clips are contiguous or non-contiguous.

4. Click **Project** on the menu bar, then click **Automate to Sequence**.

   TIP You can also use the Automate to Sequence button in the Project panel to access the Automate to Sequence dialog box.

5. In the Automate to Sequence dialog box, click the **Ordering list arrow**, click **Selection Order**, click the **Method list arrow**, click **Insert Edit**, type **0** in the Clip Overlay text box, then compare your Automate to Sequence dialog box to Figure 19.

6. Click **OK**, then compare your Timeline to Figure 20.

   The odd-numbered clips are added to the Timeline after 2.psd in the same order that they were selected in the Project panel.

(continued)

FIGURE 19
Automate to Sequence dialog box

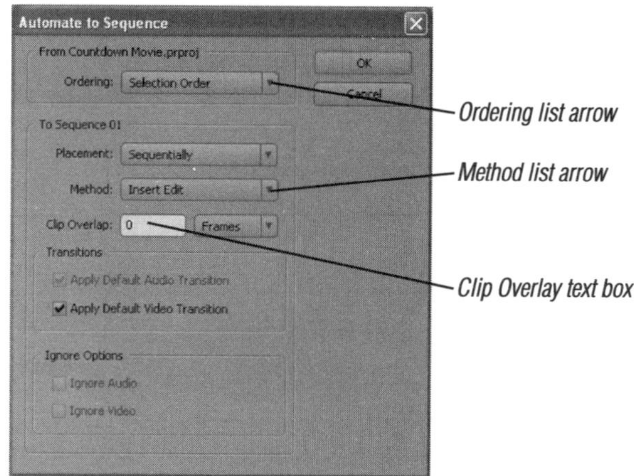

FIGURE 20
Viewing the odd-numbered clips in the Timeline

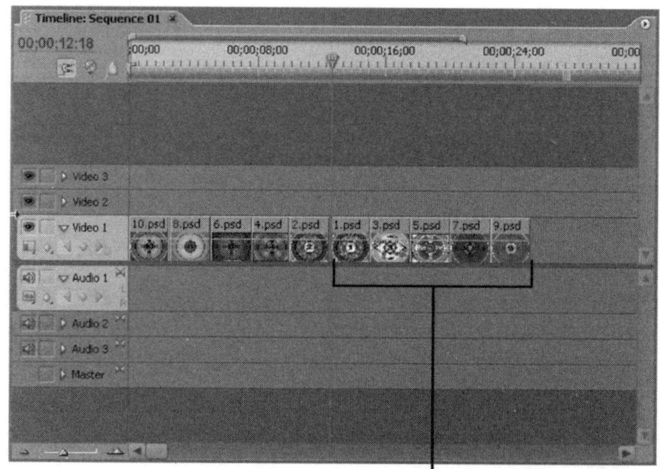

FIGURE 21

The Timeline with two sets of odd-numbered clips

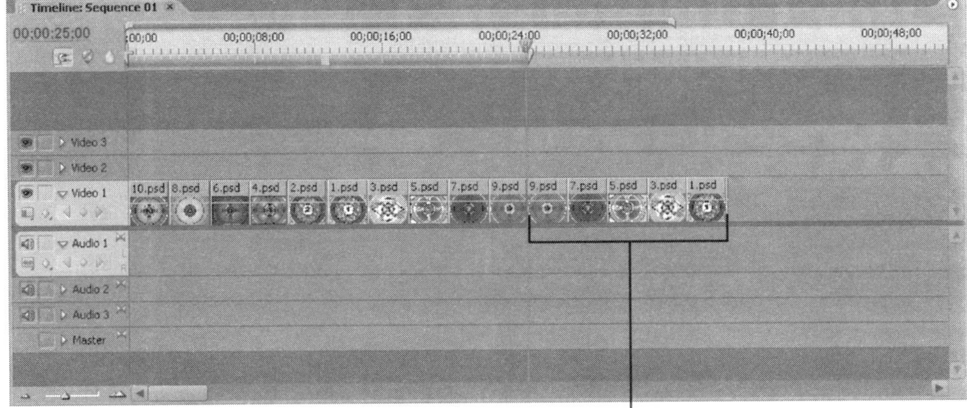

Second set of odd-numbered clips added to the Timeline in the order they were selected in the Project panel

7. Drag the **Current time indicator** to 25.0, click **9.psd** in the Project panel, press and hold **[Ctrl]**, then click **7.psd**, **5.psd**, **3.psd**, and **1.psd**.

   TIP You can also press [End] to place the Current time indicator at the end of the sequence or type 25 in the Current time display.

8. Click the **Automate to Sequence button** in the Project panel, click the **Ordering list arrow**, click **Selection Order**, if necessary, click the **Method list arrow**, click **Insert Edit**, if necessary, type **0** in the Clip Overlay text box, then click **OK**.

   The second set of odd-numbered clips is added to the end of the Timeline in descending order.

   TIP Depending on your workspace, you may not be able to see the clips at the end of the Timeline.

9. Click **Window** on the menu bar, point to **Workspace**, then click **Editing**.

   Your Timeline should resemble Figure 21.

   TIP The Editing workspace is a good choice when your sequence starts to grow: It gives you a larger view of the Timeline and displays the Tools panel next to the Timeline.

10. Save your work.

You inserted the contents of the Odd bin into the Timeline using the Automate to Sequence command.

MANIPULATE CLIPS IN THE TIMELINE

What You'll Do

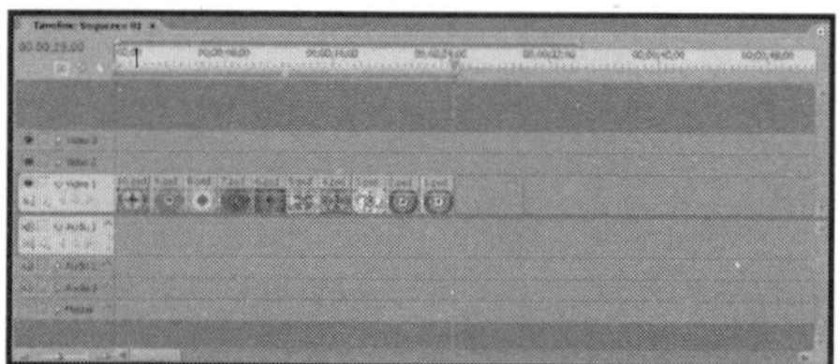

In this lesson, you will remove clips from the Timeline and rearrange the remaining clips.

Removing Clips from the Timeline

Removing a clip from the Timeline does not remove the clip from the Project panel. When you remove a clip from the Timeline, the clip is removed from your sequence, but not from the project. The only way to remove a clip from the project is to delete it from the Project panel. If you try to delete a clip that is being used in the Timeline from the Project panel, all of the instances of the clip in the Timeline will be removed. Fortunately, you will be given a warning if you try to remove a clip that is being used in the Timeline.

Director's Cut: *Valley of the Dolls*

You'll get a fine example of trendy 1960's editing techniques and a smart use of still images in 1969's infamous *Valley of the Dolls*. Having cast Patty Duke as Neely O'Hara—supposedly a gifted actress, singer, and dancer—the producers faced the problem that Patty Duke the actress was not a dancer. But rather than resort to a long shot with a body double, they instead used still images to make Neely dance.

With Patty Duke in costume—a top hat and tails—they photographed her in a series of dance poses against a red background. Then they put the photos together in sequence and—like a moving illustration in a flip-book—Neely appears not only to dance, but also to be executing some fairly complex moves! The solution was ingenious and a fine example of how still images can be animated for great effect.

Moving Clips within the Timeline

Once you have brought clips into the Timeline and begun editing, you will often want to rearrange the clips, experimenting with different sequences. Clips can be pushed left or right or repositioned between two other clips.

When you remove a clip from the Timeline, an empty space remains where the clip once was. This space will appear as a black frame when you preview your sequence, and as an empty space in your Timeline, as shown in Figure 22. It logically follows that you would then want to select all the clips to the right of the space and move them left to close the gap. You can do so using the Track Select Tool. Click the Track Select Tool in the Tools panel, click any clip, and that clip and all the clips to the right of it are selected, making it easy to move all the clips left in one quick move. You can also select multiple clips by pressing [Shift] while you click each clip with the Selection Tool. Normally, pressing [Shift] is only used to select contiguous items (items next to each other in a list or, in this case, the Timeline), however, in Premiere Pro, [Shift] is used when you need to select both contiguous and non-contiguous clips.

FIGURE 22

A space remains when a clip is removed

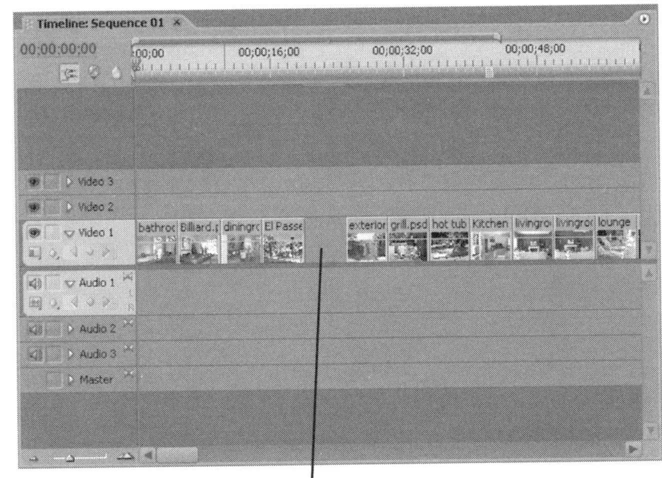

A deleted clip appears as an empty space in the Timeline and as a black frame in a movie

Remove clips from the Timeline

1. Click the **Selection Tool**, click **1.psd**, press and hold **[Shift]**, then click **5.psd** from the first set of odd-numbered clips in the Timeline.

   Both clips are selected.

2. Click **Edit** on the menu bar, then click **Clear**.

   The two selected clips are deleted from the Timeline. Your Timeline should resemble Figure 23.

   TIP You can delete clips from the Timeline by selecting them and pressing [Delete].

3. Click the first **3.psd** in the Timeline, press and hold **[Shift]**, click **7.psd**, then click **9.psd**.

4. Press **[Delete]**.

   Clips 3, 7, and 9 are deleted from the Timeline.

You removed the first set of odd-numbered clips from the Timeline.

FIGURE 23

Two clips deleted from the Timeline

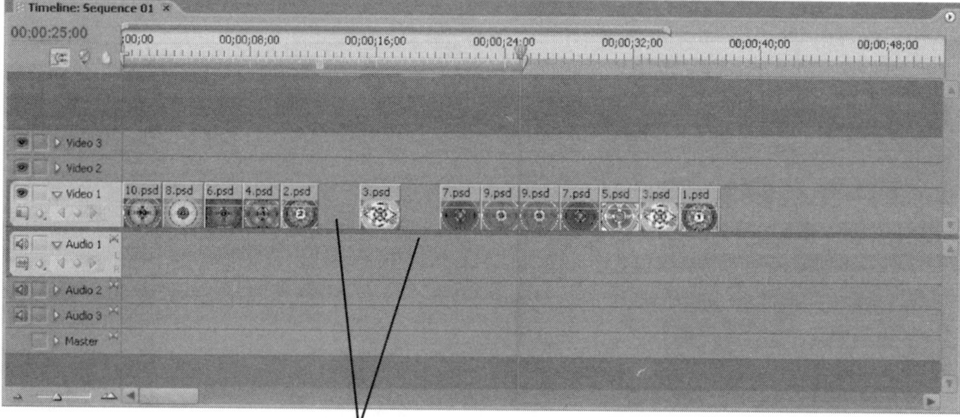

FIGURE 24

Moving clips in the Timeline

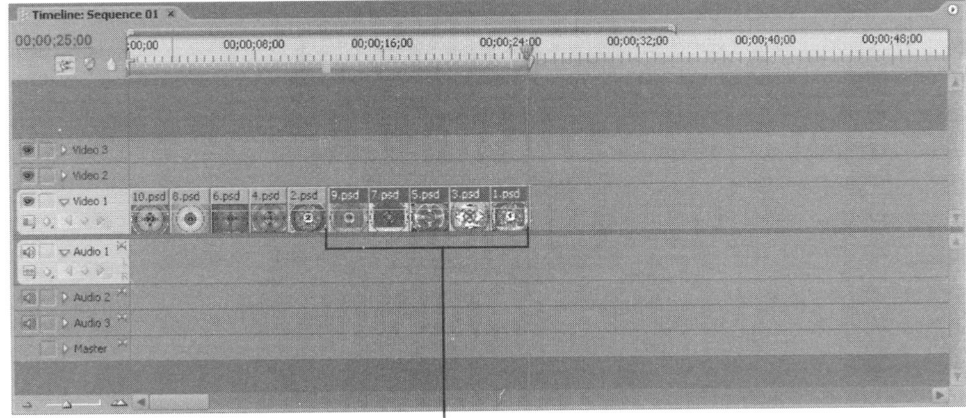

Selected clips snap to 2.psd

FIGURE 25

Ten clips in descending order

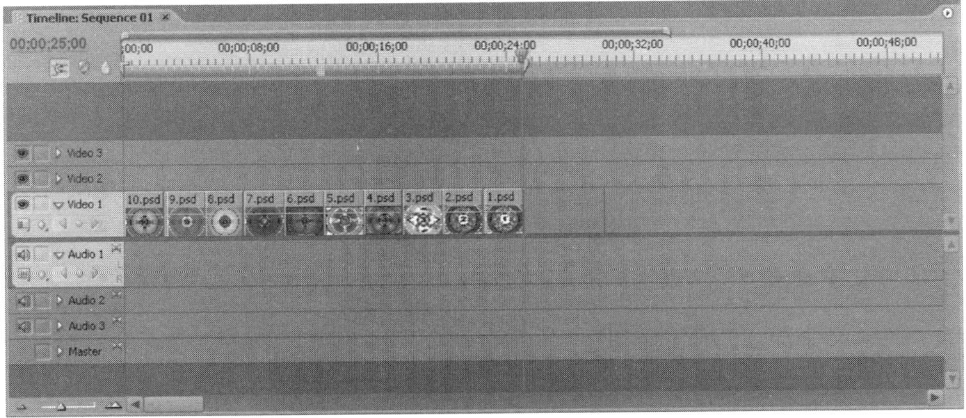

Rearrange clips in the Timeline

1. Click the **Track Select Tool**, then click **9.psd** in the Timeline.

   9.psd and all clips to the right of it are selected.

2. Position the Track Select Tool pointer over 9.psd, then click and drag to the left until the selection snaps to 2.psd.

   Your Timeline should resemble Figure 24.

3. Click the **Selection Tool** and click anywhere in the Timeline to deselect the selected clips.
4. Press and hold **[Ctrl]**, click and drag **9.psd** between 8.psd and 10.psd, then release [Ctrl].
5. Using the same steps, move the odd-numbered clips so that all the clips are in descending order, from left to right.
6. Close up any gaps in the Timeline if necessary.

   Your Timeline should resemble Figure 25.

7. Press **[Home]** on your keyboard to move the Current time indicator to the beginning of the Timeline.
8. Click the **Play button** in the Program Monitor to preview the clips in the Timeline.
9. Save your work, then close Countdown Movie.

You rearranged the order of clips in the Timeline using the Selection Tool and the Track Select Tool.

CHAPTER SUMMARY

Getting comfortable with the Premiere Pro interface should be your first priority. There is no better way to do this than to practice importing clips, creating bins, previewing clips, and bringing them into the Timeline. The Project panel offers loads of information about each clip. When you're ready to create a movie, your first step will be to import your clips and organize them in the Project panel. You can create bins and store like items in named bins. For example, you could store all of your still images in a bin named "Stills." You can use the Clip Speed / Duration dialog box to view the duration of a clip and change it if necessary. Bringing clips into the Timeline can be done by simply dragging and dropping them from the Project panel or the Source Monitor, or you can use the Automate to Sequence command. You'll want to practice moving clips in the Timeline and rearranging them as needed. The Selection Tool and the Track Select Tool will become your fast friends. One last thing: Switch to the Editing workspace to get your best view of the Timeline and access to the Tools panel.

What You Have Learned

- How to import a file into the Project panel
- How to import a folder into the Project panel
- How to create and name a new bin
- How to drag clips into bins
- How to expand and collapse bins
- How to change the duration of a still image
- How to view the width and height of a clip
- How to view and change the pixel aspect ratio of a project
- How to add clips to the Timeline
- How to insert clips in between other clips
- How to use the Automate to Sequence command
- How to delete clips from the Timeline
- How to select clips in the Timeline
- How to use the Track Select Tool to move a range of clips in the Timeline

Key Terms

Frames A series of still images that make up a movie or sequence.

Pixels Short for picture element—pixels are the smallest components of a digital image.

Pixel Aspect Ratio Pixel aspect ratio is a measurement that specifies the ratio of width to height of one pixel in a frame.

Automate to Sequence command A command that lets you add a number of clips to the Timeline in one step.

Track Select Tool A tool in the Tools panel used for selecting a clip and all clips to the right of the selected clip.

SALT
PEPPER

lu lu

chapter

3 WORKING WITH TRANSITIONS

1. Understand video transitions.
2. Add video transitions to clips in the Timeline.
3. Modify video transitions in the Effect Controls panel.
4. Set the work area bar and create previews.

chapter 3 WORKING WITH TRANSITIONS

The visual change from one clip to another is called a *transition*. Transitions are fun to work with, and Premiere Pro offers you dozens to choose from, including classics such as dissolves, wipes, and zooms. You apply transitions to clips by dragging and dropping them from the Effects panel to the clip in the Timeline. Once added to the Timeline, transitions can be previewed and modified using the Effect Controls panel. Working with transitions will test your aesthetic sense. Using too many transitions, especially those that are inappropriate for a given project, may look gimmicky and unprofessional. Though some would say that using lots of different transitions is always wrong, that is a limited view of editing, and it's a limited view of Premiere Pro. Keep in mind that Premiere Pro is not only used for editing straightforward, narrative video projects but also for creating quick, cool, animated presentations, especially with still images. A sure sign of a visually gifted editor is one who can identify the type of project in which different flashy transitions will be appropriate, and who is also confident and crafty enough to use them to generate energy, excitement, and momentum.

Tools You'll Use

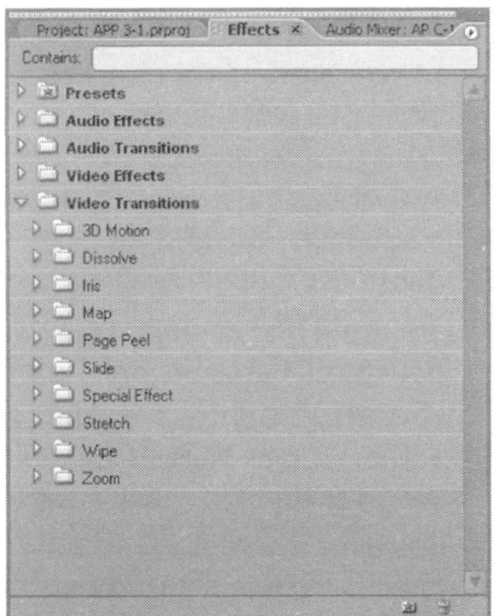

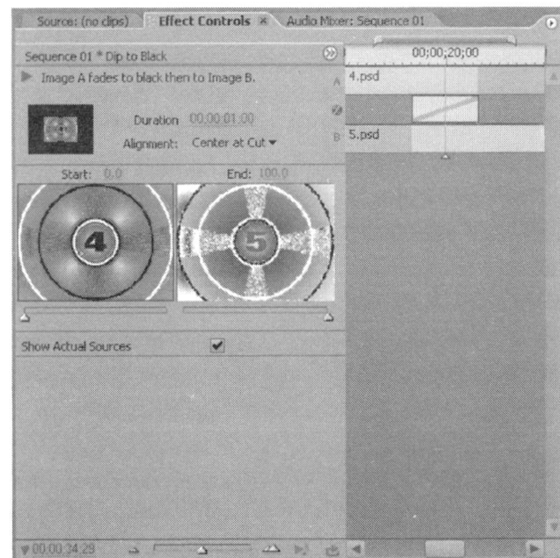

LESSON 1

UNDERSTAND VIDEO TRANSITIONS

What You'll Do

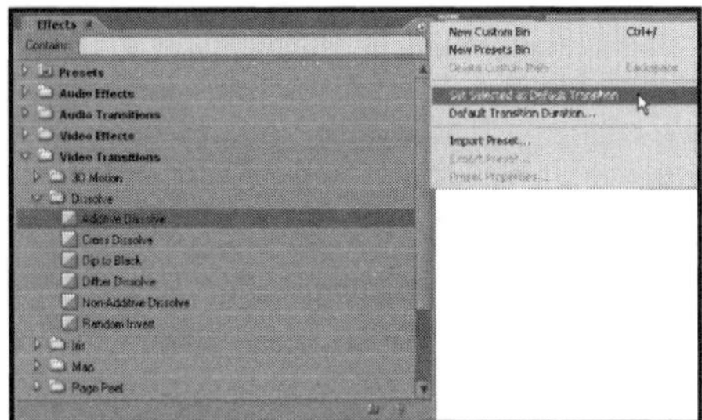

In this lesson, you will learn about video transitions in Adobe Premiere Pro.

Working with Video Transitions

Video transitions are built-in effects that Premiere Pro provides to create a visual change from one clip to another. Transitions often function as segues between clips, as when one clip fades into another. Premiere Pro offers many transitions that are "classics" and common to video editing. Examples of classic transitions are **dissolves**, in which the end of one clip fades into the beginning of the next, **wipes**, in which the first clip moves off screen to reveal the next clip, and **irises**, in which the first clip reveals the second clip using a specific shape. Video transitions are located in the Video Transitions bin in the Effects panel. Within the Video Transitions bin are 10 more bins of video-transition categories. Figure 1 shows the Video Transitions bin expanded, as well as the 3D Motion bin expanded, so that you can see the 10 3D Motion transitions available. There are also a number of video transitions available in the Presets bin, also located in the Effects panel. Preset categories, such as Mosaics and Solarizes, are shown in Figure 2. Notice the Blurs bin is expanded showing its contents. The Presets bin and all bins in the Presets bin are marked with a purple star icon to differentiate them from other transitions.

FIGURE 1

Contents of the Video Transitions bin in the Effects panel

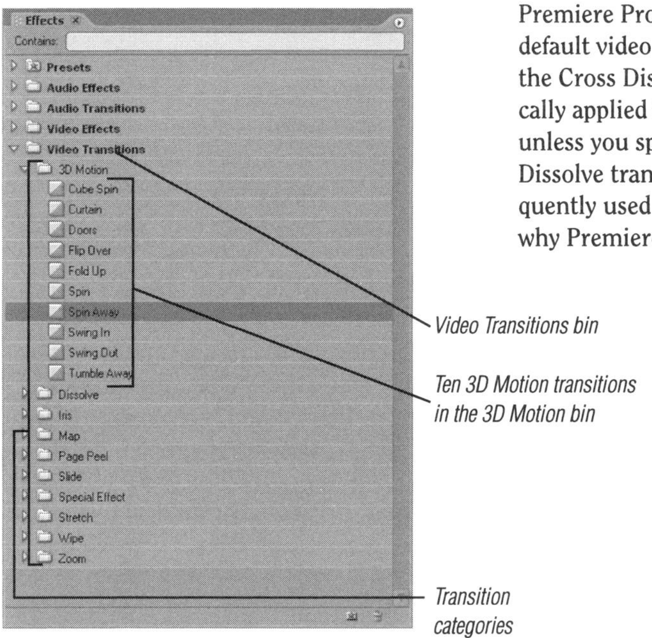

FIGURE 2

Contents of the Presets bin

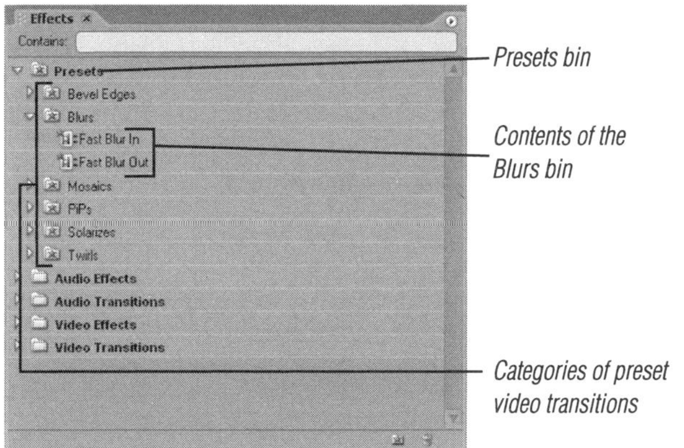

Setting the Default Video Transition

Premiere Pro uses Cross Dissolve as the default video transition. In other words, the Cross Dissolve transition is automatically applied to the clips in your sequence unless you specify otherwise. The Cross Dissolve transition is one of the more frequently used transitions, which may be why Premiere Pro uses it for its default.

You can change the default transition to one that you prefer by selecting the desired transition in the Effects panel, clicking the Effects panel list arrow, then clicking Set Selected as Default Transition. In Figure 3, the Cross Dissolve transition is the default transition. Notice the Additive Dissolve transition is selected and will become the new default transition once the command is executed. The default transition has a red outline around its icon for easy identification.

> **QUICKTIP**
>
> You can change the duration of the default transition by clicking Edit on the menu bar, pointing to Preferences, clicking General, then changing the value in the Video Transition Default Duration text box.

FIGURE 3

Setting the default transition

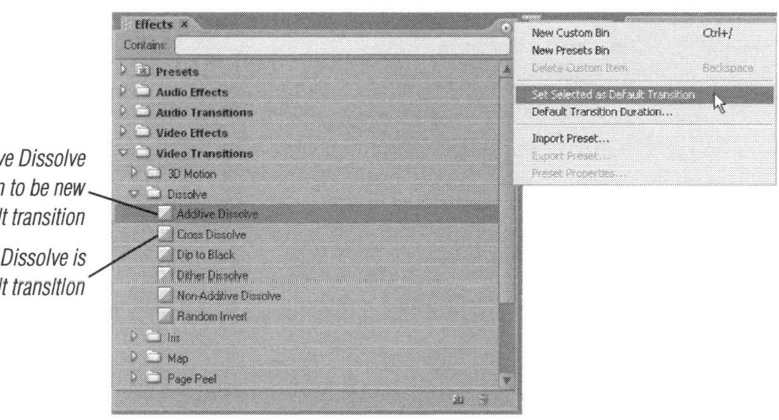

ADD VIDEO TRANSITIONS TO CLIPS IN THE TIMELINE

What You'll Do

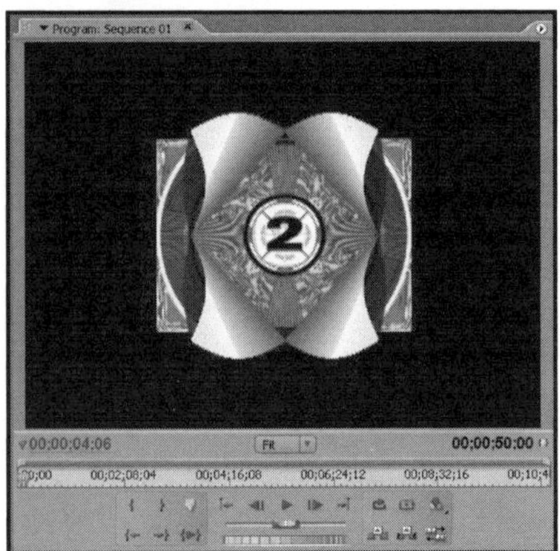

In this lesson, you will learn how to add video transitions to clips in the Timeline.

Using the Effects Workspace

If you are going to be concentrating heavily on transitions in your project, you should consider using the Effects workspace during that phase of production. As shown in Figure 4, the Effects workspace places the Effects panel to the left of the Timeline. Since transitions are applied to clips by dragging them from the Effects panel to the Timeline, this positioning is ideal. Furthermore, the placement of the Effect Controls panel, above the Timeline, is also beneficial for heavy transition editing. The Effect Controls panel is where you preview transitions as well as modify their settings.

Adding Video Transitions to Clips in the Timeline

You add video transitions to clips in the Timeline by dragging them from the Effects panel and dropping them between two clips. The line between two clips is known as the *cut line*. As you prepare to "drop" the transition, you'll see one of three icons next to the white arrow pointer—the End at Cut icon, the Start at Cut icon, or the Center at Cut icon. The icons specify how the transition will be aligned to the first or second clip in the pair. The End at Cut icon aligns the end of the transition to the end of the first clip. The Start at Cut icon aligns the beginning of the transition to the beginning of the second clip, and finally, the Center at Cut icon centers the transition over the cut line between the two clips. Figure 5 shows the End at Cut icon.

Another way to apply the default transition to clips being placed in the Timeline is to use the Automate to Sequence dialog box. Click the Apply Default Video Transition check box in the Automate to Sequence dialog box before clicking OK. This is an efficient way to apply the same transition to a number of clips and add them to the Timeline simultaneously.

Like clips, transitions can be deleted. Click a transition in the Timeline, then press [Delete]. If you have trouble selecting the transition, zoom in closer for a better view of the Timeline contents.

FIGURE 4
Using the Effects workspace

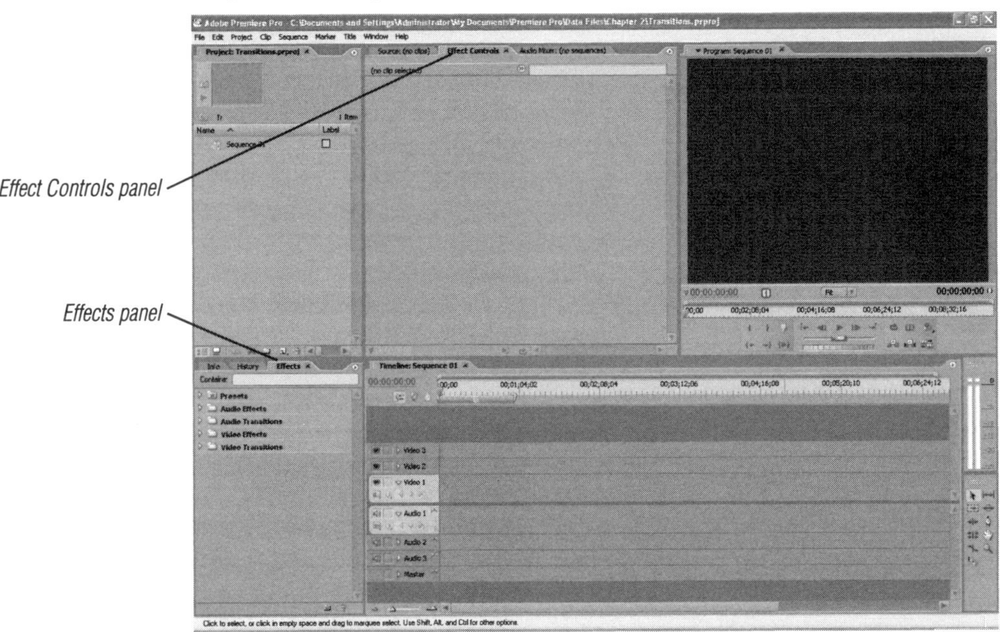

FIGURE 5
The End at Cut icon applied to 1.tif

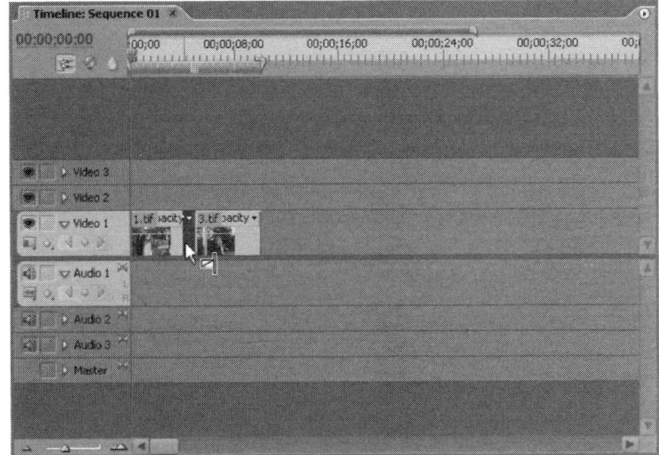

Align a transition to the end of a clip

1. Open APP 3-1.prproj, then save it as **Transitions**.

   TIP If you cannot locate a source clip in the Source Clips folder, look in the Countdown Stills folder, which is in the Source Clips folder.

2. Click **Window** on the menu bar, point to **Workspace**, then click **Effects**.
3. Expand the Countdown Stills bin, drag **clips 1.psd – 10.psd** in consecutive order into the Video 1 track in the Timeline, then zoom in, if necessary, so that your Timeline resembles Figure 6.
4. Expand the Video Transitions bin, then expand the Page Peel bin.

   TIP The Video Transitions bin is located in the Effects panel.

5. Drag the **Center Peel transition** to the left of the cut line between 1.psd and 2.psd until you see the End at Cut icon, as shown in Figure 7, then release.

   The Center Peel transition will begin at the end of 1.psd.

(continued)

FIGURE 6

Clips 1.psd – 10.psd in the Video 1 track

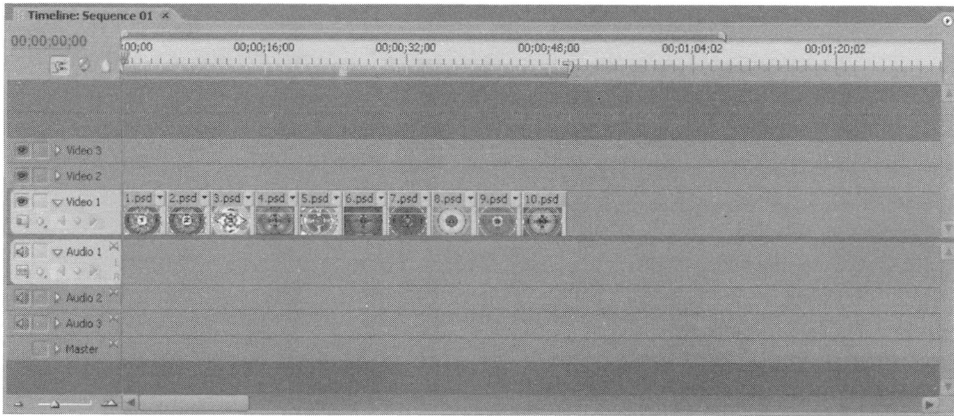

FIGURE 7

Dragging the Center Peel transition between 1.psd and 2.psd

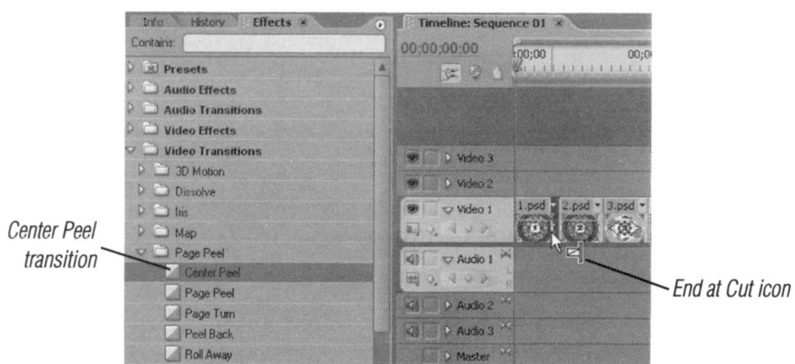

FIGURE 8

Zooming in on 1.psd to view the transition

FIGURE 9

Viewing the Center Peel transition in the Program Monitor

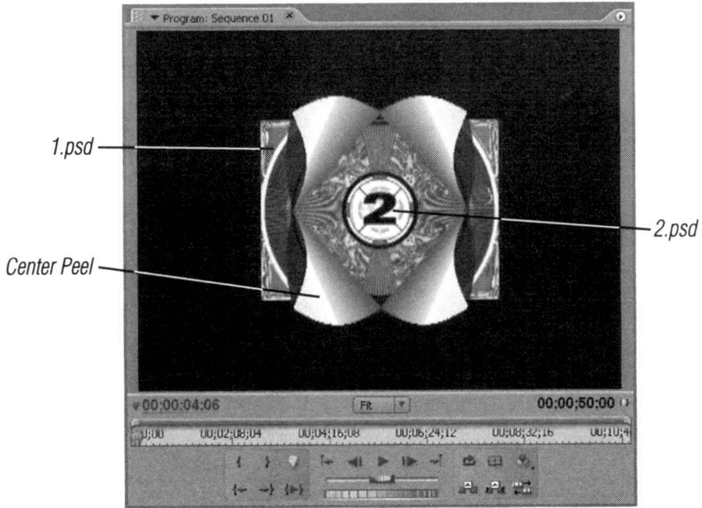

6. Zoom in on the Timeline so that your Timeline resembles Figure 8.

   Zooming in on the Timeline makes it easy for you to quickly see the name of a transition.

7. Zoom out to a zoom level you are comfortable with, then press **[Home]**.
8. Click the **Play button** in the Program Monitor to view the transition between 1.psd and 2.psd, then click the **Stop button** .

   As shown in Figure 9, the Center Peel transition begins transitioning from 1.psd to 2.psd at the end of 1.psd.

9. Save your work.

You added 10 clips to the Timeline, aligned the Center Peel transition to the end of 1.psd, then previewed the transition in the Program Monitor.

Align a transition to the beginning of a clip and between two clips

1. Collapse the Page Peels bin, then expand the Wipe bin.
2. Drag the **Band Wipe transition** to the beginning of 3.psd until you see the Start at Cut icon, as shown in Figure 10, then release.
3. Preview the transition in the Program Monitor.

   The transition does not occur until the beginning of 3.psd.
4. Collapse the Wipe bin, then expand the Dissolve bin.
5. Drag the **Additive Dissolve transition** between 4.psd and 5.psd until you see the Center at Cut icon, as shown in Figure 11, then release.

   As shown in Figure 12, the Additive Dissolve transition plays equally at the end of 4.psd and the beginning of 5.psd.

   > TIP You can preview a transition much slower by dragging the Current time indicator in the Timeline over the clips and transitions you wish to see.
6. Save your work.

You aligned a transition to the beginning of 3.psd and centered another transition between 4.psd and 5.psd.

FIGURE 10
Dragging Band Wipe to the beginning of 3.psd

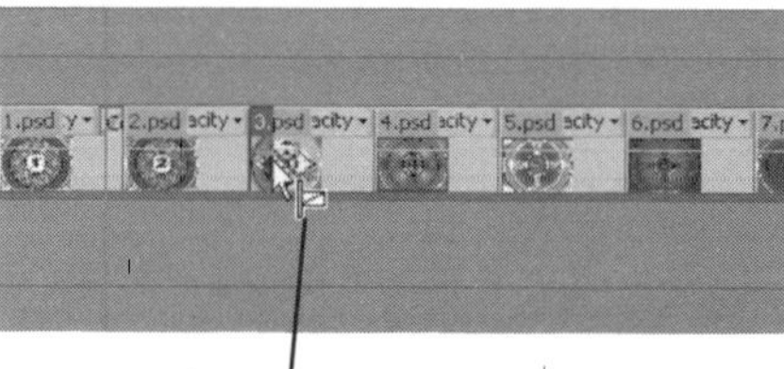

FIGURE 11
Dragging the Additive Dissolve transition between 4.psd and 5.psd

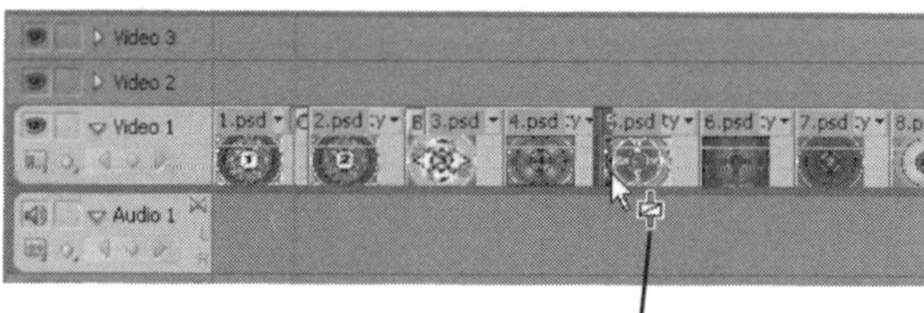

FIGURE 12
The Additive Dissolve transition plays equally at the end of 4.psd and the beginning of 5.psd

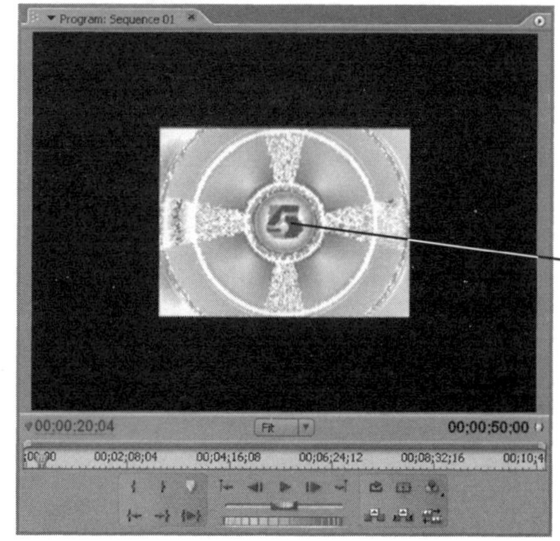

FIGURE 13

Automate to Sequence dialog box

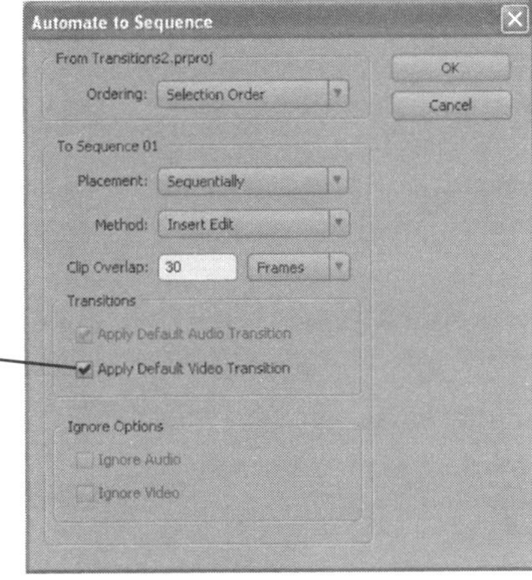

Apply the default video transition using the Automate to Sequence command

1. Click **6.psd** in the Timeline, press and hold **[Shift]**, then click **7.psd**, **8.psd**, **9.psd**, and **10.psd**.
2. Press **[Delete]**.

   The five clips are removed from the Timeline.
3. Drag the Current time indicator to the end of the sequence so that the Current time display reads 25:0.

   TIP You can also type 25.0 in the Current time display to position the Current time indicator at frame 25.
4. Click anywhere in the Project panel to deselect, click **6.psd** in the Project panel, press and hold **[Ctrl]**, then click **7.psd**, **8.psd**, **9.psd**, and **10.psd**.
5. Click the **Automate to Sequence button** on the Project panel, then choose the settings shown in Figure 13.

   Notice that the Apply Default Video Transition check box is checked.
   Clips 6 – 10 will have the Cross Dissolve transition applied to them since Cross Dissolve is the default video transition.
6. Click **OK**, press **[Home]**, then preview the entire sequence.
7. Save your work.

You deleted five clips from the Timeline, then used the Automate to Sequence command to add the five clips back to the Timeline with the default video transition applied.

LESSON 3

MODIFY VIDEO TRANSITIONS

What You'll Do

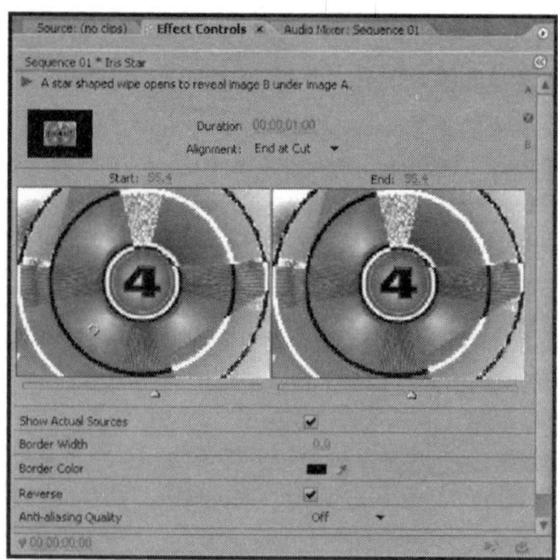

In this lesson, you will replace transitions, view transitions in the Effect Controls panel, then modify them by changing settings in the Effect Controls panel.

Replacing Transition Instances

One of Premiere Pro's great features for working with transitions is the ability to replace a transition quickly and easily. Simply select the replacement transition in the Effects panel, then drag and drop it on top of the existing transition in the Timeline. The new transition occupies the same location with the same duration.

Because replacing transitions is so easy, it allows you the freedom to experiment with different transitions as you build your project.

Modifying Transitions

As you add transitions, you'll probably find that you want to view them frequently, and after viewing them you may want to make changes to some of their properties. Premiere Pro lets you create a preview of your sequence and make any necessary changes to transitions in the Timeline. Each video transition has its own settings that can be modified in the Effect Controls panel. You can also use the Effect Controls panel to simply view how a specific transition works. As shown in Figure 14, a description of how the transition works appears at the top of the panel, as well as a thumbnail preview. The letters "A" and "B" represent the start and the end of the transition. You can also view the type of transition alignment and the transition duration. You can change the type of alignment by clicking the Alignment list arrow and choosing a different alignment option. The default duration of a video transition is 30 frames (or one second). You can click the Reverse check box to reverse the transition—the thumbnail preview will update to reflect this option. Among other settings are the Anti-Aliasing Quality, Border Color and Border Width. Click the Show Actual Sources check box to replace the "A" and "B" images with the actual clips in the Timeline. As shown in Figure 15, the Band Wipe transition is applied to 3.psd with a Start at Cut alignment. Therefore the preview shows 2.psd and 3.psd. The right side of the Effect Controls panel shows the section of the Timeline that corresponds to the transitioning clips. You can choose to hide this section for a larger view of the clip thumbnails. Finally, click the Custom button to find out how you can customize a specific transition. In Figure 16, you can customize the Band Wipe transition by changing the number of bands in the Band Wipe Settings dialog box from the default number (7) to one of your choice. The Custom button is not available for every transition. Remember, changes made in the Effect Controls panel only affect the transitions that are placed in the Timeline. These transitions are merely instances or copies of the transitions stored in the video transition bins in the Effects panel.

FIGURE 14

Band Wipe transition settings in the Effect Controls panel

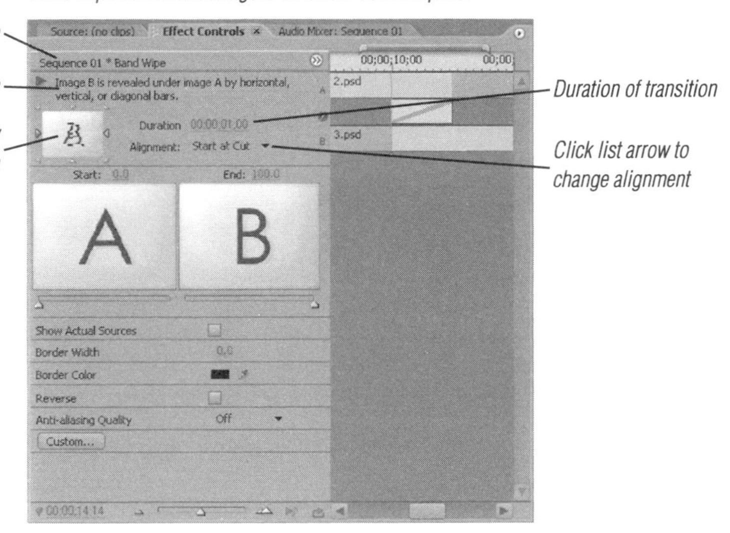

FIGURE 15

Viewing the actual sources that the transition is applied to in the Effect Controls panel

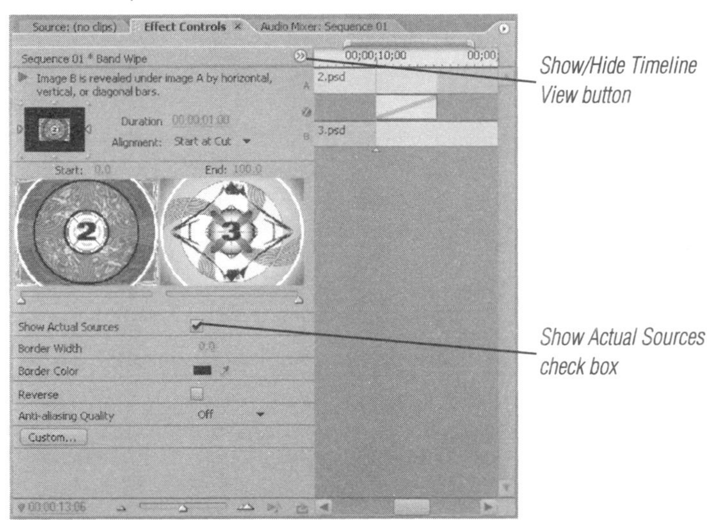

FIGURE 16

Making custom changes in the Effect Controls panel

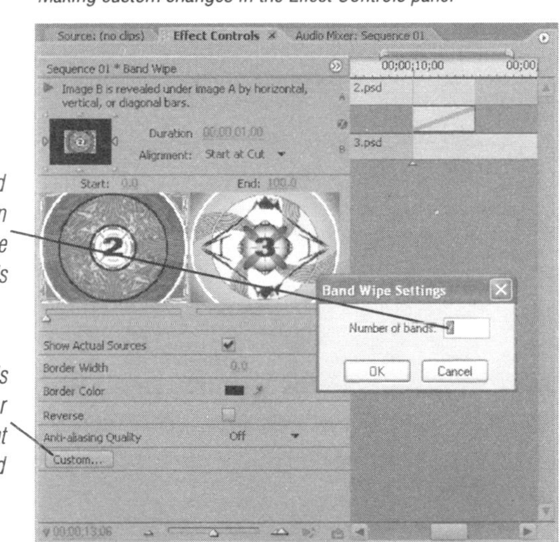

Replace transitions in the Timeline

1. Close the Dissolve bin in the Effects panel, if necessary.
2. Expand the Iris Bin, drag the **Iris Diamond transition** directly on top of the Center Peel transition aligned to the end of 1.psd, then release when you see the Center Peel transition highlighted, as shown in Figure 17.

   > TIP When one transition is directly over another, the new one will replace the existing one when you release the mouse pointer.

3. Replace the Band Wipe transition aligned to the beginning of 3.psd with the Iris Round transition.

(continued)

FIGURE 17
Replacing the Center Peel transition with the Iris Diamond transition

FIGURE 18

The Iris Star video transition

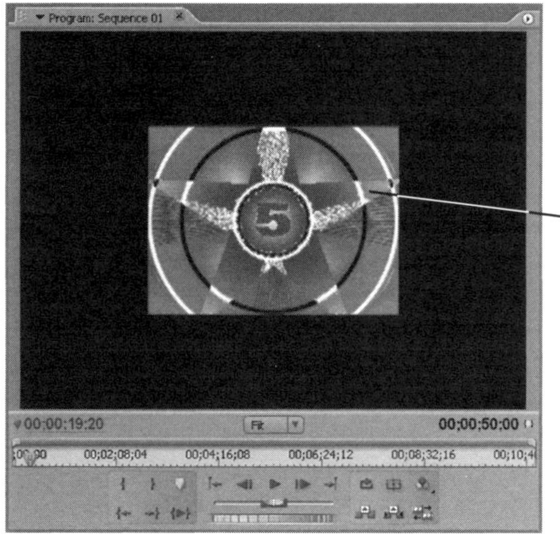

The Iris Star transition uses the shape of a star to transition from one clip to another

4. Replace the Additive Dissolve transition centered over 4.psd and 5.psd with the Iris Star transition.

   As shown in Figure 18, the Iris Star transition uses the shape of a star to transition from 4.psd to 5.psd.

5. Click the **Timeline panel** to select it, press **[Home]**, then preview your sequence in the Program Monitor.

6. Collapse all open bins in the Effects panel, then save your work.

You replaced three transitions in the Timeline with three Iris transitions, then previewed the new sequence.

Modify video transitions in the Effect Controls panel

1. Zoom in on the Timeline so that you can see the transitions clearly in the Timeline.
2. Double-click the **Iris Star transition** located between 4.psd and 5.psd.

   As shown in Figure 19, the Iris Star transition settings appear in the Effect Controls panel.
3. Drag the **slider** under the "A" image to view the transition from "A" to "B".
4. Notice the small circle in the center of the "A" image.

   This small circle represents the point where the transition occurs. The default setting is the center of the first clip.

(continued)

FIGURE 19

The Iris Star settings in the Effect Controls panel

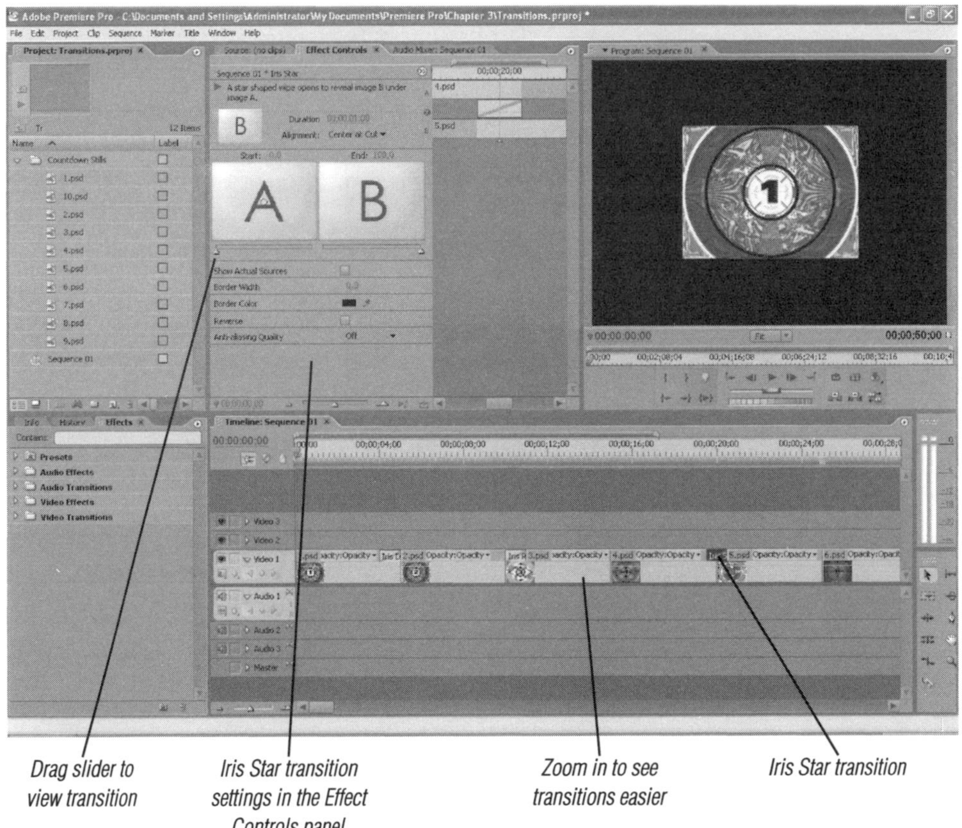

FIGURE 20

Changing the start location for the transition

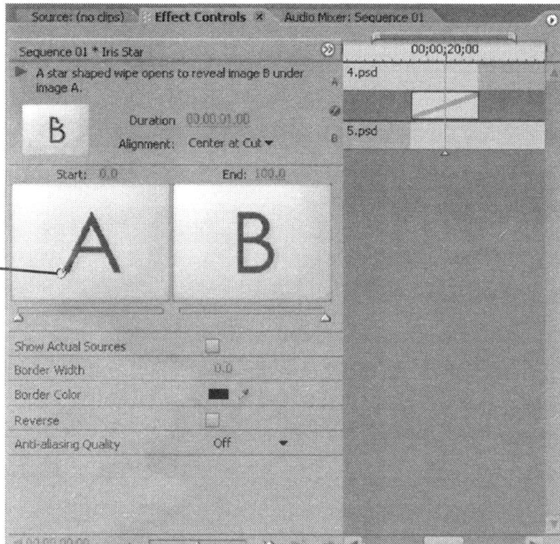

FIGURE 21

Modifications made to the Iris Star transition

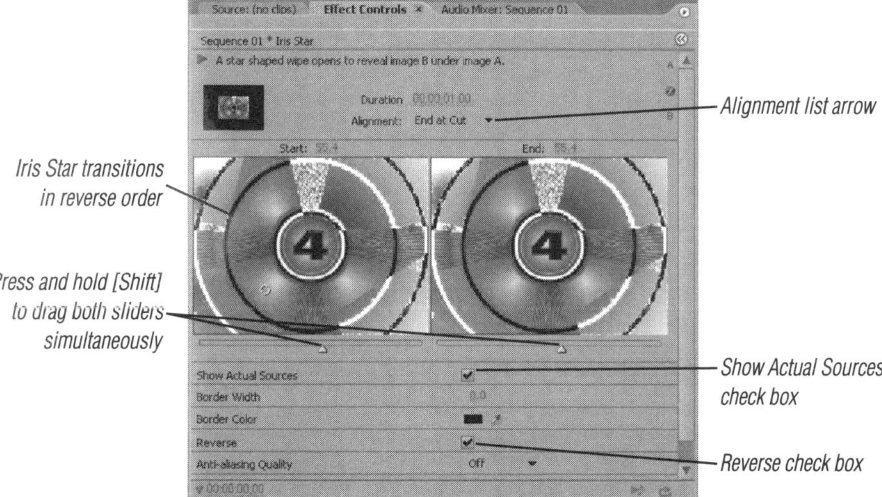

5. Drag the **small circle** to the approximate location shown in Figure 20, drag the small slider beneath "A" all the way to the right, then all the way back to the left to view the new transition location.
6. Click the **Show/Hide Timeline View button** to hide the Timeline view in the Effect Controls panel.
7. Click the **Show Actual Sources check box**, click the **Alignment list arrow**, click **End at Cut**, then click the **Reverse check box**.
8. Press and hold **[Shift]**, then drag the slider under the "A" image to see both "A" and "B" images transition simultaneously.

   As shown in Figure 21, the star shape transitions in the reverse order. Instead of starting out small and growing larger, the star starts out as a large star and decreases in size as the transition occurs over time.
9. Save your work.

You modified the Iris Star transition settings in the Effect Controls panel.

SET THE WORK AREA BAR AND CREATE PREVIEWS

What You'll Do

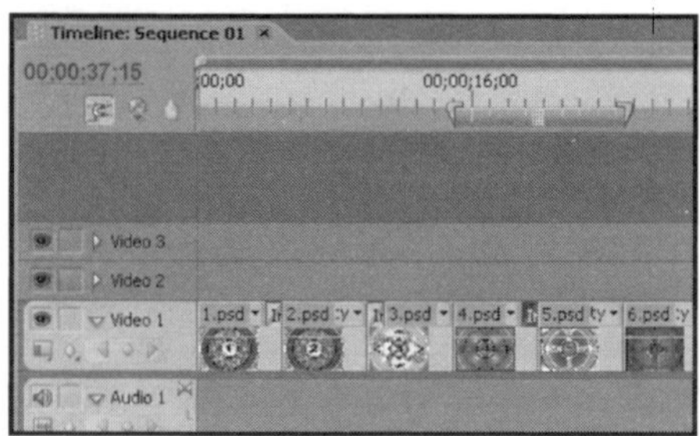

In this lesson, you will learn how to set the work area bar and how to create previews of your entire sequence or just parts of it.

Generating a Preview

Premiere uses the term "preview" generically to refer to many types of views in the Monitor windows. The formal definition of **preview**, however, is a display of contents in the Timeline shown in the Program Monitor—*at the intended frame rate*—from files generated and saved to the hard drive. You generate a preview by clicking Sequence on the menu bar, then clicking Render Work Area, or by pressing [Enter]. When you generate a preview, Premiere Pro saves files of the contents of your Timeline to your hard drive (by default). You can think of this as Premiere Pro *processing* your Timeline. Think about it: When transitions are present in the Timeline, Premiere Pro is generating entirely new content because the frames where the two clips overlap are entirely new to the project. These files must be created and saved before the Program Monitor can play the movie in real time. After the preview is rendered, the sequence plays back automatically in the Program Monitor.

Setting the Work Area Bar

When creating a preview, you can render the entire sequence or just a section of it. Sequences can become very long before you know it. You'll find that there are sections in your sequence that you may need to preview frequently—for example, a segment in which an audio clip starts at a precise point in time of a video clip. You wouldn't want to preview the entire sequence each time you wanted to preview that specific section. You can instead set the work area bar to define the exact section of the sequence you want to render as a preview. The **work area bar**, as shown in Figure 22, is the gray band positioned directly above the time ruler in the Timeline. It determines the areas of the

Timeline that will be included when you generate a preview. The work area bar can be set to generate a preview of the entire sequence or of one continuous area. You determine the length of the work area bar by resizing it, dragging the work area markers to define the beginning and end of a sequence. You can also set the work area bar by dragging the textured center left or right, then fine tuning the parameters with the work area markers. Notice also the thin red bar directly below the work area bar and directly above the clip icons. The red color indicates sections of the Timeline that have not yet been rendered. As the preview renders, the red line is replaced by a bright green bar. The color green indicates areas in the sequence that have been rendered and for which updated preview files have been generated. If you continue to edit the sequence after creating a preview, the green bar will be interrupted by red sections above the clips that have been edited. Blank areas in the Timeline are identified by a gap in the colored band. This can be very useful for spotting unwanted gaps between clips.

QUICKTIP

Pressing and holding [Alt] when clicking the work area bar extends the work area bar from the first clip in the Timeline to the last.

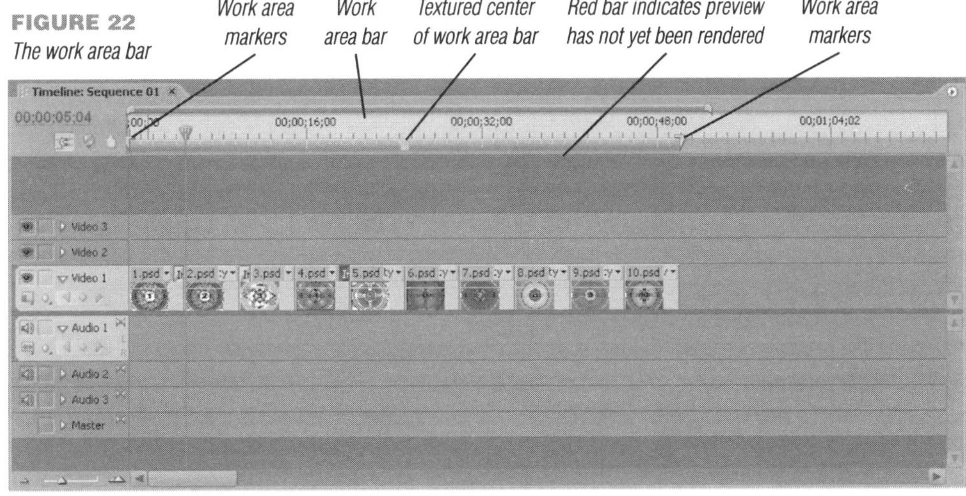

FIGURE 22
The work area bar

Set the work area bar and create a preview

1. Click and drag the textured center of the work area bar so that it starts at the beginning of clip 4.psd, as shown in Figure 23.
2. Drag the ending work area marker to the left until you reach the end of clip 5.psd, as shown in Figure 24.

(continued)

FIGURE 23
Dragging the work area bar

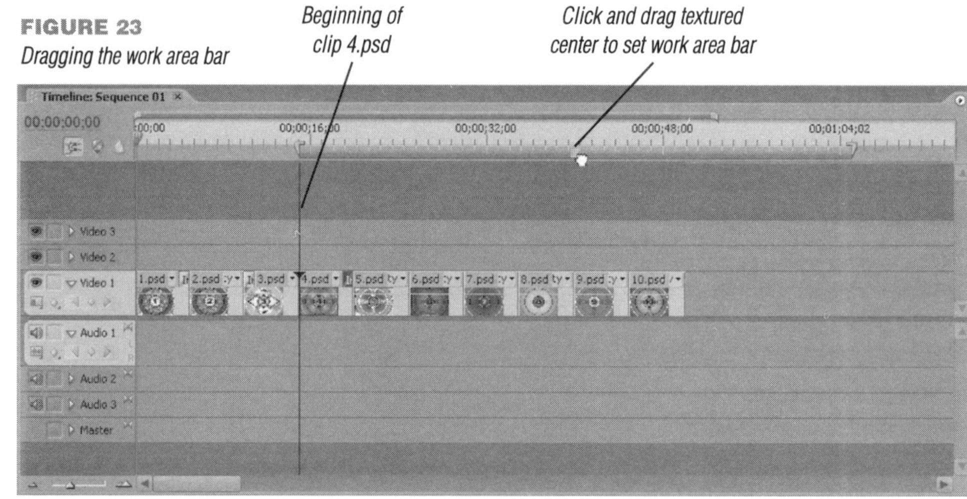

FIGURE 24
Setting the work area bar

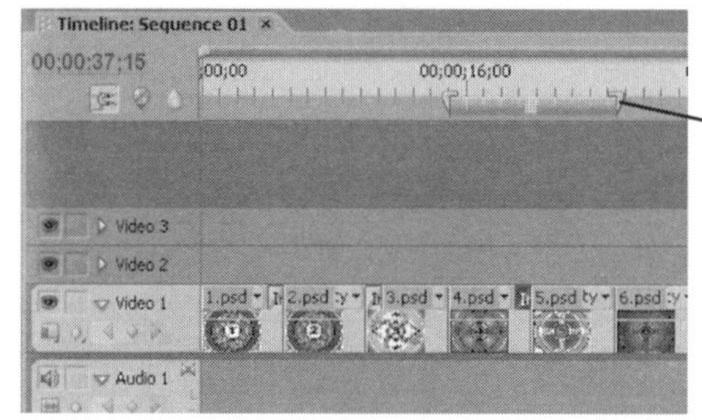

FIGURE 25
Results of rendering the work area bar

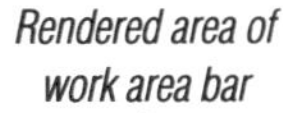

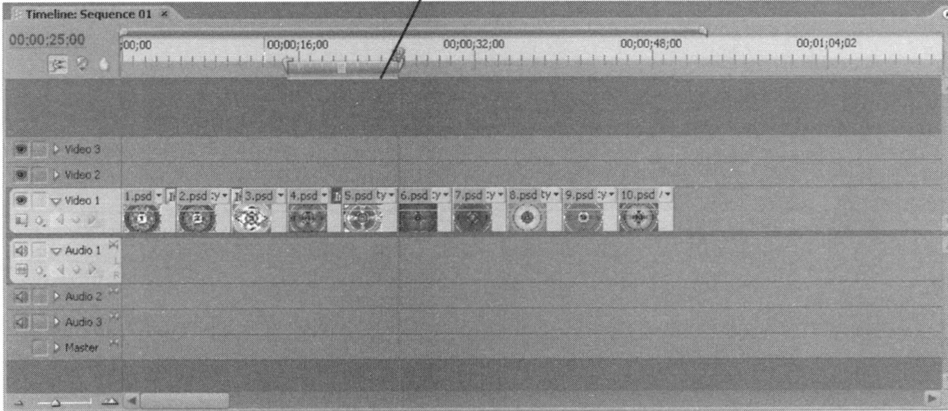

3. Press **[Enter]** to create a preview.

   Figure 25 shows the rendered area of the work area bar. On your monitor, you should see that a bright green bar has replaced the red bar over the work area bar, indicating that this section of the sequence has been rendered as a preview. Notice that only the rendered section played back in the Program Monitor.

4. Save your work, then close the Transitions project.

You set the work area bar by defining its beginning and end points, then rendered a preview.

CHAPTER SUMMARY

Video transitions are used to create a visual change from one clip to another. Typical video transitions are wipes, dissolves, and zooms. Premiere Pro has lots of fun transitions to choose from. Video transitions are categorized by type and placed in named bins in the Effects panel. Simply drag and drop a video transition into the Timeline in one of three ways: at the end of a clip, at the beginning of a clip, or centered over two clips. The method that you use will determine how one clip transitions to the next. You can easily replace transitions by again dragging and dropping a new transition over another in the Timeline. In addition, you can modify transition settings in the Effect Controls panel by double-clicking a transition in the Timeline. The Effect Controls panel allows you to view how a transition works, modify the settings, then preview it over and over until you're happy with it. Finally, when it's time for you to preview your sequence, you can set the work area bar to define exactly which part of the sequence you'd like to see. Pressing [Enter] will render a preview of the work area bar.

What You Have Learned

- How to choose the Effects workspace
- How to view video transitions in the Effects panel
- How to add transitions to the Timeline
- How to create a Start at Cut transition
- How to create an End at Cut transition
- How to create a Center at Cut transition
- How to replace a transition in the Timeline
- How to modify a transition in the Effect Controls panel
- How to set the work area bar
- How to render a preview

Key Terms

Transitions These are built-in effects that Premiere Pro provides to create a visual change from one clip to another.

Dissolves Transitions, in which the end of one clip fades into the beginning of the next.

Wipes Transitions, in which the first clip moves off screen to reveal the next clip.

Irises Transitions, in which the first clip reveals the second clip using a specific shape.

Cut line The line between two clips in the Timeline.

Preview A display of contents in the Timeline shown in the Program Monitor.

Hanoi

chapter 4 EXPLORING ESSENTIAL EDITING TECHNIQUES

1. Trim video clips.
2. Insert and overlay clips.
3. Perform a ripple edit and a rolling edit.

chapter 4 EXPLORING ESSENTIAL EDITING TECHNIQUES

As you become more experienced with Premiere Pro, you'll find yourself incorporating more audio, transitions, and special effects into your projects. You might be surprised at the sheer number of clips that you'll bring into the Timeline, and the complex interrelationships that develop between those clips. It is exactly because of these complex interrelationships that inserting a clip into an existing sequence in the Timeline can get a little bit tricky. Sometimes, you'll want the insertion to affect other clips in the sequence, and sometimes you won't. Sometimes, you'll want to insert a clip without increasing the duration of the program. Sometimes, the duration won't matter.

Premiere Pro offers a number of standard editing techniques, including inserts, overlays, three-point edits, four-point edits, ripple edits, and rolling edits. As you explore these techniques, you'll want to make mental notes of the different options each offers—and the different effect each has on other clips in the Timeline.

Tools You'll Use

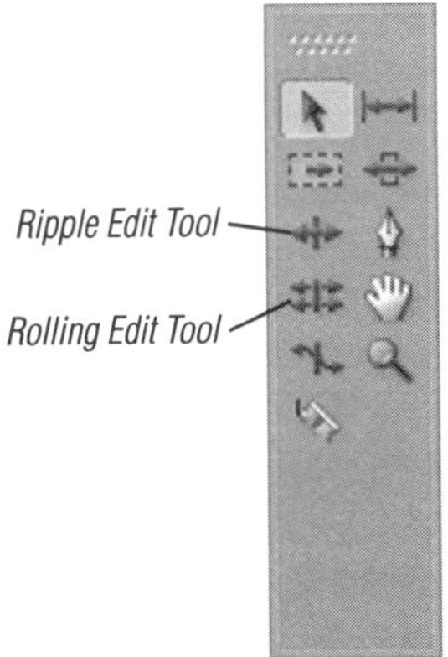

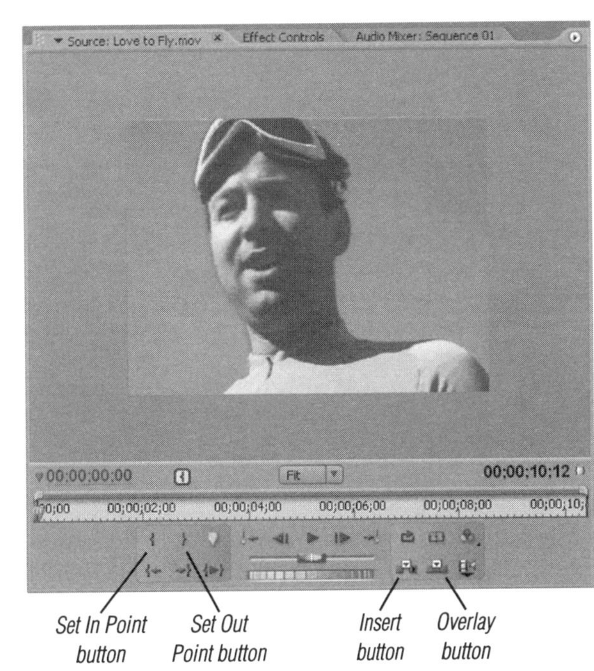

LESSON 1

TRIM VIDEO CLIPS

What You'll Do

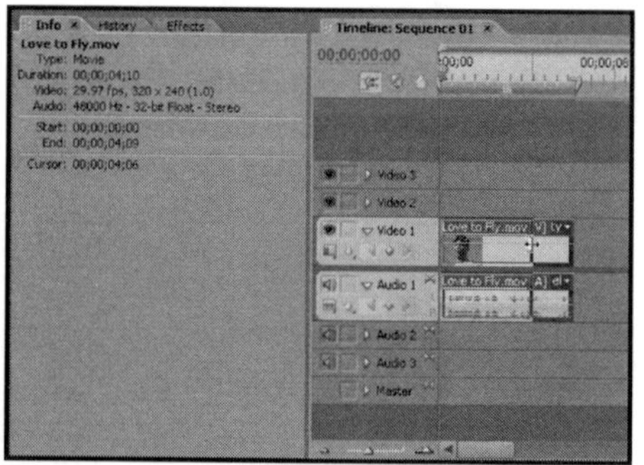

In this lesson, you will trim video clips in the Source Monitor and in the Timeline.

Trimming Video Clips

Once you've imported video, chances are you will want to use only portions of that video in your final cut. The process by which you excise a specific segment of video (or audio) for use in a project is called **trimming**. You can trim clips before you add them to the Timeline in the Source Monitor and you can also trim them in the Timeline.

Setting In and Out Points in the Source Monitor

In Points and Out Points refer to the first and last frame of a clip, respectively. When you trim clips, you change one or both points to determine which segment of the clip you want as part of your final cut. Once trimmed, the frames that come before the In Point are referred to as **head material**, and the frames that follow the Out Point are called **tail material**. When you trim a clip in the Source Monitor and add it to the Timeline, it is added at its new duration—the duration of video between the In and Out Points. Remember that the head and tail material are still available if you choose to elongate the clip in the Timeline.

QUICKTIP

The term "trim," which is used to describe the process of excising a segment of a video clip, may remind you of something being cut. However, keep in mind that when you trim a clip, you are not cutting it. You are simply choosing where you want to start the clip and where you want to end the clip.

As shown in Figure 1, setting In and Out Points is very easy to do in the Source Monitor. Move to the frame that you want as your first frame, then click the Set In Point button. Move to the frame that you want as your last frame, then click the Set Out Point button. Notice the In and Out Points in the time ruler. Also, notice that the head and tail material are still available should you choose to modify the In or Out

Points. Let's say that after you set both of your In and Out Points, you decide you want to start the clip at an earlier frame. Simply move to the new frame, then click the Set In Point button again. The new frame becomes the new In Point. The section of the clip from the In Point to the Out Point is highlighted in the time ruler. This is the section of the clip that will play if this clip is added to the sequence in the Timeline.

Modifying Trimmed Clips in the Source Monitor

The Time duration display in the Source Monitor identifies the clip's duration, as specified from the In Point to the Out Point. When you change the In or the Out Point, the new duration is reflected in the Time duration display. However, changing a clip's duration in the Source Monitor does not alter the actual duration of the original clip in the Project panel. Remember, changes made to clips in the Source Monitor or in the Timeline do not affect the original clips in the Project panel. When you work with a clip outside of the Project panel, you are working with an instance of that clip and always have access to the original clip in the Project panel. As shown in Figure 2, the clip called Love to Fly.mov has a duration of ten seconds and 12 frames, however the duration of the trimmed clip is just shy of seven seconds long. When a trimmed clip is displayed in the Source Monitor, you can view its In and Out Points in the Project panel.

FIGURE 1

Setting In and Out points in the Source Monitor

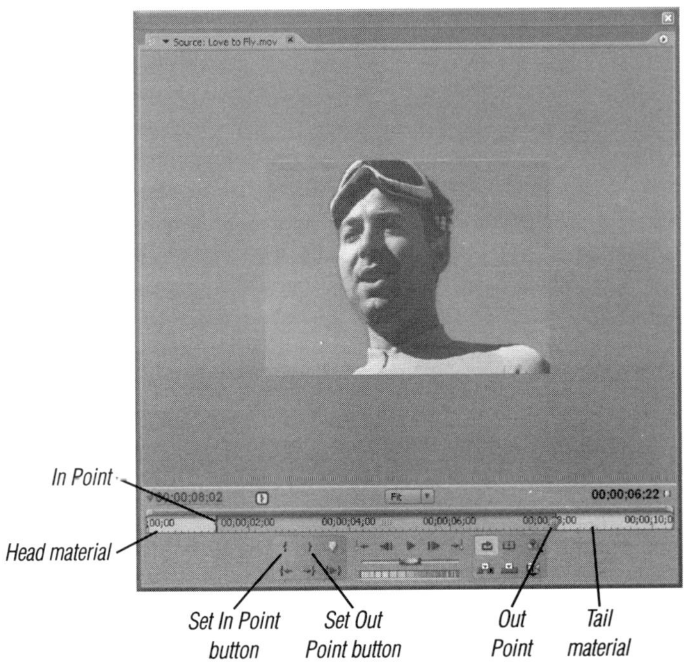

FIGURE 2

Viewing information about a trimmed clip in the Project panel

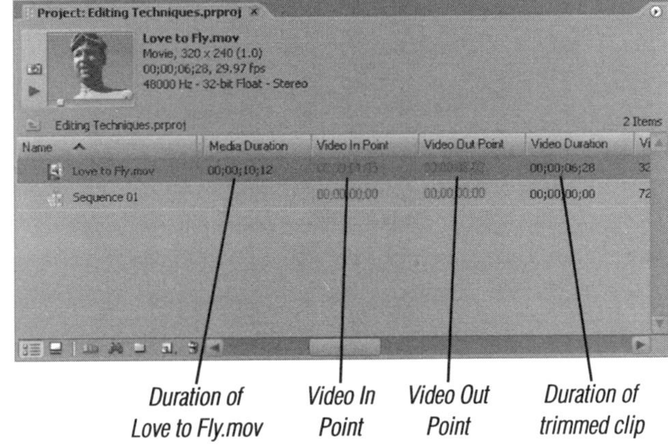

Once you've trimmed a clip in the Source Monitor, you'll want to preview it before you add it to your sequence to make sure it's trimmed to your liking. There are several buttons in the Source Monitor that will help you work with trimmed clips. You can click the Go to In Point button to "jump" to that particular frame or the Go to Out Point button to quickly place the Current time indicator at the last frame of the trimmed clip. You can also click the Play In to Out button to preview a clip from its In Point to its Out Point. You may also want to click the Loop button in order to watch a clip over and over if you need to analyze a specific segment. Undoubtedly, you'll need to adjust the In and Out Points that you set in the Source Monitor. As stated earlier, you can simply click a new location in the time ruler, then click the Set In Point button or Set Out Point button again, or you can drag the Trim-in or Trim-out icons to a new location in the time ruler. The Trim-in icon, shown in Figure 3, appears when you position your pointer near the In Point. When you see the Trim-in icon, drag the In Point left or right to define the new frame for the clip's In Point. The same is true for the Trim-out icon, as shown in Figure 4. Drag the Trim-out icon left or right, as needed, to define the clip's new Out Point.

FIGURE 3
Using the Trim-in icon to change a clip's In Point

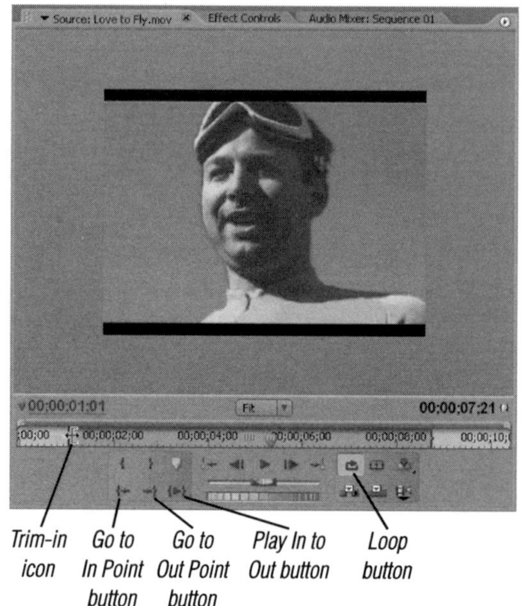

FIGURE 4
Changing a clip's Out Point using the Trim-out icon

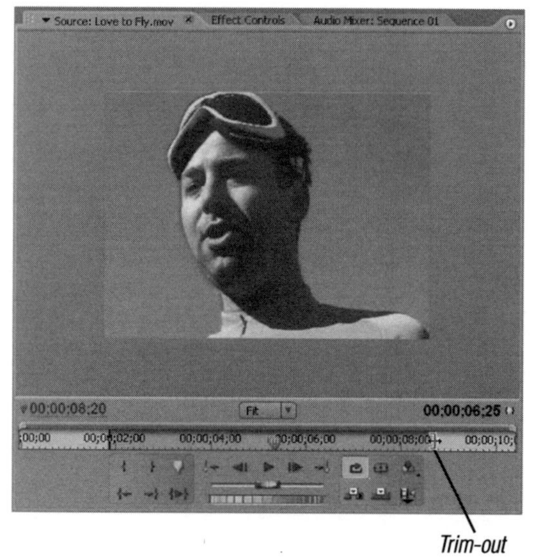

Trimming Clips in the Timeline

You can also edit the In and Out Points of clips in the Timeline using the Trim-in and Trim-out icons. In Figure 5 the Out Point of the Love to Fly.mov clip is being trimmed using the Trim-out icon. Notice that the Love to Fly.mov has both a video and an audio component. Clips that contain both audio and video components are linked. When such a clip is added to the Timeline, the audio portion is automatically added to an audio track and the video portion is added to a video track. To break the link between the audio and video clips, simply press [Alt] as you drag the Clip-in or the Clip-out icon. Trimming clips in the Timeline can be done with precision. As you drag the Clip-in or Clip-out icon, the Info

FIGURE 5
Trimming a clip in the Timeline

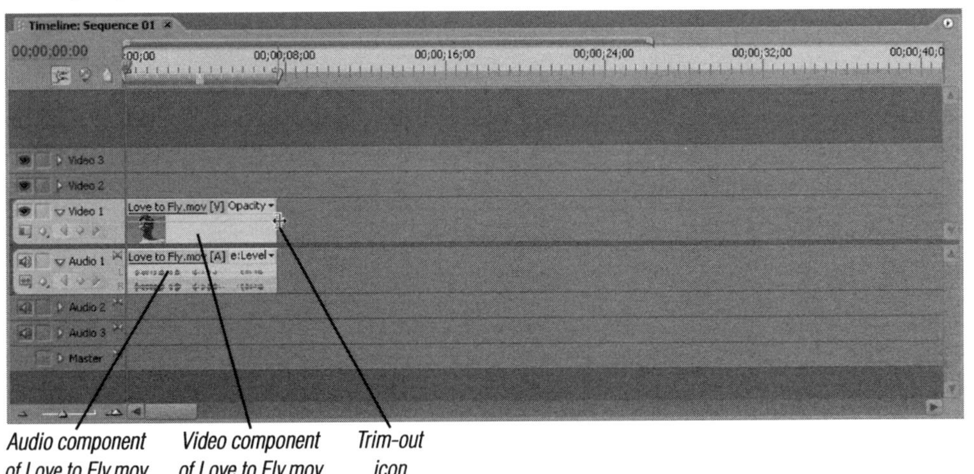

palette identifies the changing location of the clip's In or Out Point as well as the changing duration of the clip, as shown in Figure 6.

An excellent method for trimming in the Timeline is to incorporate the Current time indicator. Let's say that you want to change the Out Point of a clip. Move the Current time indicator to the frame that you want as your Out Point, then simply drag the Clip-out icon to the Current time indicator, and it will "snap" to the Current time indicator, aligning itself precisely. Make sure the Snap icon is activated in the Timeline. Finally, if you plan on trimming clips in the Timeline, rely on the Zoom buttons, slider, or Zoom Tool in the Tools panel to enlarge your view of the clips in the Timeline. This will make your work much easier.

FIGURE 6

Using the Info palette to trim a clip with precision

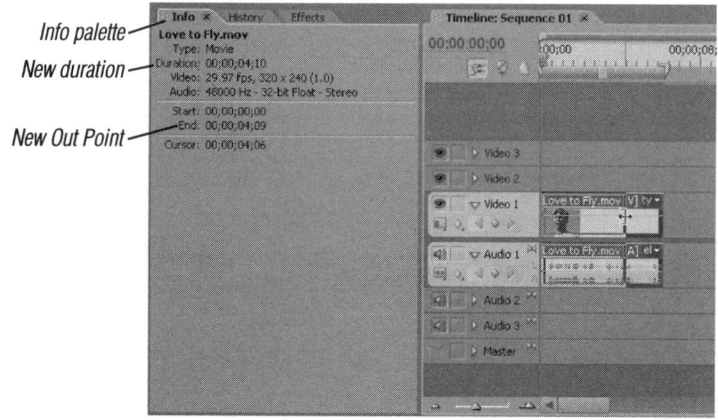

Understanding Three-Point and Four-Point Edits

Even when you think you have finished a project, you may find that you have to go back to it and make changes. In fact, as a professional editor, you will find that much of your work will be done on an already existing program or rough cut that needs reediting or fine-tuning. This can be very challenging because you will often need to replace clips without changing the duration of the entire project, or you will want the replacement to affect only certain clips, leaving others untouched. This is the type of situation that calls for three-point edits and four-point edits. The names of these standard techniques developed because you use In and Out Points to define three or four points that are involved in the edit.

For an example of a three-point edit, let's say you want a source clip to replace only a specific area of the program. You define that area in the Timeline with an In and an Out Point. Those are the first two points. You then specify one other point—the In Point or the Out Point of the source clip.

Once you have defined the three points, you execute the three-point edit by clicking the Overlay button in the Source Monitor. In a three-point edit, the three specified points can be any three of the four available points: the In or Out Point of the source clip, or the In or Out Point of the sequence.

In a four-point edit, all four points are specified and must be adhered to. In other words, the source clip—from its In Point to its Out Point—must replace all the clips in the Timeline that are specified from the In Point to the Out Point in the Timeline. A four-point edit is useful when the starting and ending points are critical in both the source and the program.

Trim video clips in the Source Monitor

1. Open APP 4-1.prproj, then save it as **I'll Fly Away**.
2. Switch to the Editing workspace, if necessary.
3. Expand the Kit Carlson bin in the Project panel, select all of the clips in the Kit Carlson bin, then drag them into the Source Monitor.

   As shown in Figure 7, you can click the Source Monitor tab to show the Source menu of available clips in the Source Monitor.

   The Updraft.mov clip is currently displayed in the Source Monitor.
4. Click the **Source Monitor tab**, then click **Steep Hike.mov** from the Source menu.
5. Play the clip in the Source Monitor to become familiar with it.
6. Drag the **Current time indicator** in the Source Monitor to frame 10:10 or type **10.10** in the Current time display.

   This is the point in the clip where Kit finishes speaking and before he moves his hand over his face.

(continued)

FIGURE 7
Viewing list of clips in the Source Monitor menu

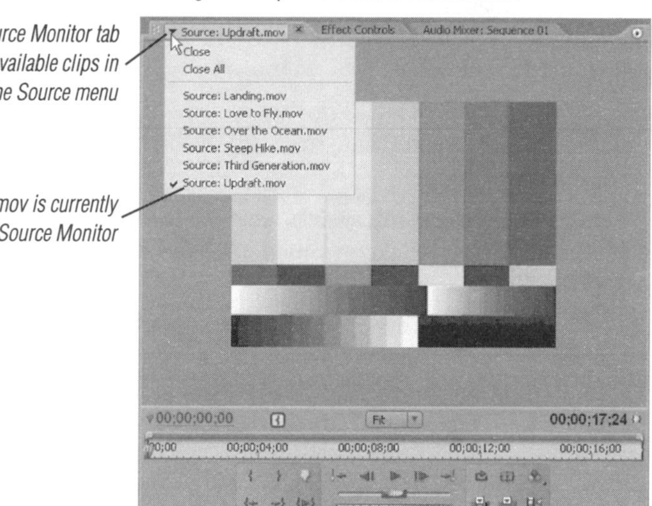

FIGURE 8

Setting a new Out Point for Steep Hike.mov

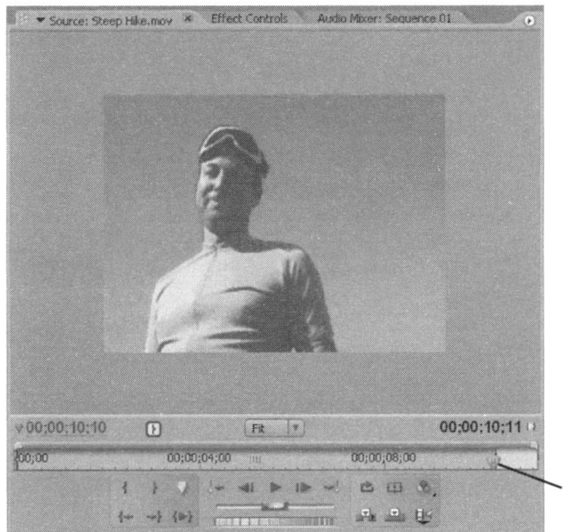

7. Click the **Set Out Point button** .

   The clip is trimmed to end at the new Out Point, as shown in Figure 8.

8. Click the **Play In to Out button** to view the newly trimmed clip in the Source Monitor.

9. Choose Third Generation.mov from the Source menu, then change its In Point to 2:05—the first frame when Kit begins speaking.

10. Set a new Out Point at 13:09.

11. Choose Over the Ocean.mov in the Source Monitor, set a new Out Point at 14:16, then save your work.

You dragged six clips into the Source Monitor, chose the Steep Hike.mov, previewed it, then changed its Out Point and previewed it again. You then modified In and Out Points for Third Generation.mov and Over the Ocean.mov.

Trim video clips in the Timeline

1. Click the **Project panel** to deselect the selected clips, then drag **Updraft.mov** to the beginning of the Video 1 track in the Timeline.
2. Drag **Landing.mov** next to Updraft.mov in the Video 1 track, then zoom in on the Timeline to view the clips easier.

   Your Timeline should resemble Figure 9.
3. Preview the contents of the Timeline in the Program Monitor to become familiar with the sequence so far.
4. Verify that the Snap icon is activated in the Timeline.

   TIP The Snap icon should looks "pressed" and light gray when activated.
5. Drag the **Current time indicator** to frame 3:16 or type **3.16** in the Current time display in the Program Monitor.
6. Position the Selection Tool over the left edge of the Updraft.mov clip and drag it slowly until you see the Trim-in icon, then drag to the right until it snaps to the Current time indicator, as shown in Figure 10.

(continued)

FIGURE 9
Updraft.mov and Landing.mov added to the Timeline

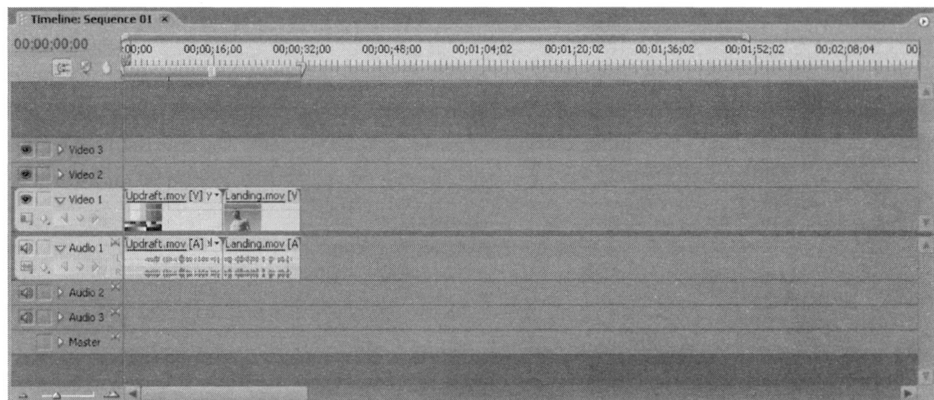

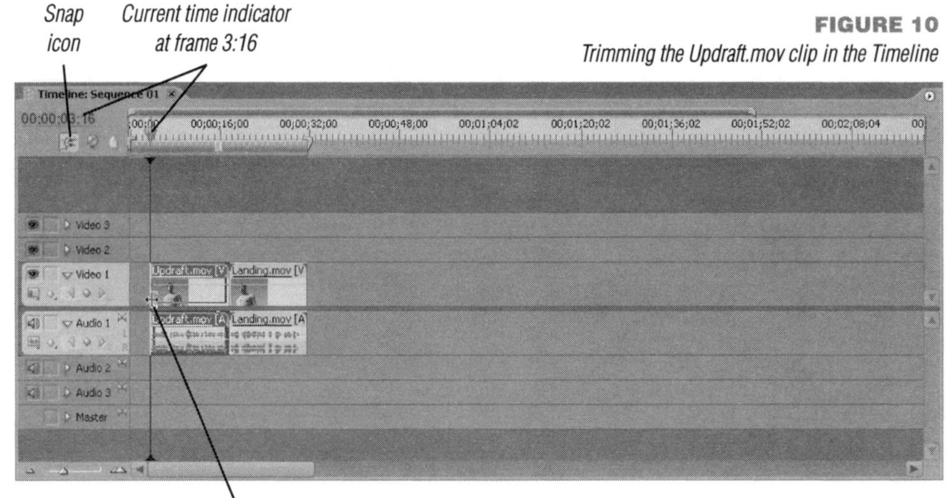

FIGURE 10
Trimming the Updraft.mov clip in the Timeline

FIGURE 11
Stopping the clip after Kit finishes speaking

Your Current time display may differ

7. Preview the sequence in the Program Monitor and press the **Stop button** right after Kit says "right on the beach."

   When you press Stop, your Program Monitor should resemble Figure 11. Your Current time display may differ slightly from the figure.

8. Position the Selection Tool at the right edge of the Landing.mov clip in the Timeline and drag it slowly until you see the Trim-out icon, then drag to the left until it snaps to the Current time indicator.

   TIP When you trim clips in the Timeline, a tooltip displays the number of frames being trimmed.

9. Click the **Track Select Tool**, click **Updraft.mov** in the Timeline, then drag the selected clips to the beginning of the Video 1 track.

10. Choose Steep Hike.mov from the Source menu, drag **Steep Hike.mov** from the Source Monitor to the right of Landing.mov in the Timeline, play the new sequence, then save your work.

You trimmed two clips in the Timeline using the Trim-in and Trim-out icons, moved the clips to the beginning of the Timeline, then added Steep Hike.mov to the Timeline.

LESSON 2

INSERT AND OVERLAY CLIPS

What You'll Do

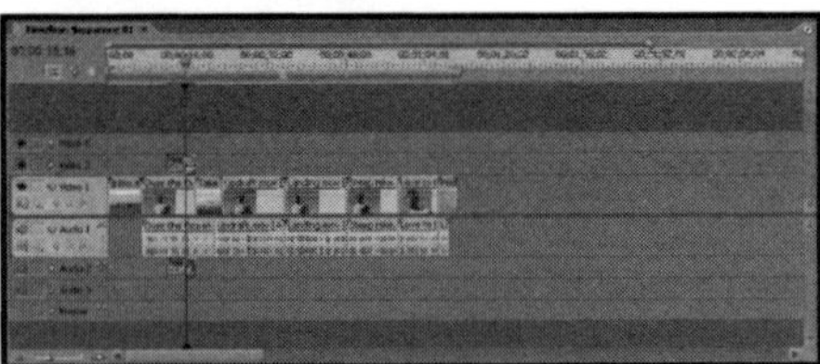

In this lesson, you will insert and overlay clips and examine the impact of doing so on clips in the Timeline.

Inserting Clips from the Source Monitor

After you've trimmed a clip in the Source Monitor, you can easily add it to the Timeline. You can drag a clip from the Source Monitor to the Timeline to add it to the Timeline or to insert it between two clips in the Timeline. To insert it between two clips, drag the clip from the Source Monitor over the point where the two clips meet in the Timeline, then release the mouse button. This point is known as the **cut line**. If you press [Ctrl] when adding the clip between two clips, the newly added clip makes room for itself, pushing the clips to the right of the insertion point further to the right. The clips on the left don't move. If you do not press and hold [Ctrl], the newly added clip replaces the clip to its right in the Timeline.

You can also insert a clip from the Source Monitor into the Timeline using the Insert button in the Source Monitor. When clicked, the Insert button inserts the current clip in the Source Monitor at the location of the Current time indicator in the Timeline. None of the clips in the Timeline are replaced, they are just displaced. If the Current time indicator is not positioned at the cut line between two clips, but instead in the middle of a clip, as shown in Figure 12, the clip in the Timeline is split into two parts, and the newly added clip is inserted

FIGURE 12
Position of Current time indicator affects clips in the Timeline when new clips are inserted

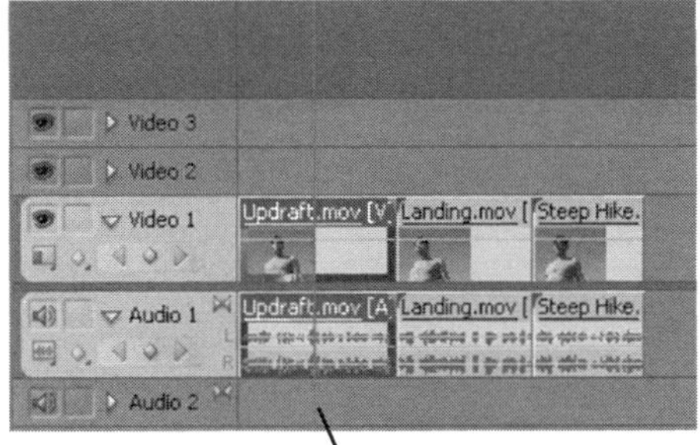

Current time indicator is placed in the middle of a clip, indicating that this clip will be split into two clips if a new clip is inserted using the Insert button

between them, as shown in Figure 13. Notice the location of the Current time indicator in Figure 12, then notice that the Over the Ocean.mov clip is inserted at that point. The Updraft.mov clip is split into two parts and the Current time indicator moves to the end of Over the Ocean.mov, as shown in Figure 13. If the Current time indicator had been located at the cut line between Updraft.mov and Landing.mov, Updraft.mov would not be affected and Landing.mov would have been pushed to the right to make room for Over the Ocean.mov.

Overlaying Clips from the Source Monitor

Like the Insert button, the Overlay button in the Source Monitor adds the current clip in the Source Monitor to the location of the Current time indicator in the Timeline. In contrast to the Insert button, the Overlay button replaces the existing material at the Current time indicator with the newly inserted clip. For example, if the clip in the Source Monitor has a duration of one minute and you click the Overlay button, the clip in the Source Monitor will replace one minute of the existing frames that are to the right of the Current time indicator in the Timeline.

FIGURE 13

Over the Ocean.mov clip inserted in the middle of Updraft.mov

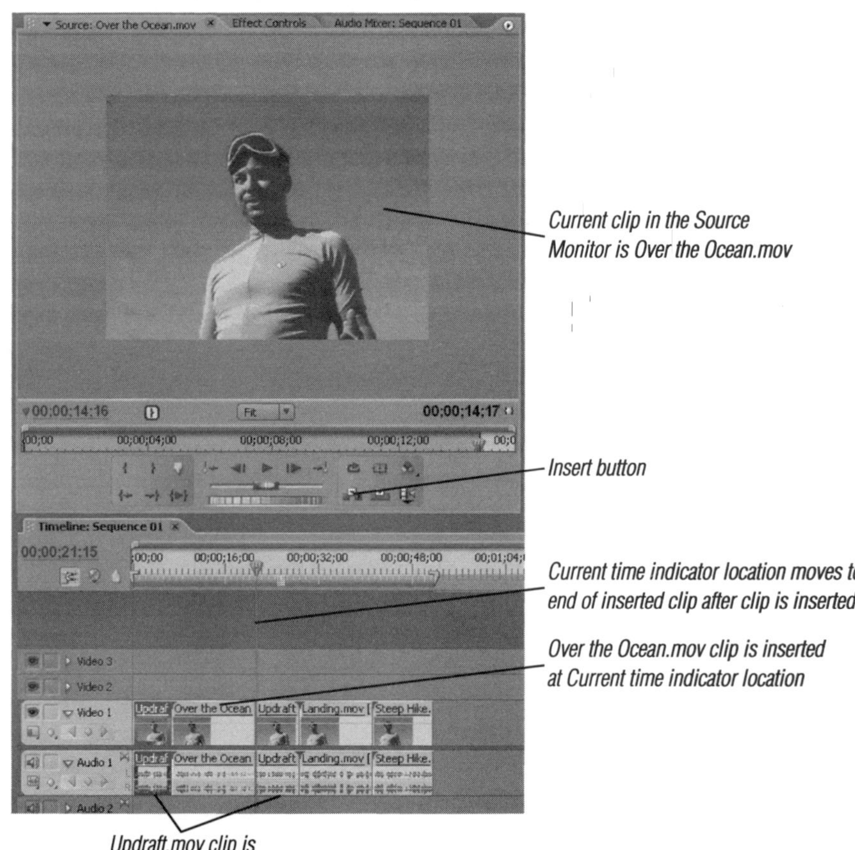

Working with Multiple Video Tracks

The Timeline has three video tracks to work with by default; however, you can have up to 99 video tracks, if needed. To change the number of video tracks in the Timeline, click Project on the menu bar, point to Project Settings, then click General. Click the Default Sequence category in the Project Settings dialog box, then click the up arrow next to Video to choose a new number of video tracks. Placing clips on different tracks has many advantages, especially for special effects and superimposing clips. In terms of inserting and overlaying clips, using a second video track is an easy way to insert a clip into the program without affecting the clips already there.

A clip positioned on a superior video track plays to the exclusion of the clips beneath it. This can be very useful when editing. For example, let's say you had a 10-second clip in the Video 1 track and you wanted a three-second clip to play in the middle of the 10-second clip. Rather than cut the 10-second clip in the Video 1 track, simply position the three-second clip on the Video 2 track, centered above the 10-second clip.

Using the Razor Tool

A quick and easy way to cut a clip into two or more clips is to use the Razor Tool. To use the Razor Tool, select it in the Tools panel, then click a clip in the Timeline at the location where you want to split the clip. After you cut a clip you can then fine tune its In and Out Points using the Trim-in and Trim-out icons. If you know exactly where you want to cut a clip, line the Razor Tool up with the Current time indicator at a specific frame before you click, as shown in Figure 14.

FIGURE 14

Aligning the Razor Tool with the Current time indicator

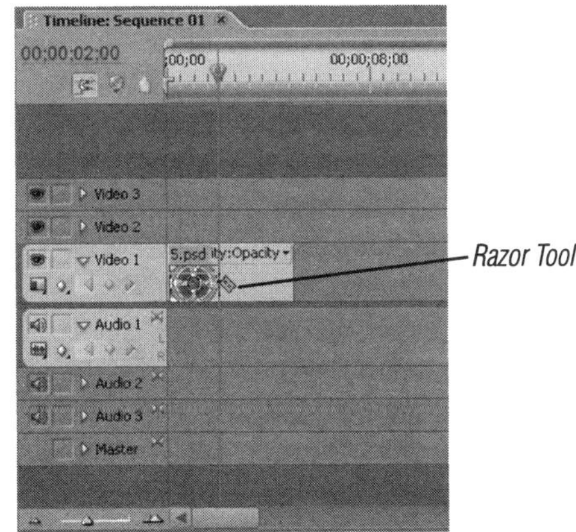

Director's Cut: Bonnie and Clyde

With his 1967 *Bonnie and Clyde*—on the surface a straightforward period piece—
director Arthur Penn (and producer Warren Beatty) bent and broke many accepted moviemaking techniques. Coming at a turbulent time in a turbulent decade, the film is subtly but unmistakably antiestablishment. The fact that it's hard to say why only contributes to its power. An example of both its rule-breaking and its impact comes midway through the film. Bonnie (Faye Dunaway) and Clyde (Warren Beatty) pick up a young man and his wife, who are impressed to meet the notorious bank robbers on the lam. Bonnie is only too happy to play to their fantasies as she regales them with tales from her adventures as an outlaw.

Bonnie has turned around fully in the front seat, and she talks to her guests in the back seat the way a mother entertains her children on a long ride. She asks the young man (Gene Wilder) what he does for a living, and her smile freezes when he says that he's an undertaker. She whips her head around, and as she turns, the camera cuts to the front seat, where we see Bonnie's head snap forward. Her smile has vanished. This is a bad omen, and she wants them out of the car . . . now.

The scene is disturbing precisely because the cut is not perfect, *intentionally*. Bonnie's head does not turn from the backseat to the front in one smooth motion. Instead, the cut overlaps, so that we see her head turn once from the backseat, then we see it again from the front seat. The force with which she whips her head around is enhanced, and so is the sense that she has two faces—smiling on the back, glowering on the front. The scene is an excellent example of the power of a sudden change in tone. It is also a reminder that "perfect" cuts are not always the most effective choice. The scene is already disturbing. The unexpected jump cut makes it jarring, too.

FIGURE 15

Dragging Over the Ocean.mov over Updraft.mov

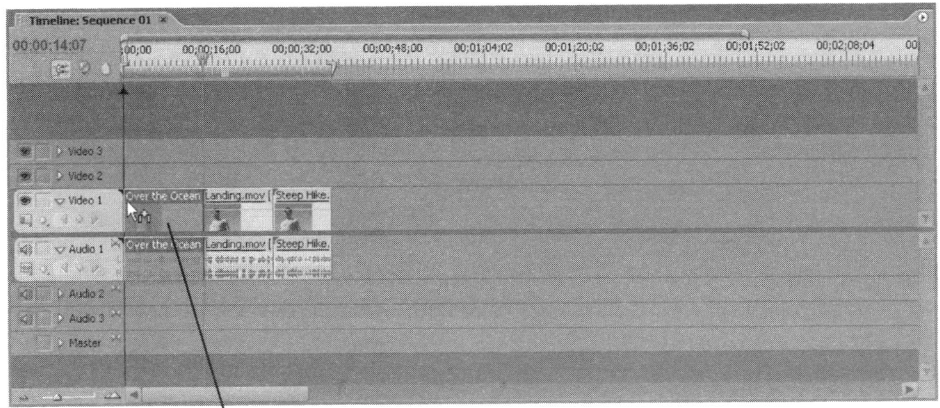

When Over the Ocean.mov is placed on top of Updraft.mov, the clip is highlighted in the Timeline

FIGURE 16

Over the Ocean.mov becomes the first clip in the Timeline

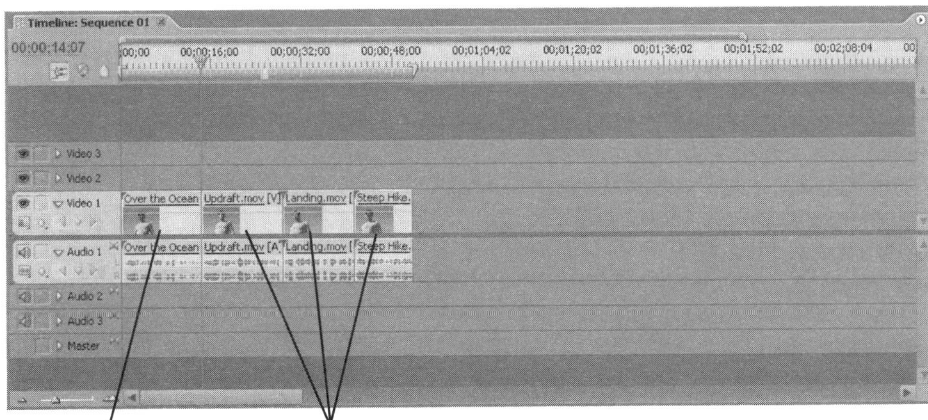

Over the Ocean.mov

Three existing clips are pushed to the right

Insert clips from the Source Monitor

1. Choose Over the Ocean.mov from the Source menu in the Source Monitor.
2. Press and hold **[Ctrl]**, drag the **Over the Ocean.mov clip** from the Source Monitor on top of the Updraft.mov clip in the Timeline, as shown in Figure 15, then release your mouse button.

   As shown in Figure 16, Over the Ocean.mov becomes the first clip in the sequence, and the three other clips are pushed to the right.
3. Choose Love to Fly.mov from the Source menu in the Source Monitor, then drag it into the Timeline, to the right of Steep Hike.mov.
4. Expand the Air Clips folder in the Project panel, select all the clips in the Air Clips folder, then drag them into the Source Monitor.

(continued)

5. Choose Intro.mov from the Source menu, position the Current time indicator all the way to the left in the Timeline, then click the **Insert button** in the Source Monitor.

   The Intro.mov clip is inserted at the beginning of the Timeline, as shown in Figure 17.

6. Click the **Current time display** in the Program Monitor, type **1.06.24**, then press **[Enter]**.

   The Current time indicator moves to the new location.

   TIP You can also enter timecode without periods.

7. Choose Peddler.mov from the Source menu, then click the **Insert button**.

   Love to Fly.mov is split to accommodate the insertion. Your Timeline should resemble Figure 18.

(continued)

FIGURE 17

Intro.mov is inserted at beginning of Timeline

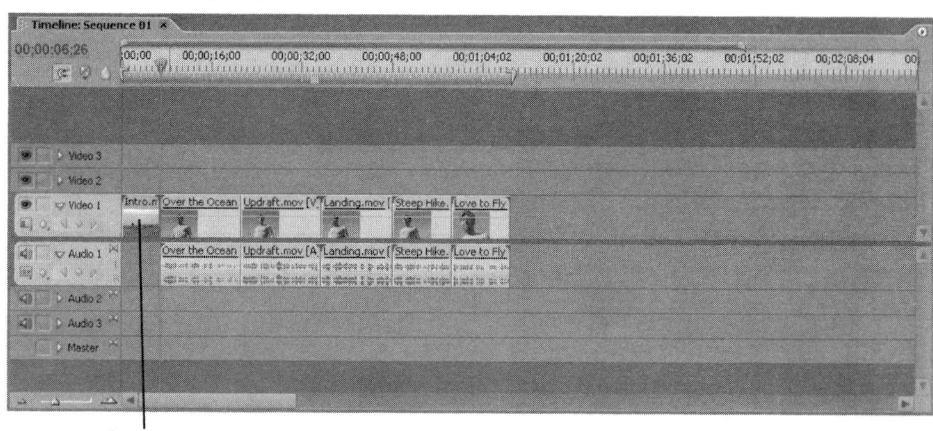

FIGURE 18

Inserting the Peddler.mov clip

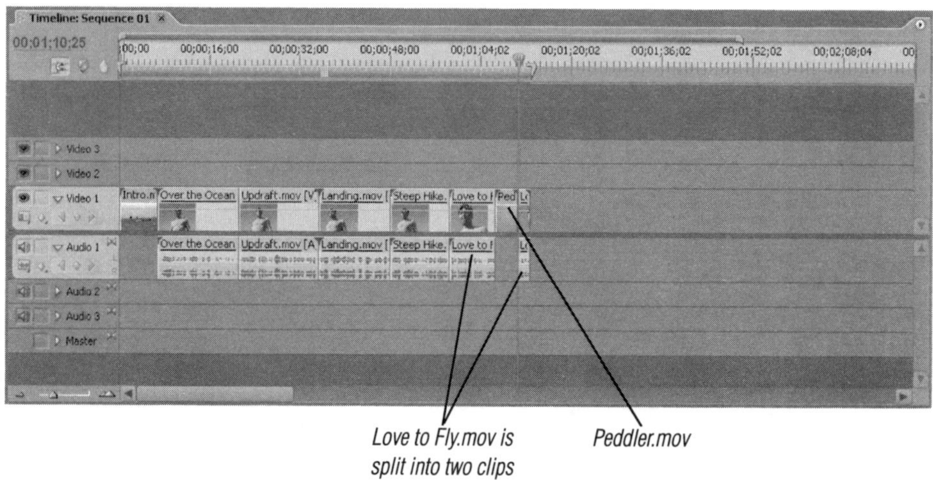

FIGURE 19
Repositioning the unlinked audio clip

8. Click the **Selection Tool** , select the last clip in the Timeline, click **Clip** on the menu bar, then click **Unlink**.
9. Click anywhere to deselect, delete the unlinked video, then drag the audio clip to the left until it snaps to the previous clip, as shown in Figure 19.
10. Press **[Enter]** to generate a preview, then save your work.

You inserted clips into the Timeline by dragging one from the Source Monitor and using the Insert button for the others.

Overlay clips in the Timeline

1. Choose Take Off.mov from the Source menu.
2. Position the Current frame indicator in the Timeline at frame 6:26 (the start of Over the Ocean.mov), then press the **Play button** in the Program Monitor to preview the Over the Ocean.mov and Updraft.mov clips.

   You are previewing clips that will be replaced by an overlay.
3. Position the Current time indicator in the Timeline at 17:17, then click the **Overlay button** in the Source Monitor.

   Take Off.mov is inserted at frame 17:17, replacing a video portion of Over the Ocean.mov and changing the In Point of Updraft.mov, as shown in Figure 20.
4. Generate a preview.

You used the Overlay button in the Source Monitor to replace portions of two clips in the Timeline with a clip in the Source Monitor.

FIGURE 20
Overlaying Take Off.mov

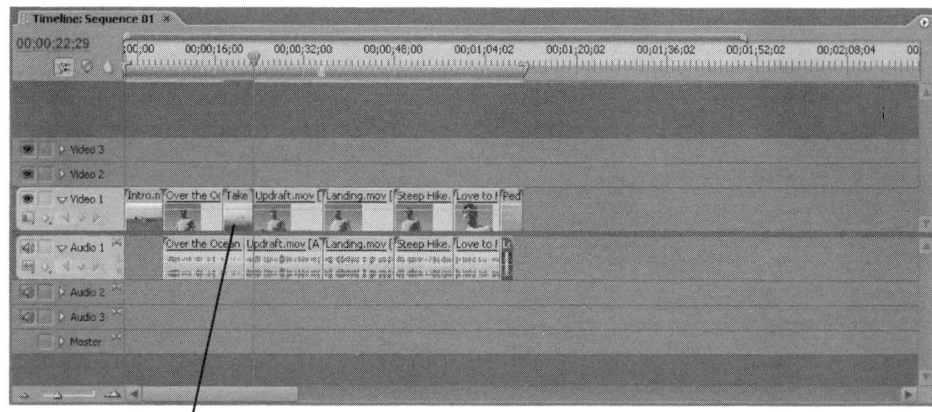

Take Off.mov is overlaid in the Timeline and replaces part of Over the Ocean.mov

FIGURE 21

Adding Spiral.mov to the Video 2 track

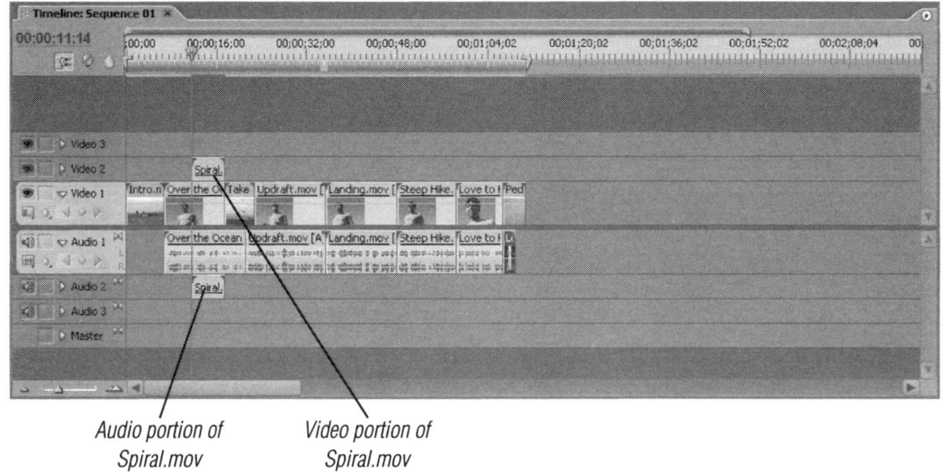

FIGURE 22

Trimming Spiral.mov in the Video 2 track

Work with multiple video tracks

1. Position the Current time indicator in the Timeline at frame 11:14—the point where Kit finishes saying "...my favorite place to fly."
2. Choose Spiral.mov from the Source menu, then press the **Play button** to preview it in the Source Monitor.
3. Drag **Spiral.mov** into the Video 2 track so that it begins at the Current time indicator.

   The audio portion of Spiral.mov is positioned automatically on the Audio 2 track so as not to disturb the Audio 1 track, as shown in Figure 21.
4. Position the Current time indicator at frame 15:16—the point where Kit starts to say "jump."
5. Click the **Selection Tool**, position the pointer at the right edge of Spiral.mov, then drag the **Trim-out icon** left until it snaps to the Current time indicator, as shown in Figure 22.
6. Click **Clip** on the menu bar, then click **Unlink**.
7. Deselect, then delete the audio component of Spiral.mov.
8. Generate a preview, then save your work.

You added a video clip to the Video 2 track to play over the video clip beneath it.

LESSON 3

PERFORM A RIPPLE EDIT AND A ROLLING EDIT

What You'll Do

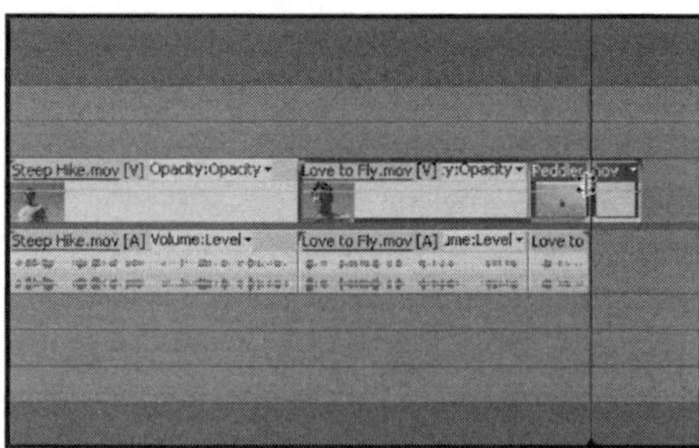

In this lesson, you will use the Ripple Edit Tool and the Rolling Edit Tool.

Using the Ripple Edit Tool

As you have already seen, you can trim clips in the Timeline by dragging their left or right edges with the Trim-in and Trim-out icons. Trimming clips using the Trim icons does not affect the other clips in the Timeline. The Ripple Edit Tool is also used to shorten or lengthen a clip, but the change "ripples" through the Timeline. If you shorten a clip using the Ripple Edit Tool, the clips to the right of the shortened clip shift left to take up the space created by the shortening, as shown in Figure 23. If you lengthen a clip, the clips to the right move to the right to create space for the lengthening. In both cases, the duration of the other clips is not affected by the ripple edit—just their location in the Timeline. However, the duration of the entire project—by definition—is changed.

FIGURE 23
Using the Ripple Edit Tool

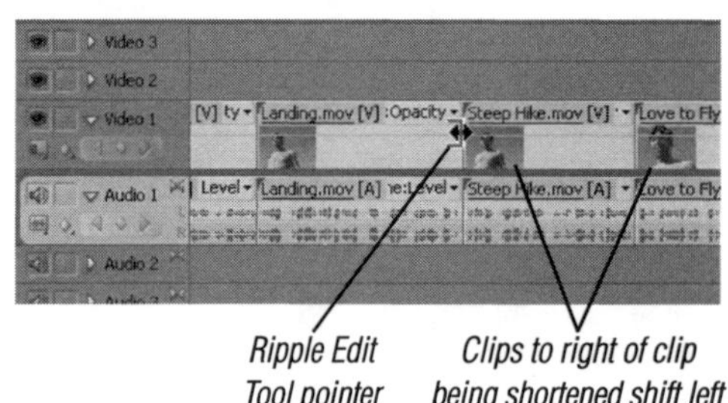

Performing a Rolling Edit

In a **rolling edit**, you shorten or lengthen a specified clip without changing the duration of the entire project. When you trim a clip with the Rolling Edit Tool, the In or the Out Point of that clip is adjusted and the duration of the adjacent clip is also adjusted so that the total duration of the two clips together remains the same.

For example, imagine two clips in the Timeline. If you use the Rolling Edit Tool to elongate the first clip by 30 frames, the In Point of the second clip will occur 30 frames later in the clip, and the duration of the second clip will therefore be reduced by 30 frames. Thus, the duration of the entire project does not change. If you were to reduce the first clip by 30 seconds, the In Point of the second clip would be moved 30 seconds earlier in the clip, and the duration of the second clip would therefore be increased by 30 frames. Figure 24 shows the Over the Ocean.mov clip being lengthened with the Rolling Edit Tool. In this example, the clip to the right of Over the Ocean.mov, Take Off.mov, is shortened by the same amount, thus maintaining the same duration of the entire sequence.

When you use the Rolling Edit Tool to shorten a clip, the clip that is adjacent to the edge you are dragging must have enough head material or tail material to fill the gap created by the shortening. If there is not enough head or tail material, you will not be able to drag the edge of the specified clip.

QUICKTIP

The Ripple Delete command on the Edit menu does exactly what its name implies. When you use the command to delete a clip in the Timeline, the deletion ripples through the Timeline, and all the clips to the right of the deleted clip shift left to fill the gap left by the deletion. The Ripple Delete command is also very useful for deleting a gap in the Timeline. Simply select the gap with the Selection Tool, then apply the Ripple Delete command. All of the clips to the right of the gap shift left to fill the gap.

FIGURE 24

Lengthening a clip with the Rolling Edit Tool

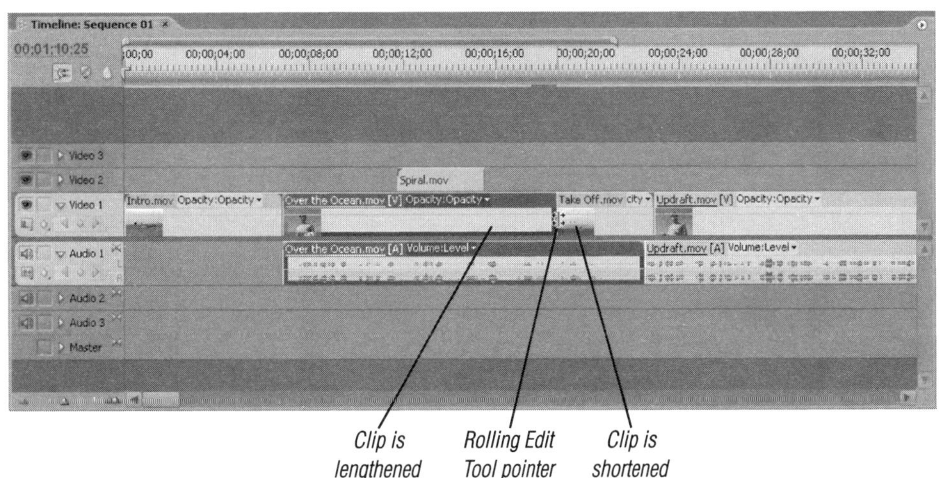

Perform a ripple edit

1. Zoom in on the Timeline to see the clips at a larger view.
2. Drag the **Current time indicator** in the Timeline to 32:27.
3. Click the **Ripple Edit Tool** , then position it over the right edge of Updraft.mov until it changes to the Ripple Edit pointer, as shown in Figure 25.

   TIP The Ripple Edit pointer looks like a red bracket. The direction of the bracket indicates which clip is being trimmed in the Timeline.

4. Drag the right edge of Updraft.mov left until it snaps to the Current time indicator.

   All of the subsequent clips shift to the left; the duration of the movie is reduced to 1:08:00.

5. Generate a preview.

Using the Ripple Edit Tool, you reduced the length of a clip, leaving no gaps in the Timeline but reducing the duration of the movie.

FIGURE 25
Preparing to perform a ripple edit

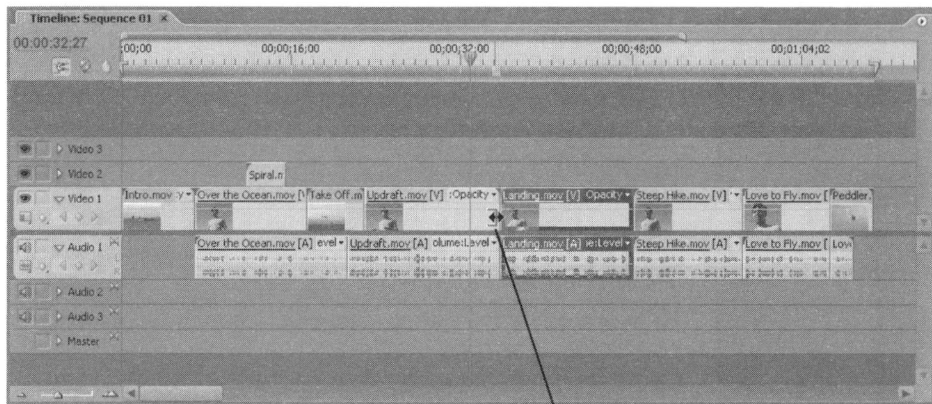

FIGURE 26
Preparing to perform a rolling edit

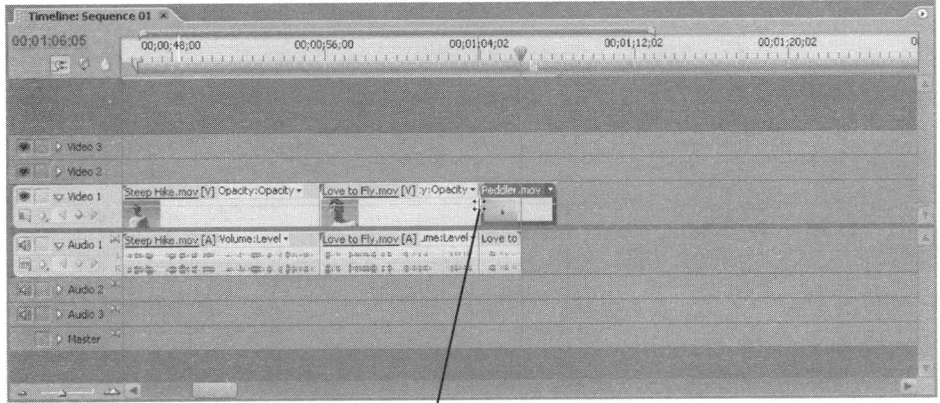

FIGURE 27
Drag Rolling Edit pointer to Current time indicator

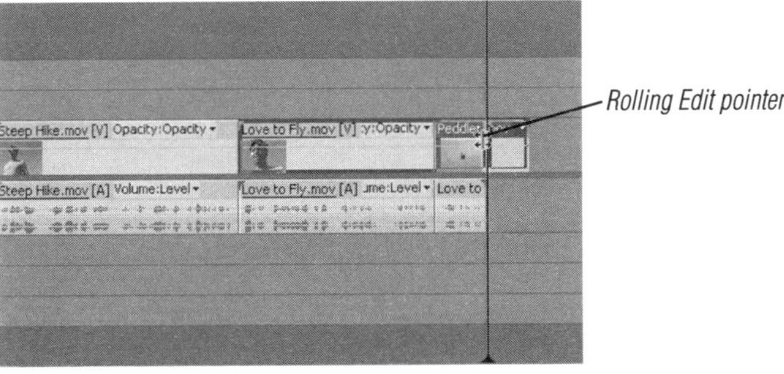

Perform a rolling edit

1. Drag the **Current time indicator** to 45:12—the beginning of Steep Hike.mov.
2. Play the movie from this frame until the end and notice that Peddler.mov is showing when Kit says "It's like total freedom."

   The duration of the sequence is one minute, eight seconds.
3. Type **1.06.05** in the Current time display in the Program Monitor, then press **[Enter]**.

   This frame marks the end of the audio portion of the Love to Fly.mov clip. You will perform a rolling edit so that Kit finishes speaking before Peddler.mov starts, without changing the duration of the entire sequence.
4. Click the **Rolling Edit Tool** in the Tools panel and position it at the right edge of Love to Fly.mov in the Video 1 track, as shown in Figure 26.
5. Drag the **Rolling Edit pointer** to the right until it snaps to the Current time indicator, as shown in Figure 27.

(continued)

As you drag the Rolling Edit pointer, the Program Monitor shows both clips being affected by the edit, as shown in Figure 28.

6. Notice that the duration of the entire sequence did not change, save your work, then generate a preview.

   Your movie should end with Peddler.mov playing without Kit speaking.

You performed a rolling edit to change the end of the sequence without changing the duration of the sequence.

FIGURE 28

Program Monitor displays both clips affected by a rolling edit

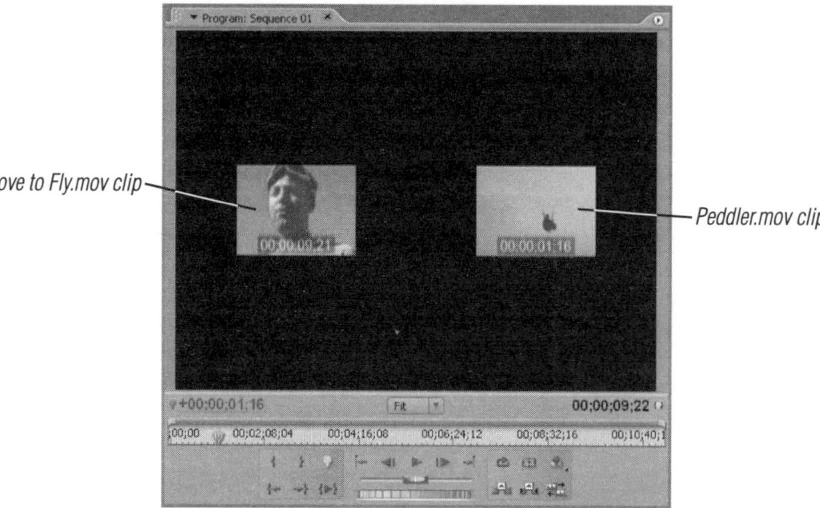

CHAPTER SUMMARY

Once you start adding clips to the Timeline, the editing process begins. It's only natural that you'll find yourself previewing your sequence repeatedly and finding areas that you'll want to change. For example, you may want to extract part of a clip instead of using all of it. You may need to lengthen one clip and shorten its neighbor without changing the duration of the sequence. Premiere Pro offers lots of ways to trim clips and manipulate their placement and length in the Timeline. You can set In and Out Points for a clip in the Source Monitor before adding it to the Timeline or you can trim a clip directly in the Timeline with the Trim-in and Trim-out icons. You can also insert a clip using the Insert button and the Overlay button in the Source Monitor. The Insert button will insert a clip at the location of the Current time indicator; and push the existing clips to the right of it. The Overlay button also inserts a clip at the location of the Current time indicator, however, the newly inserted clip replaces the same amount of video in the Timeline. For example if you overlay a ten-second clip on top of a 30-second clip, the first ten seconds of the existing clip will be replaced by the overlaid clip. Finally, the Ripple Edit Tool and the Rolling Edit Tool allow you to trim clips in the Timeline. If you shorten a clip using the Ripple Edit Tool, the clips to the right of the shortened clip shift left to take up the space created by the shortening. When you trim a clip with the Rolling Edit Tool, the In or the Out Point of that clip is adjusted and the duration of the adjacent clip is also adjusted so that the total duration of the two clips together remains the same.

What You Have Learned

- How to add multiple clips to Source Monitor from the Project panel
- How to choose a clip from the Source menu
- How to set an In Point
- How to set an Out Point
- How to trim a clip in the Timeline with the Trim-in icon
- How to trim a clip in the Timeline with the Trim-out icon
- How to insert a clip using the Insert button
- How to overlay a clip using the Overlay button
- How to create a ripple edit
- How to create a rolling edit

Key Terms

Trimming Trimming is the process by which you excise a specific segment of video (or audio) for use in a project.

Head Material The frames that come before the In Point are referred to as head material.

Tail Material The frames that follow the Out Point of a frame are called tail material.

In point The first frame of a clip—the In Point can be set using the Set In Point button.

Out point The last frame of a clip—the Out Point can be set using the Set Out Point button.

STOP
ONLY
ONLY

chapter

5 WORKING WITH AUDIO

1. Investigate audio clip properties.
2. Extract audio.
4. Unlink audio from video and adjust volume.
5. Apply and modify audio effects.

chapter 5 WORKING WITH AUDIO

Premiere Pro is usually identified as a video-editing program, but that perception overlooks its role as a powerful audio-editing program as well. With Premiere Pro, you can mix audio with professional results, and you can synchronize audio clips with video clips to create dramatic and complex relationships. In Premiere Pro, audio clips are treated much like video clips in the sense that you import them into the Project panel, drag them into the Timeline, preview them in the Source Monitor, and even add effects and transitions to them using the Effects panel. Audio clips function in the Timeline just as video clips do: They have specific durations, and they can be moved, copied, and pasted throughout the Timeline. You can set In points and Out points for audio clips.

The Audio workspace, as its name implies, is the most convenient workspace for working with audio, especially if you plan on manipulating audio clips in the Audio Mixer panel. The Audio Mixer panel allows you to record sounds directly to the Timeline while your sequence plays if you have the correct audio hardware installed on your computer.

Audio is often an extremely important component of any video presentation. With Premiere Pro, you will find that you are equipped to work with audio in ways that will challenge you and help you to translate your creative sensibilities to the fascinating world of sound.

Tools You'll Use

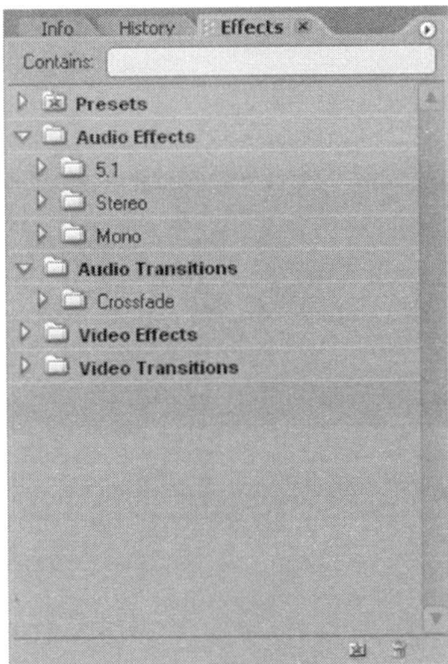

INVESTIGATE AUDIO CLIP PROPERTIES

What You'll Do

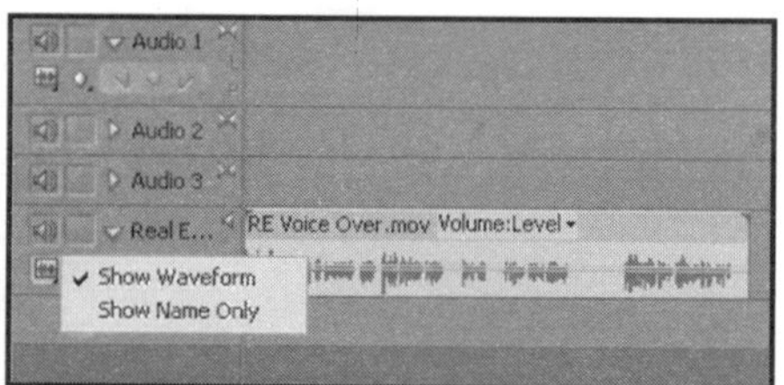

In this lesson, you will familiarize yourself with audio clip properties and audio track properties in the Timeline.

Understanding Properties of Audio Clips

You don't have to be an audio expert to play around with audio files in Premiere Pro, however, it is important to understand a few basic principles about audio clips. You can import individual audio files into Premiere Pro, such as MP3 or WAV files, or you can import video clips that have an audio component attached. Audio files are measured using kilohertz (kHz)—**kilohertz** measure how many sounds play per second on a soundtrack. 48 kHz is the default sample rate setting in Premiere Pro, as shown in Figure 1. This is a good choice because it is the same rate that audio is recorded at using digital video recorders. However, if you need to change the sample rate, the time to do it is at the beginning of the project. Click the Custom Settings tab in the New Project dialog box, click the Sample Rate list arrow, then choose the new sample rate.

Premiere Pro allows you to place three types of audio clips into the Timeline: Mono, Stereo, and 5.1 (surround sound). **Mono** audio clips have one audio channel, **Stereo** have two (left and right), and 5.1 have five. The number of channels an audio clip has is determined at the time a clip is recorded. You can easily determine what type of clip you are working with using the Project panel. As shown in Figure 2, the Audio Info column shows that the RE Voice Over.mov audio clip is a Mono audio clip. Also notice the Audio Usage column lists 1. The RE Voice Over.mov clip is being used once in the sequence. In this figure, the columns in the Project panel have been edited to feature the audio columns. Another point that you need to understand is how audio clips are added to the Timeline. As shown in Figure 3, a new project starts out with three audio tracks and one Master track in the

FIGURE 1
Custom Settings in the New Project dialog box

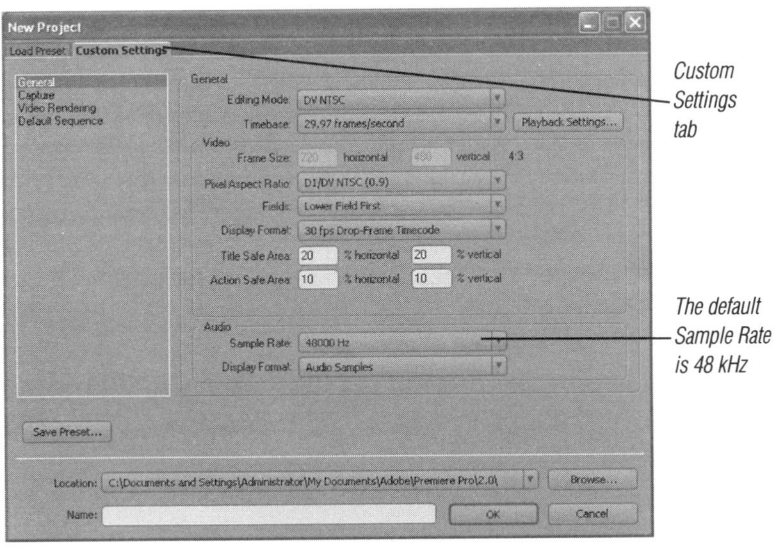

FIGURE 2
Viewing audio clip properties in the Project panel

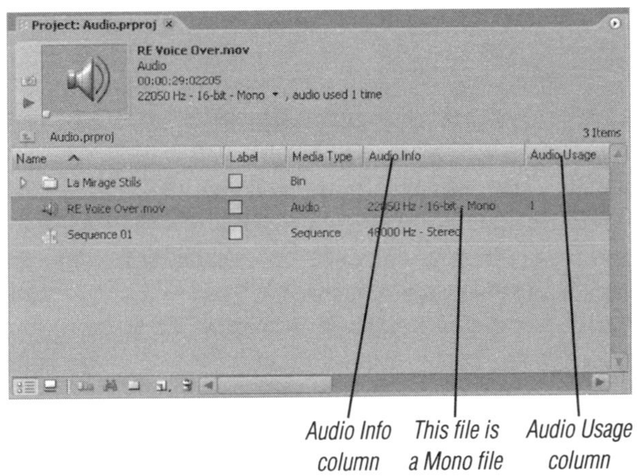

FIGURE 3
Viewing audio tracks

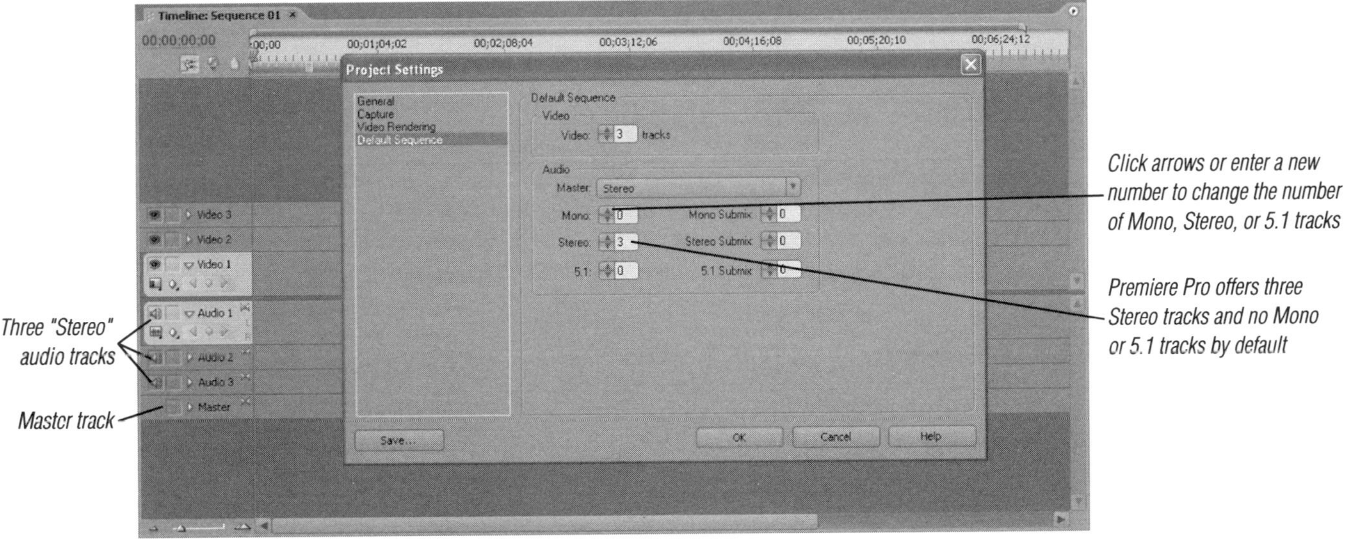

Timeline. The Audio 1, 2, and 3 tracks are designated strictly for Stereo audio clips, as shown in the Project Settings dialog box in Figure 3. Notice that there are no tracks designated for Mono or 5.1 audio clips. Regardless of how many audio clips or tracks you use or types of audio clips you use, all audio ultimately ends up on the Master track. In other words, when you are ready to export your sequence, the Master track is the only audio track that is exported. It includes all audio from the audio tracks above it. You can change the number of Mono, Stereo, or 5.1 tracks you'd like by changing the corresponding values in the Project Settings dialog box. To do so, click Project on the menu bar, point to Project Settings, then click Default Sequence. However, if you try to place a non-Stereo audio clip into the Timeline, Premiere Pro will automatically add a new track to accommodate it. Notice in Figure 4, RE Voice Over.mov is a Mono clip. It is impossible to place a Mono clip on a Stereo track. When it is added to the Timeline, a new Audio 4 track is created and it is placed on that track.

If you know in advance that you'll be using lots of audio tracks, you can add them to the Timeline by clicking Sequence on the menu bar, then clicking Add Tracks. As shown in Figure 5, you can add any number of new tracks and choose what type of new tracks are added using the Track Type menu.

QUICKTIP

You can change how Premiere Pro treats an audio clip by choosing a different type of track for it to be played on. Select the audio clip in the Project panel (before it's placed in the Timeline), click Clip on the menu bar, point to Audio Options, then click Source Channel Mappings.

FIGURE 4

Premiere Pro adds audio tracks automatically as needed

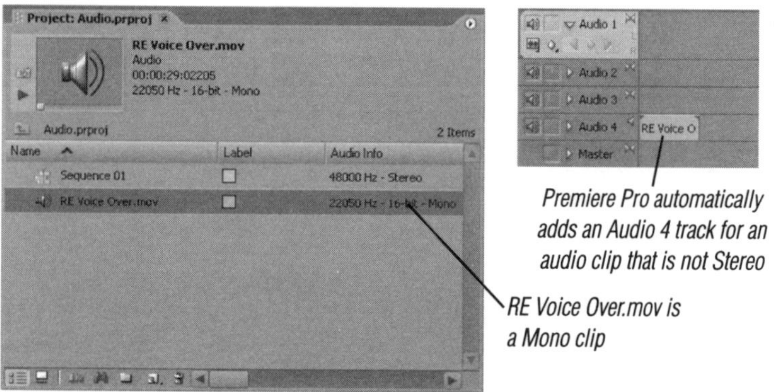

Premiere Pro automatically adds an Audio 4 track for an audio clip that is not Stereo

RE Voice Over.mov is a Mono clip

FIGURE 5

Add Tracks dialog box

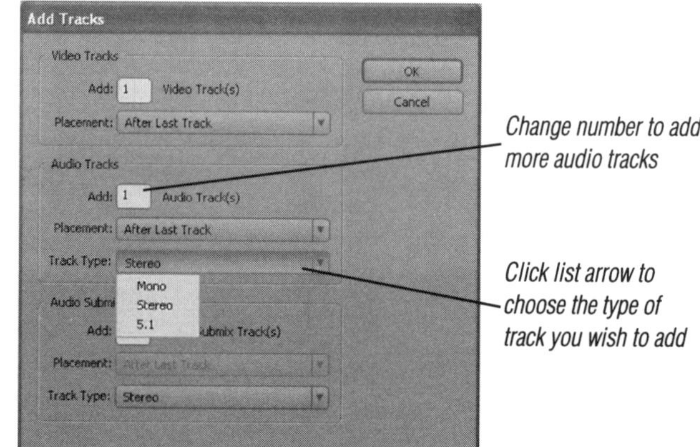

Change number to add more audio tracks

Click list arrow to choose the type of track you wish to add

Working with Audio Clips in the Timeline

When you add an audio clip to the Timeline, it will be placed in an appropriate audio track. Like video tracks, audio tracks are collapsed. You need to click the Collapse/Expand Track button to the left of the track name to expand the track and view its options. You can temporarily mute an audio track by clicking the Toggle Track Output button. You can also lock an audio track by clicking the Toggle Track Lock button. When an audio track is locked, a padlock icon appears next to the track name. You can also rename an audio track for easier identification. Just right-click the track name, click Rename, and type a new descriptive name. Figure 6 shows RE Voice Over.mov in an audio track that has been renamed. Also, note that this track is not locked nor it is muted. You can choose to view an audio clip by its name only or you can view its waveform right in the Timeline. A **waveform** is a visual display of an audio clip. To view a clip's waveform, click the Set Display Style button in the Timeline, then click Show Waveform, as shown in Figure 7.

QUICKTIP

Mono clips display one waveform in the Source Monitor and Stereo clips display two waveforms–one for each speaker.

FIGURE 6

Expanding an audio track

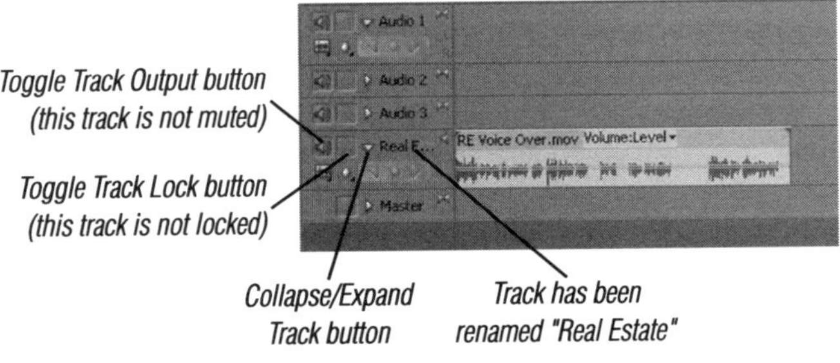

FIGURE 7

Viewing a clip's waveform

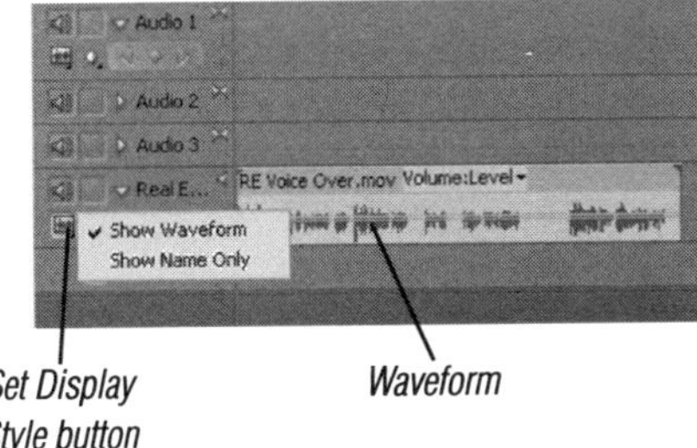

Work with an audio clip

1. Open APP 5-1.prproj, then save it as **Audio Fun**.
2. Click **Window** on the menu bar, point to **Workspace**, then click **Audio**.

   As shown in Figure 8, the Audio workspace features the Audio Mixer panel. This workspace is useful if you plan on using the Audio Mixer for recording or manipulating individual tracks. For our purposes, we do not need this workspace.
3. Click **Window** on the menu bar, point to **Workspace**, then click **Editing**.
4. Click **Wedding Music.mov** in the Project panel, then scroll to the right slowly until you see the Audio Info column, as shown in Figure 9.

   As shown in the figure, Wedding Music.mov is a Mono file. Your Wedding Music.mov file may have slightly different information under the Audio Info column, such as "22050 Hz – 32-bit Float – Mono."

   TIP When an audio clip is selected in the Project panel, you can view its properties in the Preview Area of the Project panel.

(continued)

FIGURE 8
The Audio workspace

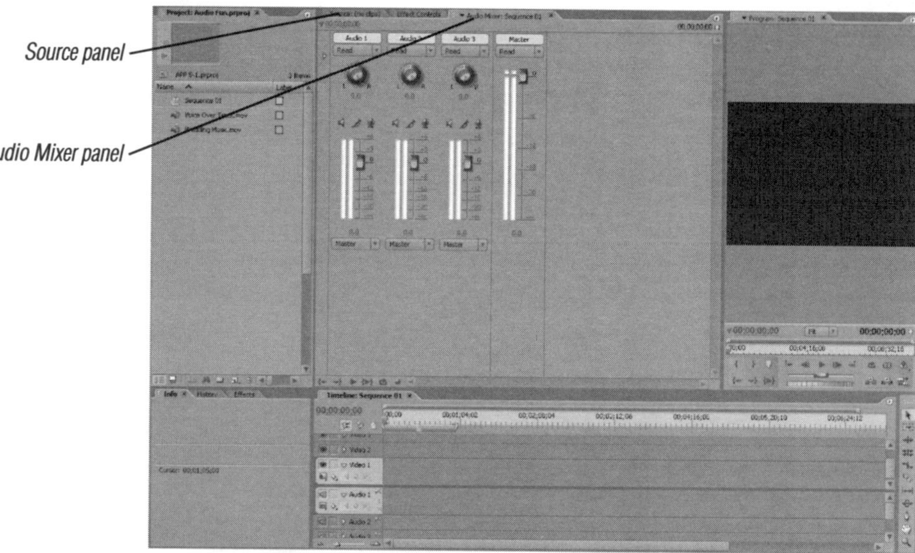

FIGURE 9
Viewing the Audio Info column

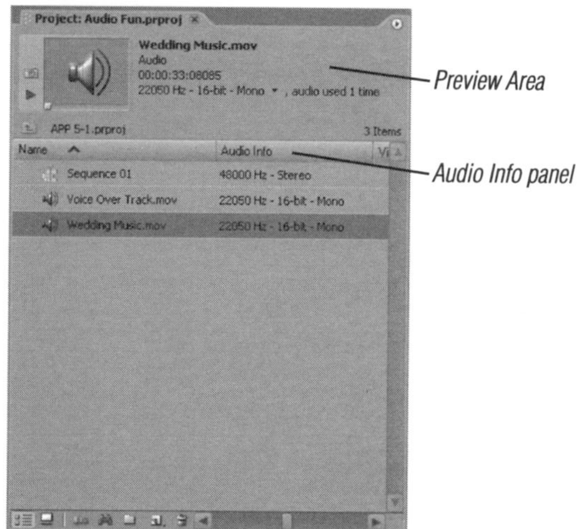

FIGURE 10

Placing Wedding Music.mov in the Timeline

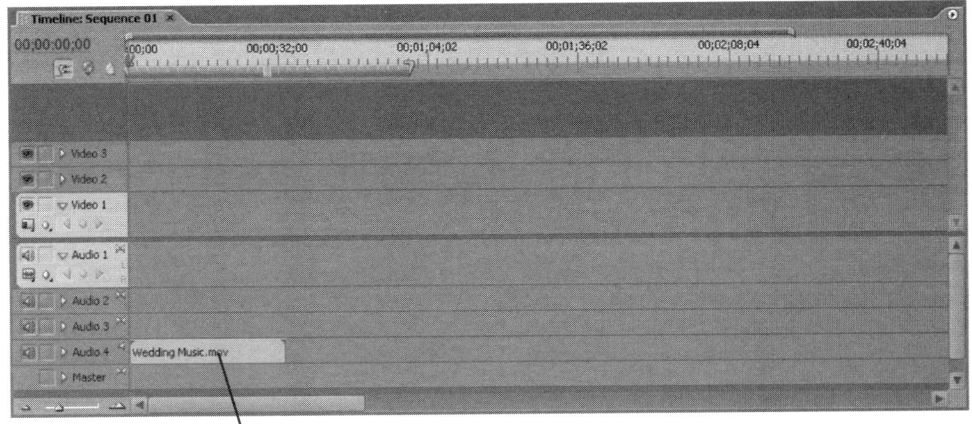

Wedding Music.mov is added to a new audio track

FIGURE 11

The Wedding audio track

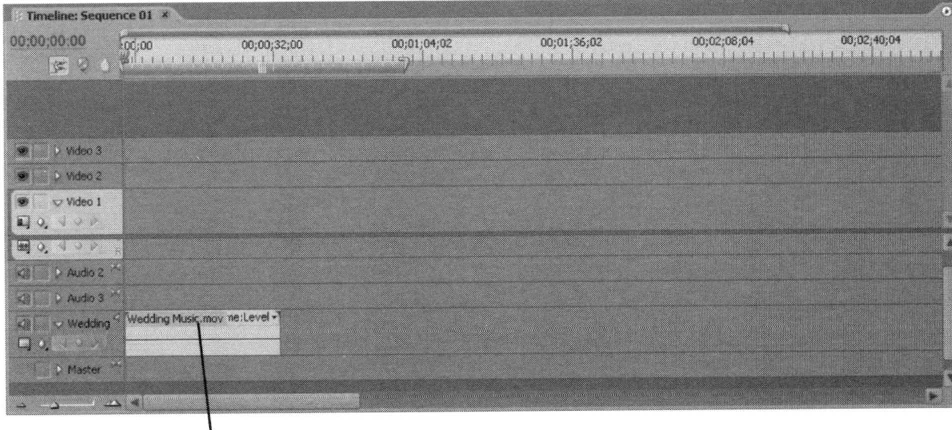

Clip shows name only

5. Drag **Wedding Music.mov** to the Timeline and try placing it in one of the three audio tracks, then release the mouse pointer.

   As shown in Figure 10, the Wedding Music.mov clip is automatically added to a new track because it is not a Stereo clip.

6. Right-click **Audio 4**, click **Rename**, type **Wedding**, then press **[Enter]**.
7. Click the **Collapse/Expand Track button** on the Wedding track to expand it, click the **Set Display Style button**, click **Show Name Only**, then compare your Timeline to Figure 11.
8. Play the movie, save your work, then close Audio Fun.

You viewed the properties of an audio clip, added it to the Timeline, changed the audio track name, and changed the view of the clip icon to view the clip name only.

EXTRACT AUDIO

What You'll Do

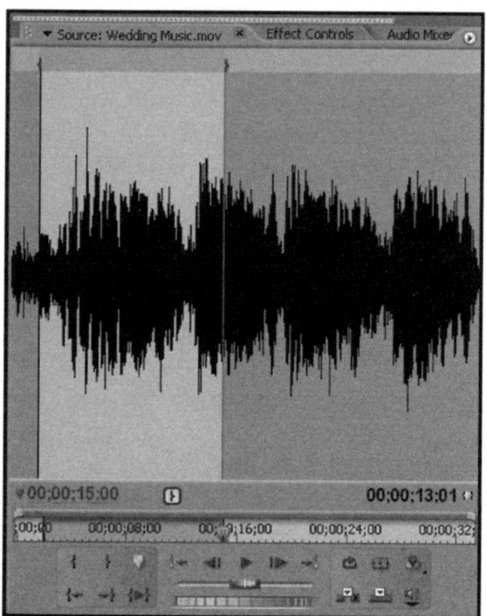

In this lesson, you will extract audio clips from an audio source file.

Working with Audio Clips

Working with audio clips is very similar to working with video clips. Both can be previewed in the Source Monitor and added to the Timeline. Audio clips function in the Timeline just as video clips do: They have a specific duration, and they can be moved, copied, and pasted throughout the Timeline.

One major behavioral difference between video clips and audio clips must be noted: When video tracks overlap in the Timeline, the clips on the superior track always play to the exclusion of the clips on the tracks beneath. In other words, when video clips overlap, you see only the top clip during playback. When audio tracks overlap, the overlapping clips "mix" together. Thus, the sounds in the overlapping areas play simultaneously.

Previewing Audio Clips

The best method for listening to and examining the contents of an audio clip is to use the Source Monitor. There the clip is displayed using the waveform as a visual reference. As with video clips, the duration of an audio clip is measured in timecode. When you position the Current time indicator, the Current time display identifies that location in timecode, as shown in Figure 12.

As with video clips, you use the Program Monitor to preview audio clips in the Timeline. Press the Play/Stop Toggle button, and the Program Monitor will play both the video and the audio. You may also scrub the Timeline, and the audio will play.

Trimming Audio Clips

Often, you will not need to use an entire audio clip in your program. Instead, you will want to cut out a segment from the source clip to use in the Timeline. Again, just like video clips, you can trim a clip by changing its In point, its Out point, or both. You can refer to Chapter 4 for a review of trimming clips.

The most precise method for trimming an audio clip is to do so in the Source Monitor. Set the Current time indicator to where you want the sound to begin, then click the Set In Point button. Set the Current time indicator to where you want the sound to end, then click the Set Out Point button, as shown in Figure 13. Then, to make sure you've captured what you want, you can click the Play In to Out button in the Source Monitor and adjust the locations of the In and Out points if necessary.

When you change the In point, the Out point, or both, you are, by definition, changing the duration of the clip. The new duration will be noted in the Source Monitor. When you add the trimmed clip to the Timeline, it is added at its new duration. In other words, nothing before the In point or after the Out point is added to the Timeline.

FIGURE 12

Viewing an audio clip in the Source Monitor

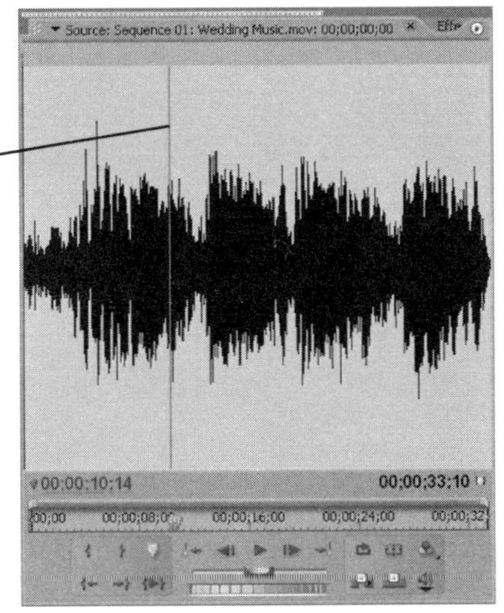

FIGURE 13

Setting In and Out points for an audio clip

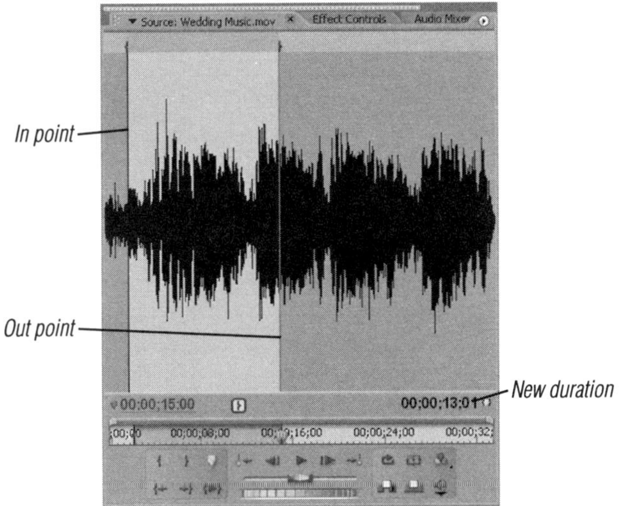

Extract One or Multiple Segments from an Audio Clip

Many times, you will want to extract numerous segments from a single audio clip. This is easy to do in Premiere Pro by setting and resetting In and Out points. Once you've set the In and Out points for your first segment, drag the clip from the Source Monitor to the Timeline. Then, change the In and Out points in the Source Monitor again; doing so will not affect the previously trimmed segment you dragged to the Timeline. With the new In and Out points set, drag the segment from the Source Monitor to the Timeline. Using this method, you can isolate and extract as many segments from a single source file as you need.

Trimming Audio Clips in the Timeline

You can trim audio clips in the Timeline the same way that you trim video clips: by dragging either edge of a clip using the Trim-in and Trim-out icons. If you move the left edge in either direction, you are changing the In point. If you move the right, you are changing the Out point, as shown in Figure 14.

It is important to remember that when you drag the edge of a clip in the Timeline, you are neither compressing the clip nor elongating it. You are literally trimming it—decreasing or increasing its duration.

FIGURE 14
Trimming an audio clip in the Timeline

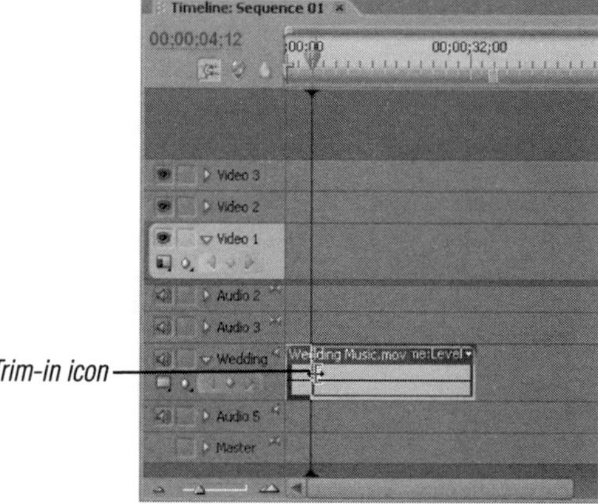

Viewing duration of clips in the Info panel

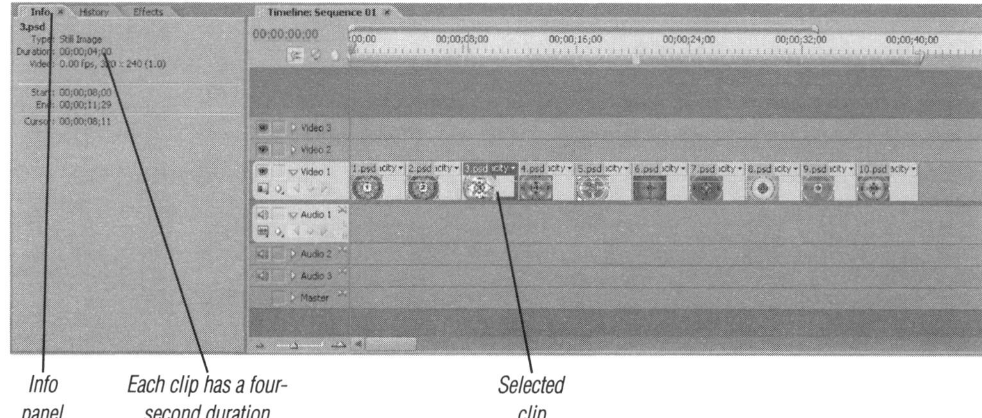

Preview and trim an audio clip in the Source Monitor

1. Open APP 5-2.prproj, then save it as **Countdown Audio**.
2. Verify that you are working in the Editing workspace, and then click each clip in the Video 1 track and view its duration in the Info panel, as shown in Figure 15.

   Each clip has a duration of four seconds.
3. Double-click **Ping.mov** to open it in the Source Monitor, then play the clip to become familiar with it.

   Ping.mov is a series of "ping" noises that occur every two seconds.

(continued)

4. Set the Current time indicator to 4:00 in the Source Monitor, then click the **Set Out Point button** .

   Your Source Monitor should resemble Figure 16.

5. Drag **Ping.mov** from the Source Monitor to the beginning of the Audio 1 track in the Timeline.

   As shown in Figure 17, the edited audio clip is the same length as 1.psd. Notice that Ping.mov falls easily into the Audio 1 track because it is a Stereo type of audio file.

(continued)

FIGURE 16
Setting a new Out point for an audio clip

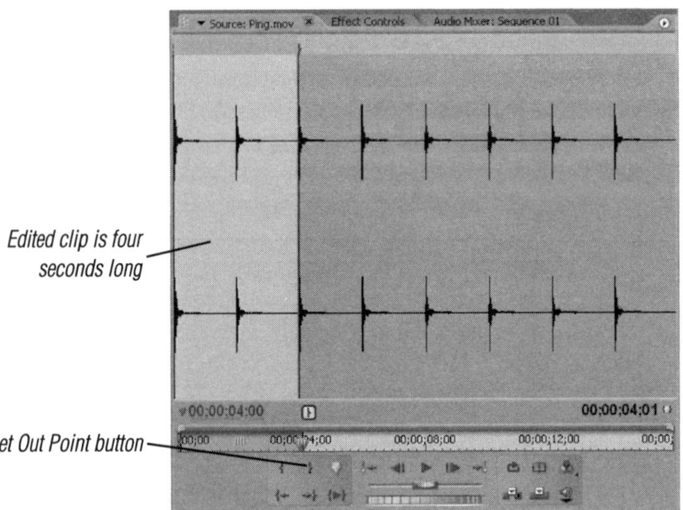

FIGURE 17
Adding Ping.mov to the Audio 1 track

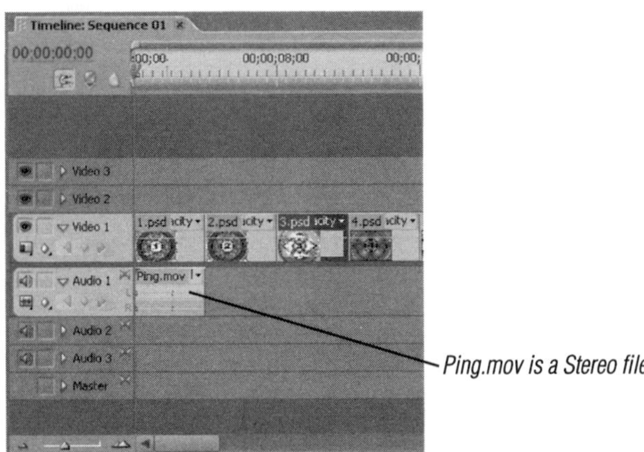

FIGURE 18

Placing Ping.mov under each still image

Ten instances of Ping.mov in the Audio 1 track

6. Repeat Step 5 nine times to place Ping.mov directly below each still image in the Video 1 track, so that your Timeline resembles Figure 18.
7. Play the sequence.

   The "ping" occurs twice during each still image.
8. Save your work.

You changed the Out point of Ping.mov in the Source Monitor, then added 10 instances of the trimmed clip to the Audio 1 track.

Trim an audio clip in the Timeline

1. Click the **Current time duration**, then type **2:00** to move the Current time indicator to frame 2:00.
2. Position the mouse pointer at the right edge of 1.psd in the Video 1 track until you see the Trim-out icon, then drag **1.psd** to the left until its right edge snaps to the Current time indicator.

   TIP Verify that the Snap icon is pressed in the Timeline if you do not feel the clips "snap" to the Current time indicator.

3. Repeat Step 2 to trim the first instance of Ping.mov so that it also snaps to the Current time indicator, as shown in Figure 19.
4. Click the **Track Select Tool**, click **2.psd**, then drag to the left until all of the clips in the Video 1 track snap to 1.psd.
5. Click the **Selection Tool**, then click another track in the Timeline to deselect all.
6. Click the **Track Select Tool**, click the second instance of Ping.mov to select all of the Ping.mov clips, then press **[Delete]**.

   Nine instances of Ping.mov are removed from the Audio 1 track.

(continued)

FIGURE 19
Trimming an audio clip in the TImeline

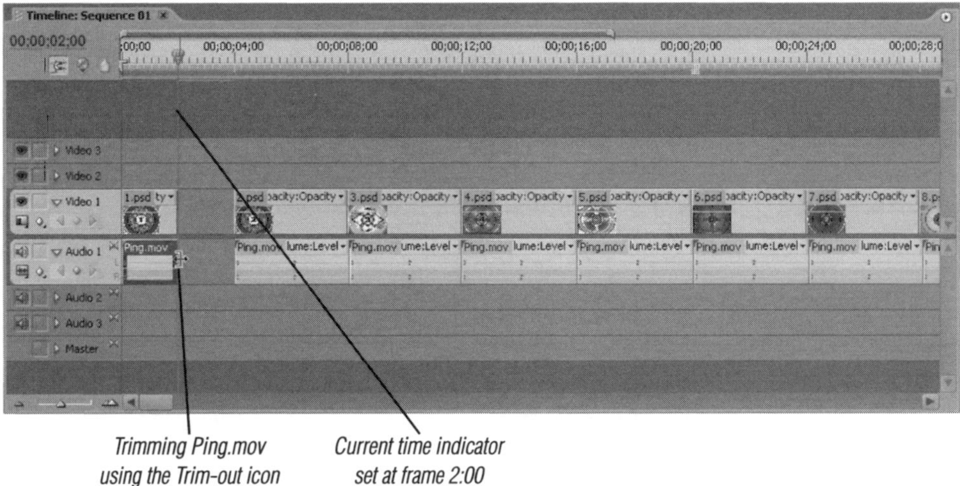

Trimming Ping.mov using the Trim-out icon

Current time indicator set at frame 2:00

FIGURE 20

Changing the Out point of Ping.mov

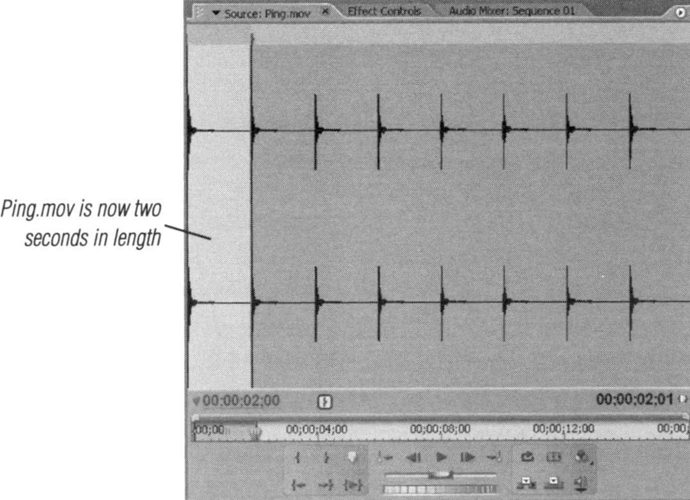

FIGURE 21

Synchronizing the audio with the video

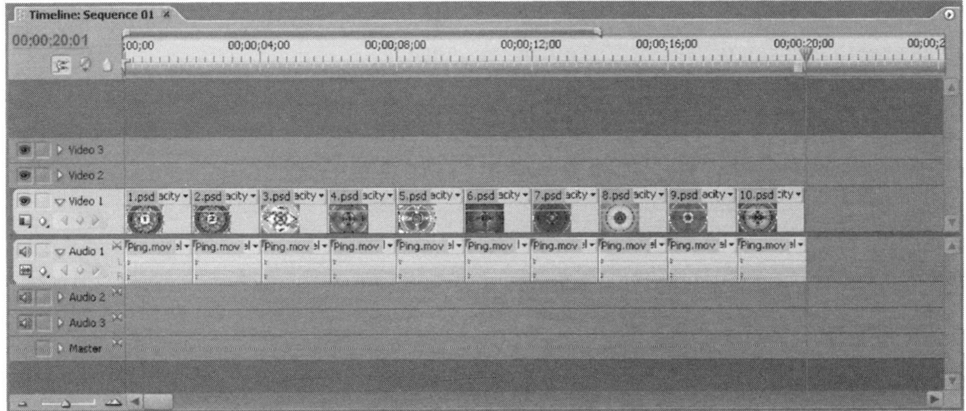

7. Repeat Steps 1 and 2 to change the duration of the remaining nine still images in the Video 1 track to two seconds each.

   TIP Each time you repeat Steps 1–2, increase the location of the Current time indicator by two seconds. For example, for 2.psd, the Current time indicator should be set to frame 4:00 before you trim it.

8. Verify that Ping.mov is still showing in the Source Monitor.

   TIP If you do not see Ping.mov in the Source Monitor, double-click Ping.mov in the Project panel.

9. Set the Current time indicator to 2:00 in the Source Monitor, then click the **Set Out Point button** to change the duration of Ping.mov from four seconds to two seconds, as shown in Figure 20.
10. Drag nine instances of Ping.mov from the Source Monitor to the Audio 1 track so that your Timeline resembles Figure 21.
11. Save your work, press **[Home]**, then play the sequence.

You trimmed each still image so that it was two seconds in length, then trimmed Ping.mov to two seconds using the Trim-out icon using the Set Out Point button in the Source Monitor. You then added nine instances of the newly trimmed audio clip from the Source Monitor to the Audio 1 track and played the synchronized sequence.

LESSON 3

UNLINK AUDIO FROM VIDEO AND ADJUST VOLUME

What You'll Do

In this lesson, you will work with audio and video clips that are linked, and you will modify the volume of audio tracks.

Working with Linked Audio and Video

When you shoot video footage with your video camera, the video and the audio are captured simultaneously. When you import the movie into Premiere Pro, the video clip is imported with the audio as one of its components. When a video clip is brought into a video track in the Timeline, the audio elements of the clip appear in an audio track, and the video and audio clips are linked. If you move one, the other moves with it. If you delete one, the other is deleted with it. If you trim one, the other is trimmed by the same number of frames.

Many times, especially with video that contains dialogue, you will want to keep the video and audio linked. In other cases, you may want to unlink the two and manipulate the audio independently from the video. In still other cases, you will want to delete either the audio or the video. You can unlink audio and video clips by selecting the linked clip in the Timeline, clicking Clip on the menu bar, then clicking Unlink. If you want to relink an audio and video clip, select both clips by clicking one, pressing and holding [Shift], clicking the other, then choosing Link from the Clip menu.

QUICKTIP

You can also unlink and relink clips by right-clicking them in the Timeline and choosing Unlink or Link.

Using the Toggle Take Audio and Video Button

There may be times when you have a great video clip and you don't necessarily need the audio section of it or vice versa. If you want to extract a portion of either the audio or video of a linked clip, you can do so in the Source Monitor by telling Premiere Pro which component you want to trim—the audio or the video. Once the linked clip is displayed in the Source Monitor, you can toggle between trimming the video component or the audio component by clicking the Toggle Take Audio and Video button in the Source Monitor, as shown in Figure 22. The button icon in this figure shows the button's default state—a filmstrip and a speakerphone icon together. Clicking the button once will show only the filmstrip icon and display the video component of the linked clip.

FIGURE 22
Toggling audio and video in the Source Monitor

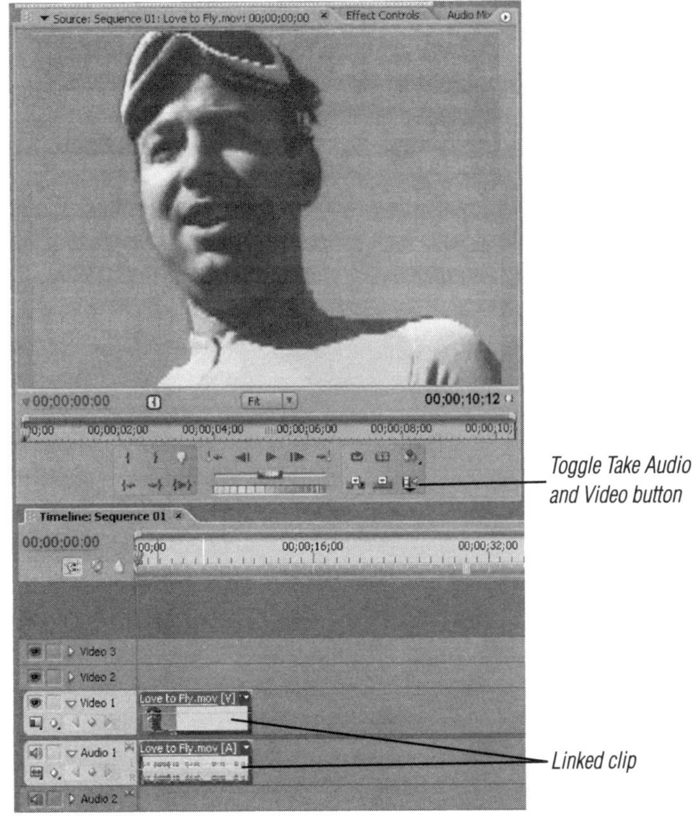

Clicking the icon again displays a speakerphone icon, which represents audio, and the Source Monitor switches to display the audio component of the linked clip. See Figure 23.

When you trim the audio or video component of a linked clip in the Source Monitor, then drag it to the Timeline, that instance of the clip is automatically unlinked and is placed in the appropriate audio or video track. In other words, if you trim the audio portion of a linked clip, then drag the trimmed audio from the Source Monitor to the Timeline, the video component of the linked clip is not included. Only the trimmed audio clip is added to an audio track.

Adjusting the Volume of Audio Clips and Audio Tracks

You can adjust the volume of audio a number of ways. Audio clips are added to the Timeline with a default volume applied, much like video clips have a default opacity setting. As shown in Figure 24, you can choose to view the volume of each individual clip or you can view the volume of the entire track. If you choose Show Clip Volume, you'll see an individual yellow line midway through each audio clip in an audio track, as shown in Figure 25. If you choose to show the volume for the track, the volume control line spans the entire

FIGURE 23

Viewing the audio component of a linked clip

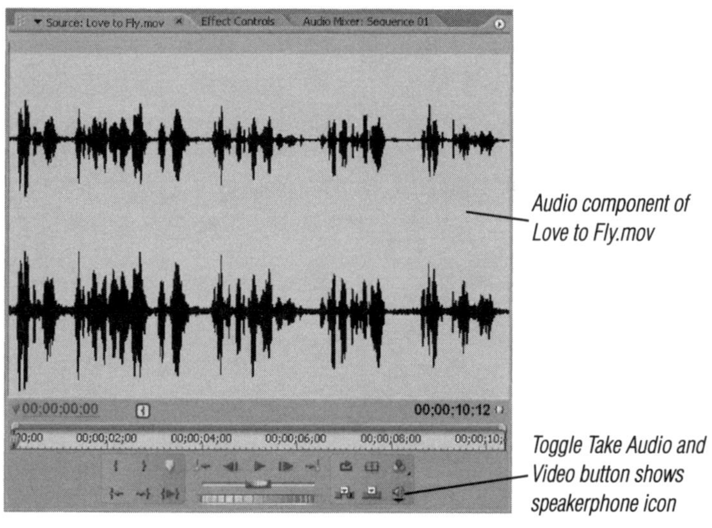

FIGURE 24

Viewing volume options for audio

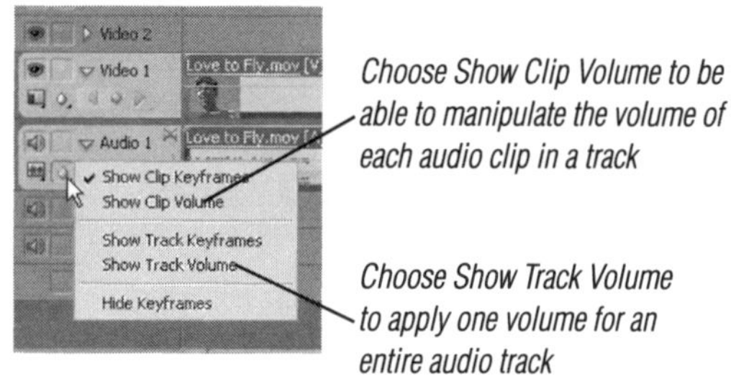

FIGURE 25

Showing the volume for each audio clip

track, as shown in Figure 26. In either case, you can drag the volume controls up or down to increase or decrease the volume for an individual clip or for the entire track. Obviously, being able to manipulate the volume for each individual clip allows you much more flexibility. It all depends on the nature of your project as to which way you'll choose to control volume. The volume setting is also available in the Effect Controls panel. Changing the volume in the Timeline or in the Effect Controls panel will be a personal choice.

Using the Audio Mixer

Premiere Pro offers an Audio Mixer panel designed to resemble a professional audio mixing console. The Audio Mixer offers a set of controls for each audio track. The audio track in the Audio Mixer is identified by a number that corresponds to the numbered audio track in the Timeline. You can use the Audio Mixer to gain very specific control of how the audio tracks in a program relate to one another—how they overlap and how they fade in and out. To open the Audio Mixer, simply choose Audio Mixer from the Window menu, or choose the Audio workspace. The Audio workspace features the Audio Mixer panel where the Source Monitor is usually located. You can also use the Audio Mixer to record sounds and voice overs directly to the Timeline, assuming you have the correct audio hardware installed on your computer.

FIGURE 26

Showing the volume for the track

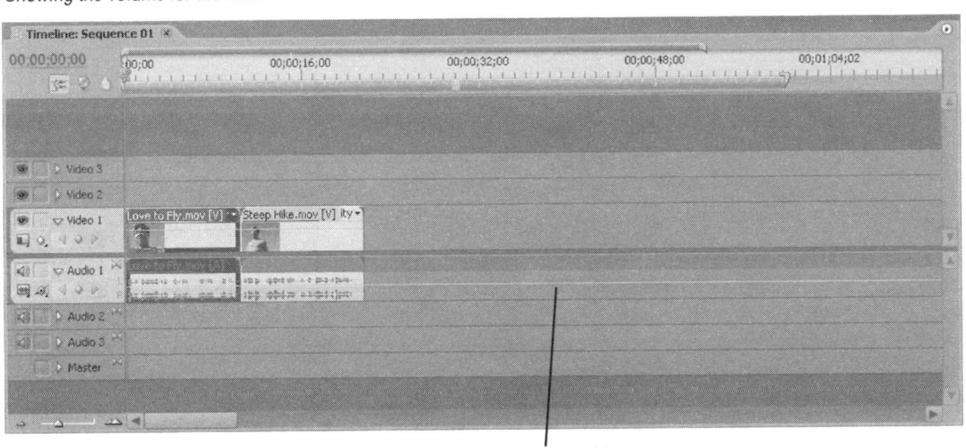

Work with linked audio and video clips

1. Open APP 5-3.prproj, then save it as **Volume**.
2. Double-click **Can Opener.mov** in the Project panel to open it in the Source Monitor, then play the Can Opener movie to become familiar with it.
3. Click the **Toggle Take Audio and Video button** in its default state, then click it again in its video state.

   You should see the audio portion of the Can Opener.mov clip in the Source Monitor, as shown in Figure 27.
4. Type **20:00** in the Current time display in the Source Monitor, then click the **Set Out Point button**.
5. Drag the trimmed audio clip to the Timeline into the Audio 2 track twice so that your Timeline matches Figure 28.

(continued)

FIGURE 27

Taking just the audio portion of a linked clip

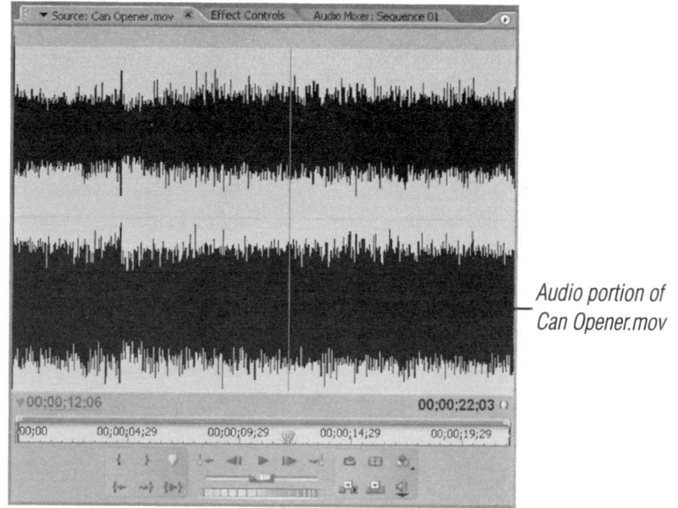

FIGURE 28

Adding Can Opener.mov to the Timeline

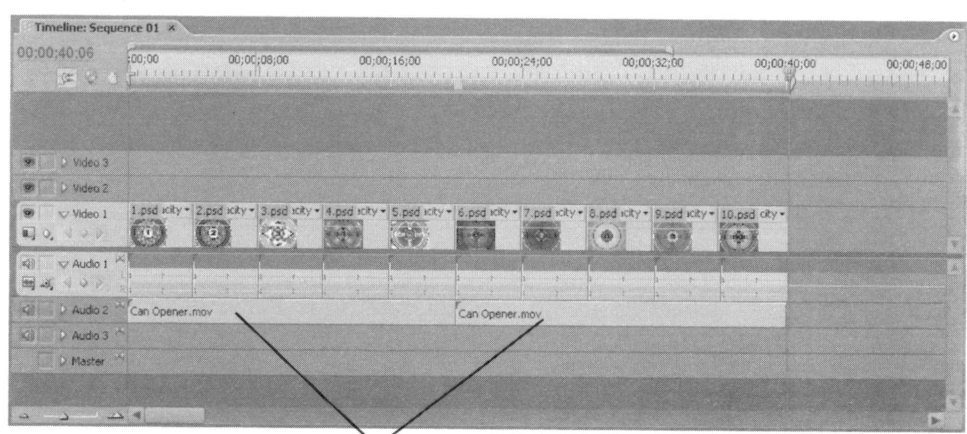

FIGURE 29

Choosing to show the volume for the entire Audio 2 track

FIGURE 30

Adjusting the volume of the Audio 1 and Audio 2 tracks

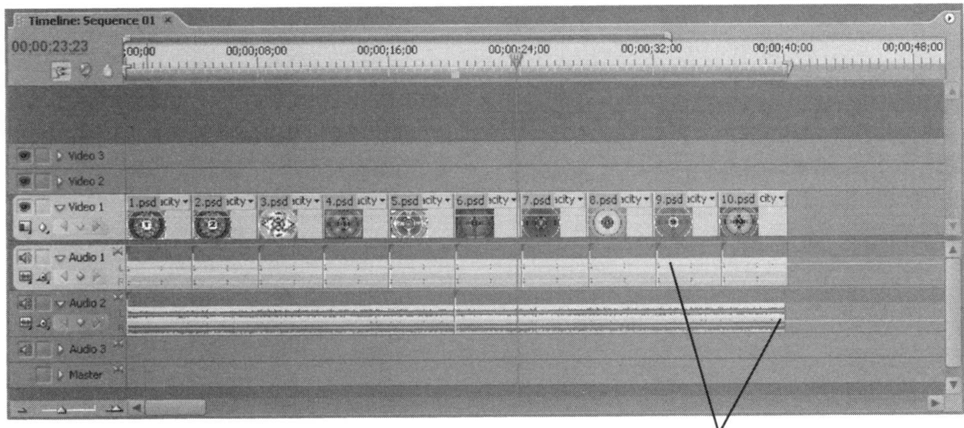

6. Click the **Collapse/Expand Track button** on the Audio 2 track, click the **Show Keyframes button,** as shown in Figure 29, then click **Show Track Volume**.

   A thin line spans the entire Audio 2 track. You are unable to manipulate the volume of the two audio clips individually.

7. Drag the **yellow line** down and watch the tooltip value change as you drag, then release the mouse pointer at any time.

   Dragging the volume control down will decrease the volume.

8. Change the volume for the Audio 1 track, this time increasing the volume of Ping.mov for the entire track.

9. Play the movie and make any necessary adjustments.

   TIP You should be able to hear the "ping" sound easily above the can opener sound.

10. Compare your Timeline to Figure 30, save your work, then close the project.

You trimmed the audio portion of a linked clip, added two instances of the trimmed clip to the Timeline, then adjusted the volume of the Audio 1 and Audio 2 tracks.

LESSON 4

APPLY AND MODIFY AUDIO EFFECTS

What You'll Do

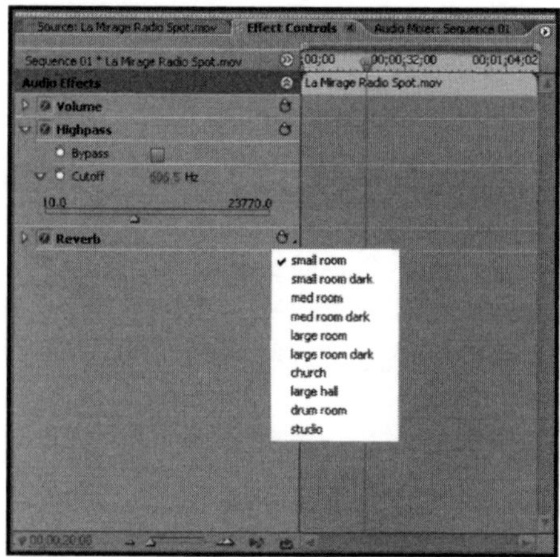

In this lesson, you will add audio effects to audio clips in the Timeline, using the Effects panel and the Effect Controls panel.

Applying Audio Effects

Premiere Pro includes audio effects which can be added to audio clips in the Timeline. Audio effects are stored in the Effects panel and categorized by type of audio file (5.1, Stereo, and Mono), as shown in Figure 31. Audio effects can be used for practical purposes, such as for filtering out unwanted background noise or boosting sound quality of a clip. They can also be used for special effects purposes, such as delays and reverberations.

FIGURE 31
Audio Effects in the Effects panel

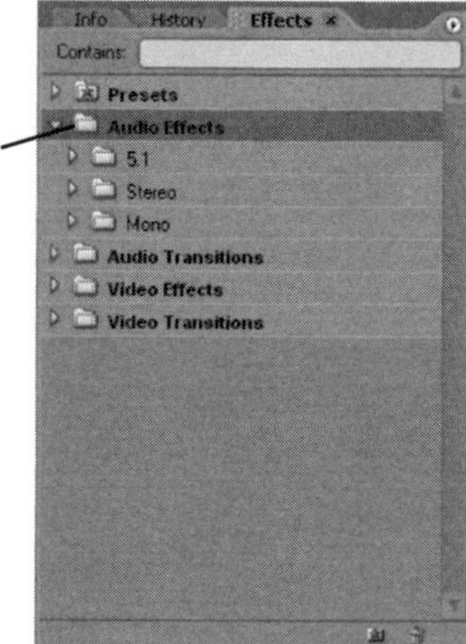

You add an audio effect to an audio clip by dragging it from the Effects panel directly on top of the clip in the Timeline. When you do so, the effect will be listed in the Effect Controls panel whenever that clip is selected in the Timeline. The other method is to select the clip in the Timeline that you want the effect applied to, then drag the effect from the Effects panel directly into the Effect Controls panel.

Whenever an audio clip is selected, the Effect Controls panel lists the effects that have been applied to the clip. The Effect Controls panel, as shown in Figure 32, is something like the command center for all the effects (video and audio) being used in a project. For example, if the effect has controls for its settings, you will manipulate those controls directly in the Effect Controls panel.

You may also use the Effect Controls panel to temporarily enable or disable an effect: Select the effect, and then click the Toggle the Effect On or Off button to the left of the effect name, which toggles between enabling and disabling the effect.

When you want to remove an audio effect, click the effect in the Effect Controls panel, click the Effect Controls list arrow, then click Delete Selected Effect.

QUICKTIP

If you have Adobe Audition installed on your computer, you can edit your audio clips in Audition using the Edit in Adobe Audition command on the Edit menu. If you select the audio clip in the Project panel, then apply the command, a new edited clip will be created and will not replace the original audio file. However, if you select an instance of the audio clip in the Timeline, then select Edit in Adobe Audition, the edited clip will replace the clip instance in the Timeline. The original clip in the Project panel will not be affected.

Working with the Highpass and Lowpass Audio Effects

The **Highpass** effect removes low frequencies from an audio clip, and the **Lowpass** effect removes high frequencies. These effects are very useful because they isolate specific areas of the audio. For example, if the sound you record sounds shrill or "tinny," the Lowpass effect can be used to mask some of the high sounds and take some of the edge off. In contrast, the Highpass effect can be used to mask the low hum often associated with background noise.

The Cutoff frequency setting allows you to set a threshold at which specific frequencies are masked.

FIGURE 32

Effect Controls panel showing audio effects

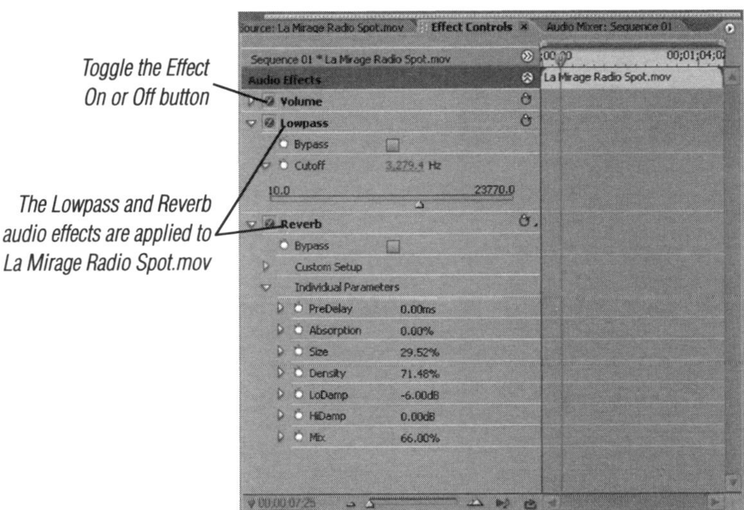

Apply the Lowpass audio effect

1. Open APP 5-4.prproj, then save it as **Real Estate**.
2. Click **Window** on the menu bar, point to **Workspace**, then click **Effects**.

   The Effects workspace is ideal for applying audio and video effects to clips in the Timeline.
3. Drag **La Mirage Radio Spot.mov** to the Timeline.

   La Mirage Radio Spot.mov is added to a new track, Audio 4, since it is a Mono type of audio file.
4. Play the sequence to hear the audio file in its entirety.
5. Expand the Audio Effects bin in the Effects panel, then expand the Mono bin by clicking the triangle icon ▷ to the left of each.
6. Drag the **Highpass audio effect** from the Mono bin directly on top of La Mirage Radio Spot.mov in the Timeline, as shown in Figure 33.
7. Play the movie again, and notice the effect on the voice over.
8. Verify that La Mirage Radio Spot.mov is still selected in the Timeline, expand the Highpass audio effect in the Effect Controls panel, then expand the Cutoff setting, as shown in Figure 34.

   TIP The Volume effect is applied to all audio clips by default.

(continued)

FIGURE 33
Applying the Highpass audio effect to La Mirage Radio Spot.mov

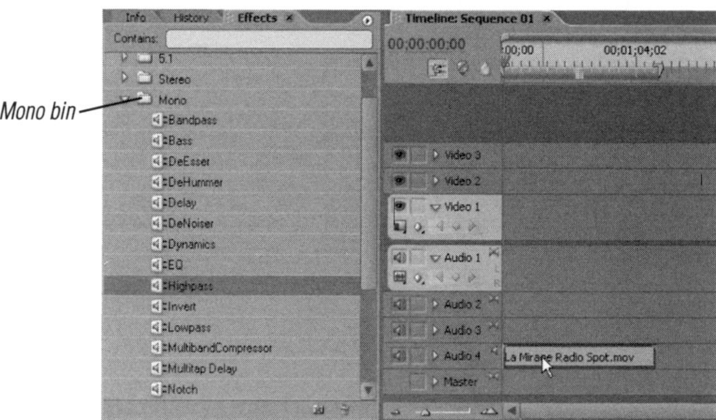

FIGURE 34
Viewing the Highpass audio effect settings in the Effect Controls panel

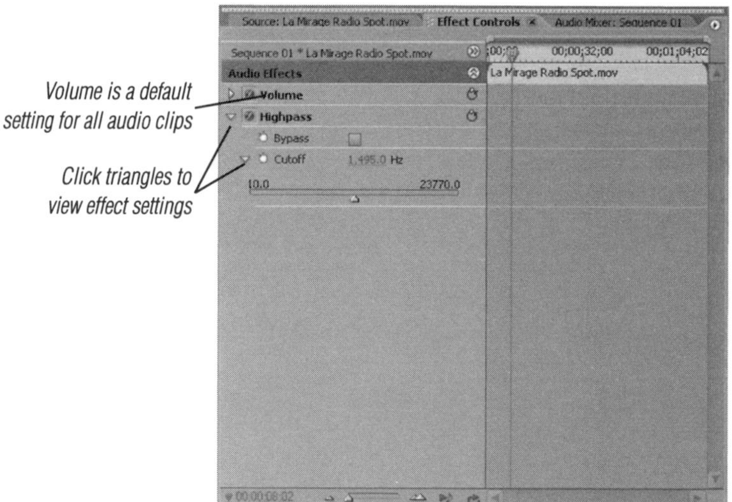

FIGURE 35

Modifying the Cutoff value for the Highpass audio effect

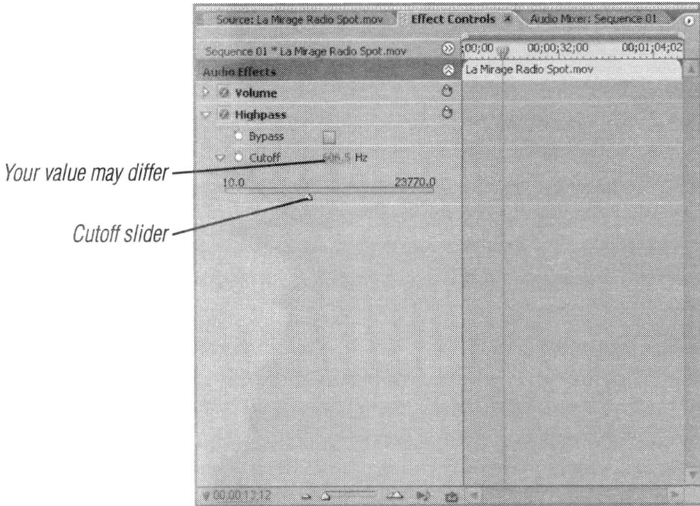

9. Drag the **Cutoff slider** to approximately 600, as shown in Figure 35, then play the movie again.

   This setting has a more realistic effect on the audio clip.

10. Save your work.

You applied the Highpass audio effect to an audio clip, then modified its settings to improve the voice over.

Apply the Reverb audio effect

1. Click **La Mirage Radio Spot.mov** in the Audio 4 track, if necessary.
2. Locate the Reverb audio effect in the Effects panel, then drag it to the Effect Controls panel.
3. Play the movie to hear how both audio effects affect the clip.
4. Click the **Reset button** next to Reverb in the Effect Controls panel to expose the pull-down menu, as shown in Figure 36.

   Notice that "small room" is selected. The speaker in the La Mirage Radio Spot clip sounds as though he is in a small room.
5. Click **large hall** from the list, then play the movie again.
6. Expand the Reverb audio effect in the Effect Controls panel, then expand the Custom Setup and Individual Parameters settings.

   You will need to experiment a lot with audio effect settings to become more knowledgeable about them.

(continued)

FIGURE 36
Viewing choices for the Reverb audio effect

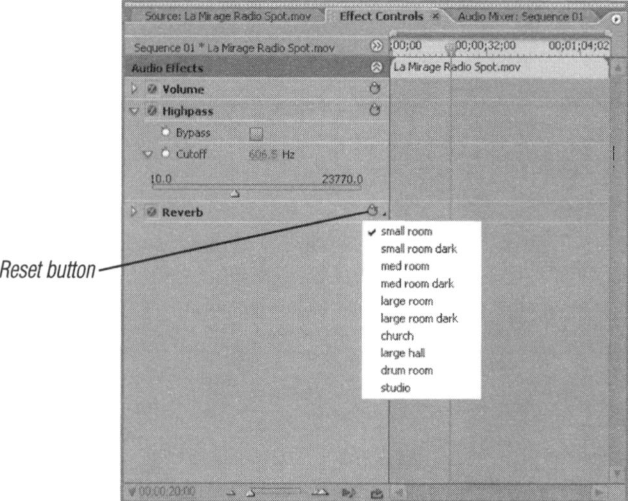

FIGURE 37

Turning the Highpass audio effect off

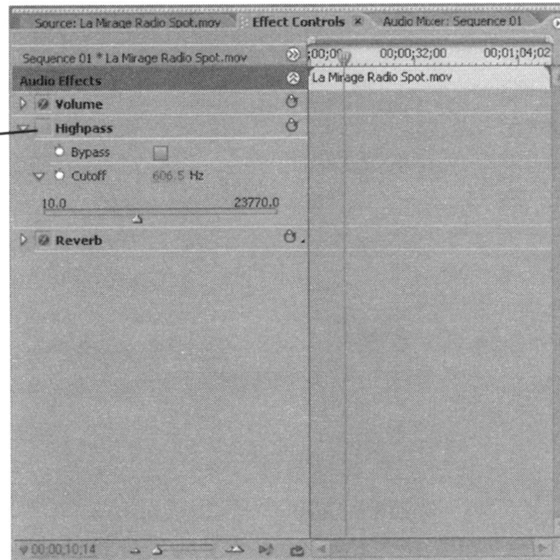

7. Collapse the Reverb audio effect, then click the **Toggle the Effect On or Off button** next to the Highpass audio effect to temporarily turn off the Highpass effect.

   Your Effect Controls panel should match Figure 37.

8. Play the sequence without the Highpass effect, then play it again with the Highpass effect.
9. Save your work, then close the Real Estate project.

You applied another audio effect to La Mirage Radio Spot.mov by dragging the effect to the Effect Controls panel. You then modified the effect settings and played the sequence with and without the Highpass effect.

CHAPTER SUMMARY

When creating a movie, nothing brings pictures alive more than sounds and voices. With Premiere Pro, not only will you be able to add sounds, music, voice overs, and sound effects to your sequence, but you'll also be able to mix sounds, adjust volume, apply audio effects, and modify audio effects to get just the right results. The Premiere Pro interface makes it very easy to work with audio. Audio files are treated just like video clips and still images. They are stored in the Project panel and added to audio tracks in the Timeline. You can trim them in the Source Monitor and add effects to them using the Effects panel. Once you start playing around with the audio effects, you may become addicted. Like all of your work in Premiere Pro, practice makes perfect!

What You Have Learned

- How to identify Mono and Stereo audio clips
- How to add audio clips to the Timeline
- How to add audio tracks
- How to expand an audio track in the Timeline
- How to view an audio clip name or its waveform in the Timeline
- How to rename an audio clip
- How to preview an audio clip in the Source Monitor
- How to trim an audio clip in the Source Monitor
- How to trim an audio clip in the Timeline
- How to unlink audio from video in a linked clip
- How to isolate audio using the Toggle Take Audio and Video button
- How to control the volume of a clip and of an entire audio track
- How to apply an audio effect to an audio clip
- How to modify audio effect settings in the Effect Controls panel

Key Terms

Kilohertz (kHz) Kilohertz is a measuring system that measures how many sounds play per second on a soundtrack.

Mono audio clips Mono audio clips have one channel.

Stereo audio clips Stereo audio clips have two channels.

Highpass Highpass is an audio effect that removes low frequencies from an audio clip.

Lowpass Lowpass is an audio effect that removes high frequencies from an audio clip.

STOP
ONLY
ONLY

7530

chapter

6 EXPLORING ADVANCED EDITING TECHNIQUES

1. Edit using Marker menu options.
2. Use the Extract and Lift buttons.
3. Change a clip's rate.
4. Use the Slip and Slide Tools.
5. Work in the Trim Monitor.

chapter 6 EXPLORING ADVANCED EDITING TECHNIQUES

Premiere Pro is very versatile. You can have fun with it, creating presentations and editing your own home movies. But Premiere Pro also doubles as a professional editing application, and it offers all of the options, tools, and techniques that you would expect to find in any professional editing suite. The Marker menu allows you to identify important frames and return to them quickly and easily. Slow motion and fast motion are easy to do in Premiere Pro; you can slow a clip down or speed it up to make it fit into a specific space in the Timeline.

The Slip and Slide Tools allow you to change In and Out Points in the Timeline while you watch those changes take place in the Program Monitor. The Trim Monitor is especially useful when you are cutting between two clips that show the same action from different angles. Once you have synchronized the action, you can move the cut interactively. As you do so, the Trim Monitor offers you a visual representation of the clip you are cutting from to the clip you are cutting to.

Tools You'll Use

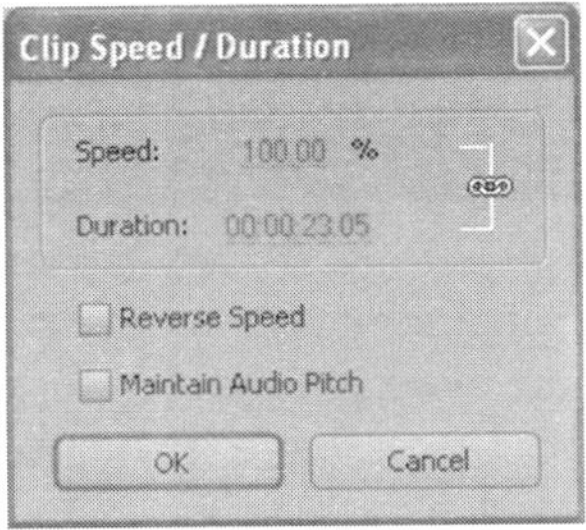

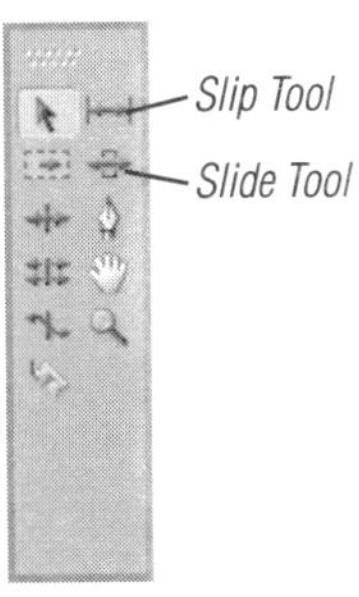

LESSON 1

EDIT USING MARKER MENU OPTIONS

What You'll Do

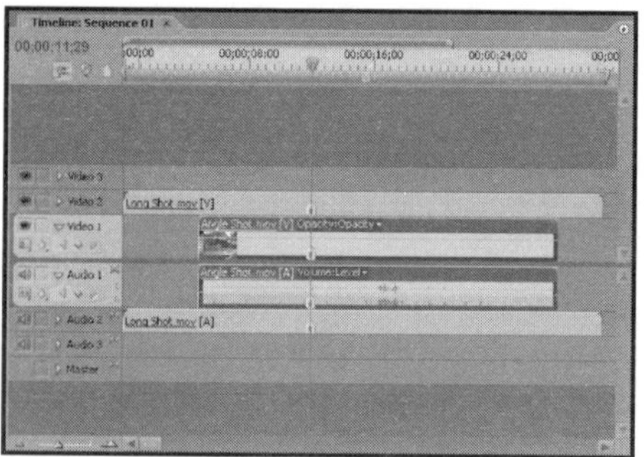

In this lesson, you will identify the same action in two clips with markers, then align the two clips at their markers.

Using Markers

You use **markers** to indicate important frames and to help you position and synchronize clips. If you had a video clip that showed a lit firecracker, for example, you might want to mark the frame where the firecracker explodes. Marking it may help you if you want to synchronize the explosion with a burst of music in the audio track, or if you want to cut from the explosion to a clip of someone's startled reaction.

There are three types of markers that you can add to clips. **Clip markers** are added to clips when they are in the Source Monitor. Adding clip markers may help you organize sections of a clip before you bring it to the Timeline. **Sequence markers** are added to clips in the Timeline. In both cases, markers are placed at the location of the Current time indicator. Markers are either numbered or unnumbered. Unnumbered and numbered markers appear as small triangular icons in the time ruler. Numbered markers show a small number within the triangular icon. Figure 1 shows both numbered and unnumbered markers in the Timeline. In addition to using the Marker menu to add an unnumbered marker to a clip in the Timeline, you can click the Set Unnumbered Marker button in the Timeline. Double-clicking a numbered marker or an unnumbered marker in the Timeline opens the Marker dialog box. The title bar in the Marker dialog box displays the marker number (for numbered markers) and the location of the marker in timecode, as shown in Figure 2.

FIGURE 1
Identifying markers in the Timeline

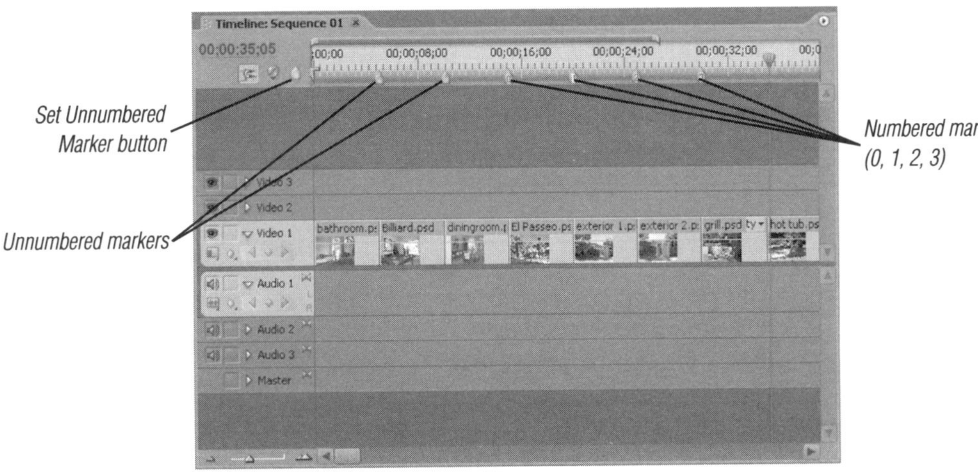

FIGURE 2
Marker dialog box

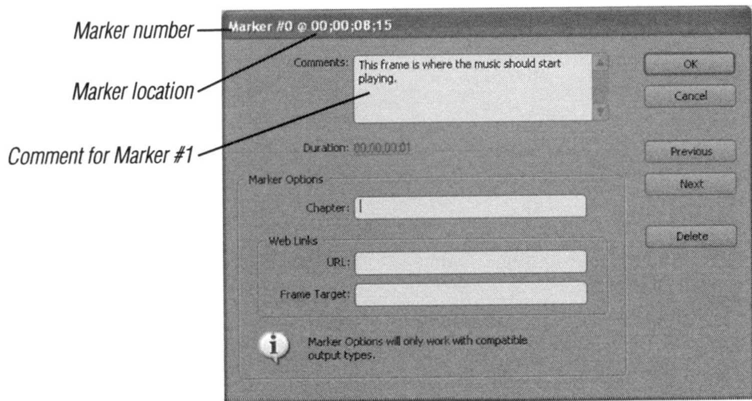

DVD markers are used specifically when you plan on outputting your project to a DVD. As shown in Figure 3, there are three types of DVD markers to choose from: Scene, Main Menu, and Stop. Like sequence markers, you can double-click a DVD marker and give it a descriptive name in the DVD Marker dialog box. You can also use the Auto-Generate DVD Markers command on the Marker menu to open the Automatically Set DVD Scene Markers dialog box, as shown in Figure 4. This dialog box lets you choose how your scene markers will be applied to the Timeline. Setting DVD markers is the first step in creating a DVD. The second step is to choose a DVD menu template from the DVD Layout command on the Window menu. DVD templates come with generic buttons that automatically link to the DVD markers that you set in the Timeline.

Markers are used only for reference and do not alter a clip or the program in any way. Once you have marked a frame, you can return to the frame by clicking the Marker menu then choosing the Go to Clip Marker or Go to Sequence Marker command. These two commands let you choose from Next, Previous, Numbered, In, or Out.

QUICKTIP

Premiere Pro assigns 0 (zero) instead of 1 (one) as the first numbered clip.

Nudging Clips in the Timeline

A very useful technique is the ability to move a clip in the Timeline left or right one frame at a time. For example, you may want to move a clip ten frames to the right to create a specific-sized gap for another clip. Or you may want to align the markers on two clips at precisely the same frame in the Timeline.

When you drag a clip, none of the windows identifies its location, and trying to drag a specific number of frames using the Info palette is very difficult. Instead, you can nudge the clip one frame at a time to the left or to the right.

Nudging a clip affects the location of that clip only. You cannot nudge a clip if it abuts another clip. In other words, you cannot nudge a clip to the right if there is another clip positioned immediately to the right. However, you can select both clips with the Range Select Tool, then nudge both clips. You can also select all clips and nudge them as a group. To nudge a clip or group of clips in the Timeline, press and hold [Alt], then press the period key [.] to shift the clip one frame to the right or the comma key [,] to shift one frame to the left.

FIGURE 3

DVD Marker menu options

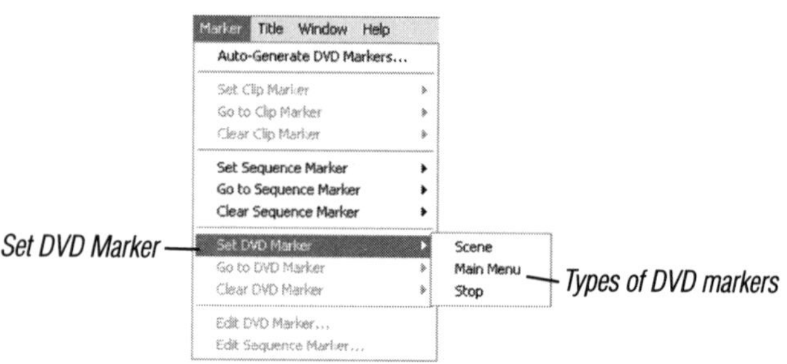

FIGURE 4

Automatically Set DVD Scene Markers dialog box

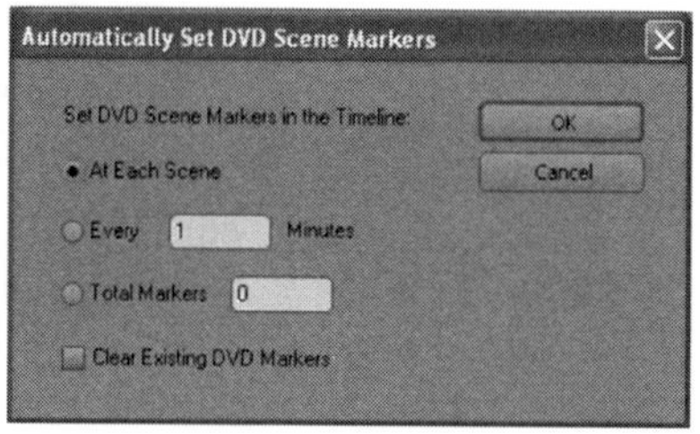

FIGURE 5
Setting a numbered marker in the Source Monitor

Set markers and align clips using markers

1. Open APP 6-1.prproj, then save it as **Mark and Lift**.
2. Choose the Editing workspace, if necessary.
3. Double-click **Angle Shot.mov** in the Project panel so that it opens in the Source Monitor, preview it, then go to frame 7:05—the frame where you first hear "action."
4. Click **Marker** on the menu bar, point to **Set Clip Marker**, then click **Next Available Numbered**.

   Numbered markers do not show a number until the clip is brought to the Timeline.
5. Drag the **Current time indicator** to the right in order to see the marker.

   Your Source Monitor should resemble Figure 5.

(continued)

6. Double-click **Long Shot.mov** in the Project panel so that it opens in the Source Monitor, then set the next available numbered marker at frame 12:02.

   The Angle Shot.mov and Long Shot.mov clips were shot simultaneously. Frame 12:02 identifies the exact same point in the action of frame 7:05 in Angle Shot.mov.

7. Drag **Long Shot.mov** from the Source Monitor to the beginning of the Video 2 track in the Timeline.

   The audio portion of Long Shot.mov is placed on the Audio 2 track.

8. Click the **Source menu** on the Source Monitor, choose Angle Shot.mov, then drag it to the beginning of the Video 1 track in the Timeline.

9. Zoom in on the Timeline so that your Timeline resembles Figure 6.

   Each clip displays a numbered marker.

10. Play the sequence and notice that you hear "action" twice.

    The markers on each clip need to be aligned so that you only hear "action" once.

(continued)

FIGURE 6
Angle Shot.mov and Long Shot.mov in the Timeline

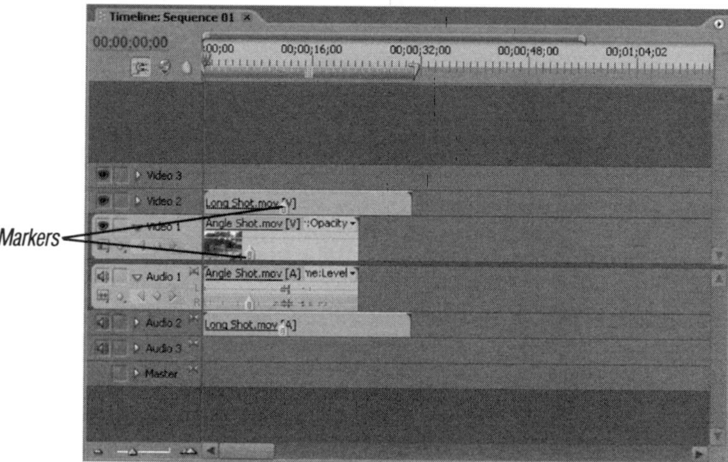

FIGURE 7

Viewing the aligned markers in the Timeline

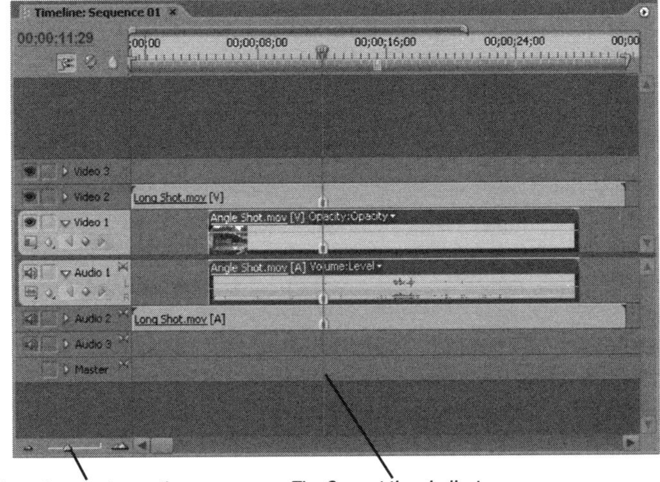

Zoom in more to see the marker locations easily

The Current time indicator can help align markers

11. Click the **Selection Tool** , if necessary, click **Angle Shot.mov** in the Timeline, press and hold **[Alt]**, then press the period **[.]** key repeatedly until the markers are aligned, as shown in Figure 7.

    TIP Use the Current time indicator to help you align the two clips along its red vertical line. Zoom in even more to see the marker locations more clearly.

12. Play the sequence again and fine tune the location of the markers if you need to.

    When playing the sequence, you should only hear "action" once.

    TIP Press and hold [Alt], then press the comma [,] key to nudge clips left one frame at a time.

13. Save your work.

You used markers to identify the same moment in two clips that were shot simultaneously. You then aligned the clips in the Timeline by aligning the markers.

Create an edit using markers

1. Double-click **Long Shot.mov** in the Timeline so that it opens in the Source Monitor.
2. Click **Marker** on the menu bar, point to **Go to Clip Marker**, then click **Numbered**.
3. Click **OK** in the Go to Numbered Marker dialog box.

   The Current time indicator moves to frame 12:02, as shown in Figure 8.
4. Click the **Set In Point button** .

   The In Point for Long Shot.mov is now the same as the first marked frame, named 0 in the Timeline.
5. Double-click **Angle Shot.mov** in the Timeline.
6. Click **Marker** on the menu bar, point to **Go to Clip Marker**, then click **Numbered**.
7. Click **OK** in the Go to Numbered Marker dialog box.
8. Click the **Set In Point button** .

   Your Timeline should resemble Figure 9.
9. Click the **Selection Tool** , drag **Long Shot.mov** to the beginning of the Timeline, then drag **Angle Shot.mov** to the beginning of the Timeline.

(continued)

FIGURE 8
Using the Go to Clip Marker command

FIGURE 9
Trimming clips to start at their markers

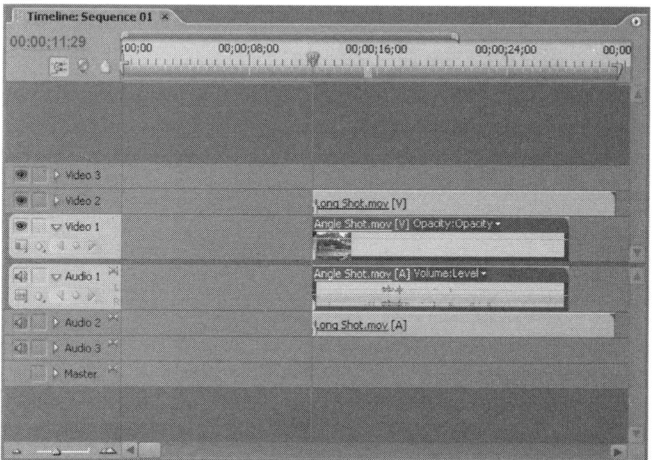

FIGURE 10

Trimming Long Shot.mov in the Video 2 track

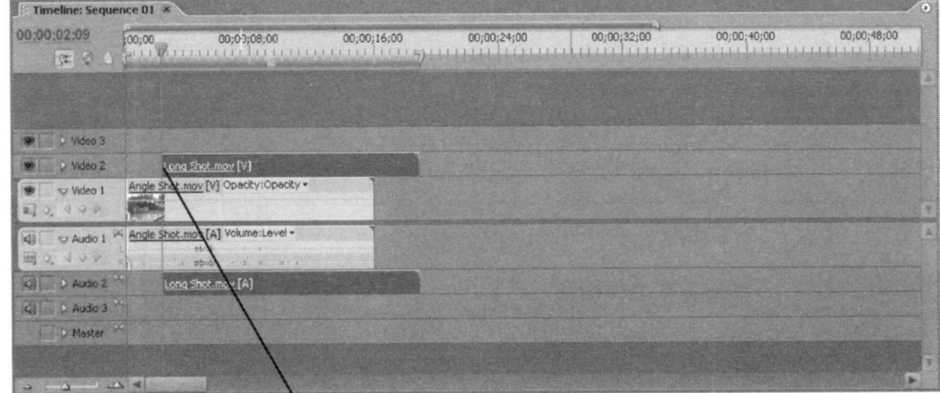

Long Shot.mov trimmed to the Current time indicator

10. Drag the **Current time indicator** to frame 2:09 in the Timeline—the frame where the man first steps up to the pool.
11. Click the **Selection Tool** , position the pointer at the beginning of the Long Shot.mov clip, then drag the **Trim-in icon** to the right, until it snaps to the Current time indicator.

    Your Timeline should resemble Figure 10.
12. Click the **Toggle Track Output button** in the Video 2 track a few times, noting the preview in the Program Monitor.

    Frame 2:09 shows the same moment in both clips—just from different angles.

    TIP The Toggle Track Output button allows you to hide and show a track's contents. When a track is hidden the "eye icon" in the Toggle Track Output button is not displayed.
13. Verify that the contents of the Video 2 track are showing by making sure the "eye icon" appears in the Toggle Track Output button on the Video 2 track, generate a preview, then save your work.

You used markers in the Source Monitor to identify the frame where you wanted to trim clips in the Timeline. You then shortened a clip in the Video 2 track to reveal the clip beneath it in the Video 1 track, thus creating a perfect cut between the two synchronized clips.

LESSON 2

USE THE EXTRACT AND LIFT BUTTONS

What You'll Do

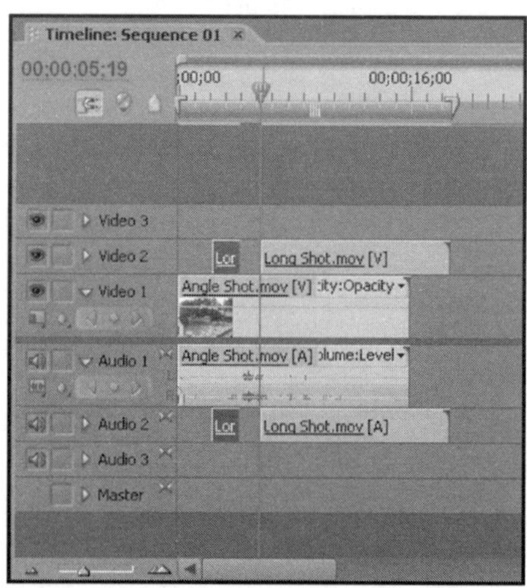

In this lesson, you will edit clips in the Timeline using the Extract and Lift buttons.

Using the Extract Button

The Extract and Lift buttons are both found in the Program Monitor, as shown in Figure 11. They look very similar to the Insert and Overlay buttons in the Source Monitor, however, they are different. You use the Extract button to remove a range of frames or a gap from the Timeline. This feature works only when you target the range of frames with In and Out Points. As with a ripple delete, the frames are deleted and the clips to the right shift left to close the gap. It is important to note that extracting removes the targeted range of frames from *all* unlocked tracks. To lock a track, click the Toggle Track Lock button in the Timeline next to the track that you want to lock. This icon is a gray square next to the Toggle Track Output button. When a track is locked, a padlock icon appears in the Toggle Track Lock button. Clicking the padlock will unlock a locked track. Diagonal lines cover the clips in a locked track.

FIGURE 11

The Lift and Extract buttons in the Program Monitor

Lift button *Extract button*

Using the Lift Button

The Lift button removes a range of frames from the Timeline, leaving a gap. The frames removed can be from a single clip or can span multiple clips. As with extracting, you target the frames you want to remove by setting In and Out Points in the Program Monitor. Lock the video and audio tracks that you do not want to be affected by the lift.

Use the Lift button

1. Position the Current time indicator at frame 4:09 in the Timeline—the frame where the man's hands first touch the water.
2. Click the **Set In Point button** in the Program Monitor.
3. Move the Current time indicator to frame 5:19, then click the **Set Out Point button** in the Program Monitor.
4. **Click the Toggle Track Lock button** next to the Video 1 track and the Audio 1 track, as shown in Figure 12.

   Only the Video 2 track and the Audio 2 track will be affected by the lift.
5. Click the **Lift button** in the Program Monitor, then unlock the Video 1 and Audio 1 tracks.

   The targeted area is removed from the Video 2 and Audio 2 tracks, as shown in Figure 13.
6. Generate a preview, save your work, then close the Project.

You set new In and Out Points in the Timeline. You locked the Video 1 and Audio 1 tracks to preserve them, then clicked the Lift button, which removed the targeted frames from the Video 2 and Audio 2 tracks, leaving a gap in the Timeline.

FIGURE 12
Locking the Video 1 and Audio 1 tracks

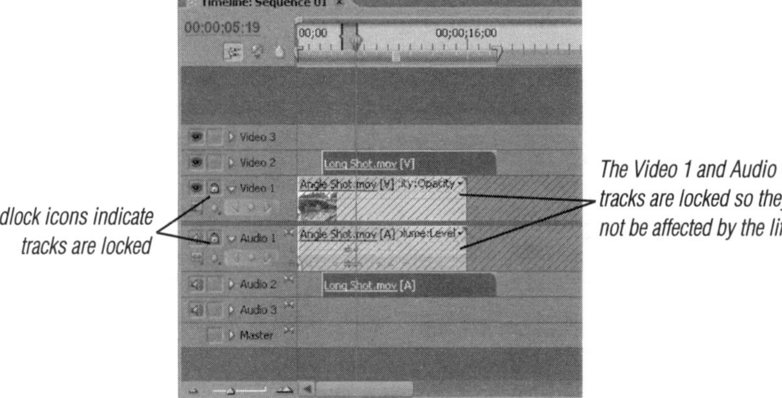

FIGURE 13
Gaps remain in the Timeline after you use the Lift button

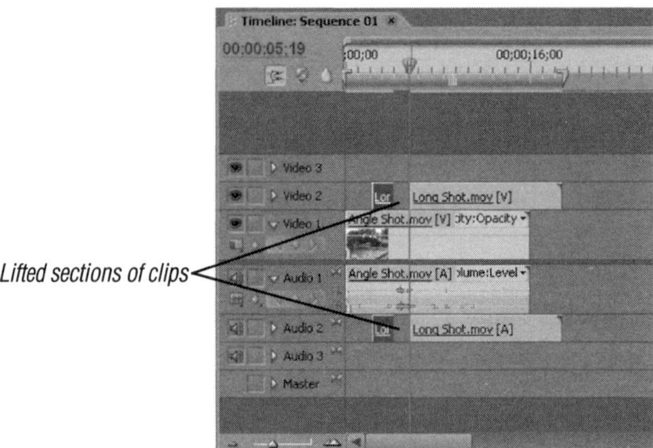

FIGURE 14
Preparing to use the Extract button

FIGURE 15
Results of the extraction

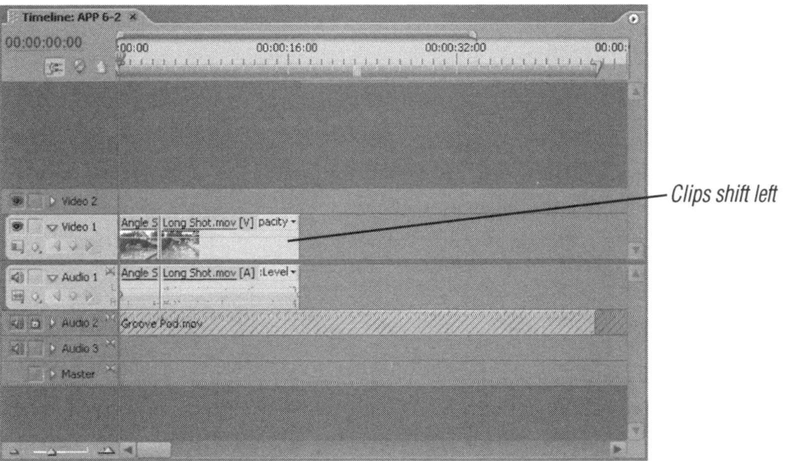

Use the Extract button

1. Open APP 6-2.prproj, save it as **Extract**, then switch to the Editing workspace, if necessary.
2. Position the Current time indicator at frame 4:00 in the Timeline.
3. Click the **Set In Point button** in the Program Monitor.
4. Position the Current time indicator at frame 32:00—the same moment as in Long Shot.mov.
5. Click the **Set Out Point button** in the Program Monitor.
6. Move the Current time indicator to the right so that you can see both the In and Out Point markers in the Timeline.
7. Zoom in on the Timeline, then lock the Audio 2 track, so that your Timeline resembles Figure 14.
8. Click the **Extract button** in the Program Monitor.

   The targeted video and audio are removed, and the material to the right of the extraction shifts left. The audio on Audio 2 is unaffected because the track is locked, as shown in Figure 15.
9. Unlock the Audio 2 track, then trim Groove Pod.mov to the left until it snaps to the right edge of the clips above it.
10. Generate a preview, then save your work.
11. Close the Extract project.

You set In and Out Points in the Timeline to define the area that you wanted to extract. You locked the Audio 2 track to protect its contents from the extraction, then clicked the Extract button in the Program Monitor.

LESSON 3

CHANGE A CLIP'S RATE

What You'll Do

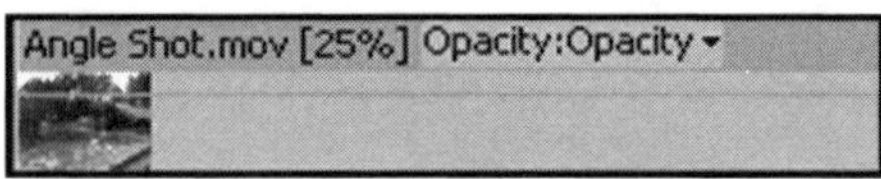

In this lesson, you will create both a slow-motion and a fast-motion effect.

Creating Slow-Motion and Fast-Motion Effects

You can make a clip run faster (fast motion) or slower (slow motion) by changing its rate. The most direct way of doing so is to select the clip in either the Timeline or in the Project panel, then change the settings in the Clip Speed / Duration dialog box.

In the Clip Speed / Duration dialog box, as shown in Figure 16, you change a clip's speed by giving it a new speed or a new duration. Choosing between the two methods is mostly a difference in preference, because each works in tandem with the other. For example, if you selected a clip whose original duration is four seconds, then you changed its rate to 200%, by default its new duration will be two seconds. Conversely, if you change its duration to two seconds, its new rate will be 200%. So, if the clip's rate and duration work in tandem, why are there two settings in the dialog box in the first place? The reason is that sometimes you'll want to use a clip at a specific rate (percentage) of its original speed, and more often you'll want to use it at a specific duration.

QUICKTIP

When a clip's speed has been changed, its new rate appears as a percentage next to the clip name in the Timeline.

Changing a clip's rate is not difficult, but understanding the difference between rate and duration can be tricky. To help you, keep the following phrases in your head: If a clip runs in slower motion, its rate decreases (50% is half as fast) while its duration increases (if it's slower, it takes longer). If a clip runs faster, its rate increases (200% is twice as fast) while its duration decreases (if it's faster, it happens quicker).

Changing the duration for a clip in the Clip Speed / Duration dialog box is not the same as the common task of changing a clip's duration. When you change a clip's duration, you are changing its In or its Out Point or both, and you are thereby changing its duration. When you modify a clip's duration in the Clip Speed / Duration dialog box, you are neither adding to nor trimming from the clip. You are either compressing the total length of a clip into a shorter duration, or you are extending the total length of a clip over a longer duration.

FIGURE 16
Clip Speed / Duration dialog box

Create a slow-motion effect

1. Open APP 6-3.prproj, then save it as **Clip Speed**.
2. Switch to the Editing workspace, if necessary.
3. Zoom in on the Timeline.
4. Position the Current time indicator at frame 3:15—the frame where the man begins his dive.
5. Click the **Timeline panel** to activate the Timeline.
6. Click **Sequence** on the menu bar, then click **Razor at Current Time Indicator**.

   The single clip is split into two at the Current time indicator, as shown in Figure 17.

(continued)

FIGURE 17
Splitting a clip into two using the Razor at Current Time Indicator command

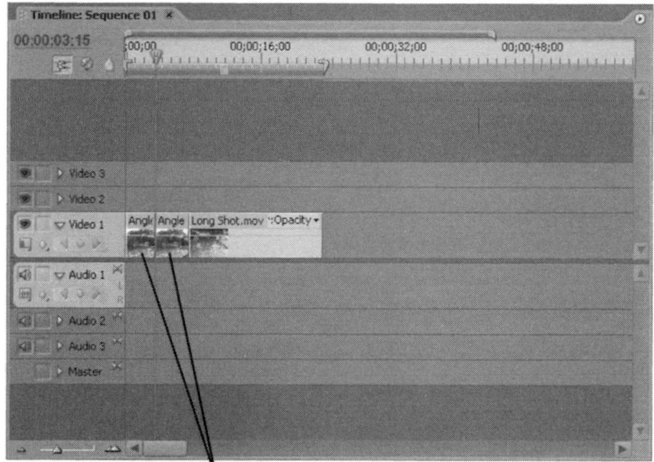

Angle.mov is split into two clips

FIGURE 18

Dragging the third Angle Shot.mov clip to the Video 2 track

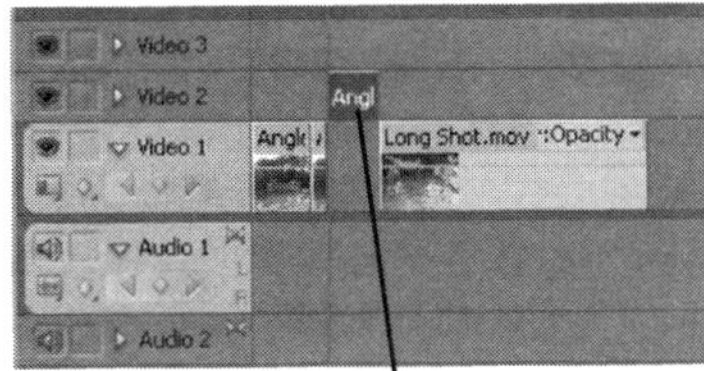

7. Position the Current time indicator at frame 4:15—when the man's feet disappear.
8. Click the **Timeline panel**, then apply the Razor at Current Time Indicator command.

   There are now three Angle Shot.mov clips in the Video 1 track.
9. Move the third clip in the Video 1 track straight up to the Video 2 track, as shown in Figure 18.

   Moving the third clip makes room for the second clip's duration to expand.

(continued)

10. Click the **Selection Tool** , click the **second Angle Shot.mov clip**, click **Clip** on the menu bar, then click **Speed/Duration**.

11. Click the number next to Speed in the Clip Speed / Duration dialog box, type **25**, then click **OK**.

    The clip's duration increases to four seconds, and the clip name changes to show that its rate is 25%, as shown in Figure 19.

    TIP You can find out a clip's duration by hovering the pointer over the clip in the Timeline until you see a tooltip of information appear.

12. Press and hold **[Ctrl]**, then drag the clip in the Video 2 track down to the Video 1 track, positioning it between the modified clip and Long Shot.mov.

13. Generate a preview, then save your work.

You used the Razor at Current Time Indicator command to split a clip into three clips. You then changed the rate of the second clip so that it runs at 25% of its original speed.

FIGURE 19
Making a clip play in slow motion

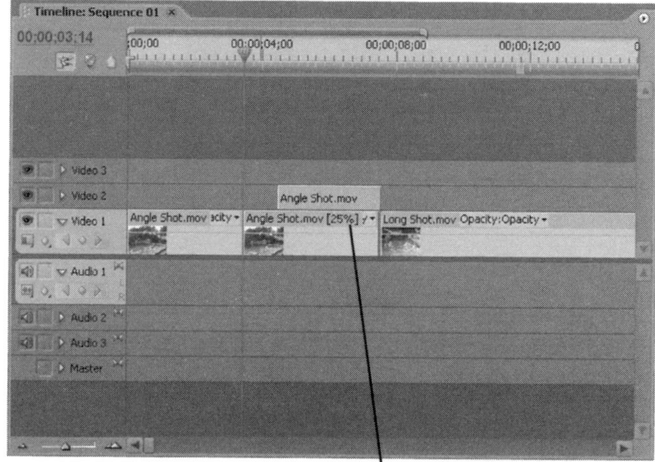

Clip is slowed down to 25%

FIGURE 20
Playing a clip in fast motion

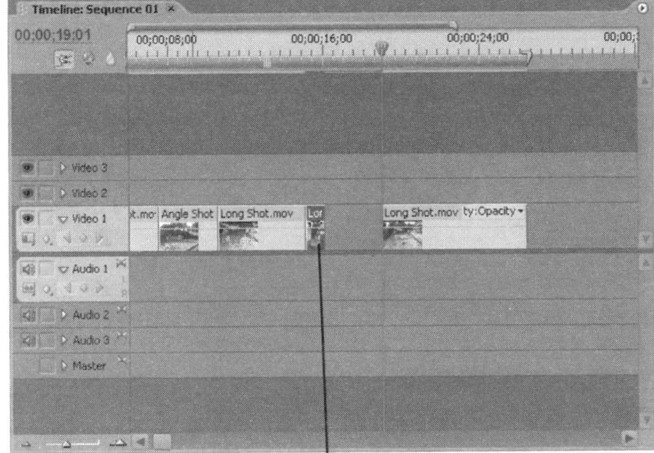

Clip is sped up to 400%

Create a fast-motion effect

1. Position the Current time indicator at 15:03—the frame where the man's feet go underwater.
2. Click the **Timeline**, then apply the Razor at Current Time Indicator command.
3. Position the Current time indicator at 19:01, click the **Timeline**, then apply the Razor at Current Time Indicator command.

   There are now three Long Shot.mov clips in the Video 1 track.
4. Click the **Selection Tool**, then select the second Long Shot.mov clip.
5. Click **Clip** on the menu bar, then click **Speed/Duration**.
6. Click the number in the Speed text box in the Clip Speed / Duration dialog box, type **400**, then click **OK**.

   The clip's duration is reduced, and its action is sped up, as shown in Figure 20.
7. Select the gap that remains, click **Edit** on the menu bar, then click **Ripple Delete**.
8. Generate a preview, save your work, then close the project.

You used the Razor at Current Time Indicator command to split a clip into three clips. You then changed the rate of the second clip so that it runs four times faster than its original speed.

LESSON 4

USE THE SLIDE AND SLIP TOOLS

What You'll Do

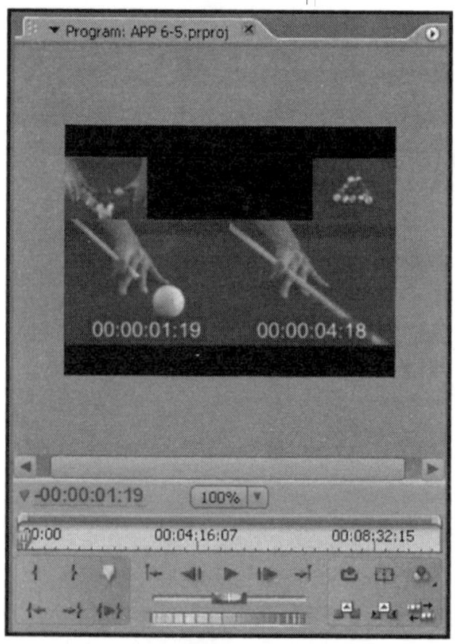

In this lesson, you will edit clips in a fixed-duration program using the Slide and Slip Tools.

Using the Slide Tool

Many times, when editing a rough cut, you will be required to adhere to the rough cut's program duration. For example, you may be given a 30-second rough cut for a 30-second commercial, and you may be instructed that, though the rough cut needs editing, no clips may be added or deleted. This can make editing more challenging, because not only can't you add or delete a clip, you also can't trim one clip without having to make up for the trim by trimming another clip.

The Slide and Slip Tools are designed for exactly this situation. Use the Slide Tool when you want to move a clip in the Timeline—making it appear earlier or later in the program—without changing the program duration. When you move a clip with the Slide Tool, the Out and In Points of the two adjacent clips move with the clip you are dragging. In other words, when you drag a clip to the right with the Slide Tool, the Out Point of the clip to the left and the In Point of the clip to the right both move right to accommodate the move.

When you move a clip with the Slide Tool, the length of the selected clip does not change; one adjacent clip is lengthened, and one adjacent clip is shortened, as shown in Figure 21. The clip that is lengthened uses its head or tail material to add to the duration. Once the head or tail material runs out, you won't be able to continue dragging the Slide Tool.

Using the Slip Tool

You use the Slip Tool when you want to change a clip's In and Out Points without changing the program duration. As you drag the Slip Tool over a clip in the Timeline, the clip itself does not move, but its In and Out Points both shift simultaneously in the direction you are dragging. If you drag right, they both shift right; if you drag left, they both shift left. Since both the In and the Out Points are shifted simultaneously, neither the clip's duration nor the program duration changes.

You can use the Slip Tool on a clip only to the extent that the clip has been trimmed and contains extra frames to accommodate the move in that direction. Put another way, once you run out of frames in one direction, you can no longer drag the Slip Tool in that direction.

The Slip and Slide Tools work in conjunction with the Program Monitor to provide a very sophisticated editing method. For example, when you drag the Slip Tool over a clip, the Program Monitor shows four clip thumbnails: The Out Point of the adjacent left clip, the In Point of the targeted clip, the Out Point of the targeted clip, and the In Point of the adjacent right clip. As you slip the targeted clip, you can watch its In and Out Point frames change and see at a glance how they will cut to the adjacent clips. See Figure 22.

FIGURE 21
Using the Slide Tool

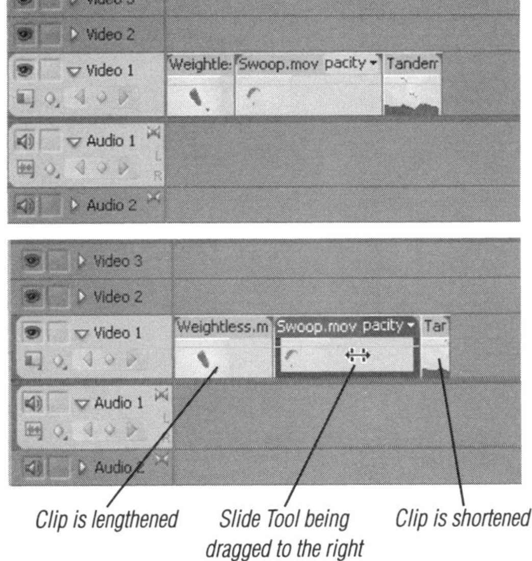

FIGURE 22
View in the Program Monitor as you use the Slip Tool

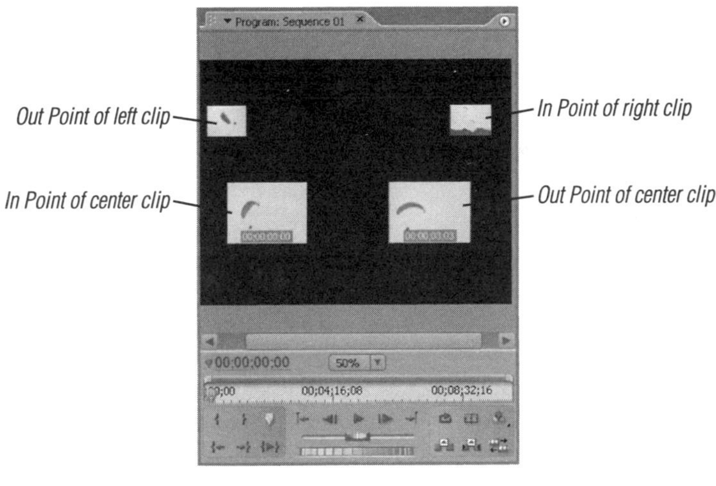

Use the Slide Tool

1. Open APP 6- 4.proj, save it as **Slide Tool**, then switch to the Editing workspace, if necessary.
2. Expand the Billiard Cuts folder, click **Slide.mov**, then click the **Play button** in the Project panel to preview the clip.
3. Zoom in on the Timeline, double-click **Slide.mov** to open it in the Source Monitor, then notice its Out Point.

   More than two seconds of tail material has been trimmed from Slide.mov.
4. Double-click **The Break.mov** in the Timeline, play the movie in the Source Monitor, and note how far into the clip the white cue ball first appears.
5. Generate a preview, then watch the entire sequence.

   The long delay from the point where the cue stick hits the cue ball in Cue.mov and where the cue ball hits the racked balls in The Break.mov makes the action seem unrealistic and needs to be fixed.
6. Click the **Selection Tool**, then position the pointer over each clip in the Timeline until you see a yellow tooltip displaying the clip's start, end, and duration.

   You may want to jot down specific numbers before performing a Slide edit—for example, you may want to calculate the number of frames a clip's In or Out Point changed to after the Slide Tool is applied.

(continued)

FIGURE 23
Using the Slide Tool

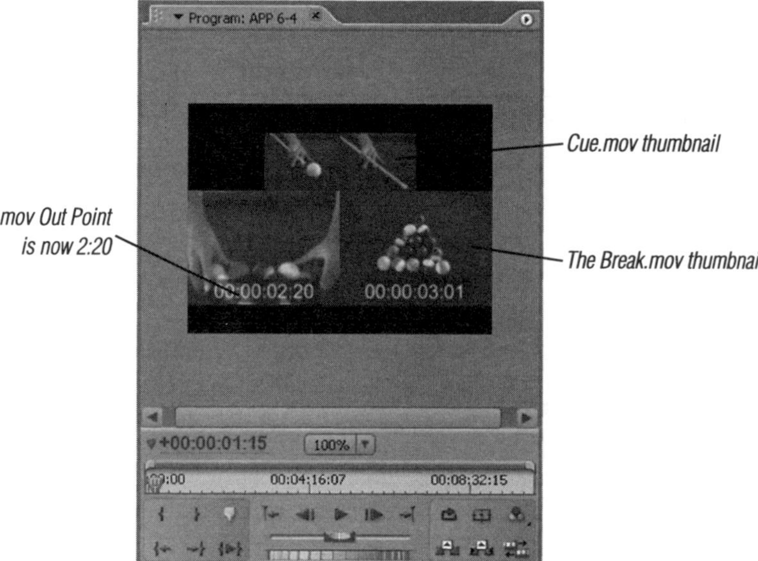

FIGURE 24
Results of using the Slide Tool

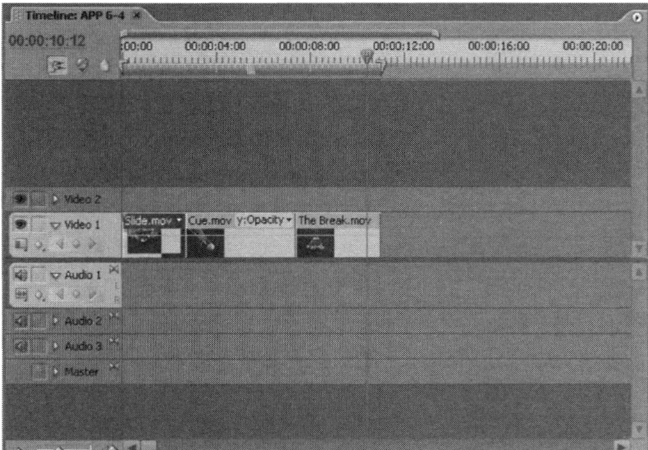

7. Click the **Slide Tool**, drag **Cue.mov** to the right until you see 2:20 in the Slide.mov thumbnail of the Program Monitor, as shown in Figure 23, then release.

   As shown in Figure 24, the duration of Cue.mov does not change. The Out Point of Slide.mov is moved to the right (one second, 15 frames to be exact), and the clip's duration is lengthened. The In Point of The Break.mov is moved to the right the same distance, and the clip's duration is shortened by the same amount. The program duration does not change.

8. Generate a preview, noting the cut between the second and third clips.

   The action is more realistic and more effective.

9. Save your work, then close the project.

You improved a cut in a sequence using the Slide Tool, thereby leaving the program duration unchanged.

Use the Slip Tool

1. Open APP 6-5.prproj, save it as **Slip Tool**, then switch to the Editing workspace, if necessary.
2. Zoom in on the Timeline, then play the sequence and watch where the second clip cuts to the third clip.

   The action of the sequence would be improved if we could see the cue stick hitting the cue ball in Cue.mov.
3. Position the Current time indicator at 4:05 so that you can see the last frame of Cue.mov in the Program Monitor.
4. Expand the Billiard Cuts folder in the Project panel, double-click **Cue.mov**, then preview it in the Source Monitor.

   The clip contains footage of the cue ball being struck by the cue.
5. Drag the **Current time indicator** to 3:00 in the Source Monitor.

   This frame is the same as the Out Point of the clip in the Timeline.
6. Drag the **Current time indicator** forward, from 3:00 to 4:17, as shown in Figure 25.

   This is a better frame for the Out Point because it comes after the cue ball has been struck.

(continued)

FIGURE 25
Choosing a better frame for an Out Point

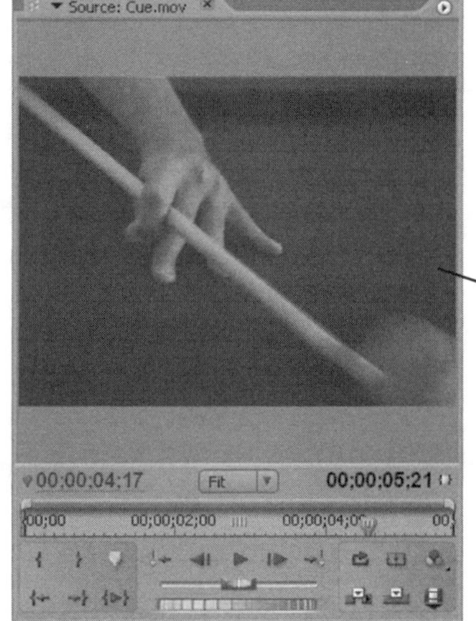

FIGURE 26
Using the Slip Tool

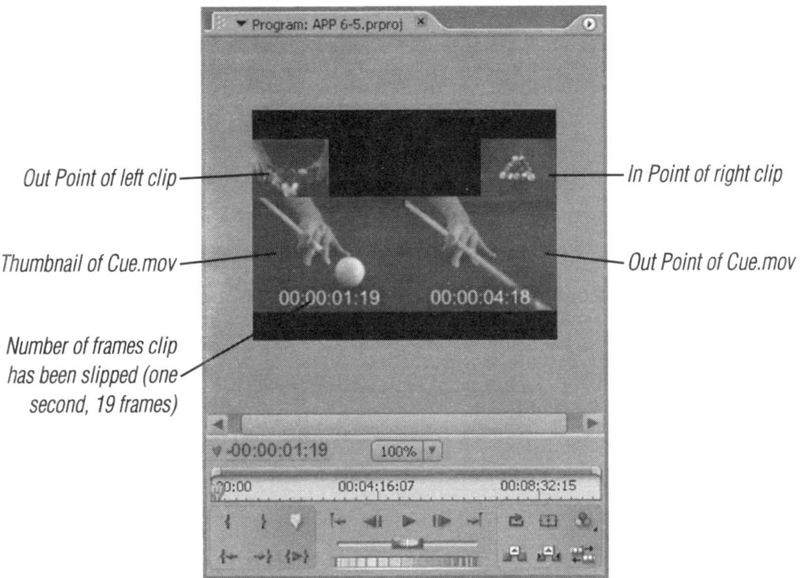

7. Click the **Slip Tool** , drag **Cue.mov** to the left until you see 1:19 in the Cue.mov thumbnail in the Program Monitor, as shown in Figure 26, then release.

   The duration of Cue.mov does not change, but its In and Out Points have moved farther into the clip.

8. Save your work, then close the project.

You identified a cut that could be improved by moving a clip's Out Point. You previewed the original clip to investigate the tail material not visible in the trimmed clip, then identified a frame that would make a better Out Point. You then used the Slip Tool to adjust the clip in the Timeline to end at that Out Point.

LESSON 5

WORK IN THE TRIM MONITOR

What You'll Do

In this lesson, you will use the Trim Monitor to edit clips precisely.

Editing in the Trim Monitor

The Trim Monitor is another way of viewing the Program Monitor. You can switch to the Trim Monitor by clicking the Program Monitor list arrow, then clicking Trim. The Trim Monitor has similar features to the Source and Program Monitors.

The Trim Monitor is very useful for fine-tuning a cut between two clips in which the action must be synchronized or when the timing is critical. When you position the Current time indicator between two clips in the Timeline, the left window in the Trim Monitor shows the Out Point of the left clip, and the right window shows the In Point of the right clip. Being able to see the frames on either side of the Current time indicator is a powerful option for making precise edits.

In the Trim Monitor, you can edit the two clips independently by using the Trim-in and Trim-out icons. This is the most powerful feature of the Trim Monitor, because it offers you the ability to cut from one clip to another with a visual reference to the Out Point of the first and the In Point of the second, as shown in Figure 27.

By default, when you trim either of the two clips in the Trim Monitor, the trim is applied to the clips in the Timeline as a ripple edit.

FIGURE 27
Trim Monitor

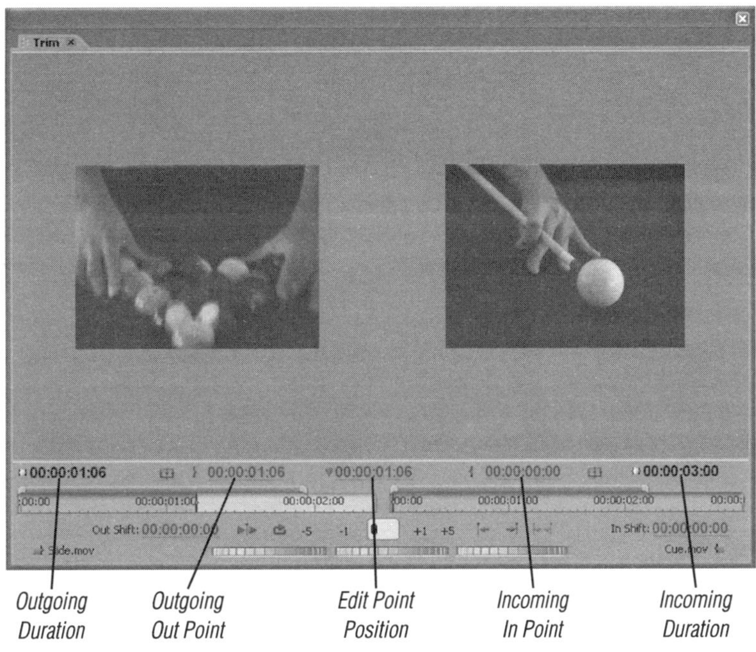

Synchronize and edit clips in the Trim Monitor

1. Open APP 6-6.prproj, then save it as **Trim Monitor**.
2. Switch to the Editing workspace, if necessary.
3. Position the Current time indicator at 9:18—the last frame of the first clip.
4. Click the **Program Monitor list arrow**, then click **Trim**.

   The Trim Monitor appears, as shown in Figure 28. It shows the last frame of Angle Shot.mov on the left and the first frame of Long Shot.mov on the right.

(continued)

FIGURE 28

Trim Monitor showing Angle.mov and Long Shot.mov

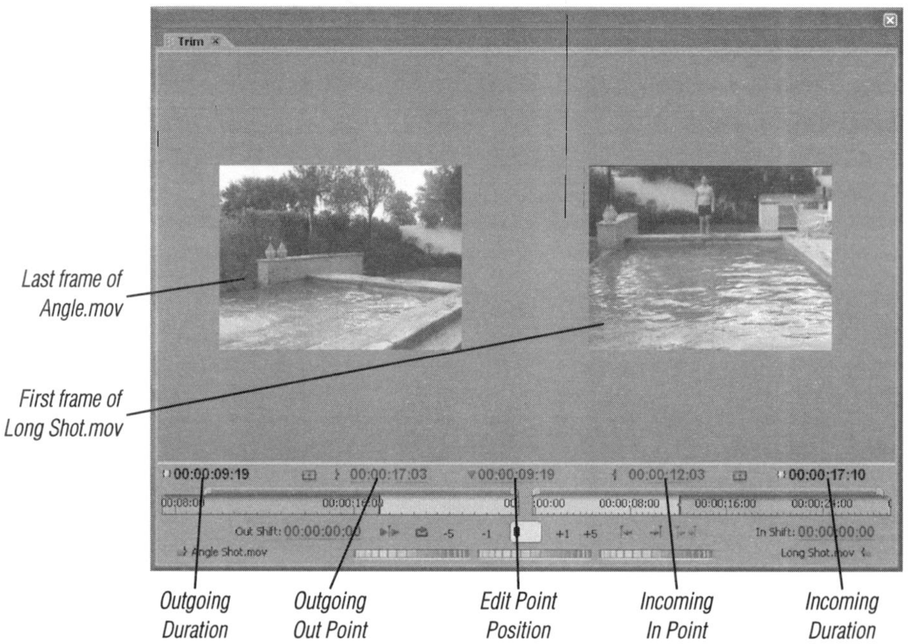

FIGURE 29

Trimming a clip in the Trim Monitor

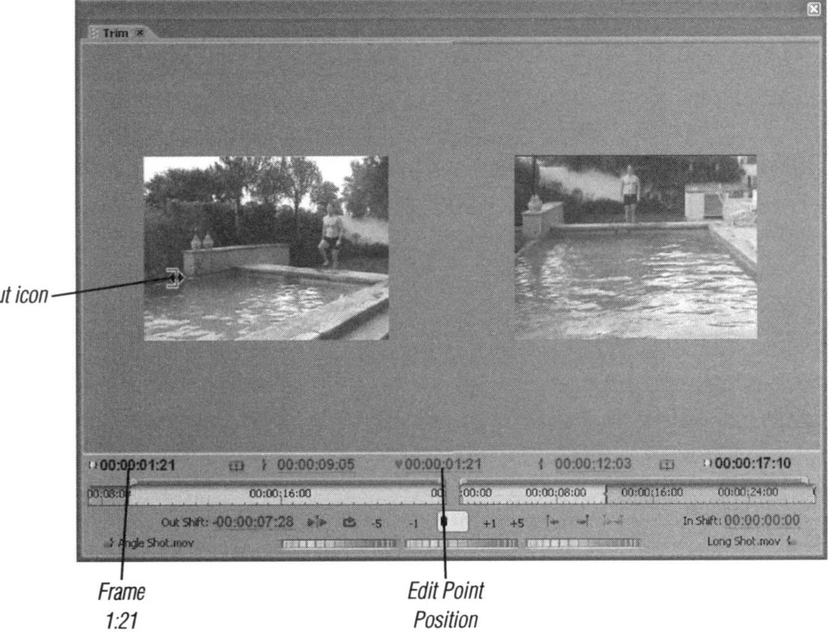

5. Position your pointer over the first clip in the Trim Monitor, then drag the **Trim-out icon** left until the Outgoing Duration reads 1:21, as shown in Figure 29.

   The trim is applied to the corresponding clip in the Timeline as a ripple edit.

6. Position your pointer over the second clip in the Trim Monitor, then drag the **Trim-in icon** right until the Incoming Duration reads 15:10.

   A ripple edit is applied to the second clip in the Timeline. The two clips appear to be synchronized in the Trim Monitor.

7. Close the Trim Monitor, then preview your new sequence in the Timeline.
8. Save your work.

You used controls in the Trim Monitor to synchronize two clips, which simultaneously applied a ripple edit to the clips in the Timeline.

Perform an interactive rolling edit in the Trim View

1. Position the Current time indicator at 1:20—the last frame of Angle Shot.mov, then display the Trim Monitor.
2. Position your pointer between the two clips in the Trim Monitor.

   The pointer becomes the Rolling Edit Tool pointer.
3. Drag the **Rolling Edit Tool pointer** right and left, notice the interactive effect on the clips in the Timeline, then release the mouse pointer.

   As you drag, the move is applied to both clips in the Timeline as an interactive rolling edit.
4. Click **Edit** on the menu bar, then click **Undo**.
5. Position your pointer between the two clips in the Trim Monitor again, then drag to the right until the Incoming Duration field reads 13:03, as shown in Figure 30.
6. Click the right side of the Trim Monitor, then click the **Trim Forward by One Frame button** +1 three times, then close the Trim Monitor.
7. Trim Groove Pod.mov in the Audio 2 track to align it with the clips above it.
8. Generate a preview, save your work, then close the project.

You performed an interactive rolling edit by dragging the Rolling Edit Tool pointer between the two clips in the Trim Monitor, relocating the cut between the two clips.

FIGURE 30
Performing an interactive rolling edit

CHAPTER SUMMARY

Chapter 6 introduced you to some advanced techniques for editing clips as well as some practical features, such as markers. Markers simply allow you to define important places in your sequence. You can add comments to markers, which is useful for long and complex sequences. DVD markers are used in conjunction with DVD templates to create DVDs from your video project.

When it comes to editing, you can change a clip's speed or duration, lift and extract clips from the Timeline, and use the Slip and Slide Tools to edit a clip's In and Out Points without affecting the duration of the entire sequence. When you move a clip with the Slide Tool, the Out and In Points of the two adjacent clips move with the clip you are dragging. As you drag the Slip Tool over a clip in the Timeline, the clip itself does not move, but its In and Out Points both shift simultaneously in the direction you are dragging. For fine-tuning a specific edit, you can use the Trim Monitor. The Trim Monitor displays the Out Point of one frame and the In Point of the frame next to it in the Timeline.

What You Have Learned

- How to set markers
- How to go to a marker
- How to move a clip one frame at a time
- How to toggle a track's output on and off
- How to lock and unlock a track
- How to extract clips using the Extract button
- How to lift clips using the Lift button
- How to use the Razor at Current Time Indicator command
- How to change a clip's rate
- How to use the Slip Tool
- How to use the Slide Tool
- How to make an edit in the Trim Monitor

Key Terms

Markers Markers are triangular icons added to clips and positioned in the time ruler to indicate important frames and to help you position and synchronize clips.

Slip Tool The Slip Tool is an editing tool that you use when you want to change a clip's In and Out Points without changing the program duration.

Slide Tool The Slide Tool is an editing tool that you use when you want to move a clip in the Timeline—making it appear earlier or later in the program—without changing the program duration.

Trim Monitor The Trim Monitor is very useful for fine-tuning a cut between two clips in which the action must be synchronized or when the timing is critical.

CAPSUL
5
MOSKVA
a.
40°
7
50°
8
60°
9
70°
10

chapter

7 WORKING WITH TITLES

1. Create and use titles.
2. Create graphics in Title Designer.
3. Insert logos into Title Designer.

chapter 7 WORKING WITH TITLES

Video editors refer to text or graphics within a video program as **titles**. The term harkens back to the early days of moviemaking, when opening credits were written—by hand—on a title card. The **title card** was filmed as a still image and then added to the beginning of a movie. This method of producing opening credits was used throughout the golden days of the Hollywood studio system. You can see elaborate examples of title cards in many classic movies from that period.

In Premiere Pro you create titles using Title Designer. Title Designer is an application unto itself, and what a powerful application it is. Essentially, it focuses on typography—working with text—and graphics. Title Designer offers a bevy of formatting options. You can align and distribute titles, apply basic formatting, such as bold, italic, and underline, as well as apply more advanced formatting options, such as tracking, kerning, and rotating. You can even change the opacity of titles and apply drop shadows to them. As a graphics utility, Title Designer has some muscle. Beyond the tools that you would expect to find—tools that allow you to create squares, circles, and lines—you might be surprised that you can also create complex gradients and fills. You can transform graphics, apply fills and strokes and, like titles, apply drop shadows and manipulate opacity settings. Premiere Pro has even included a fully functional Pen Tool that you can use to create complex shapes.

Titles add a whole new dimension to a program. More than just a simple or perfunctory add-on to the all-important video component, in and of themselves titles are an important and effective means of communication—entirely different and sometimes more powerful than a video image.

Tools You'll Use

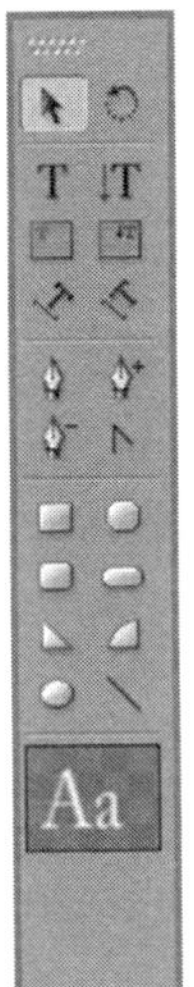

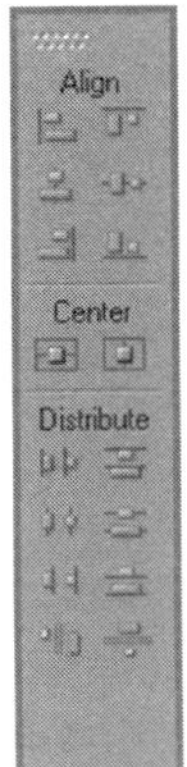

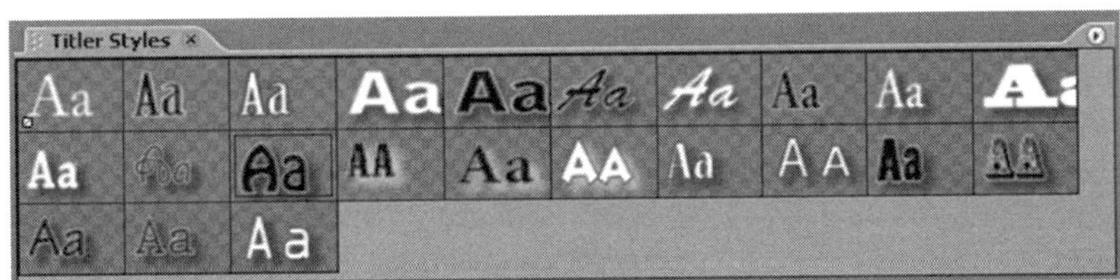

LESSON 1

CREATE AND USE TITLES

What You'll Do

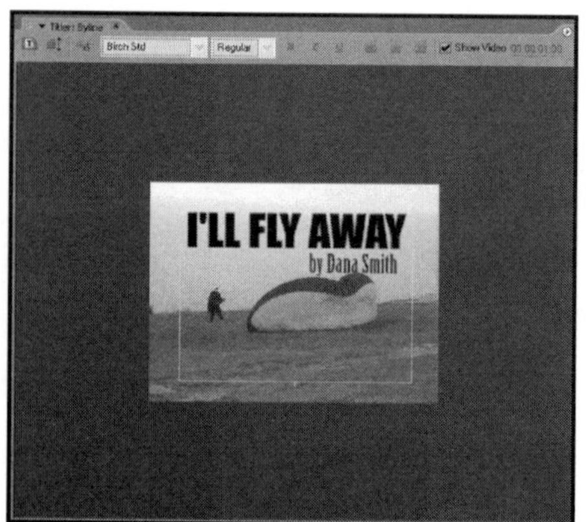

In this lesson, you will create titles in Title Designer and use them in a program.

Working with Title Designer

In Premiere Pro, you use Title Designer to add text and graphic elements, such as lines and shapes, to a video program. **Title Designer**, as shown in Figure 1, is an application that you launch to create a title. You launch Title Designer by either clicking the New Item button on the Project panel, then clicking Title from the menu, or by clicking File on the menu bar, pointing to New, then clicking Title. The New Title dialog opens, prompting you to give your title a descriptive name. Like video and audio clips, titles are clips that are housed in the Project panel with their own unique icon, as shown in Figure 2.

When creating titles, there are four more panels that you use to format your titles and graphics. They are the Title Tools panel, Title Styles panel, Title Actions panel, and the Title Properties panel. All of the title-related panels are found on the Window menu and surround the Titler panel, when accessed.

FIGURE 1

Creating titles and graphics using Title Designer

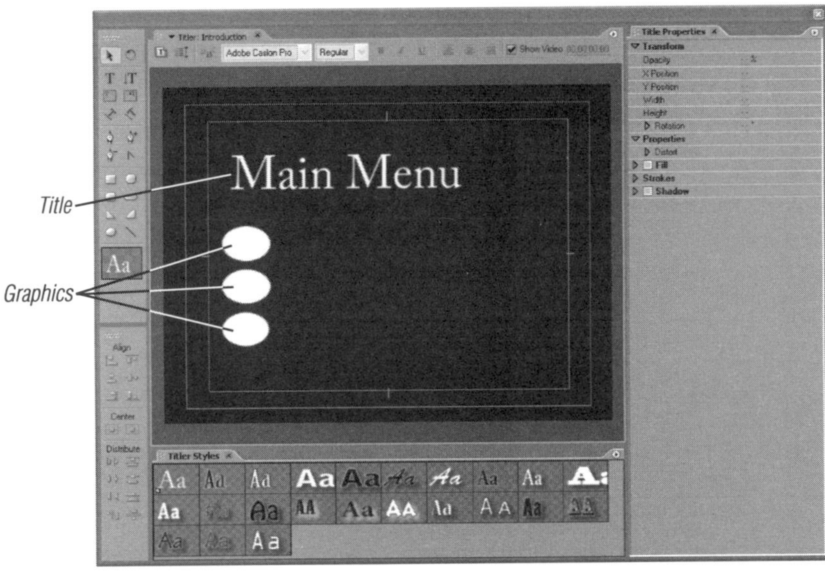

FIGURE 2

Project panel with three named title clips

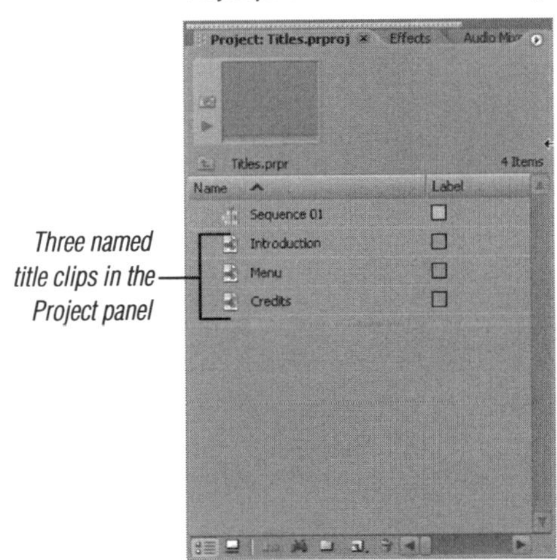

Creating Text in Title Designer

Title Designer offers powerful tools and a variety of options for creating text. If you are familiar with Adobe Illustrator or InDesign, you'll recognize the Type Tool, Area Type Tool, and the Path Type Tool. The Area Type Tool is used for filling text inside a specific shape. The Path Type Tool allows you to type text along a path. In Title Designer, you also have the ability to create vertical type, using the Vertical Type Tool, the Vertical Area Type Tool, and the Vertical Path Type Tool.

The Title Properties panel offers a complete collection of standard typographical settings, including tracking and kerning, leading, and baseline shift.

Showing Video in the Title Designer Window

When you are creating a title for a specific part of a video program, it is often helpful to view a frame from that footage in the drawing area of the Titler panel as you create the title. Displaying a frame from your program is also useful when you want to position text or graphics with a precise relationship to components of the image.

> TIP The drawing area of the Titler panel is always the same size as the project's frame size.

You can show a video frame behind the title you are designing by clicking the Show Video check box in the Titler panel, as shown in Figure 3. Notice the frame number next to the Show Video check box. You can type a new frame number in the Background Video Timecode field, and the image in the Titler panel will update automatically.

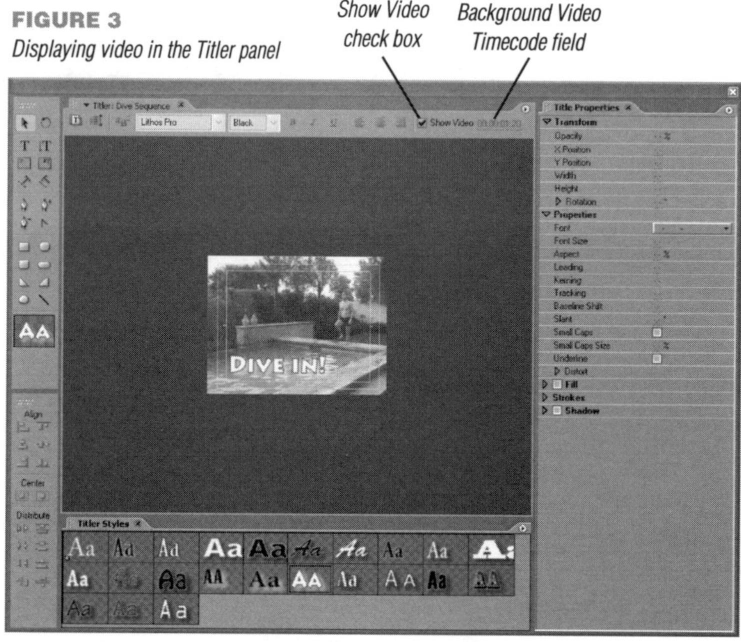

FIGURE 3
Displaying video in the Titler panel

Sampling Colors with the Eyedropper Tool

As you create text and graphics in the Titler panel, you may want to experiment with color. A fun and interesting method for choosing color involves using the Eyedropper Tool, found in the Fill section of the Title Properties panel. Select an object that you want to apply a new color to, then drag the Eyedropper pointer over the current image in the drawing area, as shown in Figure 4. The color of the selected object continually changes to the color that the Eyedropper pointer is currently over.

> TIP In addition to the image in the drawing area of the Titler panel, you can sample a color from anywhere in the Premiere Pro workspace with the Eyedropper Tool.

Adding Shadows to Text and Objects

Adding shadows to text and objects can create a very dramatic effect. The Shadow section Title Properties panel allows you to apply a shadow to a selected object. You can choose a color for the shadow as well as the angle, distance, size, spread, and opacity.

FIGURE 4
Using the Eyedropper Tool to sample color

Creating and Applying Styles

Title Designer contains 23 styles from which to choose in the Title Styles panel, and you can also create your own custom styles. Once you have customized the look of a text element—defined its font, size, color, and so on—you will find it useful to save that **style** so that you can quickly apply it to other text elements in the program.

To create a new style, click the title that the new style will be based on, click the Titler Styles panel list arrow, then click New Style. Name the style in the New Style dialog box, then click OK. The new style swatch appears in the Titlers Styles panel, as shown in Figure 5. When you save the title, the style swatch is saved with the title file and is available when you create any new titles. To apply a style, simply select an object in the drawing area, then click a style swatch from the Titler Styles panel.

Using styles is a smart working method that not only saves you time, but more important, helps you maintain consistency across multiple titles in a project.

QUICK TIP

In order to make your text really stand out, you can place it against a title bar. A title bar is simply a shape, such as a rectangle, that you position text on top of. This is a simple example of one of the many ways that you can combine text and graphics in the Title Designer window to create graphic objects and logos for your program.

FIGURE 5
Creating a new style

New style based on formatted text

Understanding Title Window Transparency

The title is the entire drawing area Titler panel. It is always the same size as the project's frame size. Anything that you create in the drawing area—text, lines, or shapes—will appear in the program with the fill color that you designate. The objects in a title are superimposed over clips that are on tracks beneath them. The other areas of the drawing area are, by default, transparent, as shown in Figure 6. The transparent areas of a title appear black in the title clip thumbnail, as shown in Figure 7.

TIP Using the Add Tracks command on the Sequence menu, you can add additional video tracks to the Timeline. All tracks higher than the Video 1 track are called **superimpose tracks** because clips on those tracks are positioned above clips on the tracks beneath them.

FIGURE 6
Viewing the transparent area of a title

Transparent area of a title

FIGURE 7
Viewing a title clip in the Preview Area of the Project panel

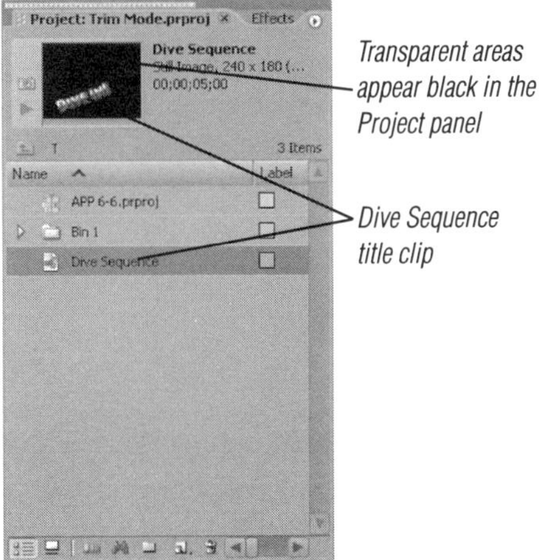

Transparent areas appear black in the Project panel

Dive Sequence title clip

Understanding Safe Title and Safe Action Margins

When you create a program for videotape or for broadcast, a television is usually the output device. When creating artwork in titles, it is important that you remember that not all televisions are the same. For example, most television sets use a process called **overscan**, which cuts off the outer edges of the picture so that the center of the image can be enlarged. The amount of overscan is not consistent across all televisions. Thus, editors have established safe zones when editing for videotape or broadcast. The Titler panel has two safe zones called the **Safe Title Margin** and the **Safe Action Margin**, as shown in Figure 8. When you are editing for broadcast or videotape, you should keep text inside the borders of the Safe Title Margin and important graphics inside the borders of the Safe Action Margin. Doing so will ensure that everything fits within the area displayed by most televisions. The Safe Title Margin is the smaller of the two because it is more critical that no text is inadvertently trimmed.

QUICK TIP

You can hide the Safe Title Margin and Safe Action Margin by clicking the Titler panel list arrow, then choosing Safe Title Margin or Safe Action Margin to remove the check mark, or by using the View command on the Title menu. By default, the Safe Title Margin and Safe Action Margin are shown in the Titler panel.

FIGURE 8

Safe Action and Safe Title Margins

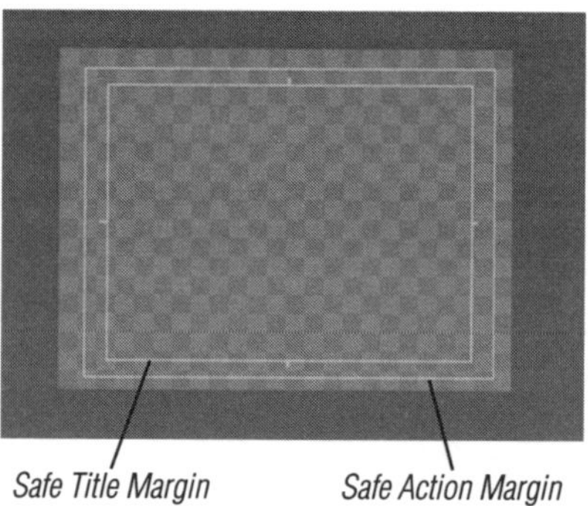

Safe Title Margin *Safe Action Margin*

Using the Color Picker

The **Color Picker** is a dialog box in which you enter values for red, green, and blue (RGB) to create a fill color for text or objects. You can enter a number from 0 to 255 in each of the text boxes. Entering zeros in each text box produces black. Entering 255 in each text box—that is, combining all three colors equally at "full-strength"—produces white.

All light sources that produce color do so based on the RGB color model. For example, flick a drop of water at your television screen, and you will see that the color image is actually created with only red, green, and blue pixels. Your computer monitor, too, is composed only of red, green, and blue pixels. The color that you perceive on either of the two screens is created from the additive properties of red, green, and blue light.

Color in film and video is also based on the RGB color model because you are capturing colors in the natural world. In Premiere Pro, when you are specifying a fill color for text or for an object, you must specify that color in RGB values. One naming convention for RGB colors uses slashes in between each value, such as 20R/40G/60B. This color name translates to 20% red, 40% green, and 60% blue. Nobody expects you to memorize RGB values for different colors. (You can specify more than 16 million!) Instead, click anywhere in the color field of the Color Picker dialog box to choose a color. You can also click and drag inside the color field, and the fill color changes interactively.

Understanding the RGB Color Model

Understanding the RGB color model requires an exploration of basic color theory. All of the natural light in our world comes from the sun. The sun delivers light to us in waves. The entirety of the sun's light, the **electromagnetic spectrum**, contains an infinite number of light waves—some at high frequencies, some at low frequencies—many of which will sound familiar to you. X-rays, gamma rays, and ultraviolet rays are all components of the electromagnetic spectrum.

The light waves that we see in our world are only a subset of the electromagnetic spectrum. Scientists refer to this subset—this range of wavelengths—as visible light. Because this light appears to us as colorless (as opposed to, say, the red light of Mars), we refer to visible light as "**white light**."

From your school days, you may remember using a prism to bend light waves to reveal what you probably referred to as a rainbow. It is through this bending—or "breaking down" of white light—that we see color. The rainbow that we are all so familiar with is called the visible spectrum, and it is composed of seven distinct colors: red, orange, yellow, green, blue, indigo, and violet.

Though the colors are distinct, the color range of the visible spectrum is infinite; for example, there's no definable place in the spectrum where orange light ends and yellow light begins.

Colors in the visible spectrum can themselves be broken down. For example, because red light and green light, when combined, produce yellow light, yellow light can, conversely, be broken down, or reduced, to those component colors.

Red, green, and blue light (RGB) are the **additive primary colors** of light. The term primary refers to the fact that red, green, and blue light cannot themselves be broken down or reduced. The term additive refers to the fact that these same colors combine to produce other colors. For example, red and blue light, when combined, produce violet hues.

As primary colors, red, green, and blue light are the irreducible component colors of white light. Therefore, it logically follows that when red, green, and blue light are combined equally, they produce white light.

Finally, you'll note that nowhere in this paradigm is the color black. That is because, in the natural world, there is no such color as black. True black is the absence of all light.

Create text in Title Designer

1. Open APP 7-1.prproj, then save it as **The Xtreme Channel**.
2. Click **Edit** on the menu bar, point to **Preferences**, click **General**, type **30** in the Still Image Default Duration text box, then click **OK**.

   Premiere Pro identifies all titles as still images. The titles that you create will have a one-second duration.
3. Click the **New Item button** in the Project panel, then click **Title**.
4. Type **Intro Title** in the Name text box of the New Title dialog box, then click **OK**.

   The Titler panel opens and the new title clip is automatically added to the Project panel.
5. Click **Window** on the menu bar, then click **Title Tools**.
6. Repeat Step 5 to show the Title Properties, Title Styles, and Title Actions panels, as necessary.
7. Click the **Show Video check box** at the top of the Titler panel, if necessary.
8. Click the **Titler panel list arrow**, click **Text Baselines** to remove the check mark, click the **Titler panel list arrow** again, then click **Safe Action Margin** to remove the check mark.

   Only the Safe Title Margin should be showing in the drawing area of the Titler panel.
9. Click the **Type Tool**, click approximately in the upper-left corner of the Safe Title Margin, then type **I'LL FLY AWAY**, as shown in Figure 9.

   The font and size of your title may differ from the figure.

(continued)

FIGURE 9
Creating a title

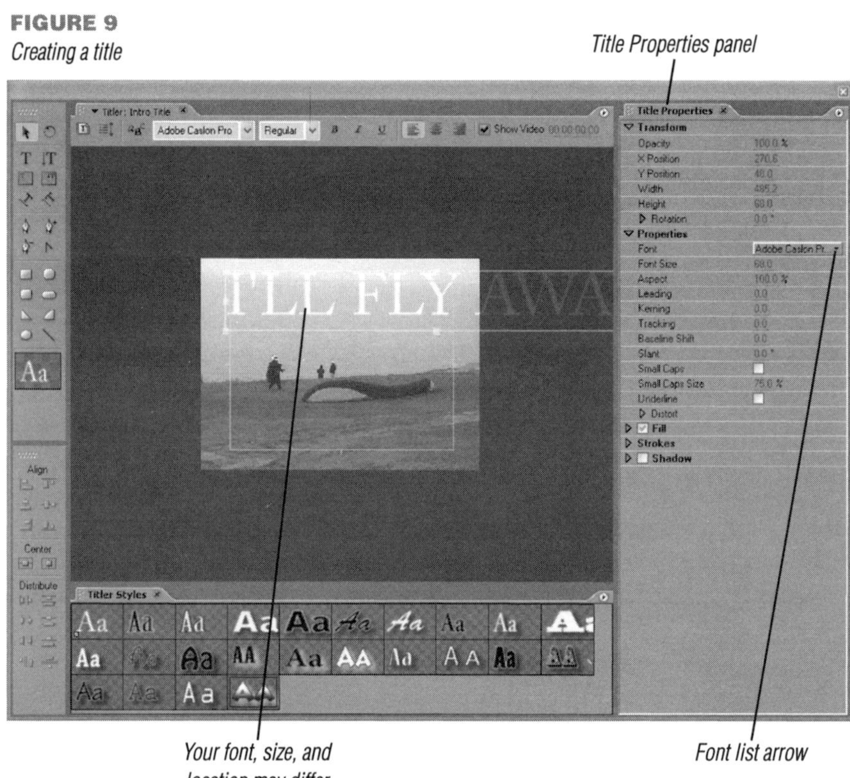

FIGURE 10
Designing a headline

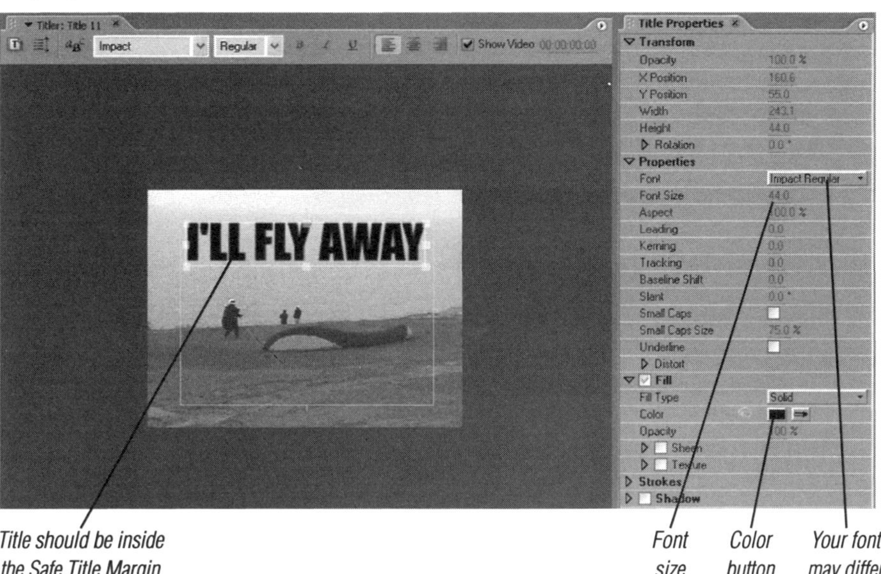

Title should be inside the Safe Title Margin

Font size

Color button

Your font may differ

10. Click the **Selection Tool**, click the **Font list arrow** in the Title Properties panel, then click **Impact**.

    When you switch to the Selection Tool, the title is automatically selected in the drawing area.

    > TIP If you do not have the Impact font, choose a similar font available on your computer.

11. Expand the Fill section in the Title Properties panel, click the **Color button** next to Color, type **0** in the R, G, and B (red, green, and blue) text boxes, then click **OK**.

    The fill color of the title changes to black.

    > TIP In the RGB color model, 0 Red, 0 Green, and 0 Blue creates black, and 255 Red, 255 Green, and 255 Blue creates white.

12. Position your pointer over the current Font Size value in the Title Properties panel, then click and drag until the value reads 44.0, as shown in Figure 10.

    When you position the mouse pointer over a value in the Title Properties panel and it changes to a double-arrow and pointing finger icon, you can click and drag the current value to change it while watching the change affect the selected item in the drawing area.

    > TIP You may need to use a different font size if you are using a different font to make your screen resemble Figure 10. Be sure that your title is inside the Safe Title Margin.

13. Save your work.

You created a new title called Intro Title, formatted it and positioned it inside the Safe Title Margin.

Add title clips to the Timeline

1. Close the Titler panel, if necessary, then zoom in on the Timeline.
2. Set the Current time indicator at frame 1:00 in the Timeline, then drag **Intro Title** from the Project panel into the Video 2 track at frame 1:00, as shown in Figure 11.
3. Click **Intro Title** in the Video 2 track, click **Clip** on the menu bar, click **Speed/Duration**, then change its duration to three seconds.
4. Preview the beginning of the sequence, stop the movie, then save your work.
5. Click the **New Item button** on the Project panel, click **Title**, name it **Byline**, then click **OK**.
6. Show all of the Title Designer panels using the Window menu, if necessary.
7. Click the **Show Video check box** in the Titler panel, if necessary, then type **1:00** in the Background Video Timecode field.

   Frame 1:00 appears in the Titler panel. Since Intro Title has been added to frame 1:00 in the Timeline, you can use it to align new titles in the Titler panel.

(continued)

FIGURE 11
Placing Intro Title at frame 1:00 in the Video 2 track

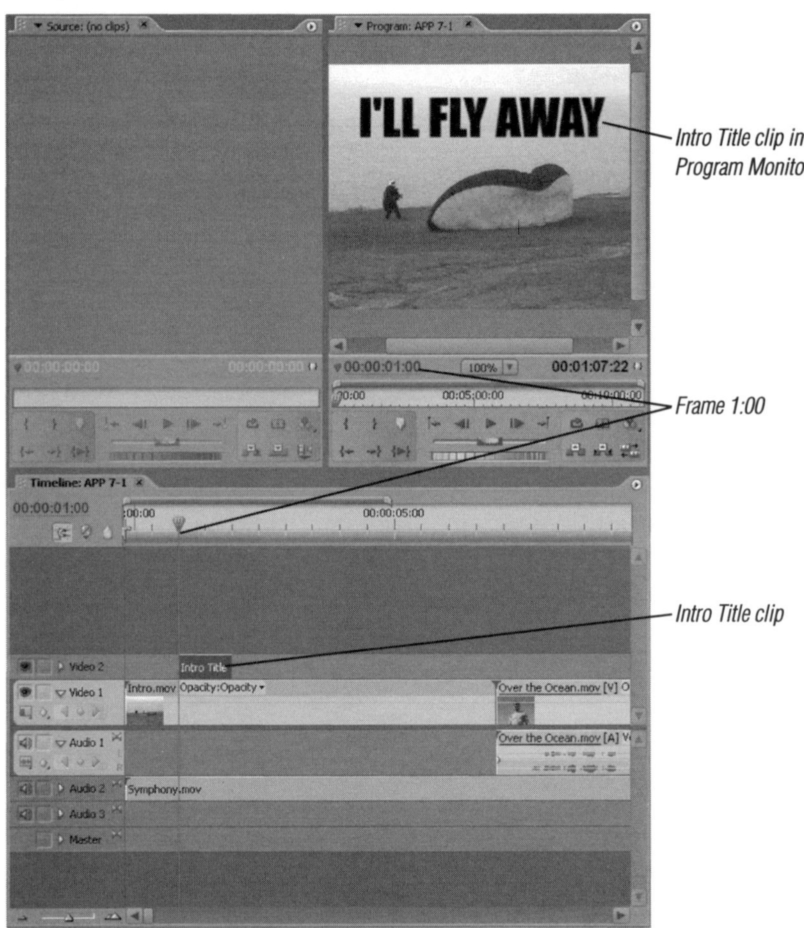

FIGURE 12
Creating the Byline title

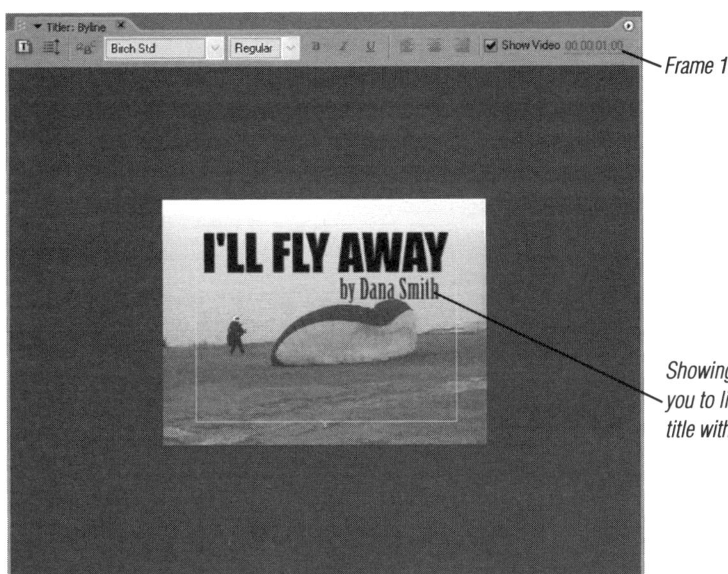

8. Click the **Type Tool** , click below "I'LL FLY AWAY," then type **by Dana Smith**.
9. Click the **Selection Tool** , click the second style in the first row of the Titler Styles panel (Birch Black 80), change the font size to 28.0, then position the byline in the approximate location shown in Figure 12.
10. Close the Titler panel, drag Byline from the Project panel next to Intro Title in the Video 2 track, change its duration to 2:26 seconds, then save your work.
11. Generate a preview, then close the project.

You added Intro Title to the Timeline, then created a new title. While creating the new title, you displayed frame 1:00 in the Titler panel. This allowed you to see the location of Intro Title in the sequence and position the new title in relationship to it.

Create a drop shadow and a new style

1. Open APP 7-2.prproj, then save it as **New Style**.
2. Double-click **Intro Title** in the Project panel.

   Intro Title opens in the Titler panel.
3. Click the **Show Video check box**, if necessary, then view frame 1:00 in the Titler panel.
4. Select "I'LL FLY AWAY," then verify that the Title Properties panel is showing.
5. Click the **Shadow check box** in the Title Properties panel, then expand the Shadow section, as shown in Figure 13.
6. Click the **Distance value**, type **5.0**, then press **[Enter]**.
7. Expand the Angle section, then drag the **angle line** to 223.

   TIP If you have trouble dragging the line to exactly 223, you can type 223 in the Angle text box.
8. Expand the Fill section, click the **Color button**, type **255** in the R, G, and B text boxes, then click **OK**.

   The title is filled with white.

(continued)

FIGURE 13
Shadow options in the Title Properties panel

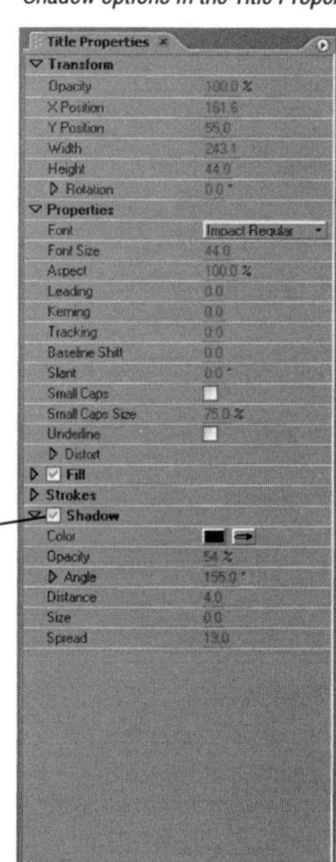

FIGURE 14
Adding a new style to the Titler Styles panel

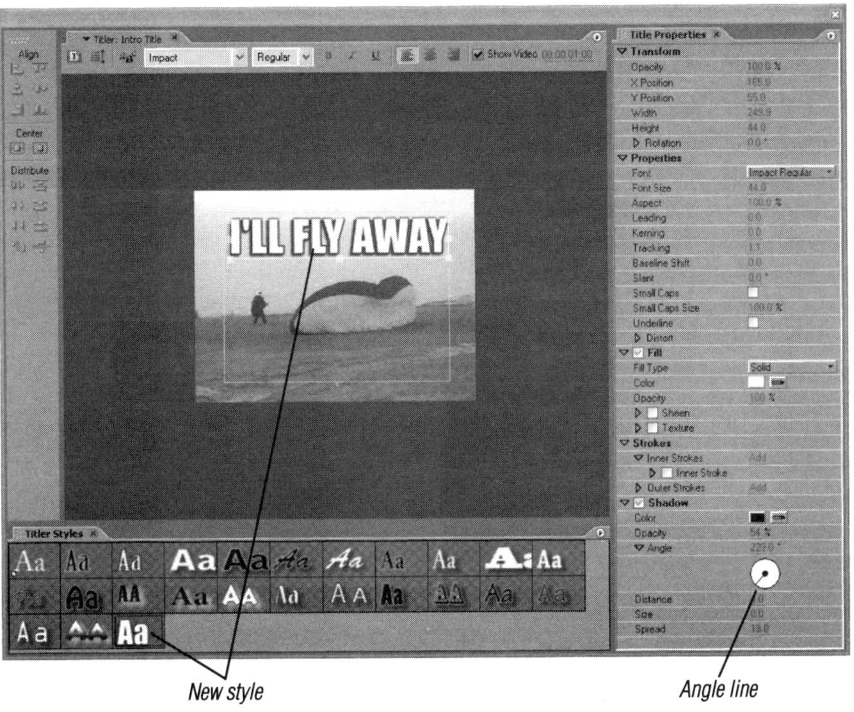

9. Display the Title Styles panel, if necessary.
10. Click the **Titler Styles panel list arrow**, click **New Style**, then click **OK** in the New Style dialog box, accepting the default name.

    All of the formatting attributes applied to "I'LL FLY AWAY" are added as a new style to the Titler Styles panel. See Figure 14.
11. Double-click **Byline** in the Project panel to open it in the Titler panel.
12. Click the **Selection Tool** , click **"by Dana Smith,"** then click the **new style** in the Titler Styles panel.
13. Change the font size to 20.0, then drag the **Byline title** inside the Safe Title Margin, if necessary.
14. Close the Titler panel, save your work, then generate a preview.

You created a drop shadow for the Intro Title clip, saved the formatting as a new style in the Titler Styles panel, then applied it to the Byline title.

LESSON 2

CREATE GRAPHICS IN TITLE DESIGNER

What You'll Do

In this lesson, you will use the tools and features in Title Designer to create graphics, transform them, apply gradients, and adjust opacity.

Creating Graphics

In addition to the text tools, Title Designer offers a variety of drawing tools, which give you the ability to create a variety of shapes—everything from simple squares and ellipses to polygons and curved objects. Just as with text, you can fill an object with color and you can add a drop shadow behind the object. Title Designer also offers you the option to transform objects. You can rotate objects and scale them. The ability to scale an object comes in handy when you are creating objects that need to be small, such as a logo to appear in the corner of the window. Instead of working painstakingly on a small object, you can create it at a larger size, then scale it down to the size you need it to be. The Title Properties panel is where all of the transform features are found. If you are familiar with Adobe Illustrator, Photoshop, or InDesign, you'll be thrilled to see the familiar Pen Tool and all of the Pen Tool accessory tools in the Title Tools panel. The ability to create vector graphics without leaving Premiere Pro will save you lots of time. You also have the added benefit of drawing a vector while seeing video behind it, if necessary.

Understanding Opacity

The term **opacity** derives from the word "opaque," which describes an object that is neither transparent nor translucent—that is, not "see through." By default, clips that you add to the Timeline are added at 100% opacity—they play to the exclusion of the clips on tracks beneath them. You can adjust the opacity of titles and objects using the Opacity setting in the Title Properties panel. Experimenting with opacity values is fun. Creating the effect of "seeing pictures through text" will make your video projects come alive.

Creating Gradients

Gradients are multi-color fills in which one color blends to another. Gradients can be created and applied to titles and objects using Title Designer. The Title Properties panel offers three types of gradients: Linear, Radial, and 4 Color. Linear and radial gradients are composed of two colors. In a linear gradient, color flows vertically, however, the angle of a linear gradient can be manipulated. Radial gradients are circular gradients in which the first color appears in the center, as shown in Figure 15. A four-color gradient uses four colors positioned at the top-left, top-right, bottom-left, and bottom-right corners of an object.

To create a gradient, first select the title or object that you would like to apply the gradient to in the drawing area of the Titler panel. Expand the Fill section of the Title Properties panel, then click the Fill Type list arrow to choose the type of gradient you want. You'll see a gradient bar with color stops beneath it, as shown in Figure 16.

FIGURE 15
Creating a linear and radial gradient

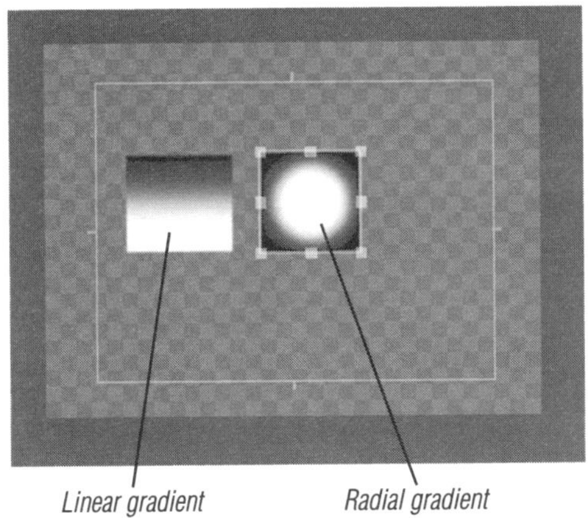

FIGURE 16
Creating a gradient

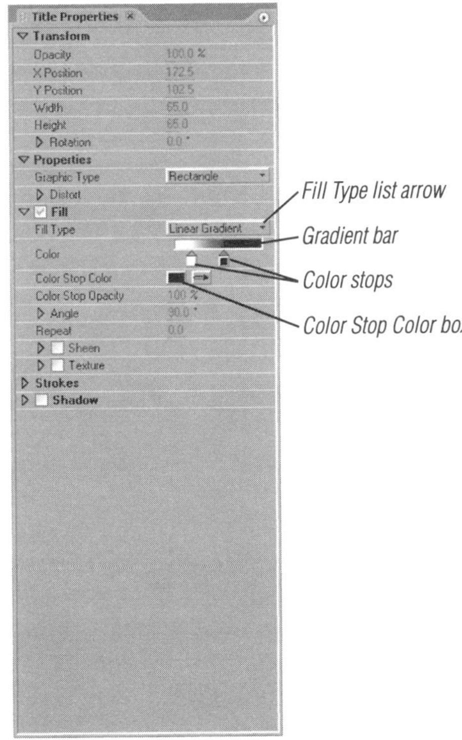

The first color stop represents the first color in the gradient and the second color stop represents the second color in the gradient. Click one of the color stops, then click the Color Stop Color box to open the Color Picker and choose the color you like. Repeat the same steps for the second color stop. The color stops serve another function: They control the length of the blend between the two colors and the way that they fill the object. The distance between the two color stops is the same as the length of the blend between the two colors that fill the object. You can adjust the gradient by moving the color stops left or right to change the location where the two colors meet. As you drag the color stops, you'll see the gradient applied to your selected object update continually. You can also change the opacity, angle, and number of times a gradient should repeat using the respective settings in the Fill section of the Title Properties panel. In Figure 17, the opacity of the second color stop (black) has been changed to 48%. You can see the checkerboard pattern behind it in the drawing area. The angle has been changed to 142.1° and the gradient has a repeat pattern of two.

QUICK TIP

When you adjust the opacity of a color stop in a gradient, only that color's opacity is changed. When you change the opacity of a selected object, it changes the opacity of the entire object.

FIGURE 17

Adjusting gradient settings

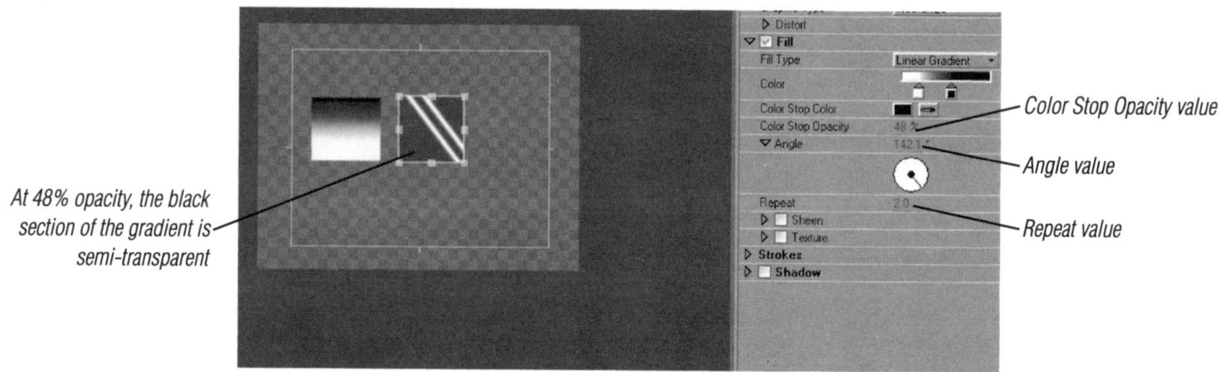

Arranging Objects in Title Designer

The Title menu offers three sets of commands that will help you select, "layer," and position titles and objects in the drawing area. Use the Select commands to select objects that may be hard to select or find because they are blocked by others. The Select commands include First Object Above, Next Object Above, Next Object Below, and Last Object Below. The Arrange commands are similar to those in most graphics applications: Bring to Front, Bring Forward, Send to Back, and Send Backward. These commands will help you stack or layer your objects and titles exactly how you want them to appear in relationship to each other. Finally, the Position commands allow you to center selected objects horizontally and/or vertically within the margins or position them in the lower third of the drawing area.

QUICK TIP

The **Ghost** fill option removes the fill from an object, thereby making its fill transparent. However, it does not remove any stroke or shadow that you have applied to the object. With this option, you can create the effect of a "hollow" stroked object that casts a full shadow. **Eliminate** is a type of fill which removes the fill and the shadow from an object.

Applying Strokes to Objects

Title Designer gives you great flexibility for adding an outline, or **stroke**, to an object or to text. Parameters that define the appearance of a stroke are its weight (thickness), color, opacity, and whether it is an inner stroke—drawn along the inner edge of an object—or an outer stroke, which is drawn along the outer edge. Strokes are created using the Title Properties panel.

In addition to the parameters listed above, Title Designer allows you to specify the type of stroke you apply. **Depth** creates a stroke that looks like a hard-edged copy placed behind the object. **Edge**, the type you will probably use most often, creates a stroke that outlines the object, along either the inner or the outer edge. **Drop Face** creates a copy of the object, which you can then offset and modify.

Create a shape

1. Click the **New Item button** on the Project panel, then click **Title**.
2. Name the new title **Background**.
3. Click the **Show Video check box** to remove the check mark.
4. Click the **Titler panel list arrow**, then click **Safe Action Margin** to show the Safe Action Margin.
5. Click the **Rectangle Tool** on the Title Tools panel, then draw a rectangle that fills the Safe Action Margin.

   Your screen should resemble Figure 18.

   > TIP The fill color of your rectangle may differ.

6. Click the **Selection Tool**, then click the **rectangle**.
7. Click the **Graphic Type list arrow** in the Title Properties panel, click **Rounded Corner Rectangle**, then change the Fillet Size to 28.5%, as shown in Figure 19.
8. Click the **Graphic Type list arrow** again, then click **Clipped Corner Rectangle**.

(continued)

FIGURE 18
Creating a rectangle

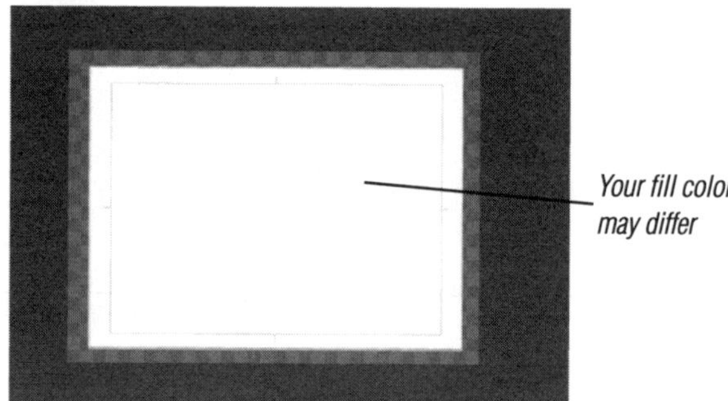

FIGURE 19
Modifying a rectangle

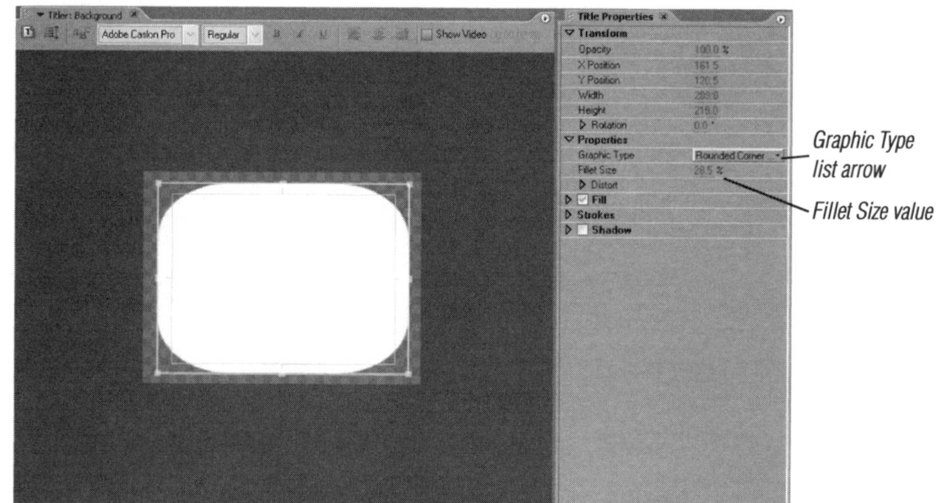

FIGURE 20
Sample of "I'll Fly Away" text

9. Using the Type Tool T, recreate the phrase "I'll Fly Away" using any font, size, style, and formatting that you wish.

   TIP Create the title outside the Safe Action Margin, then drag it on top of the rectangle when finished.

10. Click **Title** on the menu bar, point to **Position**, then click **Horizontal Center**.
11. Repeat Step 9 to center the title vertically.

    Figure 20 shows one sample of this title.
12. Save your work.

You created a new title named Background, created a rectangle that filled the Safe Action Margin, then formatted the rectangle using controls in the Title Properties panel. You then recreated the "I'll Fly Away" text and centered it horizontally and vertically in the Safe Action Margin.

Adjust opacity and create a gradient

1. Click the **Selection Tool** , then click the **"I'll Fly Away" text.**
2. Click the **Opacity value** in the Title Properties panel, then drag the pointer until the value reads 60%.

   TIP You may need to change the fill color of your text if it is too light after adjusting the opacity.

3. Click the **rectangle**, then expand the Fill section on the Title Properties panel, if necessary.
4. Click the **Fill Type list arrow**, then click **Linear Gradient**.
5. Click the **first color stop**, then click the **Color Stop Color box** to open the Color Picker, as shown in Figure 21.
6. Type **0** in the R, G, and B text boxes in the Color Picker, then click **OK**.

   You assigned black to the first color stop. Your screen should resemble Figure 22.

7. Click the **first color stop**, then change the Color Stop Opacity value to 50%.

(continued)

FIGURE 21
Choosing a color for the first color stop

FIGURE 22
A black and white linear gradient

FIGURE 23
Modifying the gradient

Drag color stops to create a similar effect

FIGURE 24
Dragging the Page Peel transition to the beginning of Intro.mov

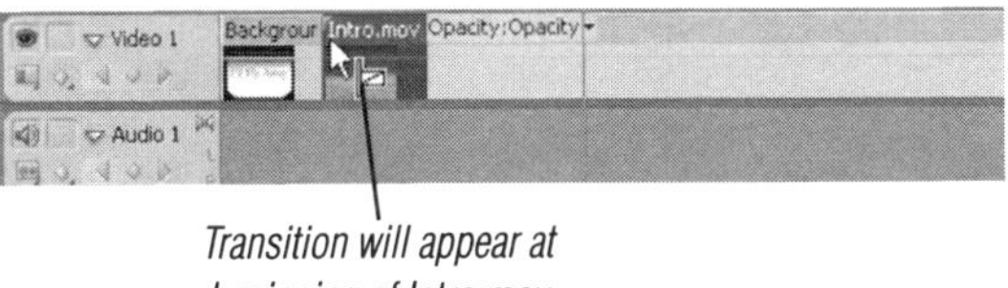

Transition will appear at beginning of Intro.mov

8. Drag the first and second color stops left and right until you are happy with the look of the gradient fill.

   Figure 23 shows one sample of a modified gradient fill.

   > TIP Watch how the gradient fill moves inside the rectangle as you drag the location of each color stop.

9. Close the Titler panel, press and hold **[Ctrl]**, and drag the **Background title** from the Project panel to the beginning of the Video 1 track.
10. Click the **Effects tab** to display the Effect panel, expand the Video Transitions bin, expand the Page Peel bin, drag the **Page Peel transition** to the beginning of Intro.mov, as shown in Figure 24.
11. Change the speed of the Background clip to 1%.
12. Delete Intro Title and Byline from the Video 2 track, then play the movie.
13. Save your work, then close the project.

You modified the opacity of the "I'll Fly Away" text, then created a linear gradient fill for the rectangle behind it. You modified the gradient by changing the opacity of the first color stop and the location where the two colors meet. You added Backround to the beginning of the Video 1 track, added a transition to Intro.mov, deleted the existing title clips from Video 2, then played the movie.

LESSON 3

INSERT LOGOS INTO TITLE DESIGNER

What You'll Do

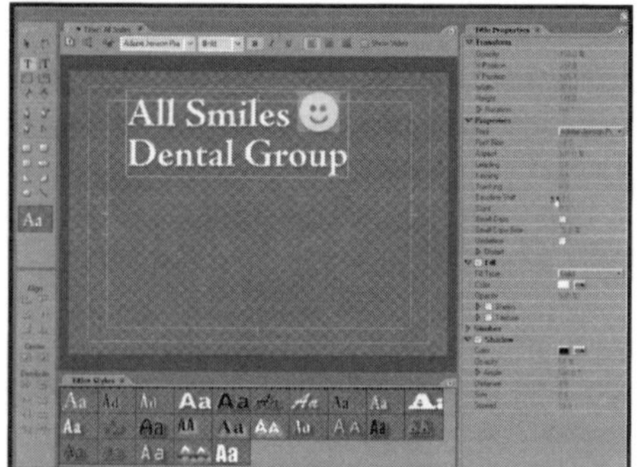

In this lesson, you will insert a logo within a title and adjust its baseline shift.

Inserting Logos

Title Designer allows you to insert your own graphics into the drawing area. Premiere Pro refers to these graphics as **logos**. Figure 25 shows the Import Image as Logo dialog box and a list of the file formats that can be inserted. This is great news for people who create their artwork in other programs, such as Adobe Illustrator or Photoshop. You can insert logos as free-standing objects or you can insert logos within a title so that the logo becomes part of the title. Figure 26 shows an example of a logo inserted into a title in Title Designer.

The smiley face was created in Adobe Illustrator CS2 and inserted into Premiere Pro. When you wish to insert a logo or graphic element within a title, click the Type Tool, click inside the title where you wish to insert the graphic, click Title on the menu bar, point to Logo, then click Insert Logo into Text. When logos are inserted within a title, they are treated just like text. You can change their font size, baseline shift, tracking, kerning and so on. Highlight the logo with the Type Tool and choose formatting options in the Title Properties panel.

FIGURE 25
Import Image as Logo dialog box

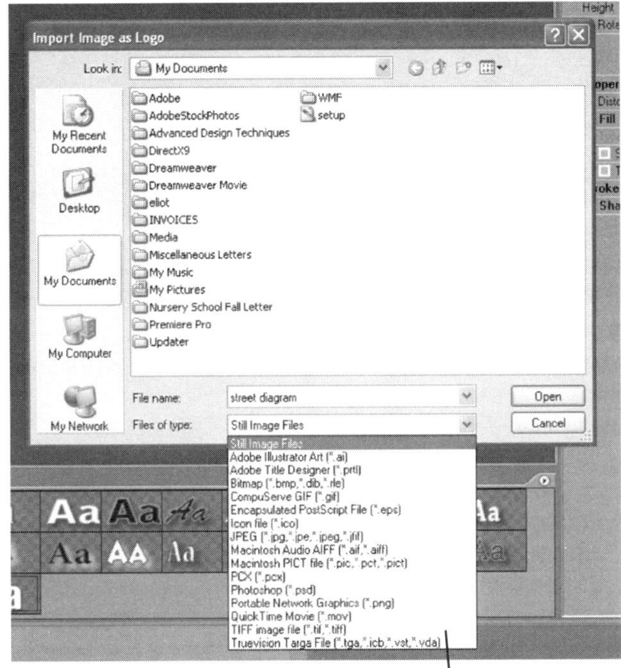

Accepted file formats formats

FIGURE 26
Inserting a logo into a title

Logo inserted into title

Create Crawling and Rolling Text

Title Designer allows you to easily create two standard types of moving text: crawls and rolls. **Crawls** refer to text objects that move horizontally across the screen, like stock quotes that you might see on a financial news channel on television. By default, crawls move from right to left (because Westerners read from left to right).

Even more familiar are **rolls**. They are the most common method for displaying credits at the end of a movie. With a roll, text moves vertically. By default, rolls in Title Designer move from the bottom to the top of the screen.

Crawls and rolls are easy to define in Title Designer. Simply set the title type to either Crawl or Roll in the Title Designer window. Note that crawls and rolls are not exclusive to text. You can create shapes and designs in a title window and set them to crawl or roll.

In most situations, text for crawls and rolls will extend beyond the drawing area in Title Designer. In other words, a sentence that crawls will probably be wider than the drawing area, and lines of text that roll will probably take up more vertical space than is available in the drawing area.

In the best-case scenario, you should define the title type as a roll or a crawl before you begin typing so that you can scroll as you type text that extends beyond the drawing area. If you don't define the type of title first, you won't be able to scroll, and you won't be able to see what you are typing after you've extended the drawing area. To define a title as a roll or a crawl, click Title on the menu bar, point to New Title, then click Default Roll or Default Crawl. Click the Roll/Crawl Options button in the Titler panel to display the Roll/Crawl Options dialog box. This dialog box allows you to further define how you'd like the roll or crawl to display. The length of the title clip in the Timeline determines the speed of the crawl or the roll. The more you increase the length of the title clip, the slower the speed. This is logical: The crawl or the roll has a longer duration to move from the start to the end of the scroll.

Insert a logo into a title

1. Click **File** on the menu bar, point to **New**, then click **Project** or click the **New Project button** in the Adobe Premiere 2.0 window.
2. Type **Logos** in the Name text box of the New Project dialog box, then click **OK**.
3. Click the **New Item button** on the Project panel, click **Title**, type **All Smiles** in the Name text box of the New Title dialog box, then click **OK**.
4. Display the Title Tools panel, if necessary.
5. Click the **Type Tool** T, click the drawing area, type **All Smiles**, then press **[Spacebar]**, as shown in Figure 27.

   Your font, font size, color, and location of "All Smiles" may differ from the figure.
6. Click **Title** on the menu bar, point to **Logo**, then click **Insert Logo into Text**.
7. Navigate to the Source Clips folder, click **Smile.ai**, then click **Open**.

   As shown in Figure 28, a smiley face icon is inserted into the text block. The icon is now part of the title and can be formatted as text.

(continued)

FIGURE 27
Typing All Smiles in the Titler panel

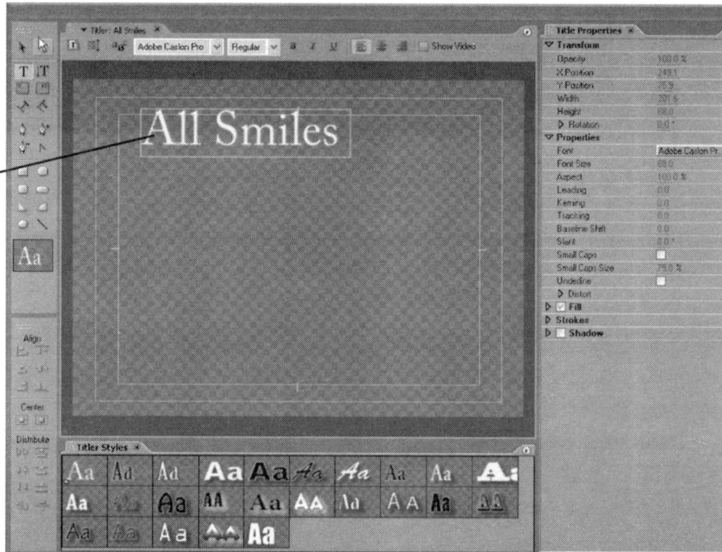

FIGURE 28
Inserting a logo into a title

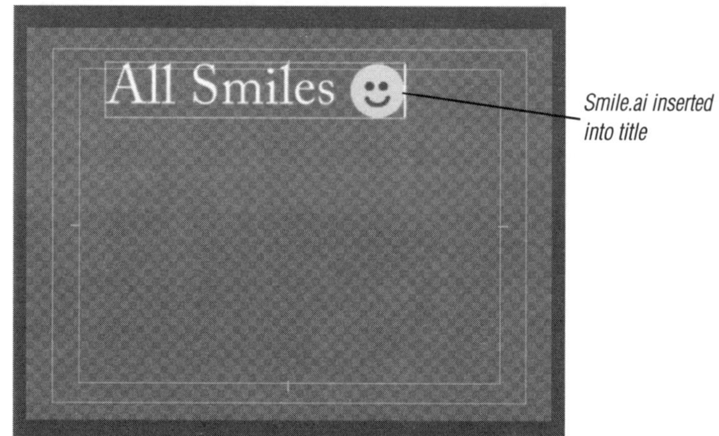

FIGURE 29

Text is highlighted and ready for formatting

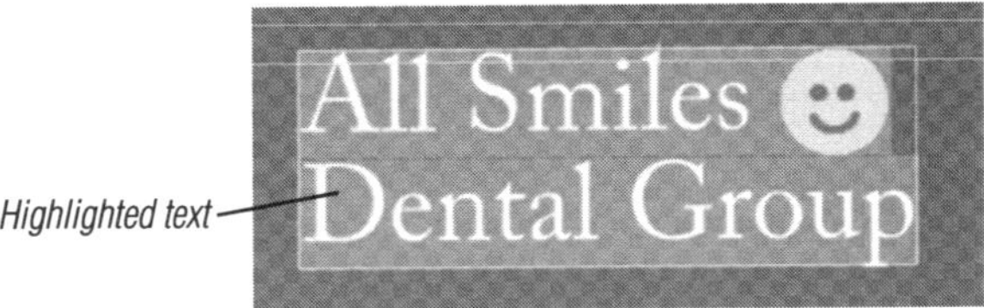

FIGURE 30

Modifying the Baseline Shift value for the icon

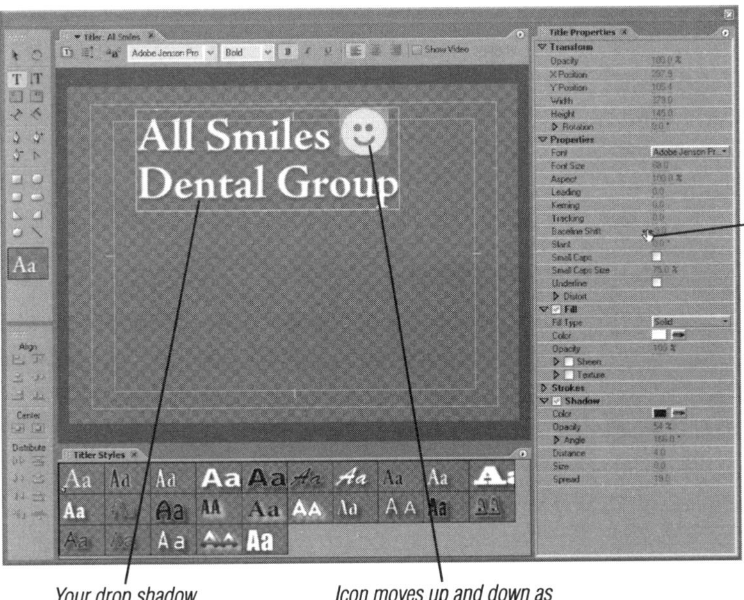

8. Press **[Enter]**, then type **Dental Group** on the next line.
9. Highlight "All Smiles Dental Group" with the Type Tool, as shown in Figure 29.
10. Choose a font of your preference, then add a drop shadow to the text, using any drop shadow settings that you like.

    TIP Use the settings on the Title Properties panel.

11. Click anywhere to deselect, then highlight the smiley face icon only.
12. Position your pointer over the Baseline Shift value in the Title Properties panel, drag it left and right to see the icon move up and down within the text block, as shown in Figure 30, then settle on a baseline shift value that works best for your title.

    Changing the baseline shift allows you to "fix" any potential problems with the design of your title.

13. Save your work, then close Logos.

You created a new title and inserted a logo into it. You then changed the font, added a drop shadow, and changed the baseline shift of the logo.

CHAPTER SUMMARY

Premiere Pro is a video-editing program; however, still images can play a big role in your final movies. Still images are illustrations, text, and bitmap images, all which can be created in other programs and stored in the Project panel. You can also create titles (text) and graphics in Title Designer—a group of five panels that allow you to create and design text and graphics within Premiere Pro. You can create vector graphics with the Pen Tool, create and modify gradient fills and strokes, and even change the opacity of objects. You can insert logos into the drawing area of Title Designer as free-standing objects or as inline graphics within a text block. When working in Title Designer, the Safe Action Margin and Safe Title Margin will help you keep your text and graphics inside the video frame boundaries. You can also choose to view a specific frame of your sequence in the background of the drawing area while you create titles or graphics. This is very helpful when you need to see how one element will be placed against another in your sequence.

What You Have Learned

- How to create text in Title Designer
- How to set the Safe Action Margin
- How to set the Safe Title Margin
- How to format a title using the Title Properties panel
- How to add a title to the Timeline
- How to apply a drop shadow
- How to create a new style
- How to adjust the opacity of a title
- How to create a gradient fill
- How to modify a gradient
- How to insert a logo into a title

Key Terms

Titles Titles are text or graphics that are part of a video program. Titles can be created within Premiere Pro using Title Designer.

Superimpose tracks Superimpose tracks are video tracks that are higher than the Video 1 track.

Safe Title Margin Safe Title Margin indicates the margin inside the drawing area of Title Designer which represents the borders that text needs to stay inside without being cut off.

Safe Action Margin Safe Action Margin indicates the margin inside the drawing area of Title Designer which represents the borders that graphics and video need to stay inside without being cut off.

Opacity The term opacity derives from the word "opaque," which describes an object that is neither transparent nor translucent—that is, not "see through."

Gradient Gradients are multicolored fills in which one color blends to another.

chapter 8

WORKING WITH VIDEO EFFECTS

1. Work with video effects.
2. Use advanced video effect techniques.
3. Use Keying effects.

chapter 8 WORKING WITH VIDEO EFFECTS

Video effects are fun. Does that really need to be said? Of course they're fun. Premiere Pro offers a number of built-in effects that allow you to manipulate the clips in your program in ways that will stretch your imagination. Distortion effects let you bend, pinch, and twirl a video clip—you can make the video appear to flow in waves or to ripple out from the center, like ripples on a pond. Blur effects do just that—blur the footage in the clip, like those used to introduce dream sequences in old movies or TV shows. You can also use them to add the effect of motion to a clip, as though something is going by so fast, "it's a blur."

Video effects are also practical. A number of effects are very useful for performing necessary tasks. The Adjust effects are a very important component of the application—they allow you to control the appearance of a clip, including the color balance and the brightness and contrast. The Levels effect gives you enormous control over the color range of the image—from shadows to highlights. The Image Control effects include Black & White, Tint, and Color Balance to name a few. The Black & White effect converts a color clip to black and white, and you can use the Tint effect to apply an overall tint to a clip. The Color Balance effect lets you adjust the hue, saturation, and lightness values of the footage.

Like transitions, video effects are applied to clips by dragging them from the Effects panel to clips in the Timeline. And also like transitions, you can modify video effects using the Effect Controls panel.

So, welcome to Chapter 8, which introduces you to quite a number of these effects. You've worked long and hard to get here. Now you're ready to work with video effects—not to just play and have fun (which you will!), but also to understand the practical and essential role effects will play in your projects.

Tools You'll Use

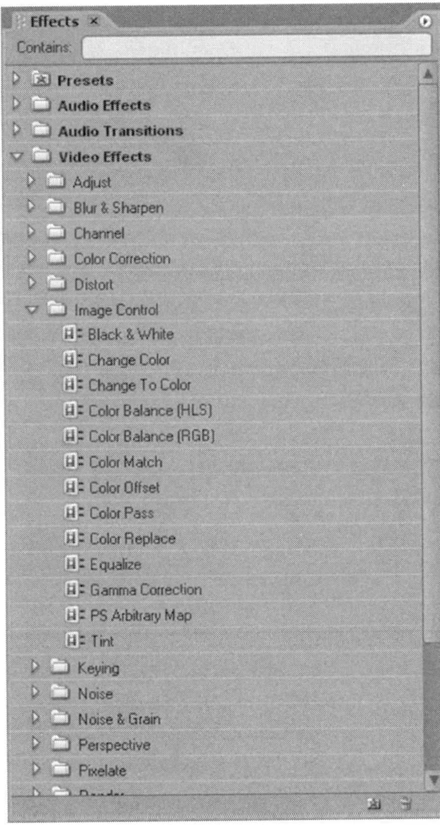

WORK WITH VIDEO EFFECTS

What You'll Do

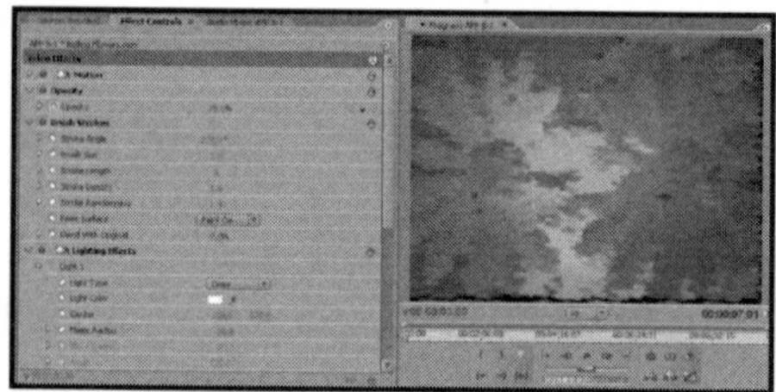

In this lesson, you will apply effects to clips and modify them in the Effect Controls panel.

Working with the Effects Panel

Premiere Pro is shipped with 17 categories of video effects that you can apply to clips in your program. **Video effects** add special visual characteristics to a clip, such as blurs, distortions, or color changes. Many effects offer simple, practical solutions. For example, the Color Balance and the Brightness & Contrast effects allow you to easily adjust the image display, much as you would on your television or on a computer monitor.

Video effects are grouped into categories in the Effects panel. You can expand a category bin to see all of the effects in that category by clicking the triangle next to the category name. In Figure 1, the Image Control bin is expanded to show the Image Control video effects. With so many video

FIGURE 1

Expanded Image Control bin in the Effects panel

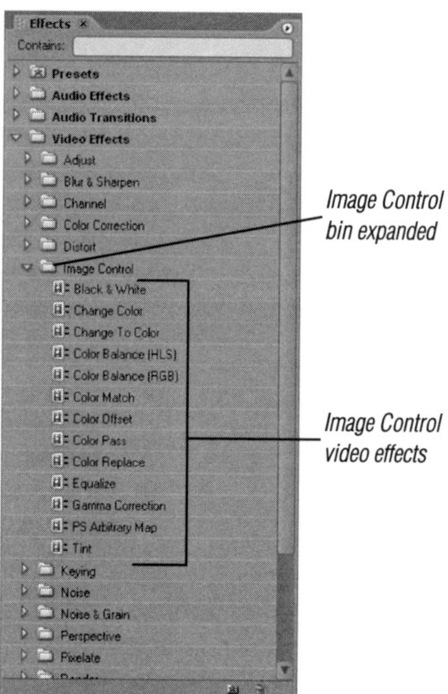

effects, you may find it hard to find a specific one or you may forget which bin it's in. You can type the video effect name or part of it into the Contains text box on the Effects panel. Every bin that contains a video effect with the text you typed in the Contains text box opens, as shown in Figure 2. In this example "Color" was typed in the Contains text box. Notice all of the possible "Color" video effects. Once you locate those hard-to-find video effects, you should consider placing them in a custom bin. You can store the effects that you use often in a custom bin by clicking the New Custom Bin button on the Effects panel, naming the folder, then storing the effects inside it. Creating custom bins gives you easy access to your favorite effects and eliminates the search process.

Applying Video Effects

You apply video effects the same way you apply video transitions: Drag them from the Effects panel onto clips in the Timeline. When you do so, a green bar appears above the clip, and the effect is listed in the Effect Controls panel. Another method for applying an effect to a clip is to select the clip in the Timeline, then drag the video effect that you want to apply to that clip directly into the Effect Controls panel.

The effect is active for the duration of the clip.

If you are planning to work with effects on a regular basis, or if you have a project that calls for effects, it's a good idea to use the Effects workspace. In the Effects workspace, the Effects panel is positioned directly to the left of the Timeline and the Effect Controls panel is displayed directly above the Timeline.

FIGURE 2

Finding a video effect quickly using the Contains text box

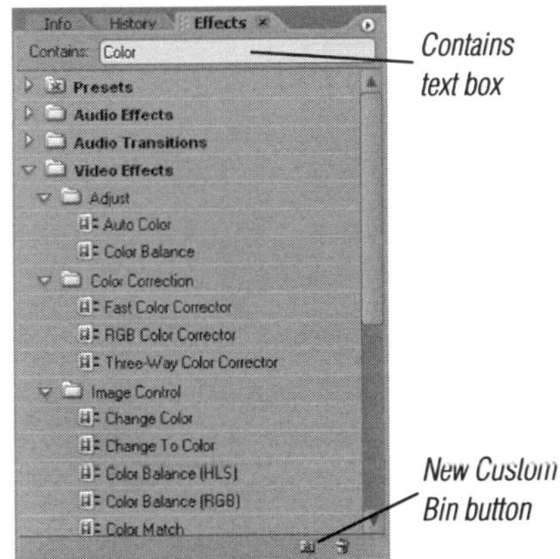

Modifying Video Effects

Like transitions, video effects are modified in the Effect Controls panel, making the Effects workspace very convenient. You must first expand the video effect name in the Effect Controls panel to view its settings. While you adjust video effect settings in the Effect Controls panel, you can view how the changes affect the clip in the Program Monitor. Figure 3 shows the Effects workspace with the Ripple video effect applied to the Balloons BW clip and the Ripple video effect settings in the Effect Controls panel. The Ripple effect has a number of options for modifying the effect.

The results of modifying a video effect can be seen immediately in the Program Monitor.

> **QUICKTIP**
>
> Click the Reset button next to a video effect in the Effect Controls panel to restore the default settings.

FIGURE 3

The Ripple video effect applied to Balloons BW

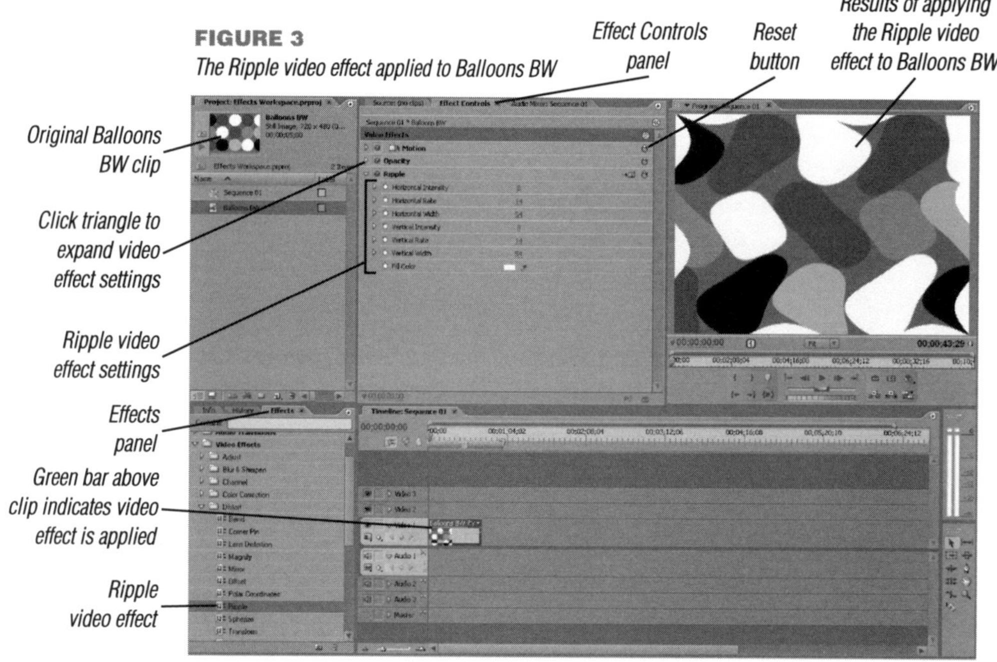

The Effect Controls panel lists each effect applied to a selected clip. When you apply an effect to a clip, the effect is—by default—active in the Effect Controls panel, as indicated by the Toggle the Effect On or Off icon. Figure 4 shows that Balloons BW now has the Lighting Effects video effect also applied to it. Click the Toggle the Effect On or Off icon to turn a video effect on or off without deleting it. This is handy when you are deciding whether you want to use a video effect or not. When you are sure you want to delete an effect, select the video effect, click the Effect Controls panel list arrow, then click Delete Selected Effect. Or, you can click Delete All Effects from Clip to remove all video effects from a clip.

QUICKTIP

Click the Show/Hide Timeline View button on the Effect Controls panel to view the Timeline location of the clip you are working with.

Some effects by their very nature cannot be customized. The Black & White effect, for example, is either active or not active—there's nothing to adjust. You'll know when a video effect does not have settings when the triangle icon does not appear next to the video effect name.

FIGURE 4

Two video effects listed in the Effect Controls panel

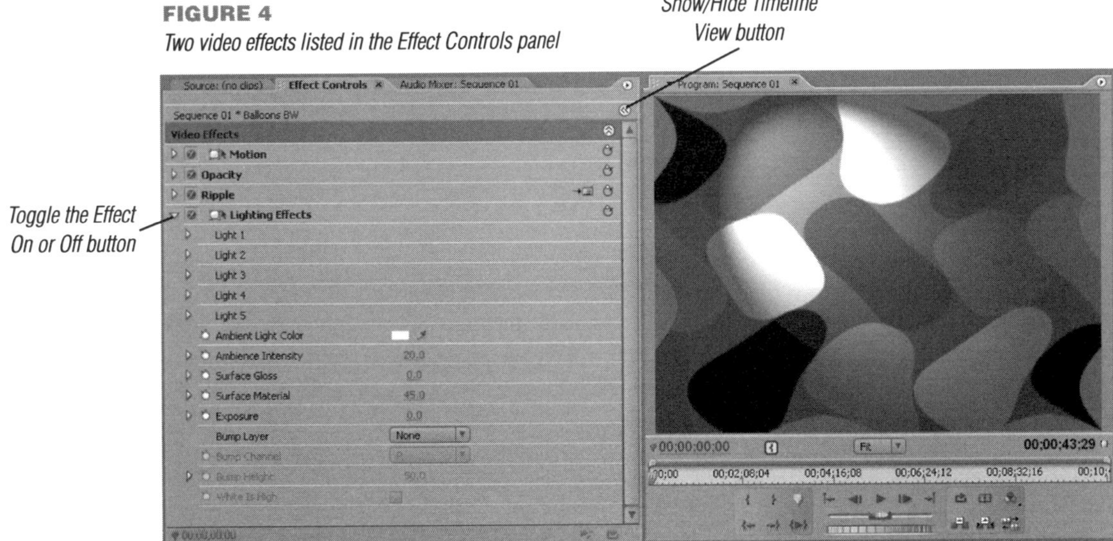

Some effects have the Setup button next to the effect name in the Effect Controls panel. Clicking the Setup button opens a Settings dialog box full of options for customizing the particular effect. Figure 5 shows the Levels Settings dialog box.

FIGURE 5

Clicking the Setup button opens the Levels Settings dialog box for the Levels video effect

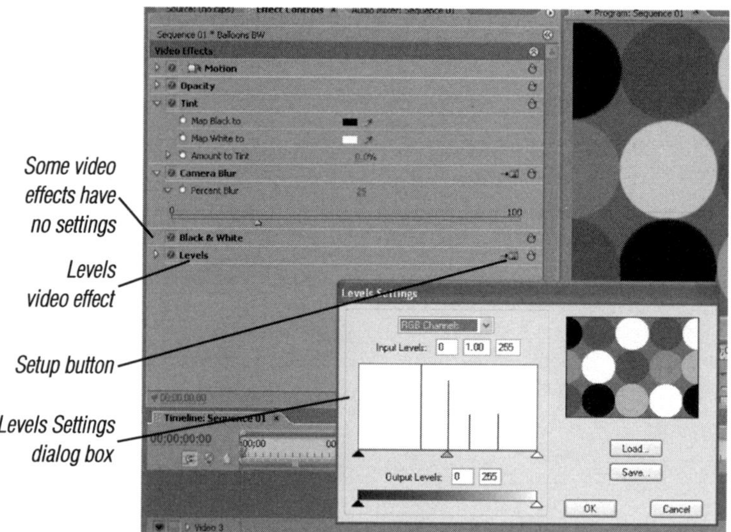

Create Custom Presets

Similar to creating custom bins to store frequently used effects, you can create **presets**—a group of specific video effect settings. Presets can be made from one or more video effects in the Effect Controls panel. For example, imagine that you have a project in which you need to convert hundreds of still clips to black and white, then map all of the black pixels to a specific color. You could select the Black & White video effect, then the Tint effect with the correct Map Black To setting, click the Effect Controls panel list arrow, then click Save Preset. Once named, the new preset is stored in the Presets bin in the Effects panel. To apply a preset, simply drag it onto a clip. To view the properties of a preset, click the clip in the Timeline that has the preset applied to it, then view the preset properties in the Effect Controls panel.

Applying the Emboss Effect

The Emboss effect, found in the Stylize bin, removes the color from an image and replaces it with a predominantly gray fill. The effect makes the clip appear stamped or raised by tracing the image's edges with white for the highlights and black for the shadows. Figure 6 shows the Emboss effect applied to a video frame. The effect is very dramatic when applied to text, as shown in Figure 7.

FIGURE 6
Emboss effect applied to a video frame

Image before Emboss effect applied

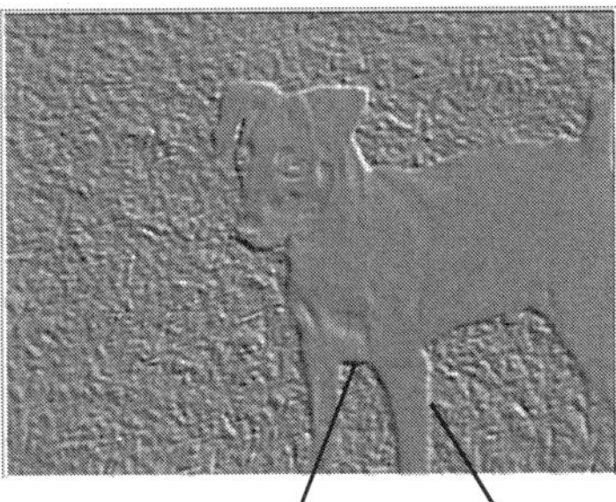

Black shadow

White highlight

FIGURE 7
Emboss effect applied to text

Text before Emboss effect applied

Modifying an Embossed Clip with the Levels Effect

The Levels effect allows you to manipulate the color of a clip's pixels. With digital imagery and video, pixels are assigned a number. In a black-and-white image, each pixel has a number from 0–255, with 0 being black, 255 being white, and 128 being the gray midpoint. The Levels effect manipulates the color of a clip's pixels by manipulating these numbers.

You can create special effects, like the example shown in Figure 8, by combining the Levels effect with transparency keys. You'll learn about transparency keys in Lesson 3.

In this example gray pixels were removed, the white highlights and black shadows were isolated, then the title was superimposed over a background image.

Modifying the Opacity of a Clip

By now you've probably noticed that clips in the Timeline have the word Opacity in the clip icon. This is especially noticeable when you zoom in on the Timeline, as shown in Figure 9. All clips have default Opacity and Motion settings applied. (See Chapter 9 to learn about motion and animation.) Changing the opacity of a clip makes it more "see-through." Opacity is modified in the Effect Controls panel the same way you modify a video effect. Simply expand the Opacity setting, then change the Opacity value or drag the thin orange line within the clip up or down to change the opacity setting. A tooltip appears as you drag, displaying the current value.

FIGURE 8
Using transparency and the Levels effect together

Gray pixels are made transparent using the Levels effect

FIGURE 9
Default Opacity applied to clips

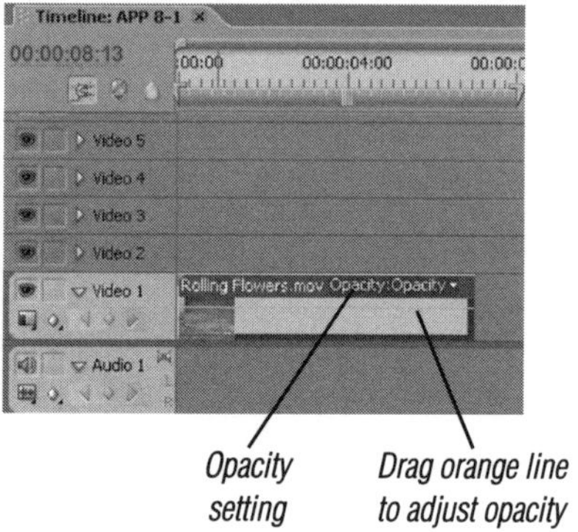

Opacity setting

Drag orange line to adjust opacity

Understanding the Color Balance (HLS) Effect

Every frame in a video program is composed of colored pixels. Color in a pixel is defined by three properties: hue, lightness, and saturation. The **hue** is the name of the color; yellow and green are hues. Digital imagery uses a color model based on a color wheel that has 360 hues available to define a pixel. Each pixel is defined by only one hue. **Lightness** and **saturation** modify the pixel's hue. Lightness has a range from 0–100 that darkens or lightens a hue. A lightness value of 100 creates a white pixel, regardless of the hue. A lightness value of 0 creates a black pixel.

Saturation has a range from 0–100 that identifies the intensity of the pixel. The greater the saturation value, the more intense the color of the pixel would be. The Color Balance (HLS) effect allows you to manipulate the hue, lightness, and saturation values of a clip. This effect can be used for practical purposes, such as increasing the saturation value slightly to intensify the color of a dull clip. It can also be used for dramatic color effects, such as changing the hues of all the pixels in a clip. Don't confuse the Color Balance (HLS) effect with the Color Balance effect. The former allows you to manipulate a clip's hue, saturation, and lightness values. With the latter, you manipulate the clip's RGB values.

Apply video effects

1. Open APP 8-1.prproj, save it as **Third Eye Yoga**, then play the movie.
2. Click **Window** on the menu bar, point to **Workspace**, then click **Effects**.
3. Position the Current time indicator at frame 3:00.
4. Zoom in on the Timeline, search for the Brush Strokes video effect in the Effects panel, then drag **Brush Strokes** onto Rolling Flowers.mov in the Video 1 track.

   A green bar appears at the top of the clip icon, denoting that an effect has been applied to the clip, and the effect is listed in the Effect Controls panel, as shown in Figure 10.
5. Expand the Brush Strokes effect in the Effect Controls panel.
6. Change the Brush Size to 3.0.

(continued)

FIGURE 10
Applying the Brush Strokes effect

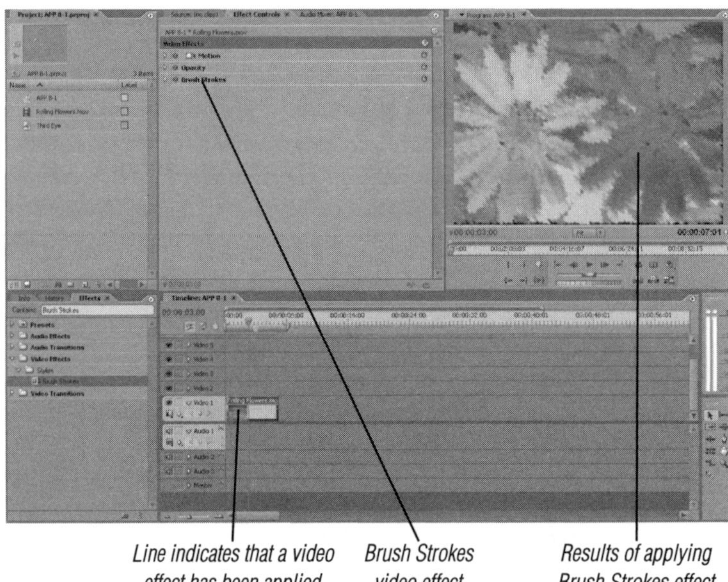

FIGURE 11
Effect Controls panel

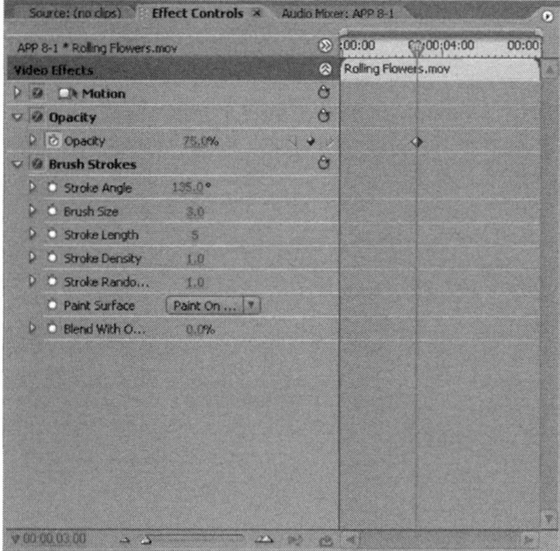

FIGURE 12
The Omni light type applied to Rolling Flowers.mov

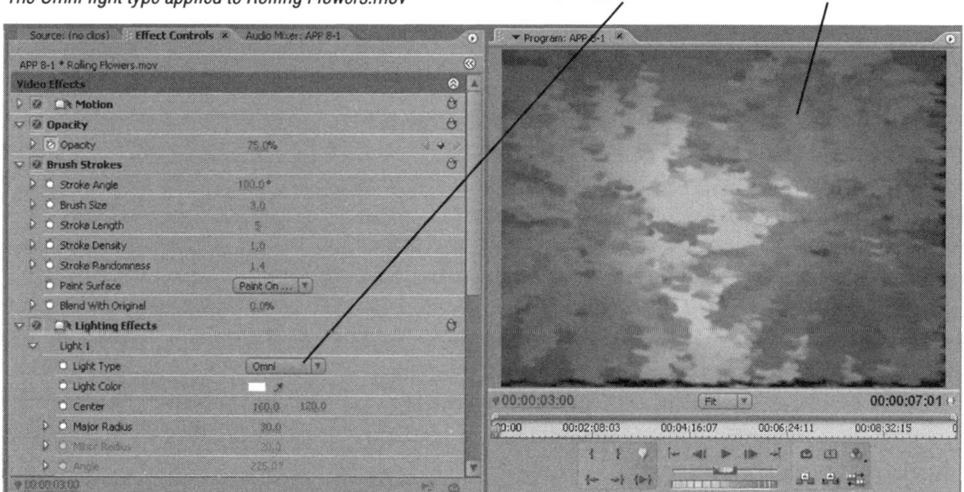

7. Expand the Opacity effect, then change the Opacity setting to 75%.

   Compare your Effect Controls panel to Figure 11.

8. Search for the Lighting Effects video effect, then drag it to the Effect Controls panel.

9. Expand Lighting Effects in the Effect Controls panel, expand Light 1, click the **Light Type list arrow**, then click **Omni**.

   The view in your Program Monitor should resemble Figure 12.

   TIP Unlike the figure in the book, your image will be in color.

10. Press **[Home]** then drag the **Current time indicator** over the Timeline to "scrub" the sequence.

11. Save your work.

You applied the Brush Strokes video effect to Rolling Flowers.mov by dragging it from the Effects panel onto the clip in the Timeline, then you applied the Lighting Effects video effect to the selected Rolling Flowers.mov clip by dragging the effect to the Effect Controls panel.

Modify video effects

1. Click **Rolling Flowers.mov** in the Video 1 track, if necessary.
2. Collapse the Brush Strokes effect in the Effect Controls panel.
3. Scroll down in the Effect Controls panel until you see Ambience Intensity, then expand Ambience Intensity.
4. Drag the **Ambience Intensity slider** to 60.0, then drag the **Current time indicator** to frame 4:10.
5. Compare your screen to Figure 13, then save your work.

You modified the settings of the Lighting Effects video effect to adjust the Ambience Intensity setting.

FIGURE 13
Modifying the Lighting Effects video effect

Ambience Intensity setting

FIGURE 14

Emboss video effect applied to the Third Eye clip

FIGURE 15

Renaming the Video 2 and Video 3 tracks

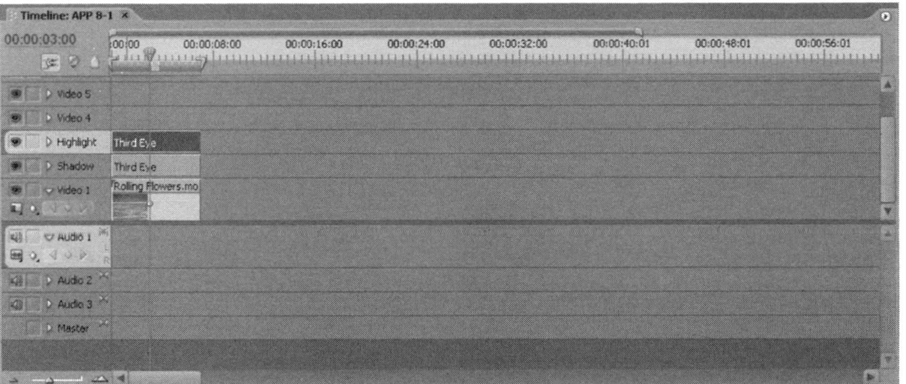

Apply the Emboss effect and rename tracks

1. Drag the **Third Eye title clip** from the Project panel to the beginning of the Video 2 track.
2. Find the Emboss video effect, and drag it onto Third Eye in the Video 2 track.

   Your Program Monitor should resemble Figure 14.

   TIP Adjust the font size of the Third Eye title clip if your text is larger then the text displayed in Figure 14.

3. Expand the Emboss effect, then expand the Relief setting in the Effect Controls panel.
4. Drag the **Relief slider** in the Effect Controls panel back and forth as you watch the changes in the Program Monitor, then settle on a value of .75.
5. Drag another instance of Third Eye to the Video 3 track, directly above Third Eye in the Video 2 track.
6. Repeat Steps 2–4 to apply the Emboss effect to the clip in the Video 3 track.
7. Right-click **Video 3** in the Timeline, then click **Rename**.
8. Type **Highlight**, then press **[Enter]**.
9. Rename the Video 2 track **Shadow**.
10. Compare your Timeline to Figure 15, then save your work.

You applied the Emboss effect to two title clips, modified the Relief value for each, then renamed the two tracks that each contain an embossed title.

Modify an embossed clip with the Levels effect

1. Click the **Toggle Track Output button** in the Highlight track to hide the track contents.
2. Find the Levels video effect in the Video panel, then drag it onto Third Eye in the Shadow track.
3. Click the **Setup button** beside Levels in the Effect Controls panel to open the Levels Settings dialog box.
4. Drag the **white triangle** in the Input Levels section left, until the rightmost Input Levels text box reads 128, as shown in Figure 16, then click **OK**.

   Each pixel in the image with a numerical value of 128 or higher will be white, thus isolating the black pixels against a white background.
5. Apply the Multiply Key effect, then drag the Current time indicator over the contents in the Timeline.

   Your Program Monitor should resemble Figure 17.

   > TIP When using the Multiply Key effect, anything multiplied with black becomes black, and anything multiplied with white retains its color. See more about transparency keys in Lesson 3.

(continued)

FIGURE 16
Levels Settings dialog box

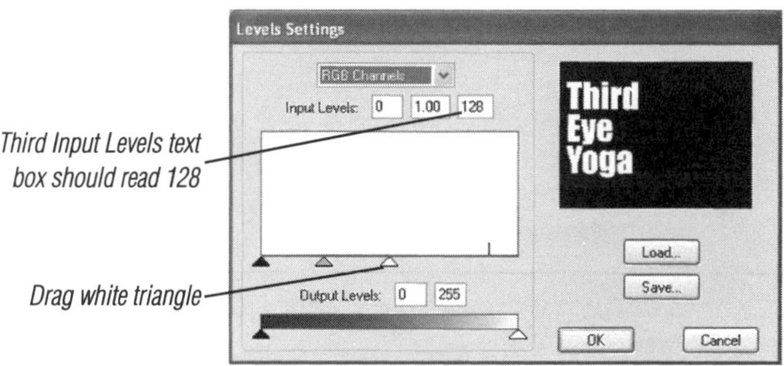

FIGURE 17
Showing the shadow against the image

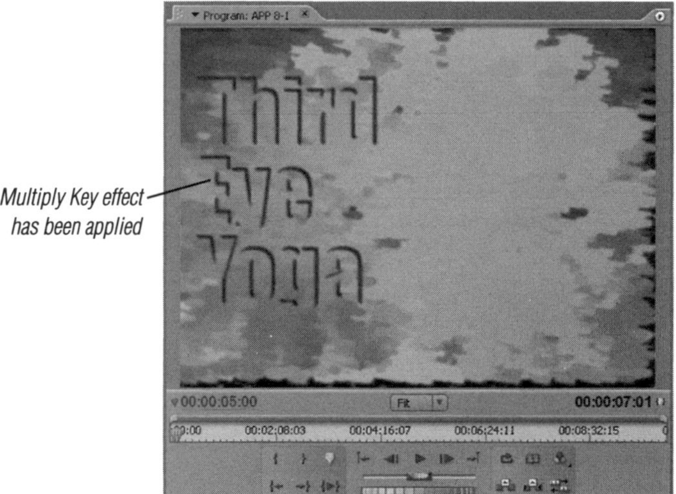

FIGURE 18
Isolating the white pixels against a black background

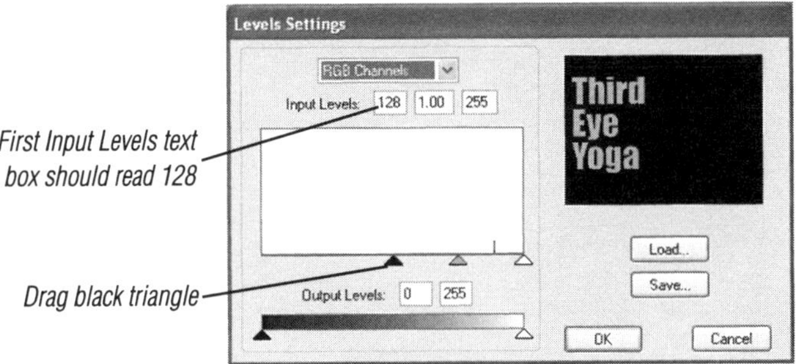

FIGURE 19
Showing the shadow and the highlight

6. Click the **Toggle Track Output button** (in its off state) in the Highlight track to show the track contents, click **Third Eye** in the Highlight track, then drag the **Levels effect** into the Effect Controls panel.
7. Click the **Setup button** next to Levels in the Effect Controls panel, drag the **black triangle** in the Input Levels section right until the leftmost Input Levels text box reads 128, as shown in Figure 18, then click **OK**.

   Each pixel in the image with a numerical value of 128 or lower will be black, thus isolating the white pixels against a black background.
8. Apply the Screen Key effect to Third Eye in the Highlight track, then generate a preview.

   Your Program Monitor should resemble Figure 19.

   TIP The Screen Key effect functions as the opposite of the Multiply Key. See Lesson 3 for more about transparency keys.
9. Close the project.

You manipulated two embossed clips with the Levels effect. For the first embossed clip, you isolated the black pixels against a white background, then applied the Multiply Key to make the white pixels transparent. For the second embossed clip, you isolated the white pixels against a black background, then applied the Screen Key effect to make the black pixels transparent.

LESSON 2

USE ADVANCED VIDEO EFFECT TECHNIQUES

What You'll Do

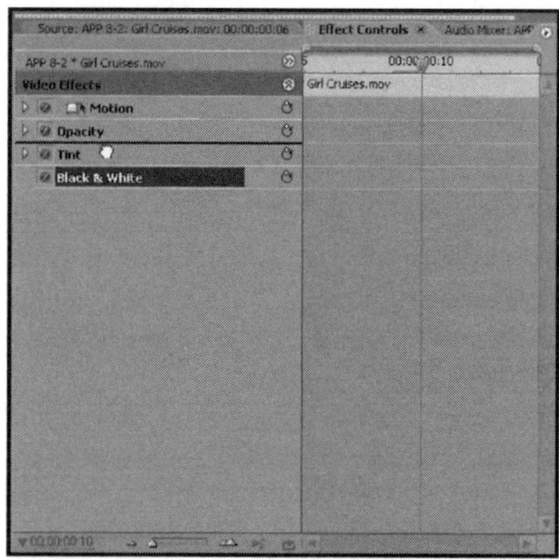

In this lesson, you will learn skills for managing effects, including how to sequence effects to achieve a specific result and how to copy effects between clips.

Understanding the Tint Effect

The Tint effect is very useful for applying an overall tint or "colorizing" a clip. Often, the effect desired from the Tint effect is created by applying the effect to a black-and-white image.

Using the Tint effect, you can alter the color information of an image or a clip using the controls in the Effect Controls panel. You use the Map Black To button to assign a different color to the darker pixels of the clip, and you use the Map White To button to assign a different color to the lighter pixels. Intermediate pixels are assigned intermediate values. The Amount slider specifies the intensity of the effect.

Changing the Order of Applied Effects

The order in which you apply multiple effects will determine the resulting appearance of the clip. When you apply the first effect, it appears at the top of the Effect Controls panel. When you apply the next effect, it appears below the first effect in the Effect Controls panel. Premiere Pro applies effects in sequence, starting with the effect at the top of the Effect Controls panel. You can change the order of effects in the Effect Controls panel by dragging effects above and below one another. Figure 20 shows an example of a clip with two effects applied to it. Since the Black & White effect is applied after the Tint effect, the Tint effect is nullified.

Understanding the Color Replace Effect

The Color Replace effect produces results that are similar to that of the Tint effect. However, the Color Replace effect uses a different procedure to produce the effect. Using the Color Replace effect, you replace all the occurrences of a sampled pixel with a different color. You can increase the similarity value to broaden the range of pixels—in addition to the sampled color—that will be replaced with the new color. By default, the lightness values of the replaced pixels are maintained; thus the effect is achieved by changing only the hue of the pixels. The result is the same as multiplying a color over specific areas of an image.

You can override the default function that preserves the replaced pixels' lightness value by clicking the Solid Colors check box in the Color Replace Settings dialog box. The replaced pixels take on the replacement color's hue and its lightness value.

Copying Effects between Clips

Once you have applied an effect or a series of effects to a clip, it is easy to apply those effects—with their identical settings—to other clips. The Paste Attributes command on the Edit menu allows you to paste effects from one clip to another.

> TIP You can also use the Paste Attributes command to copy opacity settings and motion settings between clips.

Changing Video Effect Settings in the Timeline

Just as you can adjust opacity in the Timeline by dragging the thin orange line up or down, you can also adjust the individual settings that are available with applied video effects. Each clip shows the Opacity setting in the clip title, by default. Click Opacity to view a drop-down menu with all of the video effects applied to the clip. Notice in Figure 21, two effects are applied to the clip: Tint and Black & White. Black & White is unavailable (or grayed out) because it does not offer any settings. However, the three Tint settings appear as a submenu. Because the Amount to Tint setting is chosen, Amount to Tint replaces Opacity in the clip icon. Dragging the orange line will now affect the Amount to Tint setting and the new value will be reflected in the Effect Controls panel.

FIGURE 20

Black & White effect nullifies the Tint effect

FIGURE 21

Making changes to video effects in the Timeline

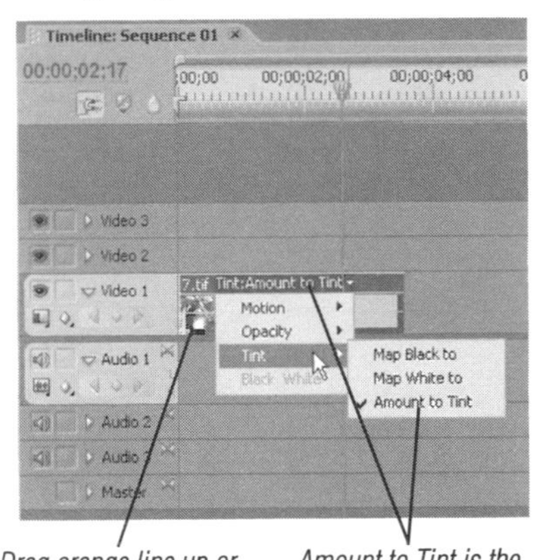

Drag orange line up or down to change the Amount to Tint value in the Tint video effect

Amount to Tint is the active setting

Apply the Tint effect

1. Open APP 8-3.prproj, then save it as **A Day at the Races**.
2. Zoom in on the Timeline and click **Girl Cruises.mov** in the Video 1 track.
3. Drag the **Current time indicator** to frame 10:00.
4. Find the Tint effect, drag it into the Effect Controls panel, expand the Tint effect, then click the **Map Black To button** to open the Color Picker dialog box.
5. Create a color that is 120R/36G/0B, then click **OK**.
6. Click **0.0%** next to Amount to Tint, type **36** in its place, then press **[Enter]**.

   Notice on your Program Monitor, the dark areas of the image are brown instead of black. See Figure 22.
7. Save your work.

You applied the Tint effect to a clip, changing the shadow areas of the image to a brown hue.

FIGURE 22
Applying the Tint effect to Girl Cruises.mov

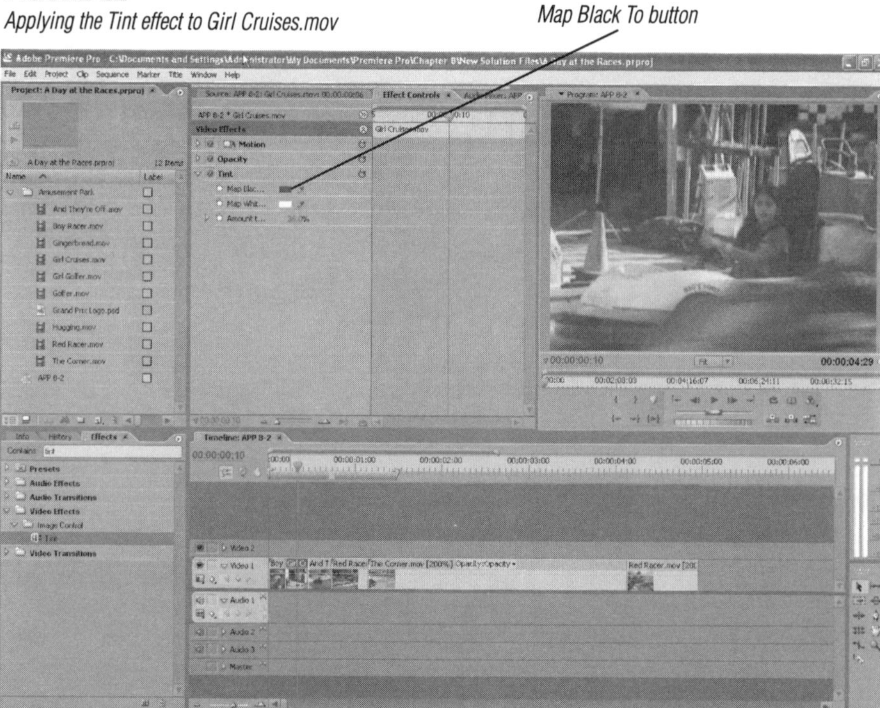

FIGURE 23
Black & White effect nullifies the Tint effect

FIGURE 24
Changing the order of effects in the Effect Controls panel

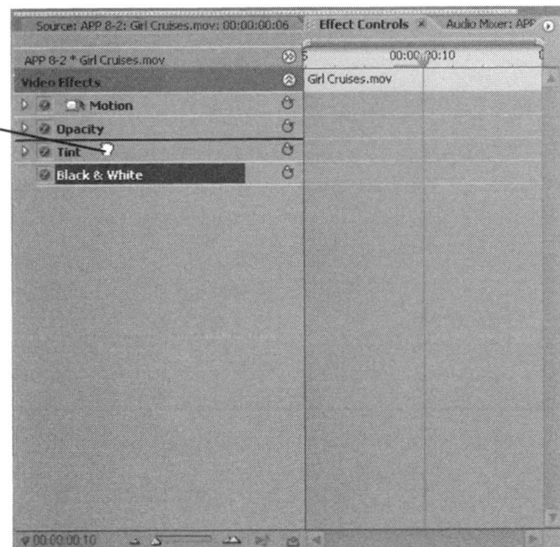

Change the order of applied effects

1. Verify that Girl Cruises.mov is selected, then drag the **Black & White effect** to the Effect Controls panel.

   As shown in Figure 23, the tint is lost to the Black & White effect.
2. Collapse the Tint effect in the Effect Controls panel.
3. Using Figure 24 as a guide, drag the **Black & White effect** above the Tint effect in the Effect Controls panel, then release the mouse pointer.
4. Click the **Show/Hide Timeline View button** , if necessary, to show the Timeline in the Effect Controls panel.
5. Drag the **Current time indicator** in the Effect Controls panel.

   The view in your Program Monitor shows that the Tint effect is applied after the Black & White effect. The new brown tint replaces all of the black pixels in the image.
6. Save your work.

You applied the Black & White effect, then repositioned it above the Tint effect in the Effect Controls panel, causing the tint to be applied after the Black & White effect.

Use the Color Replace effect

1. Verify that Girl Cruises.mov is selected, then find and drag the **Color Replace effect** to the Effect Controls panel.
2. Click the **Setup button** next to Color Replace to open the Color Replace Settings dialog box.
3. Move the pointer over the Clip Sample image, then click the **Eyedropper pointer** in the location shown in Figure 25.

   The Target Color button changes to show a white color sampled from the Clip Sample window.
4. Click the **Replace Color button**, create a color that is 255R/255G/175B, then click **OK**.

   As shown on your screen the new color is a light yellow.
5. Drag the **Similarity slider** to 48 so that your Color Replace Settings dialog box resembles Figure 26, then click **OK**.

   48 colors that are similar to the target color will be replaced with the replace color.
6. Save your work.

You used the Color Replace effect to change the highlight colors of a clip.

FIGURE 25
Sampling a color to be replaced

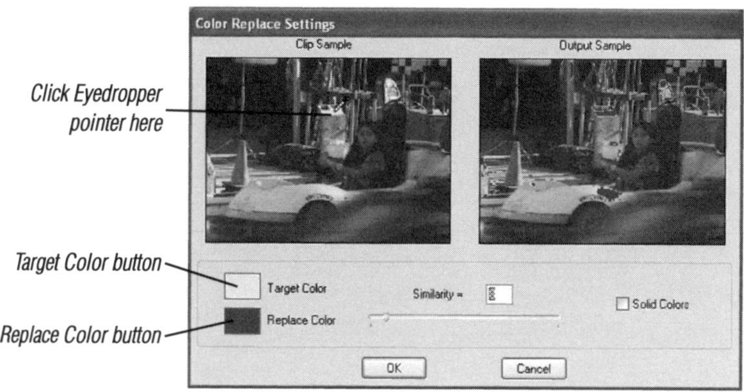

FIGURE 26
All Target Color pixels will be replaced by the Replace Color pixels

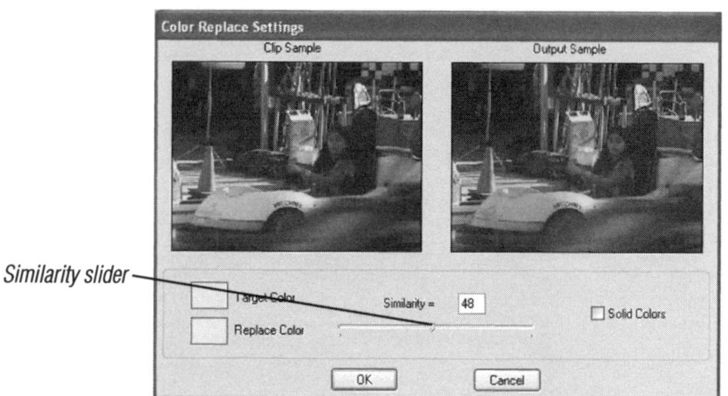

FIGURE 27

Removing all effects from And They're Off.mov

Effects are removed from And They're Off.mov

The view in your Program Monitor will show And They're Off.mov in color

Copy video effects between clips

1. Verify that Girl Cruises.mov is selected in the Timeline, click **Edit** on the menu bar, then click **Copy**.
2. Click **Boy Racer.mov** (the first clip in the Timeline), click **Edit** on the menu bar, then click **Paste Attributes**.
3. Drag the **Current time indicator** over Boy Racer.mov in the Timeline or in the Effect Controls panel.

   The same video effects are applied to Boy Racer.mov.
4. Click the **Track Select Tool**, then click **And They're Off.mov** in the Timeline to select it and the remaining clips in the Timeline.
5. Click **Edit** on the menu bar, then click **Paste Attributes** again.

   The video effects are applied to all clips in the sequence.
6. Click the **Selection Tool**, click the **Timeline** to deselect all, click **And They're Off.mov** in the Timeline, click the **Effect Controls panel list arrow**, then click **Delete All Effects from Clip**.

   As shown in Figure 27, And They're Off.mov has no effects applied to it in the Effect Controls panel.
7. Play the movie, save your work, then close the project.

You copied the effects from one clip and applied them to all of the clips in the sequence using the Paste Attributes command. You then selected one clip and removed all effects from it.

LESSON 3

USE KEYING EFFECTS

What You'll Do

In this lesson, you will experiment with the transparency keys.

Understanding Transparency Keys

When editing video, you can show one clip through another using transparency. A clip with 100% opacity is completely opaque. A clip with 0% opacity is completely transparent, allowing other clips to show through it. Clips with opacity percentages higher than 0% and lower than 100% are semitransparent. Clips below them become partially visible, creating the effect that you are watching two clips simultaneously. Using a transition that fades one clip into another is an example of transparency at work.

You use transparency keys to make specific parts of an image transparent. Transparency keys work by identifying pixels in an image that match a predefined color and making those pixels transparent or semitransparent. Keys are essential to the process of compositing. To create special effects, a subject or a scene is shot against a color screen. Once the video is digitized, the color screen is made transparent—or "keyed out"—using a transparency key. The remaining nontransparent elements are then placed over a second clip—usually a background of some sort, often a hand-painted still image—and the result is a composite. The new background is visible wherever the first clip is transparent, and the effect is that the foreground is truly a part of and belongs with the background.

Working with transparency is a blast. It challenges your ability to think creatively and strategically. It also gives you the opportunity to create some really cool special effects.

Making Clips Transparent

Superimposing means playing one clip on top of another. In Premiere Pro, when one clip is superimposed over another, only the clip in the topmost video track is displayed when you preview or export your final movie. When you add a clip to a superimposed track, you can add transparency so that the clips beneath it partially appear as well.

> TIP You cannot apply transparency to clips in the Video 1 track.

You will often hear superimposing referred to as **keying** or **matting**; in fact, Premiere Pro uses the term "Keying" to categorize the keys in the Effects panel, as shown in Figure 28. The 17 methods for creating transparency in the Keying bin are referred to as **keys**. You choose a key based on the types of clips you are working with, their content, and the type of effect you are trying to achieve.

FIGURE 28

Keying effects in the Effects panel

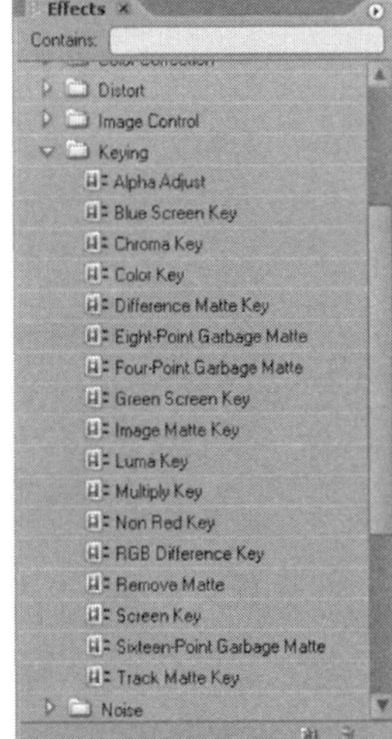

Using Keys

You use keys for a variety of purposes. Keys are sophisticated enough to allow you to "key out" specific areas of a frame. See Table 1 for a description of some commonly used keys.

When you work with titles, remember that they are created with a default transparency that results in a transparent background; only the objects with fill colors you create in Title Designer will appear when you preview. However, if you want to add a transparency key to a title, the transparent background loses its default transparency and functions as a black background.

Using the Multiply Key Effect

You use the Multiply Key effect when you want to make one clip transparent and superimpose it over another. With the Multiply Key effect, you are not keying out anything from the clip. Instead, you are changing the clip from functioning as opaque to functioning as transparent. When you use the Multiply Key effect, some degree of darkening occurs in the image as a result of the overlapping colors. There are two important points to remember when using the Multiply Key effect: Anything multiplied with black becomes black, and anything multiplied with white retains its color.

Using the Garbage Matte Effect

The Garbage Matte effect is found in the Keying bin of the Video Effects bin; however, its job is not to key anything. Instead, its job is to crop an undesirable element from your clip. You won't find "Key" in wthe Garbage Matte name. The Garbage Matte effect is available in Four-Point or Eight-Point. In Figure 29, the Eight-Point Garbage Matte effect is applied to the still image. Notice that there are eight selection handles around the image in the Program Monitor. The Four-Point Garbage Matte effect offers four selection handles. To see these handles, you must first select the effect name in the Effect Controls panel, then manipulate the handles as needed in the Program Monitor.

FIGURE 29

Results of applying the Eight-Point Garbage Matte effect

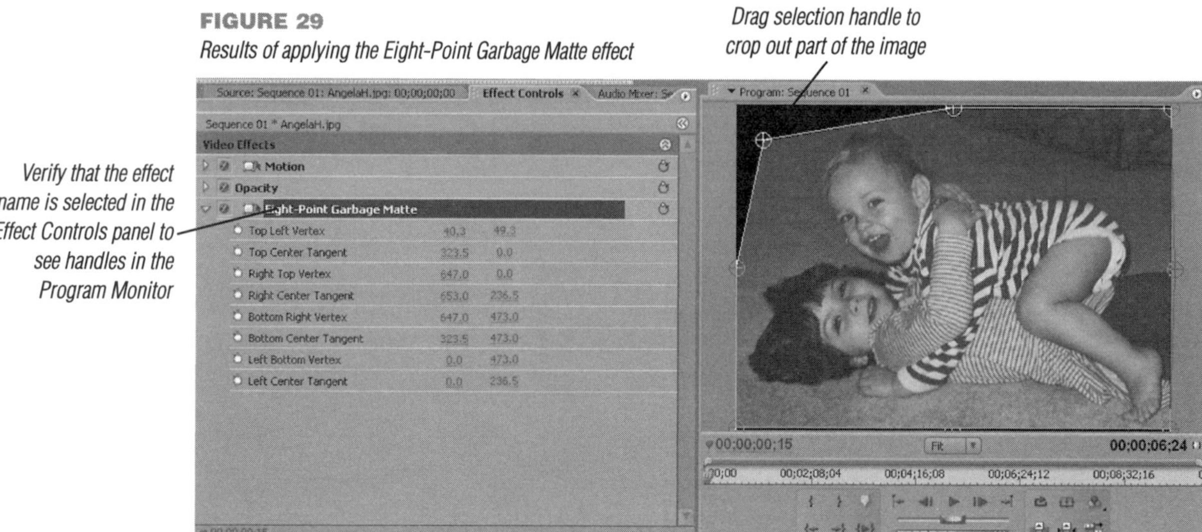

Table 1: Commonly Used Keys

Name of key	Function of key
Multiply Key	The Multiply Key effect works by multiplying the color values in two overlapping clips, then divides the sum by 255.
Green Screen Key and Blue Screen Key	The Green Screen and Blue Screen Keys are used to remove green or blue backgrounds from clips. Using the Green Screen or Blue Screen Keys to remove a background is a choice you make during the production stage of your project, long before you are editing in Premiere Pro. When you shoot footage against a green screen, for example, that green would be referred to as your **key color.** Everything that you want to key out should be green, and everything that you plan to be opaque should be any color other than green. Green and blue are favored as key colors, especially when you are shooting a person, because green and blue don't interfere with skin tone.
Chroma Key	The Chroma Key functions on the same idea as the Green and Blue Screen Keys, but it allows you to select any color as your transparent area. This comes in handy if you can't videotape footage against a green or blue background because of conflicting colors. You can shoot against any solid-color background and then key it out with the Chroma Key.
Track Matte Key	With the Track Matte Key, you need three clips, each on their own track. The track matte or simply matte is placed on the topmost track. It creates transparent areas in the clip that is superimposing the background clip. Usually, the clip being used as a track matte is a black-and-white still image. In every case, the black areas are opaque and the white areas are transparent. Gray areas that are not completely transparent. The resulting effect is that a clip plays through the white areas of the track matte.
Screen Key	The Screen Key functions as the opposite of the Multiply Key. With the Screen Key, black areas are transparent and white areas are opaque.
Garbage Matte	The Garbage Matte allows you to crop an undesired element from a clip using four or eight selection handles in the Program Monitor.

Use the Multiply Key effect

1. Open APP 8-4.prproj, then save it as **Orange Water**.
2. Click **Window** on the menu bar, point to **Workspace**, then click **Effects**.

   The transparency keys are in the Effects panel. The Effects workspace makes it very convenient to apply keys to clips in the Timeline.
3. Preview the contents of the Timeline, then drag **Orange Title** into the beginning of the Video 2 track.
4. Expand the Video Effects bin, then expand the Keying bin in the Effects panel.
5. Drag the **Multiply Key effect** on top of the Orange Title clip, as shown in Figure 30.

(continued)

FIGURE 30
Dragging the Multiply Key effect on top of Orange Title

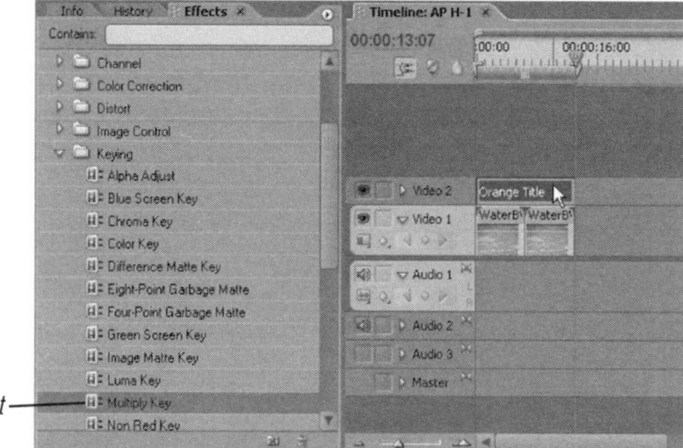

FIGURE 31

Result of applying Multiply Key effect

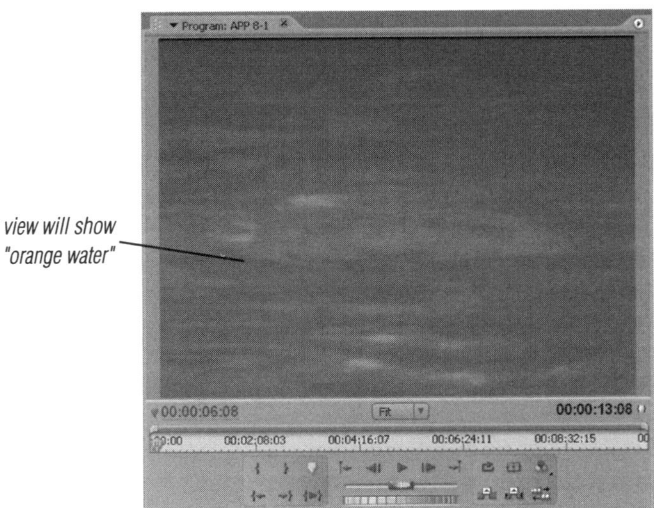

Your view will show "orange water"

Your Program Monitor should resemble Figure 31.

6. Double-click **Orange Title** in the Timeline to open it in Title Designer.
7. Click the **New Title Based on Current Title button**, name the new title **Lime Title**, then click **OK**.

   The New Title Based on Current Title button creates a duplicate title of the current title in the Titler panel. You can save time by duplicating a title when you need to apply the same formatting attributes to multiple titles.
8. Verify that the Title Properties panel is open, expand the Fill section, click the **Color box** to open the Color Picker, type **50** in the R text box, **255** in the G text box, **50** in the B text box, then click **OK**.

(continued)

9. Close the Titler panel, then replace Orange Title in the Timeline with Lime Title.

10. Apply the Multiply Key effect to Lime Title, then generate a preview.

    Your Program Monitor should resemble Figure 32.

11. Save your work, then close the project.

You positioned a title containing an orange fill in the Video 2 track. You then applied the Multiply Key effect, making the orange fill transparent, creating the effect of "colorizing" the footage on the Video 1 track. You then changed the color of the title, thus changing the color of the effect.

FIGURE 32
Applying the Multiply Key effect to Lime Water

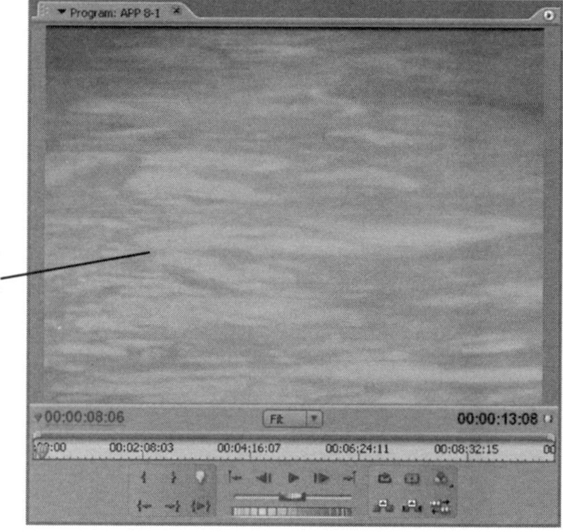

Your view will show "lime water"

FIGURE 33
Viewing Xtreme Logo in the sequence

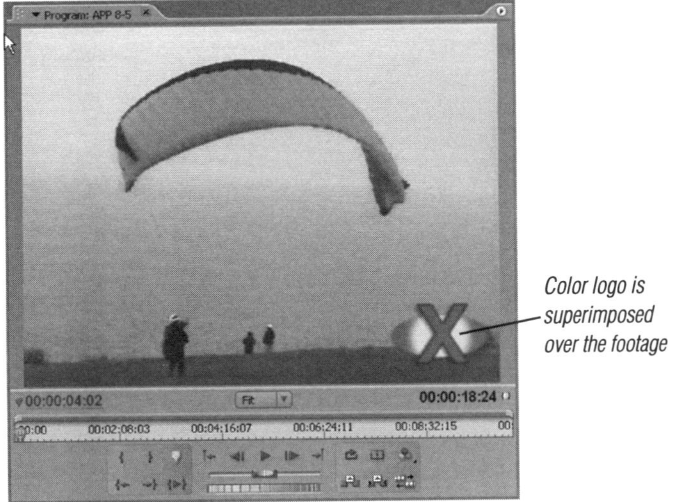

Color logo is superimposed over the footage

FIGURE 34
Changing the fill color of the logo to white

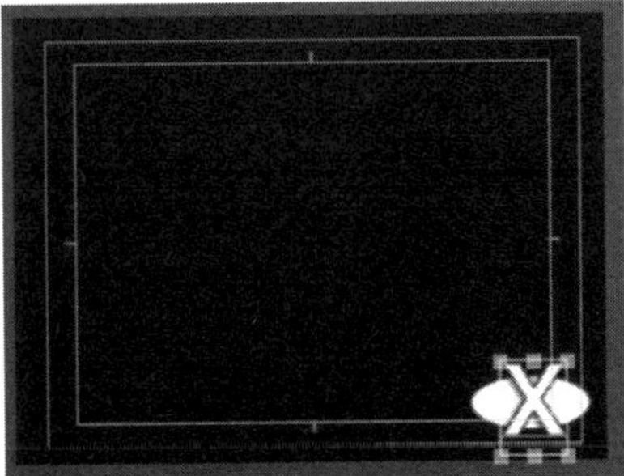

Make a white background transparent

1. Open APP 8-5.prproj, then save it as **Transparent Logo**.
2. Zoom in on the Timeline, if necessary, then play the sequence in the Timeline to become familiar it.

   The background of Xtreme Logo in the Video 3 track is transparent by default, and the color logo is superimposed over the footage, as shown in Figure 33.

   > TIP The font used for the "X" in the Xtreme Logo may differ on your computer.

3. Click the **Selection Tool** , then double-click **Xtreme Logo** in the Timeline to open it in the Titler panel.
4. Click the **New Title Based on Current Title button** , name the new title **Xtreme White**, then click **OK**.
5. Click the oval behind the X, expand the Fill section of the Title Properties panel, click the **Fill Type list arrow**, click **Solid**, then change its fill color to white (255R/255G/255B).

   > TIP Click the Color box to open the Color Picker to create white.

6. Click the **X**, then change its fill color to white so that your drawing area resembles Figure 34.

(continued)

7. Close the Titler panel.
8. Delete Xtreme Logo in the Timeline, then replace it with Xtreme White.
9. Extend the length of Xtreme White to frame 18:23, as shown in Figure 35.
10. Drag the **Multiply Key effect** from the Keying bin in the Video Effects bin on top of Xtreme White in the Timeline, then play the movie.

    The areas of the title that you changed to white are transparent, but the background of the title—with the Multiply Key—is no longer transparent; it is black.
11. Double-click **Xtreme White** in the Timeline to open it in the Titler panel, draw a rectangle that exceeds the Safe Margin Area slightly on all sides, then fill the rectangle with white.
12. Click **Title** on the menu bar, point to **Arrange**, then click **Send to Back** so that your drawing area resembles Figure 36.

(continued)

FIGURE 35
Extending Xtreme White to frame 18:23

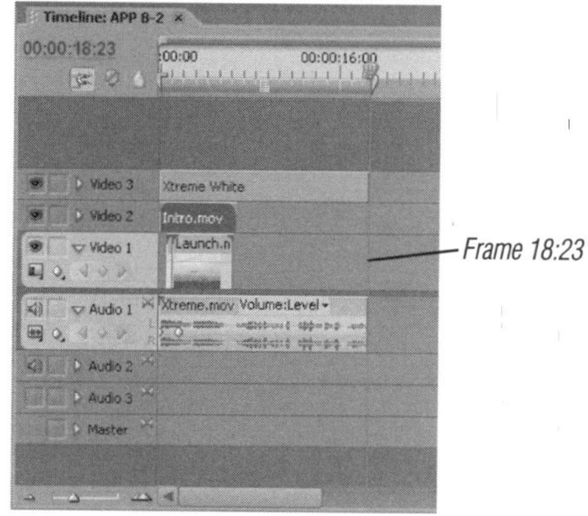

FIGURE 36
Creating a white rectangle behind the Xtreme White logo

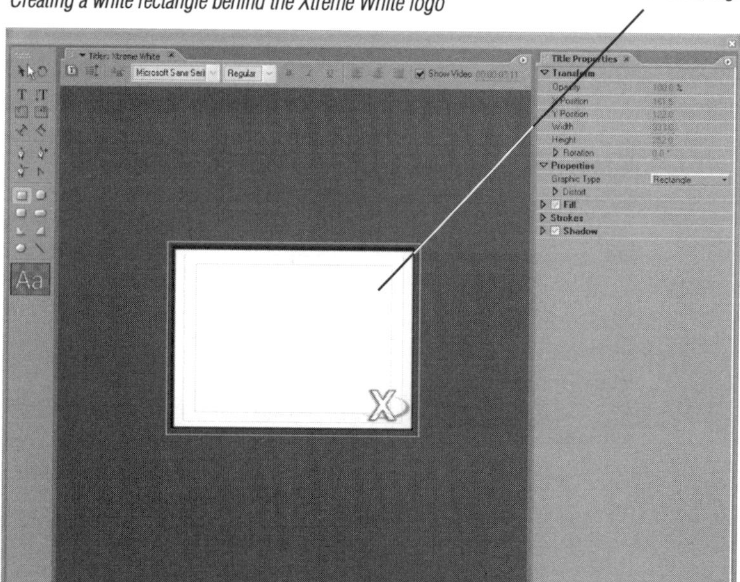

FIGURE 37
White background made transparent with the Multiply Key effect

13. Close the Titler panel, play the movie again, and notice that the white areas of the Xtreme White title are now transparent, as shown in Figure 37.
14. Save your work, then close the project.

You changed the fill color of Xtreme Logo to white and created a white rectangle to act as the title background. You then applied the Multiply Key effect to the title clip in the Timeline to make the logo and the title background transparent.

CHAPTER SUMMARY

Video effects are very similar to video transitions. You drag video effects directly over clips in the Timeline or to the Effect Controls panel. You can modify video effect settings in the Effect Controls panel and watch the changes take place on your clips in the Program Monitor. The key to understanding video effects will be when and where to use them in your Premiere Pro projects. Video effects that you use will entirely depend on the type of results you need. It may be wise to take some time and practice with video effects. For those of you who work in Photoshop, you'll be familiar with some of the Adjust effects, such as Levels and Brightness & Contrast. You can place all of your favorite effects in a custom bin in the Effects panel for easy access.

What You Have Learned

- How to apply a video effect to a clip in the Timeline
- How to modify a video effect in the Timeline
- How to restore video effect settings
- How to use the Setup button
- How to remove effects from a clip
- How to show the Timeline in the Effect Controls panel
- How to modify the opacity of a clip
- How to rename tracks
- How to use the Levels Settings dialog box
- How to apply the Tint effect
- How to change the order of effects in the Effect Controls panel
- How to use the Color Replace effect
- How to copy effects between clips
- How to use the Multiply Key effect

Key Terms

Video effects Video effects add special visual characteristics to a clip, such as blurs, distortions, or color changes.

Presets Presets are groups of specific video effect settings that are named and stored in the Effects panel as one effect and applied to clips in the Timeline.

Keying Keying is another term for superimposing—or creating transparency in specific areas of a clip.

PAN AMERICAN WORLD AIRWAY
PAA
DOUGLAS

chapter 9 ANIMATING CLIPS

1. Animate a clip using keyframes.
2. Modify keyframes.
3. Animate a video effect.

chapter 9 ANIMATING CLIPS

An animation is essentially different from a video: With video, you capture live action and reproduce it using a series of still images. With an animation, there is no live action—motion is created synthetically using a series of still images. This is why such classic cartoons as Bugs Bunny, Mickey Mouse, and The Flintstones all appropriately fall under the title of Animation Arts—they are all "animated" by stringing together a series of still drawings.

Animation is created in Premiere Pro using keyframes. **Keyframes** are locations in the Timeline where you define how something will look before the animation begins and how it will look when the animation ends. For example, if you wanted to animate a title so that it "grows" from frame 1 to frame 100, you would create a keyframe at frame 1 and choose a beginning size for the title, then you'd create a keyframe at frame 100 and enlarge the title to the size that it should grow to. Premiere Pro does the rest of the work for you. Frames 2 through 99 will be interpolated, meaning Premiere Pro will look at frame 1 and frame 100 and figure out how much the title should increase in size at each in-between frame. This process is also referred to as "in-betweening" or simply "tweening" in the world of animators.

Animation can be especially effective when transparency is used. You can make a clip appear over time by modifying the amount of opacity at keyframes.

Tools You'll Use

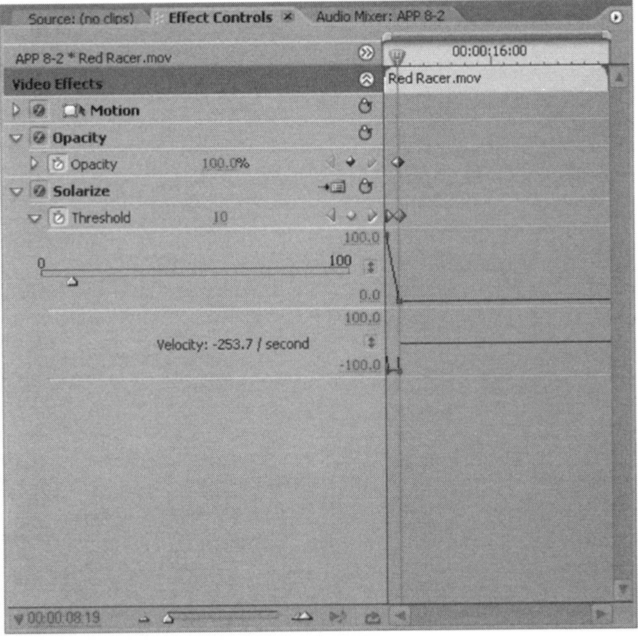

ANIMATE A CLIP USING KEYFRAMES

What You'll Do

In this lesson, you will animate a clip by rotating it 90°.

Identifying the Role of Animation

Animation is a common component to most video presentations. A title moving across the screen, as you would see at the beginning or end of a TV show, is an example of video animation. Crawls and rolling credits are classic examples of title animation. You will often see title animation in promotions for movies or TV shows—especially action movies—in which the movie's name zooms in from nowhere, getting bigger and bigger, or it floats across the screen or rotates like a cartwheel, as shown in Figure 1.

FIGURE 1
An animated title

In Premiere Pro, animation is not limited to animating titles—video clips can be animated too. For example, you might design a sequence with one video clip as a background and other smaller clips moving in the foreground, as shown in Figure 2.

Often, you will find that the most effective animations involve both transparency and animation. In Figure 3, the backgrounds of the three flower clips have been keyed out, creating a dramatic effect. Working with animation will further strengthen your understanding of and fluency with transparency.

FIGURE 2
Animated clips moving across a background video clip

FIGURE 3
Animating clips with transparency

Identifying Properties to Animate

As you have already learned, each clip has a default Opacity and Motion setting applied, once it is placed in the Timeline. These settings can be modified in the Effect Controls panel, much like modifying video effects and video transitions. Premiere Pro even lists Motion and Opacity under the Video Effects heading in the Effect Controls panel, as shown in Figure 4. In Figure 4, Motion and Opacity have been expanded in order for you to see all of the default settings that can be modified. Up until this point, you have learned to modify an entire clip. For example, if you changed the opacity of a clip to 75%, that clip's opacity remained at 75% for its entire duration. With keyframes, you can animate opacity so that a clip could be almost invisible at the start of a sequence and become visible as the Current frame indicator moves forward in the Timeline. To do so, you would set the opacity of your first keyframe to 0% or close to it, then set the opacity of your last keyframe to 100%. Premiere Pro interpolates the in-between frames and increases opacity accordingly.

FIGURE 4

Viewing default settings for clip

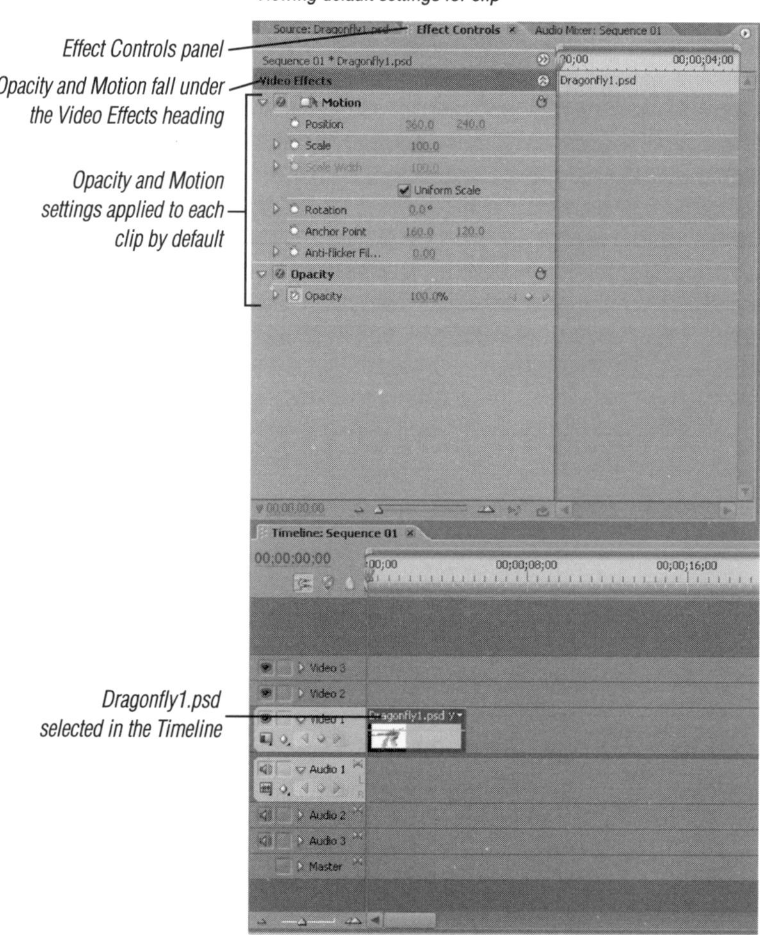

Adding Keyframes to a Clip

In order to create an animation of any kind, you need to start out with at least two keyframes—one where you want the animation to begin and the other where you want it to end. You can always add additional keyframes later to further modify your animation. When you are ready to add your first keyframe, position the Current time indicator on the exact frame where you want to place the keyframe. When working with keyframes, it is helpful to zoom in on the Timeline so that you are placing keyframes with accuracy.

Click the Toggle Animation button next to the property that you want to animate. Toggle Animation buttons, as shown in Figure 5, look like tiny stopwatch icons. You need to expand the effect that you want to modify in order to see them. Clicking the Toggle Animation button once is all you need to do to add your first keyframe, last keyframe, and any more that you decide upon. If you click the Toggle Animation button again, you will remove all keyframes from a clip. Figure 5 shows the Toggle Animation button turned on for Scale and Opacity and turned off for the Position, Rotation, Anchor Point, and Anti-Flicker filters. Notice also the keyframe in the Timeline section of the Effect Controls panel. Keyframes are represented by diamond-shaped icons.

QUICKTIP

The Toggle Animation button next to Opacity is always on by default.

FIGURE 5

Viewing the Toggle Animation button

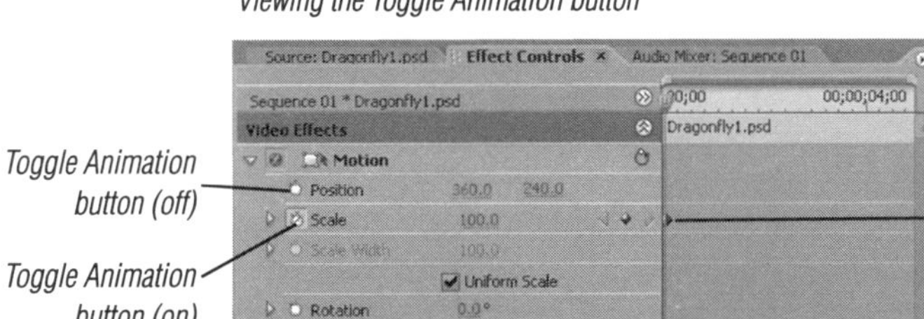

When you're ready to position your next keyframe, drag the Current time indicator to the frame where you want to position it. Notice in Figure 6, the Current time indicator in the Effect Controls panel and the Timeline move together. Notice that the Effect Controls panel offers zoom controls and a Current time display field for zooming in on the Timeline panel in the Effect Controls panel. Relying on the Timeline view in the Effect Controls panel may be easier if you are working with a very long sequence. However, the most reliable way to position a keyframe at an exact frame is to enter the frame number in the Current time display, then press [Enter]. The Current time indicator jumps to that frame in both the Effect Controls panel and the Timeline.

FIGURE 6
Viewing the Current time indicator

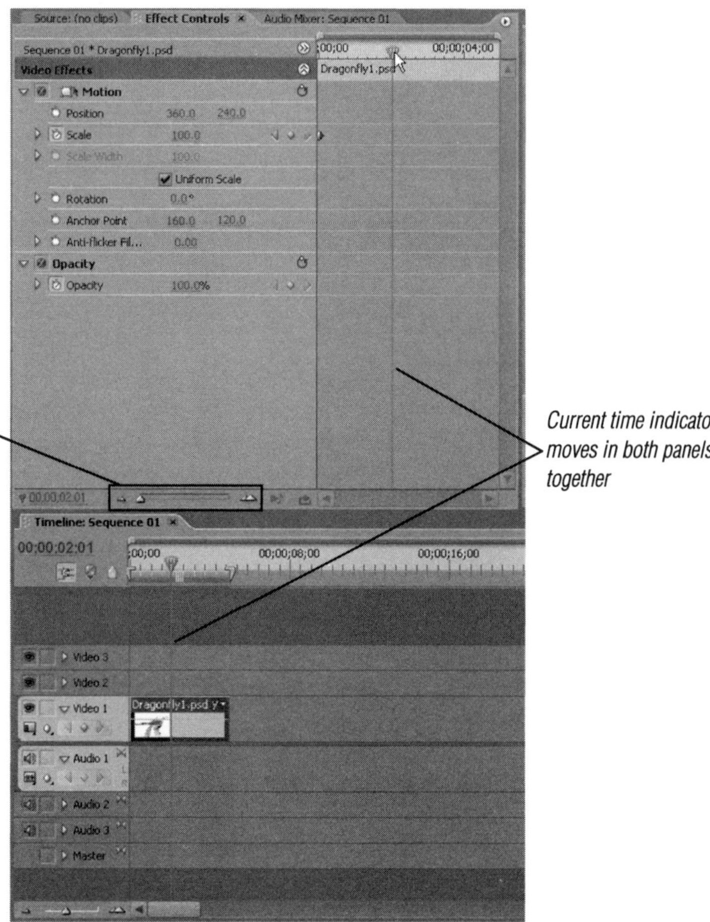

Click the Add/Remove Keyframe button, shown in Figure 7, to add a keyframe at the new location of the Current time indicator. Once you have a number of keyframes, you can move to them easily by clicking the Go to Previous Keyframe or Go to Next Keyframe button in the Effect Controls panel.

QUICKTIP

Clicking the Add/Remove Keyframe button will add or remove a keyframe from the location of the Current time indicator. Clicking the Toggle Animation button removes all keyframes for a specific property from the clip.

The Timeline offers the same controls for adding keyframes and moving to keyframes, as shown in Figure 8. In order to access these controls, you must first make sure the track is expanded. You can then choose to hide or show keyframes by clicking the Show Keyframes button and choosing the appropriate choice from the menu, as shown in Figure 9.

QUICKTIP

The Video 1 track is the only track that is expanded by default when you start a new project.

FIGURE 7
Adding the second keyframe

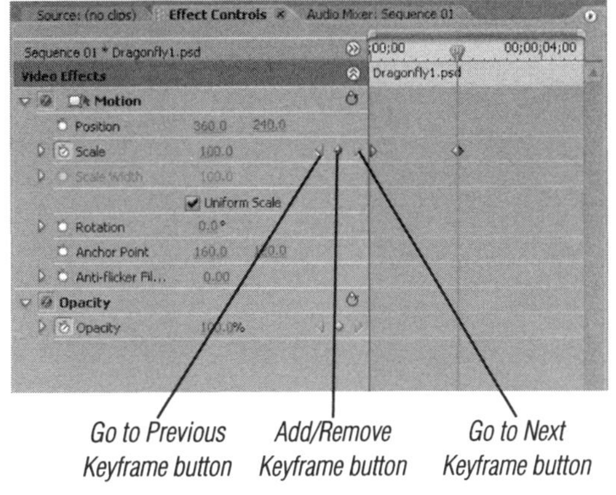

FIGURE 8
Keyframe controls in the Timeline

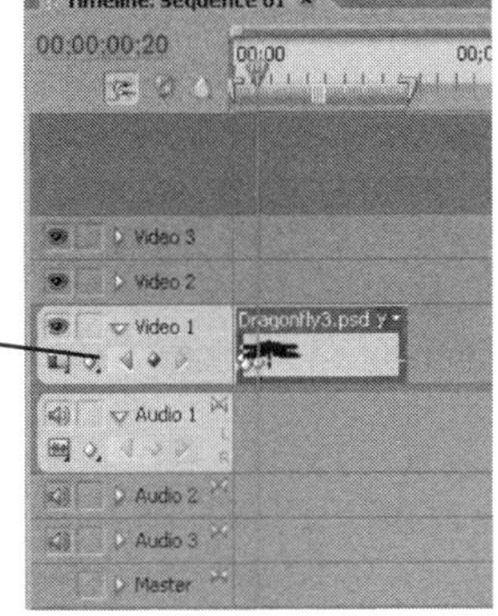

FIGURE 9
Viewing the Keyframe menu

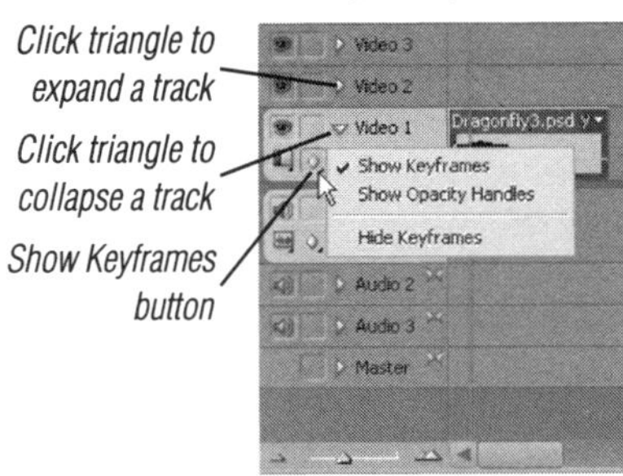

Add keyframes to a clip

1. Open APP 9-1.prproj, then save it as **Dragonfly**.
2. Switch to the Effects workspace, if necessary.
3. Drag **Dragonfly1.psd** from the Project panel into the Video 1 track in the Timeline, zoom in on the Timeline, then select Dragonfly1.psd.
4. Expand the Motion and Opacity settings in the Effect Controls panel so that your screen resembles Figure 10.

(continued)

FIGURE 10
Default motion and opacity settings for selected clip

FIGURE 11
Setting the Current time indicator at the very beginning of the Timeline

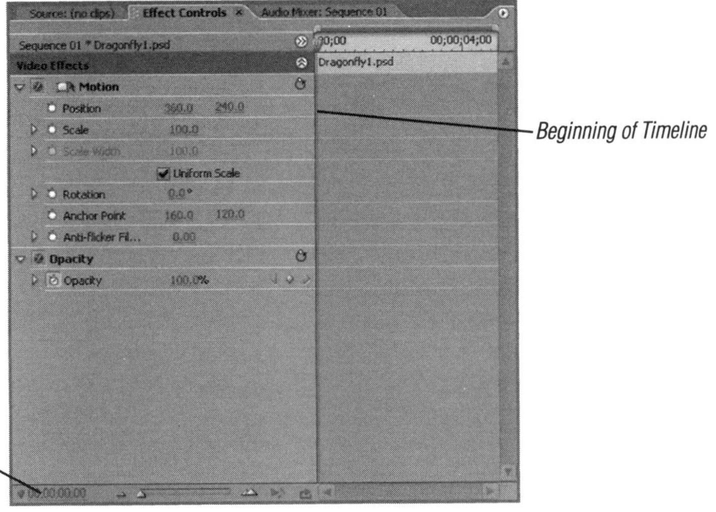

FIGURE 12
Setting the Rotation value for the second keyframe

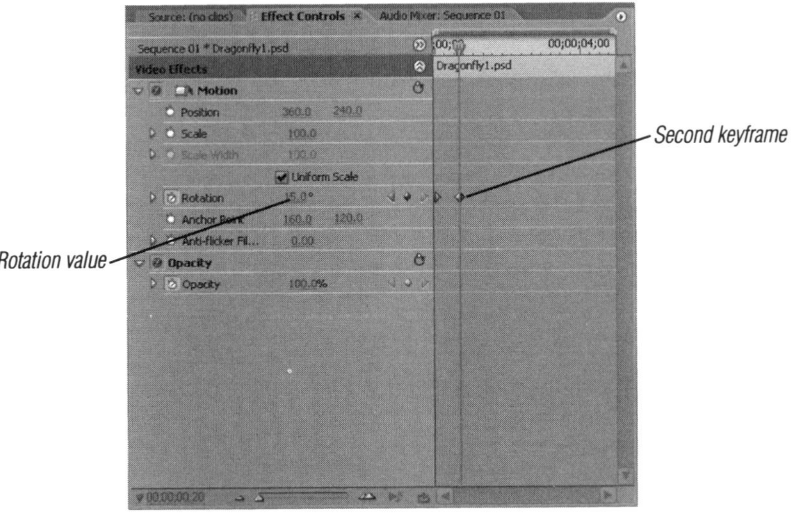

5. Click the **Current time display** in the Effect Controls panel, type **0**, then press **[Enter]**.

   As shown in Figure 11, the Current time indicator moves to the very beginning of the Timeline in the Effect Controls panel. Notice that the Current time indicator also moves to the same location in the Timeline.

6. Click the **Toggle Animation button** to the left of Rotation in the Effect Controls panel.

   A keyframe is automatically added to the Timeline.

   TIP Clicking the Toggle Animation button automatically adds the first keyframe to the location of the Current time indicator.

7. Click the **Current time display**, type **20**, press **[Enter]**, then click the **Add/Remove Keyframe button** in the Rotation section of the Effect Controls panel.

8. Click the **Rotation value**, type **15**, then press **[Enter]**.

   Your Effect Controls panel should resemble Figure 12. The dragonfly image will rotate from 0° to 15° over the first 20 frames in the sequence.

(continued)

9. Repeat Steps 7 and 8 using 40 for the Current time display value and 30 for the Rotation value.

   TIP The Current time display changes to 1:10 because 20 frames plus 20 frames is equal to 1 second and 10 frames.

10. Repeat Steps 7 and 8 again, using 60 for the Current time display value and 45 for the Rotation value.

    Your Effect Controls panel should resemble Figure 13.

11. Play the sequence so far, then save your work.

    Dragonfly1.psd rotates from 0 degrees to 45 degrees over the first 80 frames in the sequence.

You created a simple animation by creating four keyframes and increasing the Rotation value 15 degrees for each keyframe.

FIGURE 13

Four keyframes applied to Dragonfly1.psd

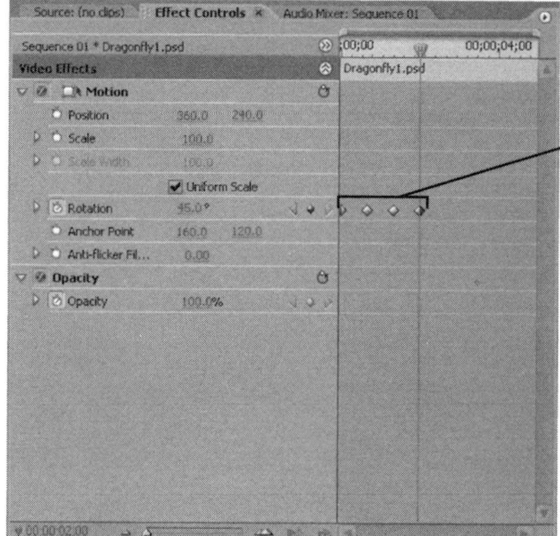

FIGURE 14
Expanding the Scale section

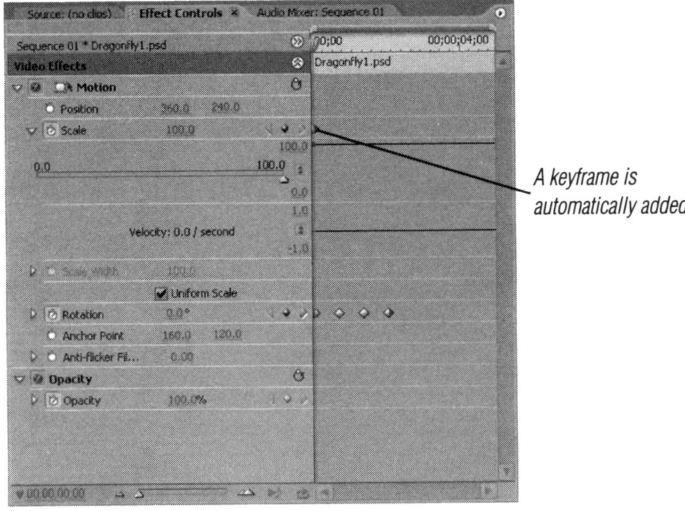

FIGURE 15
Animating the Scale property of Dragonfly1.psd

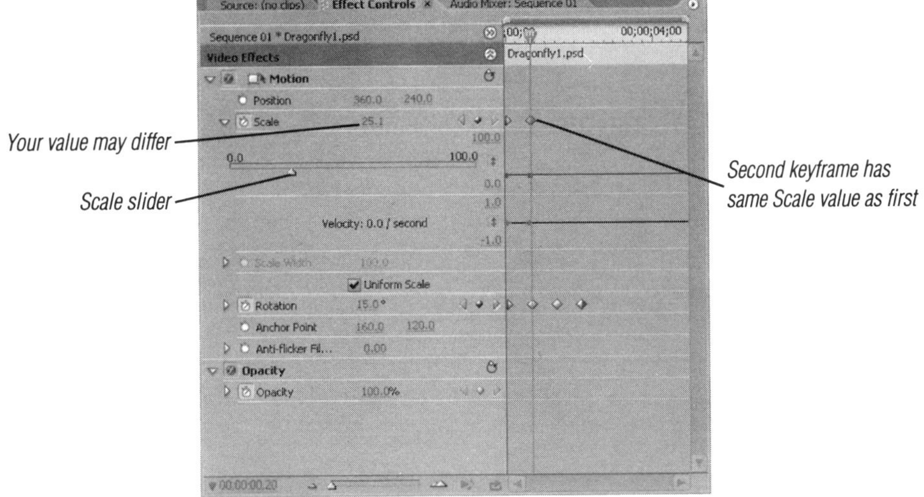

Animate two properties of a clip

1. Click the **Go to Previous Keyframe button** four times so that your Current time indicator is placed on the first keyframe in the Effect Controls panel.
2. Click the **Toggle Animation button** to the left of Scale in the Effect Controls panel, then expand the Scale section so that your Effect Controls panel resembles Figure 14.

   A keyframe is added in the Scale section in the Effect Controls panel.
3. Drag the **Scale slider** to approximately 25.

   Your value may differ slightly from 25.
4. Click the **Go to Next Keyframe button** in the Rotation section to advance to frame 20, then add a new keyframe in the Scale section so that your Effect Controls panel matches Figure 15.

   New keyframes are created with the exact setting of the previous keyframe. Notice that the second keyframe has the same scale value as the first keyframe.

(continued)

5. Position the mouse pointer over the tiny black square directly under the second keyframe in the Scale section of the Effect Controls panel, as shown in Figure 16.

   These small black squares represent the current scale value at each keyframe. You can drag a square up or down and watch the new scale value appear in the Scale section of the Effect Controls panel.

6. Drag the **small square** to approximately 50, as shown in Figure 17, then release the mouse pointer.

   The dragonfly image will increase in size from frame 1 to frame 20.

7. Click the **Go to Next Keyframe button** in the Rotation section to advance to frame 40, add a new keyframe in the Scale section, then drag the **third black square** to approximately 75.

8. Repeat Step 7 to add a fourth keyframe at frame 60, then drag the **fourth black square** to 100.

FIGURE 16

Positioning the mouse pointer over the black square

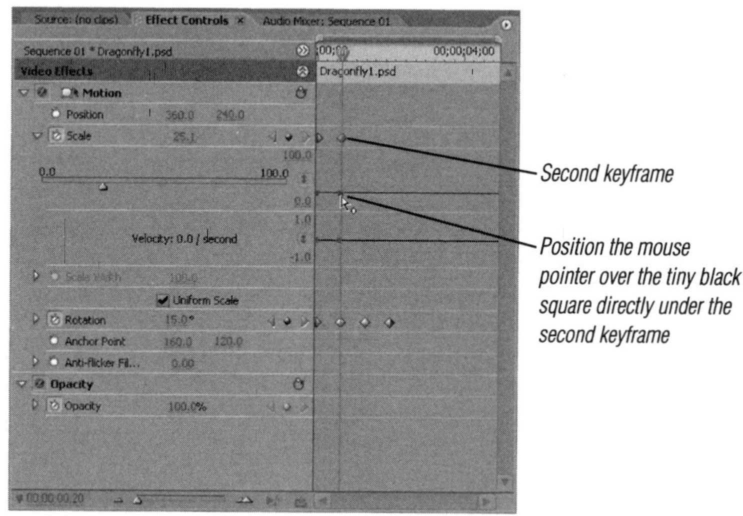

FIGURE 17

Changing the Scale value for the second keyframe

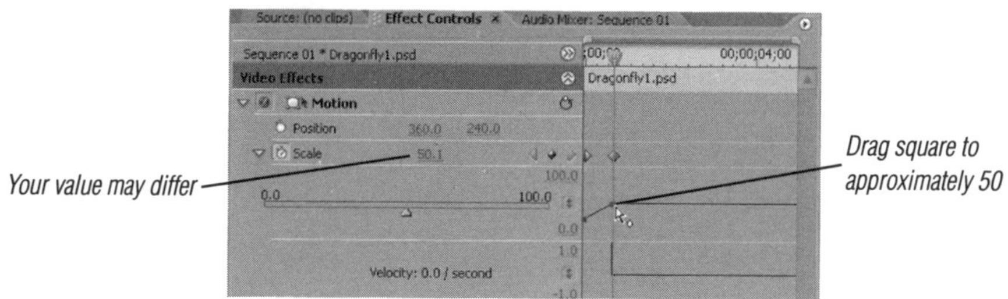

FIGURE 18
Effect Controls panel

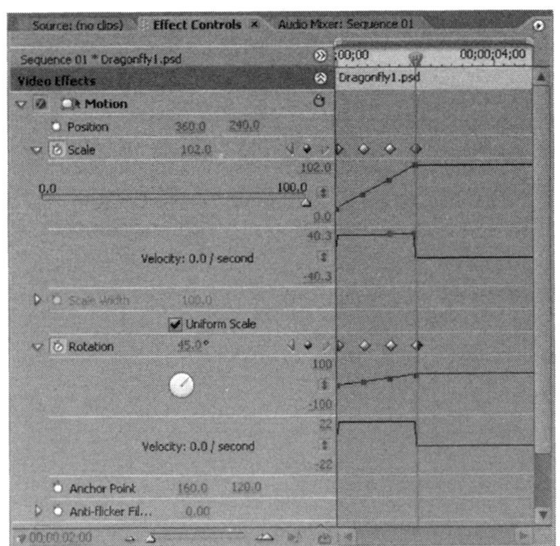

9. Expand the Rotation section in the Effect Controls panel, then compare your Effect Controls panel to Figure 18.

   The Rotation section also offers handles for manipulating the rotation values applied to keyframes.

10. Play the sequence, save your work, click **File** on the menu bar, then click **Close**.

    The dragonfly rotates and "grows" over the first two seconds of the sequence.

You animated the size of the dragonfly image over four keyframes.

LESSON 2

MODIFY KEYFRAMES

What You'll Do

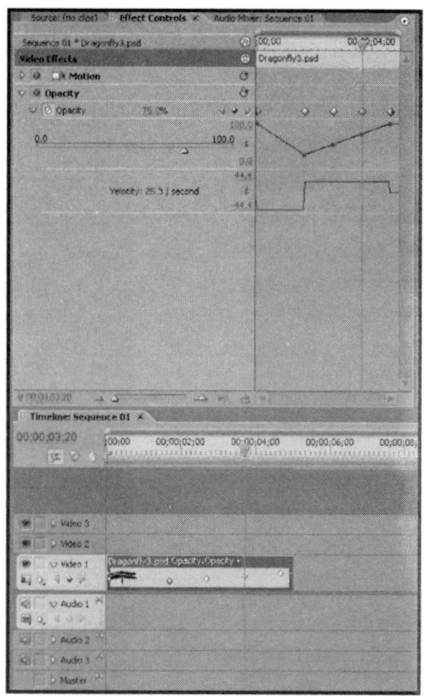

In this lesson, you will modify the animation created in Lesson 1 by making changes to the keyframes in the Effect Controls panel and in the Timeline.

Modifying Keyframes

When you create an animated sequence, you'll probably find that you need to preview your sequence over and over, making slight changes each time to get the exact outcome you want. This may mean that you have to add additional keyframes, delete keyframes, or space keyframes closer together or farther apart. You already know how to add keyframes. To delete keyframes, you simply select the keyframe, then press [Delete]. The animation will be updated based on the removal of the keyframe.

If you find that your animation moves too fast, you can slow it down by spreading it out over more frames. You can move keyframes in the Timeline by selecting them and dragging them to a new location. The reverse is also true. To speed up an animation, move your keyframes closer together. When there is less time (fewer frames) for a clip to change, the change happens faster. When there is more time for a change to occur, the animation is slower.

Finally, you can modify a keyframe's property settings after you have set them initially. Use the Go to Next Keyframe or Go to Previous Keyframe button to select the keyframe you want to modify, then adjust the appropriate settings in the Effect Controls panel.

Copying and Pasting Keyframes

When you add a new keyframe to a sequence, it has the exact properties as the keyframe before it, until you change them. In other words, if your second keyframe has an opacity setting of 50%, the next keyframe you add has an opacity setting of 50%. Typically, you add a keyframe because you want to change the properties which will make a change in the animation. In this example, you'd probably want the opacity to gradually increase or decrease, so you would set the opacity of the third keyframe to a higher percentage, such as 75%, or a lower percentage, such as 25%. There are times, however, when you'll want to match the exact properties of one keyframe to another. For example, you may want your animation to end exactly how it began. In this example, you'd want your first and last keyframes to have identical properties. You can copy and paste the properties of a keyframe to another location in the Timeline using the Effect Controls panel. Simply click the keyframe that has the properties you want to copy, click Copy or press [Ctrl][C], set the Current time indicator to the frame where you would like to paste the new keyframe, then click Paste or press [Ctrl][V]. Make sure you copy and paste keyframes in the Effect Controls panel. If you try to select a keyframe in the clip in the Timeline, you'll select the entire clip.

Adjust keyframe locations

1. Open APP 9-2.prproj, then save it as **Tweaking**.
2. Play the animation to become familiar with it.

   The opacity values starts out at 100%, drops to 13.5, jumps to 76.9, then ends at 100%. The locations of each keyframe are 0, 1:09, 2:10, and 3:23.
3. Click **Dragonfly3.psd** in the Timeline to select it, click the **Current time display** in the Program Monitor, type **4.20**, then press **[Enter]**.
4. Click the **Add/Remove Keyframe button** in the Timeline.

   As shown in Figure 19, the fifth keyframe is placed at frame 4:20.
5. Move the Current time indicator to frame 1:20, then drag the **second keyframe** to frame 1:20, as shown in Figure 20.

   Don't worry about the vertical location of the keyframe within the clip – you'll adjust the opacity setting later.

   > TIP One way to make sure the keyframe is placed exactly at frame 1:20 is to click the Go to Previous Keyframe button, then click the Go to Next Keyframe button and look at the Current time display in the Program Monitor. If it displays 1:20, you know the keyframe is positioned correctly.

(continued)

FIGURE 19
Adding a fifth keyframe to the sequence

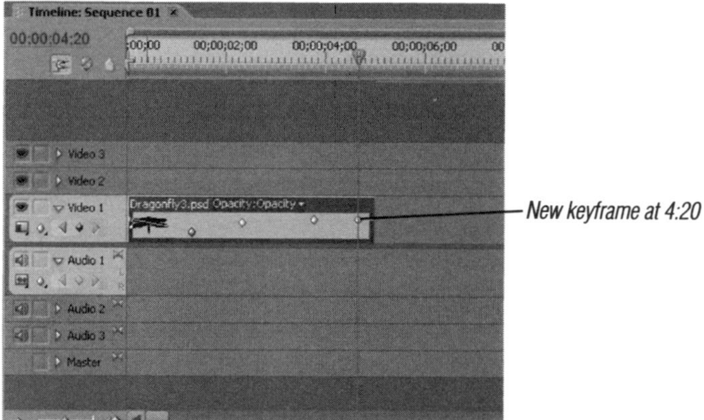

FIGURE 20
Changing the location of a keyframe

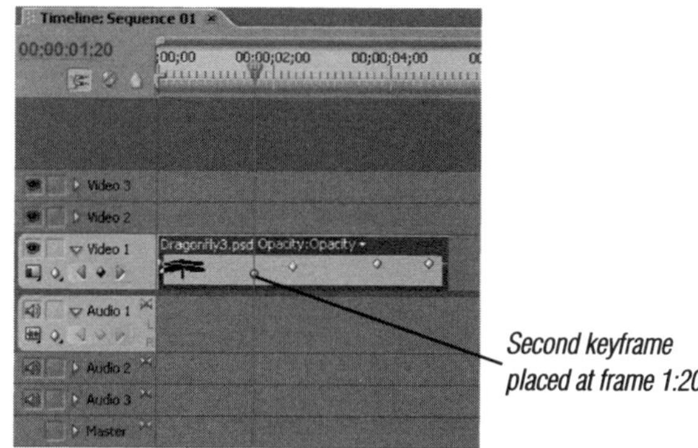

FIGURE 21
Five keyframes set at specific locations

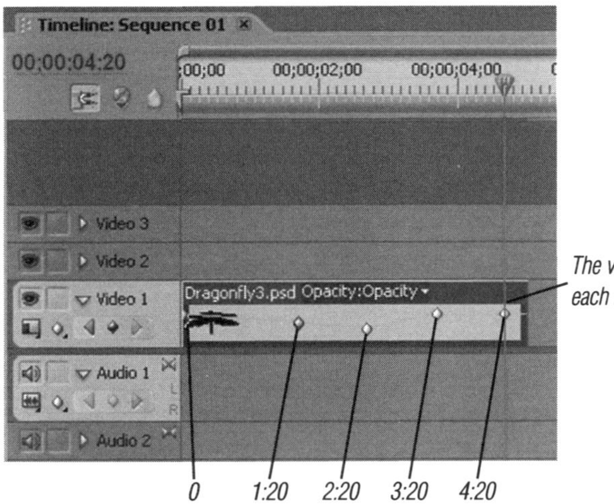

6. Click the **third keyframe**, then drag it to 2:20, watching the frame number on the yellow tooltip change as you drag.

   TIP Relying on the tooltip to show you the location of the keyframe is another way to place a keyframe accurately.

7. Move the third keyframe to 3:20 using the method of your choice, then verify that your five keyframes are set at 0, 1:20, 2:20, 3:20, and 4:20.

   Your Timeline should resemble Figure 21.

   TIP The vertical location of your five keyframes within the clip icon will differ from the figure.

8. Save your work.

You added a keyframe at frame 4:20, then changed the locations of keyframes 2, 3, and 4 to 1:20, 2:20, and 3:20.

Copy and paste a keyframe

1. Click the **Go to Previous Keyframe button** in the Timeline three times, so that your Current time indicator is placed on the second keyframe at frame 1:20.
2. Change the opacity setting of keyframe 2 to 25% in the Effect Controls panel.

   TIP Type 25 in the Opacity field in the Effect Controls panel to make sure the value is exactly 25%.

3. Click the **Go to Next Keyframe button** to change the opacity values of keyframe 3 to 50% and keyframe 4 to 75%, as shown in Figure 22.

(continued)

FIGURE 22

Adjusting the opacity of keyframes 2, 3, and 4

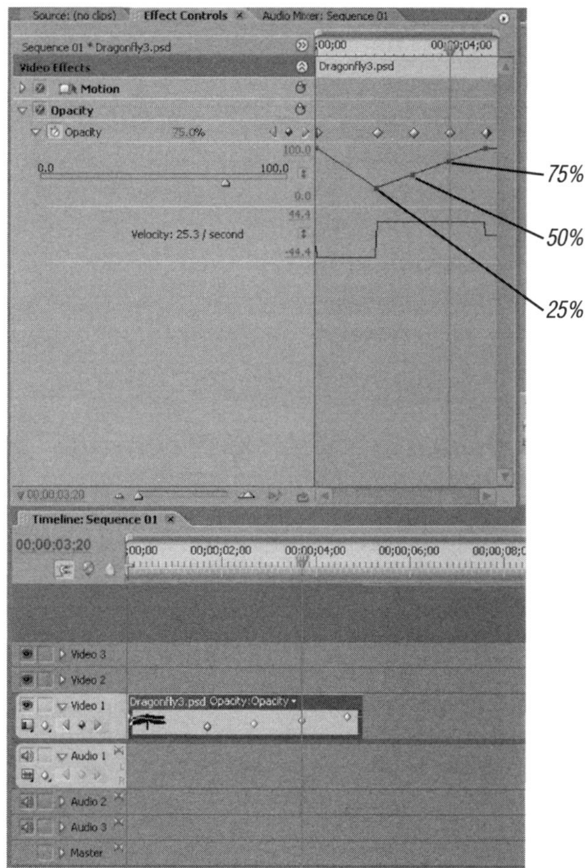

FIGURE 23
Preparing to delete a keyframe

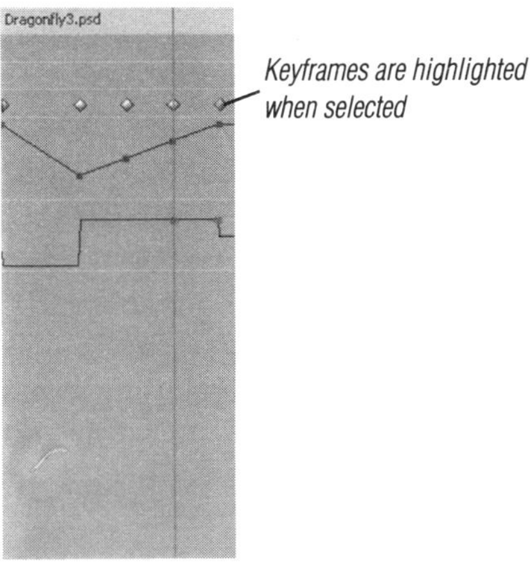

FIGURE 24
Copying and pasting a keyframe

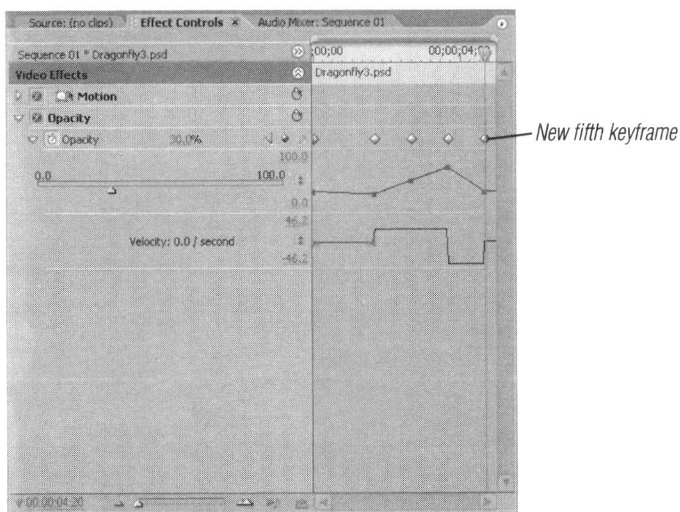

4. Click the **fifth keyframe** in the Effect Controls panel, as shown in Figure 23.

   Keyframes are highlighted when selected.

5. Press **[Delete]** to remove the keyframe.

   The keyframe is removed from the sequence.

6. Click the **Go to Previous Keyframe button** three times to select the first keyframe, then change its opacity setting to 30%.

7. Position the Current time indicator at frame 4:20.

8. Click the **first keyframe** in the Effect Controls panel to select it, press **[Ctrl][C]** to copy it, then press **[Ctrl][V]** to paste it at the location of the Current time indicator.

   The new fifth keyframe has the identical opacity property as keyframe 1. Compare your Effect Controls panel to Figure 24.

9. Save your work, click **File** on the menu bar, then click **Close**.

You changed the opacity of three keyframes, deleted the last keyframe, adjusted the opacity of the first keyframe, then copied the first keyframe and pasted it at frame 4:20 so that it would have the exact same opacity setting as keyframe 1.

LESSON 3

ANIMATE A VIDEO EFFECT

What You'll Do

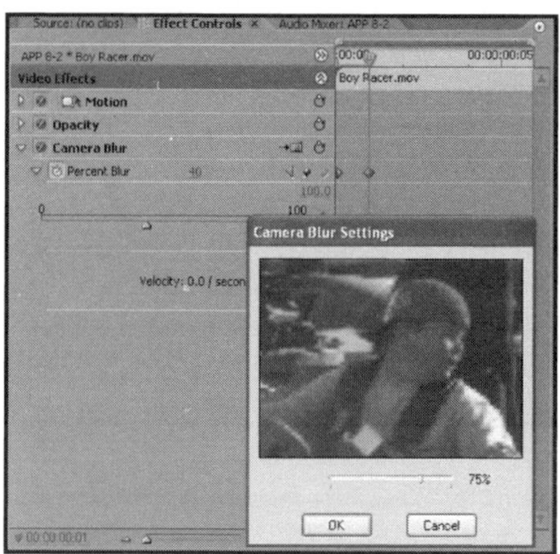

In this lesson, you will use keyframes to control how a video effect is applied to a clip.

Working with Keyframes and Video Effects

By default, when you apply a video effect to a clip, the effect is active for the duration of the clip. Many times, however, you will want more control of how the video effect plays during the clip. For example, you might want it to play only during specific portions of the clip, or you might want the effect to play at varying intensities.

Premiere Pro uses keyframes to change a video effect over time and to determine when and how an effect will play within a clip. For example, instead of applying a blur effect to a clip for its entire duration, you could edit your sequence so that the clip's appearance alternates from blurry to clear repeatedly. Using your knowledge of keyframes and the Effect Controls panel, you can create some very creative and complex sequences. To animate a video effect, you use the exact steps that you would to animate other clip properties, such as Motion and Opacity. Figure 25 shows a clip with the Gaussian Blur video effect applied. Notice that there are two keyframes in the Effect Controls panel. The first has a Blurriness value of 0% and the second has a Blurriness value of 25%. So far, the clip will start out completely clear and gradually become blurry as it approaches the second keyframe.

Using Presets

Presets are video effects that already have settings assigned to them. Some presets have keyframes in place for instant animation. Premiere Pro comes with six categories of presets, and you can save and name your own for future reference. Presets are great if you want to learn more about keyframes: Choose a preset that uses keyframes, such as a Solarize preset, locate the keyframes, and look at the settings and how the clip is affected when the sequence is played back. Presets are also useful when you want to apply a quick special effect without doing any of the work. When you select a clip and drag a preset to the Effect Controls panel, all of the detail is presented immediately. You do not need to expand any of the settings. Figure 26 shows the Twirl preset applied to The Corner.mov.

FIGURE 25

Gaussian Blur video effect applied to a clip

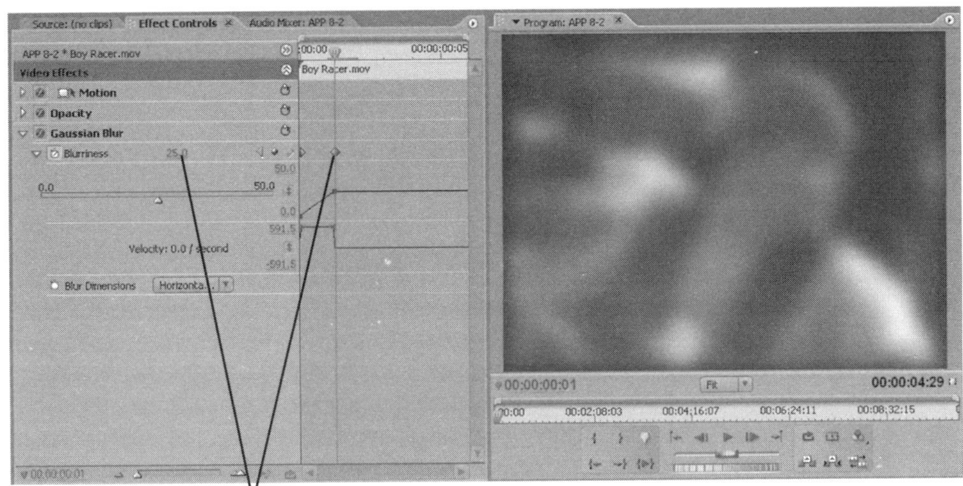

FIGURE 26

Viewing the Twirl preset in the Effect Controls panel

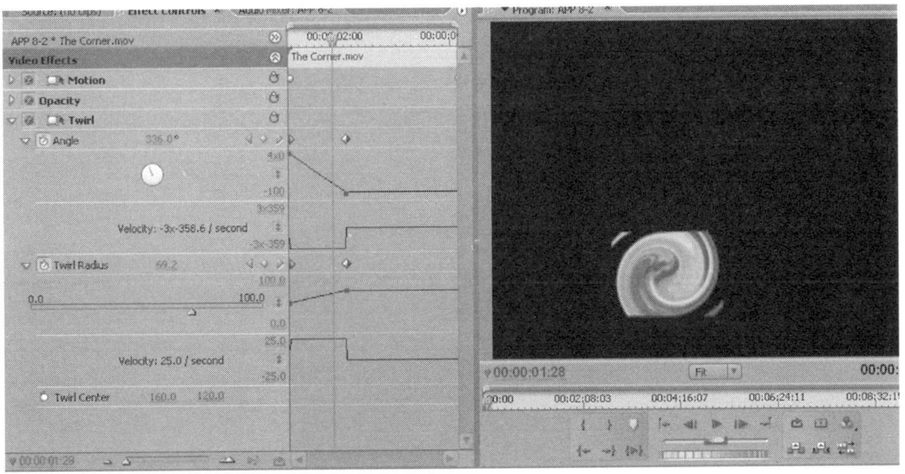

Animate a video effect using keyframes

1. Open APP 9-3.prproj, then save it as **Race Cars**.
2. Zoom in on the Timeline and verify that you are using the Effects workspace.
3. Click the **Timeline panel**, then click **[Home]** to place the Current time indicator at the beginning of the Timeline.
4. Click **Boy Racer.mov** in the Timeline.
5. Expand the Video Effects panel, then type **blur** in the Contains text box in the Effects panel.

   All of the available Blur video effects are displayed in the Effects panel, as shown in Figure 27.
6. Drag **Camera Blur** to the Effect Controls panel, expand Camera Blur, expand Percent Blur, then click the **Toggle Animation button** next to Percent Blur so that your Effect Controls panel matches Figure 28.

   A keyframe is added at frame 0.

(continued)

FIGURE 27
Finding the Blur video effects in the Effects panel

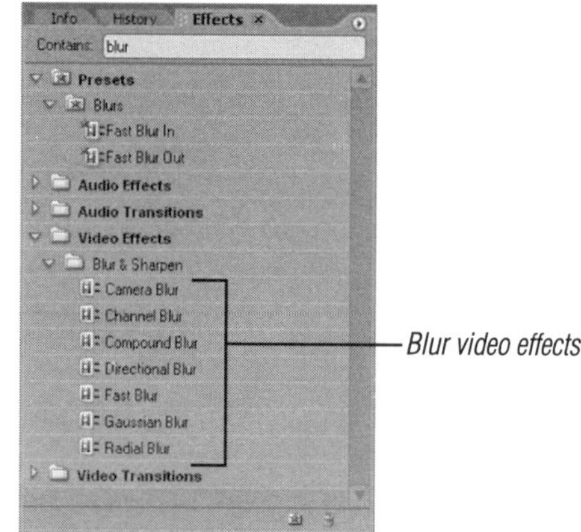

FIGURE 28
Default Camera Blur settings

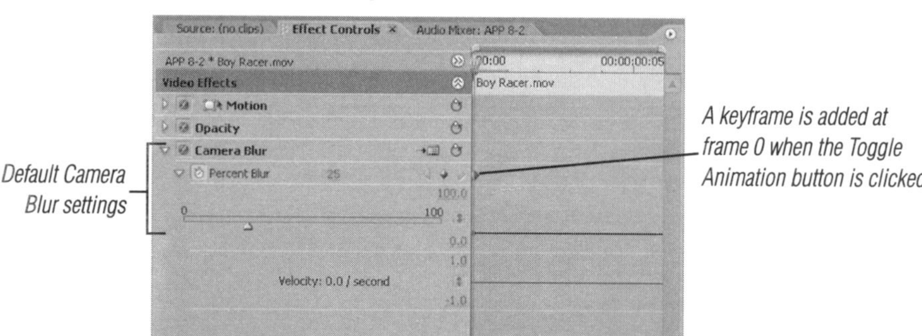

FIGURE 29
Setting the blur amount to 75% for the second keyframe

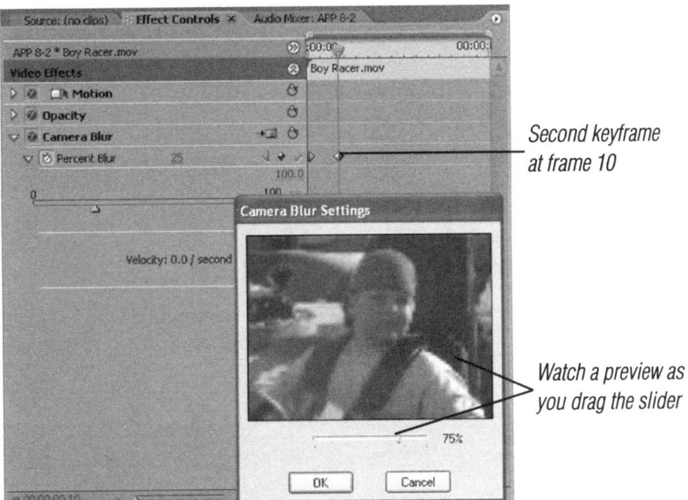

7. Click the **Setup button** next to Camera Blur to open the Camera Blur Settings dialog box.

   The default Camera Blur setting is 25%.

8. Drag the **slider** in the Camera Blur dialog box left and right to see the effect on the clip, then click **Cancel**.
9. Set the Current time indicator to frame 10, then add a keyframe.
10. Click the **Setup button**, change the value to 75%, then compare your screen to Figure 29.
11. Click **OK**, then render-scrub the movie to watch the Camera Blur effect.
12. Add a third keyframe at frame 20, then change the blur value to 95%.

(continued)

13. Clear the contents of the Contains text box, expand the Video Transitions bin, expand the 3D Motion bin, then drag the Doors video transition over Boy Racer.mov and Girl Cruises.mov.

> TIP You should see the Center at Cut icon when the transition is directly over both clips because Racer Boy.mov does not have tail material and Girl Cruises.mov does not contain head material. If the clips had tail and head material, respectively, you could transition the end of the Boy Racer.mov clip or the beginning of Girl Cruises.mov.

14. Render-scrub the beginning of the sequence, save your work, then close the Race Cars project.

    As shown in Figure 30, video transitions can be used on top of video effects to segue from one clip to another.

You used keyframes to change settings in the Camera Blur video effect applied to Boy Racer.mov. You then used the Doors video transition to transition from Boy Racer.mov to Girl Cruises.mov.

FIGURE 30

Using a video transition with a video effect

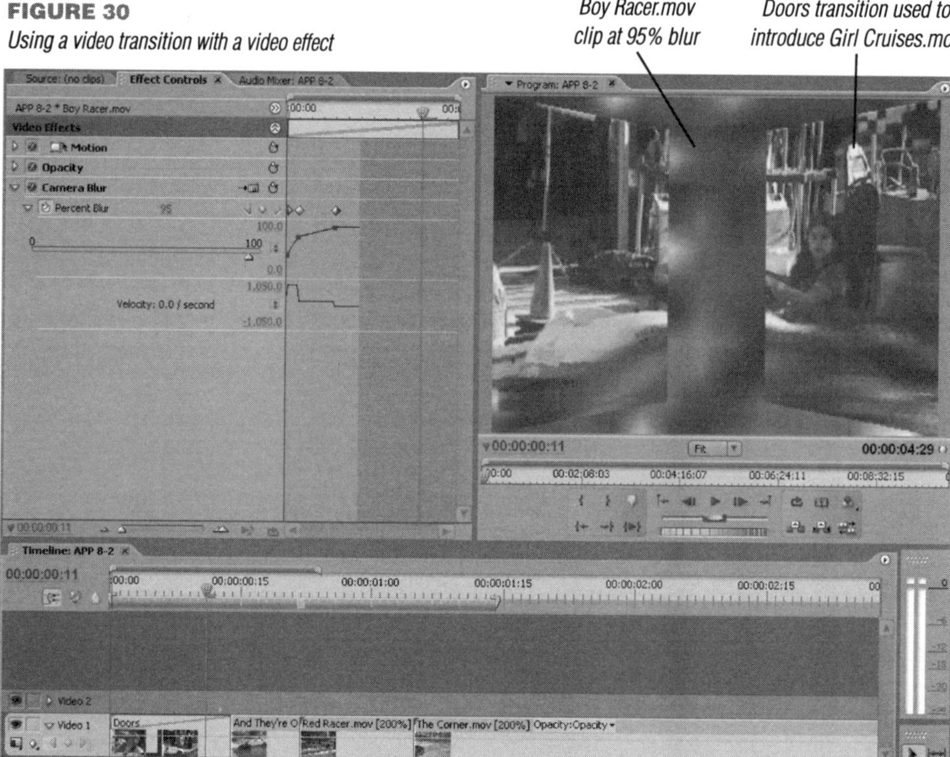

FIGURE 31
Viewing the end of the Fast Blur In preset

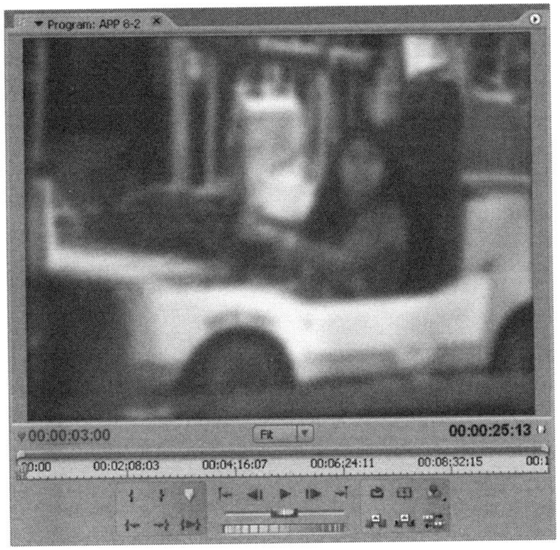

Use a preset to animate a video effect

1. Open APP 9-4.prproj, then save it as **Preset**.
2. Verify that you are using the Effects workspace.
3. Click **Boy Racer.mov** in the Timeline, then expand the Presets bin in the Effects panel.
4. Expand the Mosaics bin, then drag **Mosaic In** to the Effect Controls panel.
5. Render-scrub Boy Racer.mov to watch the effect.
6. Click **Girl Cruises.mov**, expand the Blurs bin, then drag **Fast Blur In** to the Effect Controls panel.
7. Position the Current time indicator at frame 3:00.

   As shown in Figure 31, the image starts to come into focus at this frame.
8. Apply the Solarize In preset to Red Racer.mov.
9. Generate a preview.
10. Click each clip in the Timeline and adjust any keyframe locations or keyframe settings in the Effect Controls panel to your liking, if necessary.
11. Save your work, then close the Preset project.

You applied three presets to three clips in the Timeline and generated a preview.

CHAPTER SUMMARY

The ability to manipulate properties of a clip while it is playing will take your Premiere Pro movies to an entirely new level. Using keyframes, you can manipulate clip properties such as rotation, size, opacity, and video effects. For example, you can make a clip fade, grow, or spin as it plays by assigning keyframes to it. You need at least two keyframes to create an animated sequence. At each keyframe you adjust the property setting, and the frames between the two keyframes will "react" to what is before and what is after them—the in-between frames are interpolated and the end result is an animated sequence. For example, you could set the opacity of a clip to 10% at the first keyframe and to 100% at the last keyframe. As the clip is played in the sequence, its visibility will gradually increase from 10% to 100%. The duration of this change depends on how far the two keyframes are spread apart. The farther apart the keyframes, the longer the change to the clip will occur over time. Sometimes moving keyframes apart makes for a smoother animation.

What You Have Learned

- How to use the Toggle Animation button
- How to add keyframes to the Timeline
- How to change clip properties at keyframe locations
- How to rotate a clip using keyframes
- How to go to the next and previous keyframes
- How to delete a keyframe
- How to resize a clip using keyframes
- How to move keyframes
- How to copy and paste keyframes
- How to animate a video effect
- How to use a preset

Key Terms

Animation Animation is motion that is created synthetically using a series of still images.

Keyframes Keyframes are locations in the Timeline where you define how something will look before the animation begins and how it will look when the animation ends.

Interpolation Interpolation is the process in which the frames between two keyframes are created automatically based on the keyframe settings. Interpolation is also known as "tweening" or "in-betweening."

PAN-AMERICAN-WORLD-AIRWAYS
PAA
DOUGLAS

chapter 10

EXPLORING EXPORT OPTIONS

1. Export a movie and a frame.
2. Export an edit decision list.
3. Export a filmstrip.

chapter 10 EXPLORING EXPORT OPTIONS

You can export your Premiere Pro program in a variety of ways. You can create a movie file that you can use in other projects or play on your computer screen. You can export a single frame, a segment of the Timeline, or the entire program. You can export the program as a file that can be opened and manipulated in other software programs, such as Adobe Photoshop. You can even export a program directly to videotape or as a DVD. Movies can also be exported as AAF (Advanced Authoring Format) and OMF (Open Media Framework) so that they can be edited in other programs, such as Final Cut Pro.

Premiere Pro offers a number of options for exporting movies. When you export movies, you determine a number of important specifications, such as file type, frame size, frame rate, and compression. You also choose whether you want the exported movie to contain video, audio, or both.

In addition to exporting movies, you can export an edit decision list (EDL). **EDLs** are text files that contain all of the edits you made in creating the program. Professional video production facilities can use your EDL as a map to recreate your work on a high-end editing suite or just as a simple reference document when they are outputting your project.

Exporting is often the most exciting step in the overall editing process because it's when you finally get to see the results of your work as a freestanding, real-time movie!

Tools You'll Use

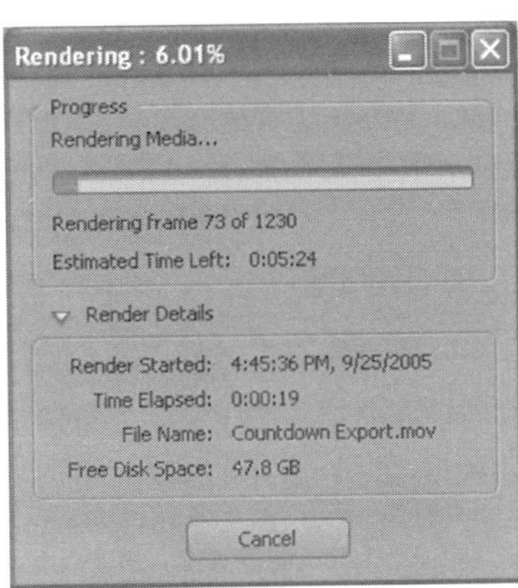

LESSON 1

EXPORT A MOVIE AND A FRAME

What You'll Do

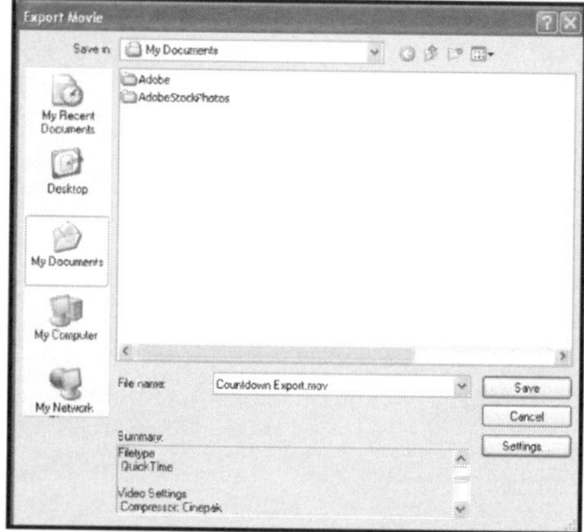

In this lesson, you will explore options for exporting a movie and a single video frame.

Exporting a Movie

When you export a movie, you create a file that is generated from the Timeline. The Export Movie Settings dialog box allows you to choose specifications for the movie you are creating.

You make essential choices as to what you are exporting from the Timeline in the General window of the Export Movie Settings dialog box. The File Type menu allows you to choose from a number of file types—though QuickTime and Microsoft AVI are the most commonly used formats.

The Range menu allows you to specify where in the Timeline the movie is being generated. You can choose to export the entire program or only a range of clips. If you choose Work Area Bar in the Range menu, the work area bar defines the area of the Timeline that will be exported. If you choose Entire Sequence in the Range menu, the entire contents of the Timeline will be exported.

Note also that you use this window to determine whether video, audio, or both are being exported from the Timeline.

Figure 1 shows the Export Movie Settings dialog box. You make more specific choices pertaining to the final movie, including the frame size and the frame rate, by making choices in the Video, Keyframe and Rendering, and Audio categories of the dialog box. It is always best for your output frame size and frame rate to match those with which the project's source clips were captured.

Keep in mind that your choice of frame size will have great impact on the file size of the exported movie. Just a small increase in frame size will result in a much higher file size. Therefore, if you are exporting a movie for your own use on your own computer, you may find 320 × 240 or 240 × 180 to be the most satisfying choice—a big enough frame size for viewing and a small enough file size to manage.

You can also choose a compression algorithm from the Compressor menu in the Video window. Because movie files can become substantially large in file size, it is most often necessary to use compression when creating them. If you are exporting a movie for your own use, use a common compression algorithm, such as Cinepak. This will greatly reduce the size of the resulting movie file.

The Quality slider offers you further control for reducing file size. Remember, the cost for a reduction in file size is always a loss of image quality. Therefore, it is usually best to keep the Quality value at 100% and allow the compression algorithm to do the work in reducing the file size.

> **QUICKTIP**
>
> If you are exporting a movie for broadcast, CD-ROM, or any other medium that requires specific standards, it is highly recommended that you use a professional video production facility and that you follow that facility's guidelines when exporting your project.

In the Audio window, shown in Figure 2, you have options for exporting audio from the audio tracks. For better audio quality in the exported file, choose a higher Sample Rate value. A lower Sample Rate value will reduce processing time and file size. As with frame size and frame rate, it is best to output the audio at the same sample rate at which it was captured.

FIGURE 1

Export Movie Settings dialog box

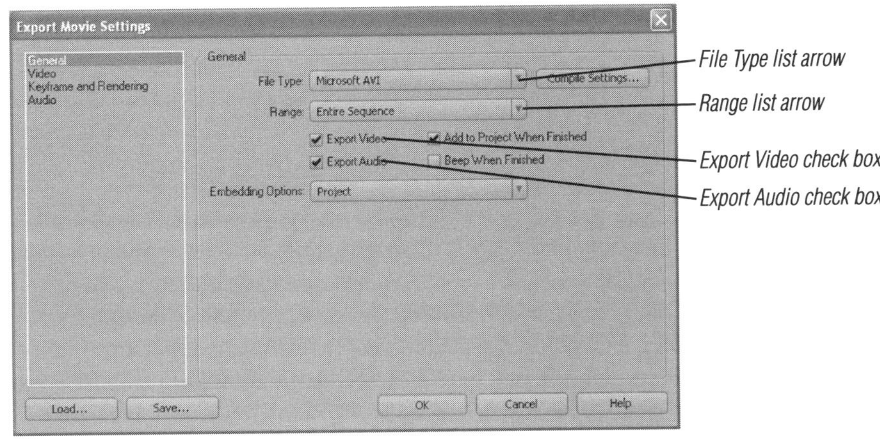

FIGURE 2

Audio section of the Export Movie Settings dialog box

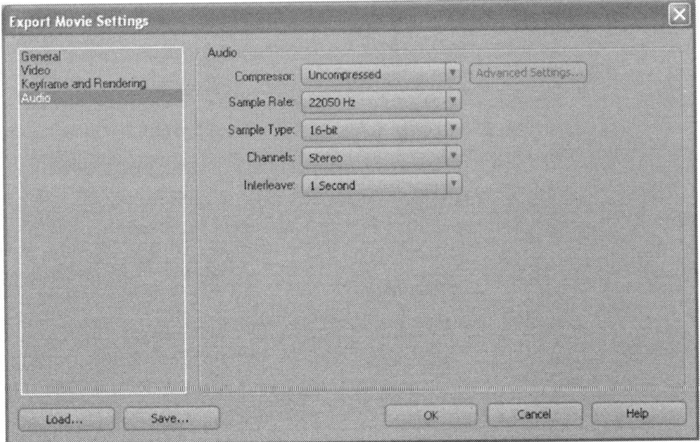

From the Sample Type menu, choose a higher bit depth, and choose Stereo from the Channels menu for better quality. Stereo provides two channels of audio; Mono provides one channel. It is suggested that you choose 16-bit Stereo, as that is the target for CD-quality audio.

The Compressor menu allows you to choose a compression algorithm for the audio output. Your options depend on the file type chosen in the General window. However, since audio does not take up nearly as much disk space as video, most editors choose not to compress audio at all.

QUICKTIP

Click the Add to Project When Finished check box if you want the exported movie to be added to the Project panel and click the Beep When Finished check box if you want an auditory signal that the rendering process is complete.

Exporting a Frame

When working with source clips in the Timeline, you may want to isolate a single frame and use it as a still image in the project. This is an easy task to accomplish. Simply position the Current time indicator at the frame you want to export, click File on the menu bar, point to Export, then click Frame. Click the Settings button and choose a file format for the exported frame. TIFF is a good choice for a format that is compatible with most other graphics programs. You also have the choice of Windows Bitmap, Targa, or GIF. Once exported, the frame is saved as a file that can be used as a source clip or in another software program.

QUICKTIP

You can import a Premiere Pro project into Adobe After Effects, however, the reverse is not true. If you want to import a movie that you have been working on in After Effects, save it as a QuickTime movie or similar file format that can be imported into Premiere Pro.

FIGURE 3

Verifying that the work area bar covers the entire sequence

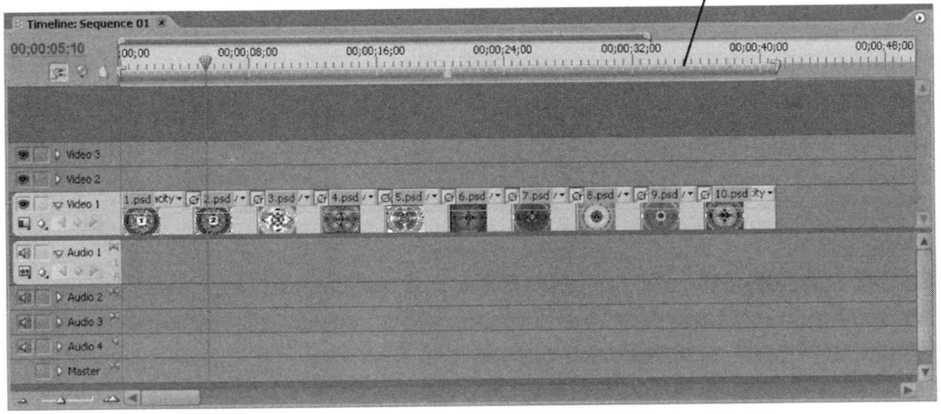

Work area bar

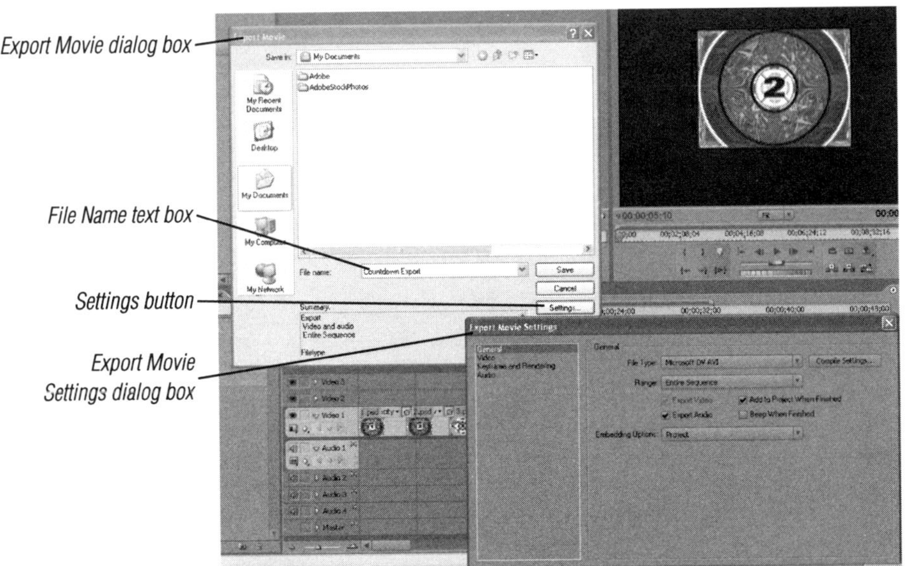

FIGURE 4

Export Movie and Export Movie Settings dialog boxes

Export a movie

1. Open APP 10-1.prproj, then save it as **QuickTime Movie**.
2. Zoom in or out of the Timeline so that you can see the entire sequence.

   A preview of the sequence has been rendered.
3. Verify that the entire sequence is covered by the work area bar, as shown in Figure 3.
4. Click the **Timeline panel**, click **File** on the menu bar, point to **Export**, then click **Movie**.

   The Export Movie dialog box opens.

   TIP If Export is grayed out on the File menu, click the Timeline panel and try again.
5. Navigate to the drive and folder where you plan on storing the movie, type **Countdown Export** in the File Name text box, then click **Settings**, as shown in Figure 4.

   The Export Movie Settings dialog box opens.
6. Click the **File Type list arrow**, then click **QuickTime**.
7. Verify that the Range setting is set to Entire Sequence, then click the **Add to Project When Finished check box**, if necessary.

(continued)

8. Click the **Video category** on the left side of the dialog box.
9. Click the **Compressor list arrow**, then click **Cinepak**, then click **OK**.
10. Before clicking Save, notice the Summary section in the Export Movie dialog box, as shown in Figure 5.

    You can quickly summarize the settings you chose and if you forgot one or if one is incorrect, you can click Settings again before exporting the movie.
11. Click **Save**.

    As shown in Figure 6, the Rendering dialog box appears, showing progress made in exporting the movie.

    TIP Click the Render Details arrow in the Rendering dialog box to view more details about the rendering process, such as the amount of time elapsed.
12. When the export process is complete, locate Countdown Export.mov in the Project panel.

You exported your entire sequence as a QuickTime movie.

FIGURE 5
Viewing the Summary information in the Export Movie dialog box

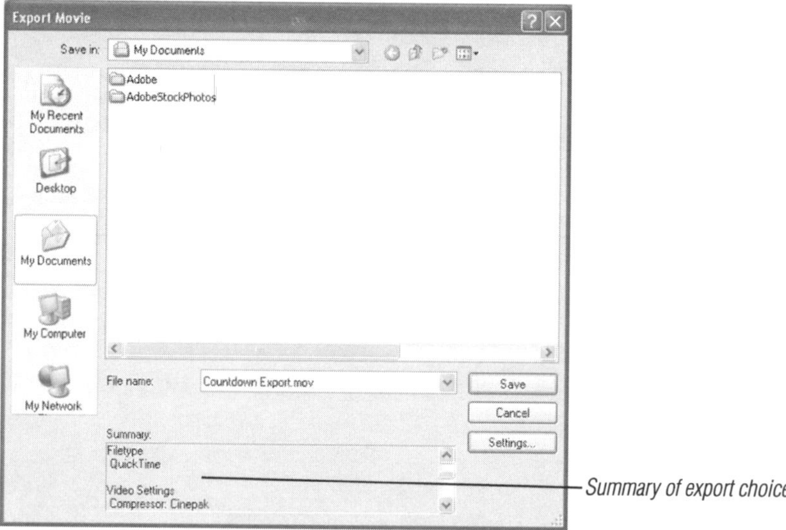

FIGURE 6
Rendering dialog box

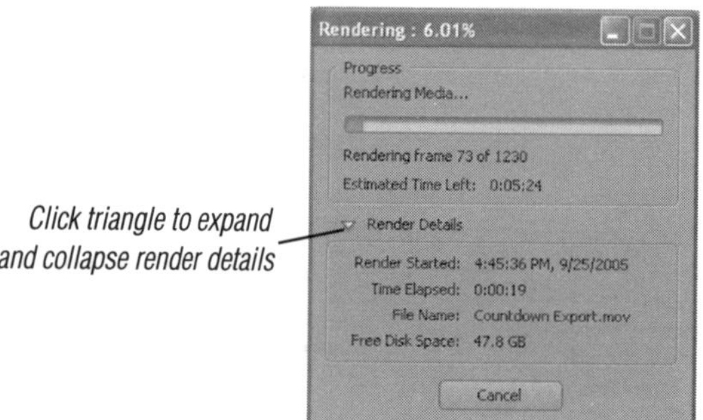

FIGURE 7
Frame 16:16 to be exported

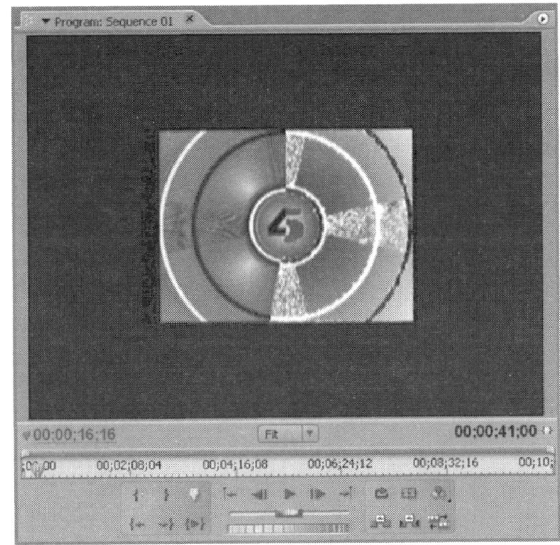

FIGURE 8
Viewing Transition frame.tif in the Source Monitor

Export a frame

1. Position the Current time indicator at frame 16:16.

   Your Program Monitor should resemble Figure 7.

2. Click the **Timeline panel**, click **File** on the menu bar, point to **Export**, then click **Frame**.

   TIP If Export is grayed out on the File menu, click the Timeline panel and try again.

3. Type **Transition frame** in the File Name text box in the Export Frame dialog box, then click **Settings**.

4. Click the **File Type list arrow**, click **TIFF**, verify that the Add to Project When Finished check box is checked, click **OK**, then click **Save**.

5. Double-click **Transition frame.tif** in the Project panel to view it in the Source Monitor.

   Your screen should resemble Figure 8. You can now use Transition frame.tif in the sequence.

You exported frame 16:16 as a TIFF file and had it added to the Project panel automatically. You then viewed the new still clip in the Source Monitor.

EXPORT AN EDIT DECISION LIST

What You'll Do

In this lesson, you will export a generic edit decision list.

Exporting an Edit Decision List

An edit decision list (EDL) is a file that lists all of the edits that you've made in a project. When you are creating a video program on your computer, and you are working in tandem with a professional video production facility, the facility will often ask you to generate an EDL when it comes time for them to step into the production process. Because the EDL functions as a "road map" of your edits, the facility can actually feed the text file into their "high-end" editing suite and—using your supplied source clips—recreate your work on their editing suite. With this method, you get to create your program yourself in Premiere Pro, but your results are delivered from a professional editing device.

The choice to work with an EDL in this manner is not one that you make on your own. If you are working with a video production facility, be sure to ask them if they want you to deliver an EDL at the output stage. To export a EDL, click File on the menu bar, point to Export, then click Export to EDL. As shown in Figure 9, the EDL Export Settings dialog box lets you choose exactly what to include.

FIGURE 9
EDL Export Settings dialog box

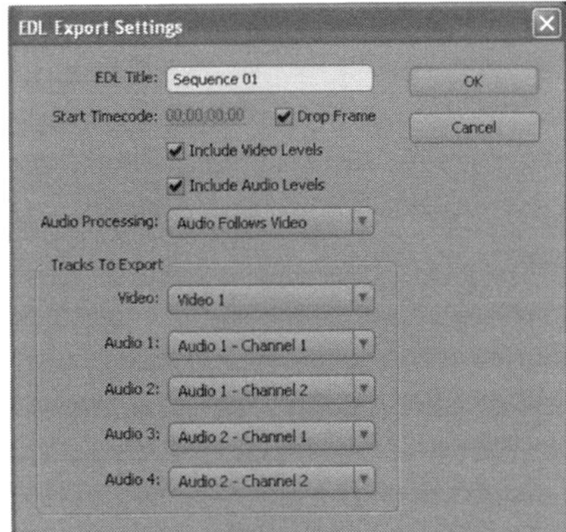

Choosing a File Format

Premiere Pro offers a number of file formats that you can choose from when exporting your program. The format you choose will depend largely on the type of program you've created. If you are working with a professional video production facility, rely on their guidance for choosing a file format.

QuickTime, Windows Bitmap, Filmstrip, Animated GIF, GIF, Targa, TIFF, Uncompressed Microsoft AVI, Microsoft AVI, Microsoft DV AVI, and Windows Waveform are the file formats you can choose for exporting video and audio files. TIFF, GIF, Targa, and Windows Bitmap are designed for exporting still images.

Managing File Size and Disk Space

The keys to managing memory-intensive video projects can be found primarily in two stages of any projects: input and output. When you capture video in your camera and then download it to your computer, it is downloaded and saved as a video file. In most cases, that "raw footage" will not have been compressed, and the file size will be enormous. You may download a minute or so of video and be surprised to find that it's taking up 300 MB of disk space on your computer! One simple solution is to only download those sections of footage that you want to work with. Then, use Premiere Pro to manage the file size issues surrounding the project.

Your choice of frame size and frame rate greatly influences the file size of the program when it is output as a movie. The larger the frame size, the larger the number of pixels per frame, thus more memory is required. The higher the frame rate, the more frames in the program, thus more memory is required.

At the output stage, choosing a compression algorithm (or Codec) for the project will substantially reduce the file size of the resulting movie. Premiere Pro offers many compressors. In this book, you will use Cinepak, which is standard and common to most computer systems.

FIGURE 10

Making choices in the EDL Export Settings dialog box

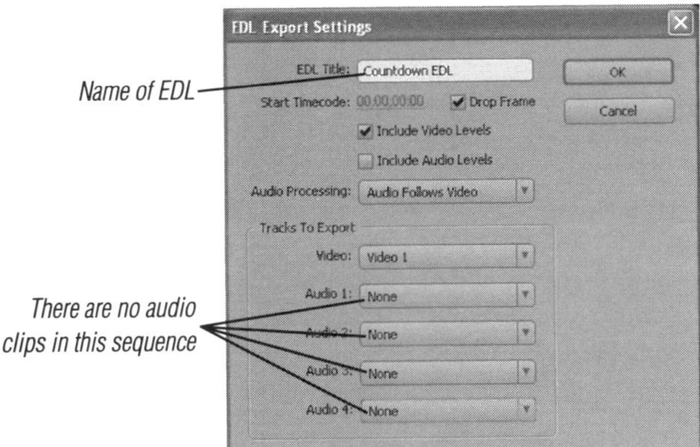

Export to an EDL

1. Click the **Timeline panel**, click **File** on the menu bar, point to **Export**, then click **Export to EDL**.
2. Type **Countdown EDL** in the EDL Title text box.
3. Remove the check mark in the Include Audio Levels check box.

   There are no audio tracks in the sequence.
4. Click each **Audio Track list arrow**, then click **None**, so that your EDL Export Settings dialog box matches Figure 10.
5. Click **OK**, accept the file name supplied in the Save Sequence as EDL dialog box, then click **Save**.
6. Close the project.

You exported a movie to an edit decision list (EDL).

LESSON 3

EXPORT A FILMSTRIP

What You'll Do

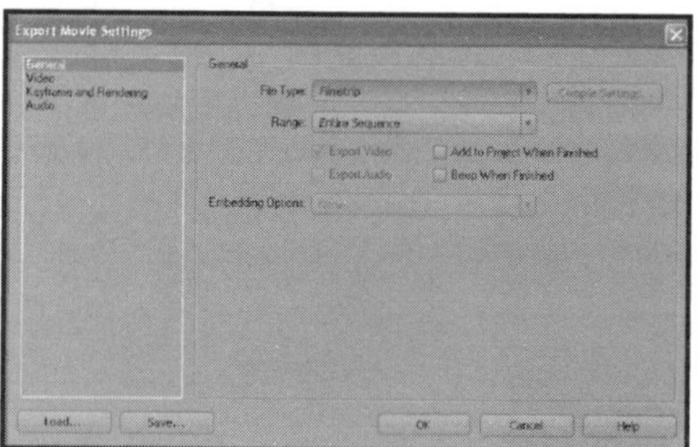

In this lesson, you will export a project as a Filmstrip file.

Exporting a Filmstrip

When you export a sequence as Video, you can choose Filmstrip as the file type to generate a Filmstrip file. Filmstrip files can be opened and manipulated in Adobe Photoshop.

Though Premiere Pro's Effects panel offers a number of the same color control options that you will find in Photoshop, there are many ways to manipulate a clip in Photoshop that Premiere Pro just doesn't offer.

Photoshop is especially effective in allowing you to isolate and manipulate specific areas of an image. For this reason alone, you may want to export a clip—or an entire movie—from Premiere Pro to Photoshop. Only the Filmstrip file format can be opened in Photoshop.

The Filmstrip file format does not export audio clips, nor does it offer a compression algorithm. Therefore, Filmstrip files almost always have large file sizes.

You can either export the entire sequence or a range of frames between In and Out points. When you export a range of the Timeline, every frame is exported with the file. Those frames are identified in the Photoshop file by their corresponding timecode and frame number. Among a number of functions, you can use Photoshop's selection tools to isolate specific areas in each frame, as shown in Figure 11. You can then manipulate only those areas, as shown in Figure 12.

Once you are finished manipulating the frames in Photoshop, you can then import the file back into Premiere Pro and use it as part of the program. However, because the Filmstrip file will almost certainly have a large file size, you may want to export the Filmstrip file as a QuickTime or Microsoft AVI movie file and then delete the Filmstrip file.

FIGURE 11
Selecting specific areas of frames in Photoshop

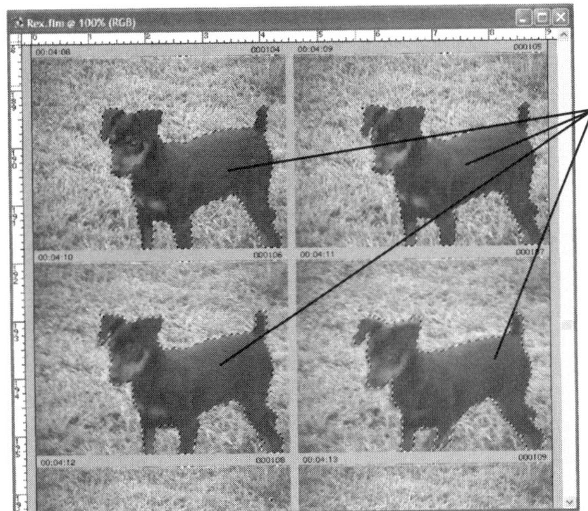

FIGURE 12
Manipulating specific areas in Photoshop

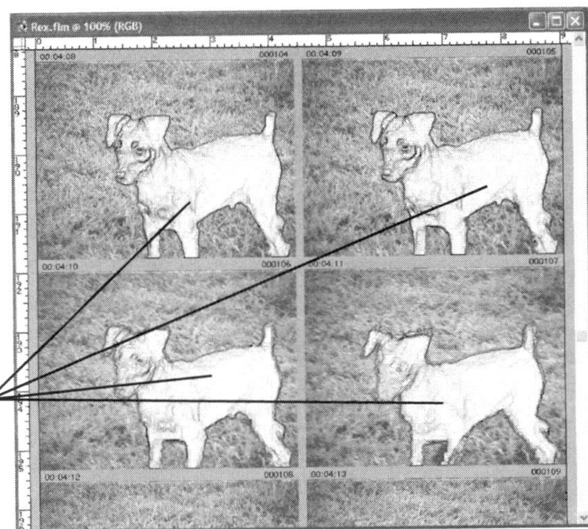

Export to DVD

You can export your movie as a DVD if your computer has a DVD burner installed. The DVD that you export will be very simple. It will not have menus or buttons, but if your sequence has DVD markers assigned, viewers can navigate to those places in the DVD using the previous and next buttons on a DVD remote control. To create a more sophisticated DVD, you'll need a program such as Adobe Encore DVD. You can use Premiere Pro's Adobe Media Encoder command to export your sequence as MPEG2. MPEG2 files are used in DVD-authoring programs.

Export a Filmstrip

1. Open APP 10-2.prproj, then save it as **Filmstrip to Photoshop**.
2. Zoom in on the Timeline, then drag the **Current frame indicator** across the clips to preview the sequence.
3. Click **File** on the menu bar, point to **Export**, then click **Movie**.
4. Type **To Photoshop** in the File Name text box, then click **Settings**.
5. Click the **File Type list arrow**, then click **Filmstrip**.
6. Click the **Range list arrow**, then click **Entire Sequence**.
7. Remove the check mark in the Add to Project When Finished check box, so that your Export Movie Settings dialog box matches Figure 13.
8. Click **Video** on the left side of the dialog box, then verify that the Frame Size is set to 320 x 240 and the Frame Rate is set to 29.97.
9. Click **OK**, then click **Save**.

   Figure 14 shows the Filmstrip open in Photoshop.
10. If you have Photoshop, open To Photoshop.flm to view it, then quit Photoshop and return to Premiere Pro.
11. Save your work, then close the project.

You exported a project as a Filmstrip file.

FIGURE 13
Exporting a Filmstrip file

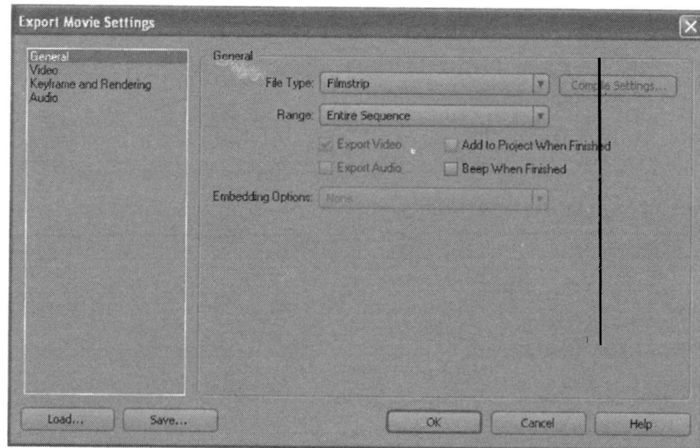

FIGURE 14
Viewing a Filmstrip file in Photoshop

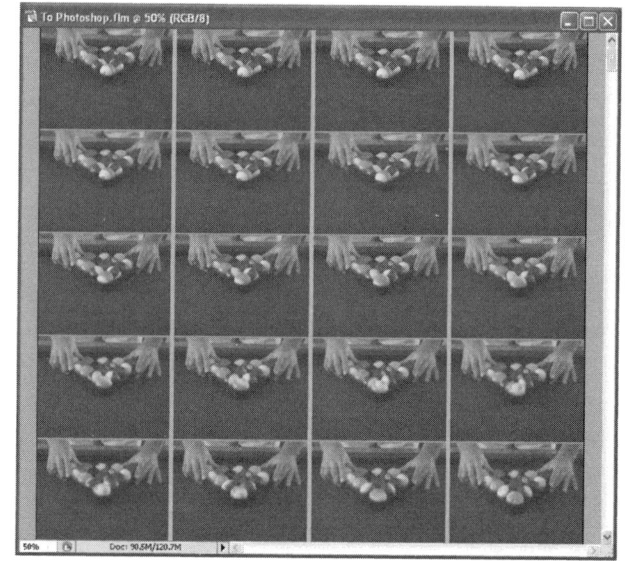

CHAPTER SUMMARY

Exporting is the final process in using Premiere Pro. There are a number of formats that you can export your sequence as—it all depends how and where you are going to use it. You can import individual frames in a number of file formats that can be used in a digital editing program or on the Web. You can export an entire movie or the section of the sequence defined by the work area bar. When exporting a movie, you can choose video, audio, or both. DVDs can be created from your sequence, assuming you have a DVD burner installed on your computer. You can also export your movies as Filmstrip files that can be opened and manipulated in Photoshop. An edit decision list, or EDL, is a record of all of your edits. EDLs are typically used when you are having a professional production facility output your movie.

What You Have Learned

- How to export a movie
- How to export a frame
- How to export an EDL
- How to export a Filmstrip

Key Terms

EDL EDL stands for Edit Decision List. An EDL is a file that you can export from Premiere. It is a record of all of your edits in your project. EDLs are used by professional production facilities to output movies on high-end equipment.

Filmstrip file A Filmstrip file is a file format that exports the entire sequence or a range of frames to an .flm file. In an .fml file, each frame is exported with the file. Filmstrip files can be opened in Photoshop for further modifying.

10°
0°
NR'328

Additive primary colors. Red, green, and blue light (RGB) are the additive primary colors of light. The term *primary* refers to the fact that red, green, and blue light cannot be broken down or reduced.

Animation. Animation is motion that is created synthetically using a series of still images.

Audio Mixer panel. The Audio Mixer panel allows you to make adjustments to audio tracks while listening to them and viewing video at the same time.

Automate to Sequence command. This command lets you add a number of clips to the Timeline in one step.

Bins. Bins are folders that you can create, using the Bin button, to store loose clips.

Clips. This term refers to the video, audio, still pictures, and graphics used in a project.

Clip markers. Clip markers are added to clips when they are in the Source Monitor.

Color Picker. The Color Picker is a dialog box in which you enter values for red, green, and blue (RGB) to create a fill color for text or objects.

Crawls. Crawls refer to text objects that move horizontally across the screen, such as stock quotes that you might see on a financial news channel on television.

Current time display. The Current time display identifies how far along you are into a sequence during playback.

Current time indicator. The Current time indicator (represented by a light-blue triangle) shows exactly which frame is being displayed.

Cut line. This is the line between two clips in the Timeline.

Depth. Depth is a type of stroke that looks like a hard-edged copy placed behind the object.

Dissolves. Dissolves are transitions in which the end of one clip fades into the beginning of the next.

Drop Face. Drop Face is a type of stroke that creates a copy of the object, which you can then offset and modify.

DVD Markers. DVD Markers are used specifically when you plan to output your project to a DVD.

Edge. Edge is a type of stroke that outlines the object along either the inner or the outer edge.

Effect Controls panel. The Effect Controls panel offers you options for changing an effect's settings.

Effects panel. The Effects panel includes special effects that you can apply to your video. These special effects are categorized into folders: Presets, Audio Effects, Audio Transitions, Video Effects, and Video Transitions.

Electromagnetic spectrum. The electromagnetic spectrum is the entirety of the sun's light, which contains an infinite number of light waves—some at high frequencies and some at low frequencies.

EDL. EDL stands for *Edit Decision List*. An EDL is a file that you can export from Premiere. It is a record of all of your edits in your project. EDLs are used by professional production facilities to output movies on high-end equipment.

Eliminate. Eliminate is a type of fill that removes the fill and the shadow from an object.

Filmstrip file. This is a file format that exports the entire sequence or a range of frames to an .flm file. In an .flm file, each frame is exported with the file. Filmstrip files can be opened in Photoshop for further modifying.

Frames. Frames are series of still images that make up a movie or sequence.

GLOSSARY

Frame rate. Frame rate is a measurement of the number of still images that make up one second of motion.

Ghost. The Ghost fill option removes the fill from an object, thereby making its fill transparent.

Gradients. Gradients are multicolor fills in which one color blends to another. Gradients can be created and applied to titles and objects using Title Designer.

Head Material. This refers to the frames that come before the In Point in a trimmed clip.

Highpass. Highpass is an audio effect that removes low frequencies from an audio clip.

History panel. This panel allows you to go back to any previous state of the project since it (the project) was opened.

Hue. The hue is the name of a color.

In Points and Out Points. In Points and Out Points are places that you can set in the Source Monitor to trim a clip or in the Timeline to crop part of a sequence.

Info panel. As its name suggests, the Info panel provides information about a selected clip or source file, a location in the Timeline, or other notations.

Interpolation. Interpolation is the process in which the frames between two keyframes are created automatically based on the keyframe settings. Interpolation is also known as *tweening* or *in-betweening*.

Irises. These are transitions in which the first clip reveals the second clip using a specific shape.

Keyframes. Keyframes are locations in the Timeline where you define how an object will change during an animated sequence.

Keying. This is another term for superimposing clips in order to create transparency in specific areas of a clip.

Keys. Keys are video effects used to create transparency. There are 17 keying effects available in Premiere Pro.

Kilohertz. Audio files are measured using kilohertz (kHz), which measure how many sounds play per second on a soundtrack.

Logos. Premiere Pro refers to logos as graphics that you insert into the drawing area of Title Designer.

Loop button. When clicked, the Loop button plays a sequence repeatedly, until you click it again to turn off looping.

Lowpass. Lowpass is an audio effect that removes high frequencies from an audio clip.

Markers. Markers are visual icons you use to indicate important frames and to help you position and synchronize clips.

Mono audio clips. Mono audio clips have one channel.

Opacity. The term *opacity* derives from the word *opaque*, which describes an object that is neither transparent nor translucent—that is, an object that is not see-through.

Overscan. Overscan is a process that most televisions use to cut off the outer edges of the picture so that the center of the image can be enlarged.

Pixels. Pixels—short for *picture elements*—are the smallest components of a digital image.

Pixel aspect ratio. Pixel aspect ratio is a measurement that specifies the ratio of width to height of one pixel in a frame.

Play/Stop Toggle button. The Play/Stop Toggle button is used for playing and stopping the sequence.

Presets. Preset are a group of specific video effect settings. Presets can be made from one or more video effects in the Effect Controls panel.

Preview. A preview is a display of contents in the Timeline shown in the Program Monitor—at the intended frame rate—from files generated and saved to the hard drive.

Program Monitor. This is the monitor used to display the contents of the Timeline.

Project panel. The Project panel is where you import, organize, and store references to video clips and still imagery.

Reference files. When files are imported into Premiere Pro, only a reference is imported. Reference files are linked to the original files on your computer.

Rolling edit. In a rolling edit, you shorten or lengthen a specified clip without changing the duration of the entire project. The In or Out Point of that clip is adjusted, and the duration of the adjacent clip is also adjusted so that the total duration of the two clips together remains the same.

Rolls. Rolls are the most common method for displaying credits at the end of a movie. With a roll, text moves vertically. By default, rolls in Title Designer move from the bottom to the top of the screen.

Safe Action Margin. This is a guide within the Titler window, showing the frame important graphics should be inside of to avoid being cut off.

Safe Title Margin. This is a guide within the Titler window, showing the frame titles should be inside of to avoid being cut off.

Sequence markers. Sequence markers are added to clips in the Timeline.

Slide Tool. This is an editing tool you use when you want to move a clip in the Timeline—making it appear earlier or later in the program—without changing the program duration.

Slip Tool. This is an editing tool you use when you want to change a clip's In and Out Points without changing the program duration.

Source Monitor. The Source Monitor is used to preview a source clip.

Step Back button. This button is used to move backward through your sequence one frame at a time.

Step Forward button. This button is used to move forward through your sequence one frame at a time.

Stereo audio clips. Stereo audio clips have two channels.

Stroke. This describes an outline added to the edge of a graphic or text. Strokes can be added in Title Designer.

Superimpose tracks. All tracks higher than the Video 1 track are called superimpose tracks because clips on those tracks are positioned above clips on the tracks beneath them.

Tail material. These are the frames that come after the Out Point in a trimmed clip.

Time duration display. The Time duration display indicates the total duration of the contents in the Timeline.

Time ruler. The time ruler displays the duration of a clip in the Source Monitor and the duration of a sequence in the Program Monitor.

Timecode. Timecode is the method for counting frames and for measuring time in a video project.

Timeline panel. The Timeline panel is where you assemble and edit your video. It contains all of the source clips that are used in the project, including video and audio, as well as title cards, transitions, and special effects.

Title. Video editors refer to text or graphics within a video program as titles. Titles can be created in Title Designer within Adobe Premiere Pro 2.0.

Title Designer. Title Designer is an application built into Adobe Premiere Pro 2.0 that you use to create text or graphics (titles).

Tools panel. The Tools panel offers tools for working in the Timeline, such as the Hand Tool, the Zoom Tool, the Selection Tool, and the Track Select Tool.

Transition. The visual change from one clip to another is called a transition.

Trim Monitor. The Trim Monitor is very useful for fine-tuning a cut between two clips in which the action must be synchronized or when the timing is critical.

Trimming. The process by which you excise a specific segment of video (or audio) for use in a project is called trimming.

Video effects. Video effects add special visual characteristics to a clip, such as blurs, distortions, or color changes.

Video transitions. These are built-in effects that Premiere Pro provides to create a visual change from one clip to another.

Waveform. A waveform is a visual display of an audio clip.

White light. White light is a term given to visible light that appears colorless.

Wipes. These are transitions in which the first clip moves off the screen to reveal the next clip.

Work area bar. The work area bar is the gray band positioned directly above the time ruler in the Timeline. It determines the areas of the Timeline that will be included when you generate a preview.

A

B

C

INDEX

D

E

F

G

H

I

J

K

L

M

N

S

T

License Agreement/Notice of Limited Warranty

By opening the sealed disc container in this book, you agree to the following terms and conditions. If, upon reading the following license agreement and notice of limited warranty, you cannot agree to the terms and conditions set forth, return the unused book with unopened disc to the place where you purchased it for a refund.

License:

The enclosed software is copyrighted by the copyright holder(s) indicated on the software disc. You are licensed to copy the software onto a single computer for use by a single user and to a backup disc. You may not reproduce, make copies, or distribute copies or rent or lease the software in whole or in part, except with written permission of the copyright holder(s). You may transfer the enclosed disc only together with this license, and only if you destroy all other copies of the software and the transferee agrees to the terms of the license. You may not decompile, reverse assemble, or reverse engineer the software.

Notice of Limited Warranty:

The enclosed disc is warranted by Thomson Course Technology PTR to be free of physical defects in materials and workmanship for a period of sixty (60) days from end user's purchase of the book/disc combination. During the sixty-day term of the limited warranty, Thomson Course Technology PTR will provide a replacement disc upon the return of a defective disc.

Limited Liability:

THE SOLE REMEDY FOR BREACH OF THIS LIMITED WARRANTY SHALL CONSIST ENTIRELY OF REPLACEMENT OF THE DEFECTIVE DISC. IN NO EVENT SHALL THOMSON COURSE TECHNOLOGY PTR OR THE AUTHOR BE LIABLE FOR ANY OTHER DAMAGES, INCLUDING LOSS OR CORRUPTION OF DATA, CHANGES IN THE FUNCTIONAL CHARACTERISTICS OF THE HARDWARE OR OPERATING SYSTEM, DELETERIOUS INTERACTION WITH OTHER SOFTWARE, OR ANY OTHER SPECIAL, INCIDENTAL, OR CONSEQUENTIAL DAMAGES THAT MAY ARISE, EVEN IF THOMSON COURSE TECHNOLOGY PTR AND/OR THE AUTHOR HAS PREVIOUSLY BEEN NOTIFIED THAT THE POSSIBILITY OF SUCH DAMAGES EXISTS.

Disclaimer of Warranties:

THOMSON COURSE TECHNOLOGY PTR AND THE AUTHOR SPECIFICALLY DISCLAIM ANY AND ALL OTHER WARRANTIES, EITHER EXPRESS OR IMPLIED, INCLUDING WARRANTIES OF MERCHANTABILITY, SUITABILITY TO A PARTICULAR TASK OR PURPOSE, OR FREEDOM FROM ERRORS. SOME STATES DO NOT ALLOW FOR EXCLUSION OF IMPLIED WARRANTIES OR LIMITATION OF INCIDENTAL OR CONSEQUENTIAL DAMAGES, SO THESE LIMITATIONS MIGHT NOT APPLY TO YOU.

Other:

This Agreement is governed by the laws of the State of Massachusetts without regard to choice of law principles. The United Convention of Contracts for the International Sale of Goods is specifically disclaimed. This Agreement constitutes the entire agreement between you and Thomson Course Technology PTR regarding use of the software.